"At last the complex relationship between the creation of a film and the day-to-day production management and coordination of that film is spelled out in clear, readable, and accurate detail. Deborah has written a wonderful book which should be extremely helpful to novice low-budget independent filmmakers and seasoned professionals alike."

— **Sharon McGowan**
Independent Producer and Assistant Professor
University of British Columbia Film Program

"The most definitive production guide I have ever read. A must for anyone who wants to understand the production process."

— **Louis Melville**
Co-Chairman, New Producers Alliance

"An exhaustive overview full of practical knowledge!!!"

— **Dan Ochiva**
Editor, *Millimeter Magazine*

"An invaluable and comprehensive guide. Deborah Patz has drawn on her own experience and has written a thoroughly researched and helpful book."

— **Norman Jewison**
Producer/Director, *The Hurricane, Moonstruck, Fiddler on the Roof*

"Deborah prepares you for any situation the PM and PC will encounter throughout the life of a project. From the initial interview to the wrap party, this book guides you on how to be prepared and how to act professionally in every circumstance."

— **Chris Robertson**
www.hollywoodwritersblock.com

"This is one of the most insightful industry books I've ever seen. Anybody going into this industry should read it."

— **Seaton McLean**
President, Motion Picture Production
Alliance Atlantis Communications, Inc.

MICHAEL WIESE PRODUCTIONS
www.mwp.com

Since 1981, Michael Wiese Productions has been dedicated to providing novice and seasoned filmmakers with vital information on all aspects of filmmaking and videomaking. We have published more than 60 books, used in over 500 film schools worldwide.

Our authors are successful industry professionals — they believe that the more knowledge and experience they share with others, the more high-quality films will be made. That's why they spend countless hours writing about the hard stuff: budgeting, financing, directing, marketing, and distribution. Many of our authors, including myself, are often invited to conduct filmmaking seminars around the world.

We truly hope that our publications, seminars, and consulting services will empower you to create enduring films that will last for generations to come.

We're here to help. Let us hear from you.

Sincerely,

Michael Wiese
Publisher, Filmmaker

PRODUCTION MANAGEMENT 101

The Ultimate Guide to Film and Television Production
Management and Coordination

DEBORAH S. PATZ

Published by Michael Wiese Productions
11288 Ventura Blvd., Suite 621
Studio City, CA 91604
tel. (818) 379-8799
fax (818) 986-3408
mw@mwp.com
www.mwp.com

Cover design: Art Hotel
Book layout: Gina Mansfield
Editor: Brett Jay Markel

Printed by Sheridan Books, Ann Arbor, Michigan
Manufactured in the United States of America

©2002 by Deborah S. Patz
This is the second edition of *Surviving Production* by Deborah S. Patz

ISBN 0-941188-45-0

Library of Congress Cataloging-in-Publication Data

Patz, Deborah S. , 1963-
    Production management 101 : the ultimate guide to film and television
    production management and coordination / by Deborah S. Patz.
        p. cm.
Rev. ed. of: Surviving production, c1997.
    ISBN 0-941188-45-0
    1. Motion pictures--Production and direction.   2. Television--Production and direction.
    I. Title: Production management 101. II. Patz, Deborah S., 1963-
    Surviving production. III. Title.

PN1995.9.P7 P38 2002
791.43'023—dc21

2002006943

for Laura
who was there at the beginning

and for Ken and Jordan
who fill my life with love, joy, and inspiration

ACKNOWLEDGMENTS

There are so many wonderful people and companies to thank, since this industry is very much the coming together of many minds. Beyond all the crews and the co-workers I have worked with over the years that have given me, and continue to give me, the forum to learn so much about the business of filmmaking, I must acknowledge with great thanks:

Michael Wiese and Ken Lee for making this project come to life and shine around the world, and for encouraging the book's expansion.

Cheryl Wagner, Rob Mills, and Nadine Henry of Radical Sheep Productions for their support when it really counted. Helena Cynamon, Mickey Rogers, and Teri Woods-McArter for the opportunity of a lifetime. Elizabeth Friesen and William Barron for a whole new wonderful and exciting perspective on filmmaking. Seaton McLean, Jamie Paul Rock, and John Calvert for my many precious years at Atlantis. The Canadian Film Centre for creating a terrific testing ground for the book. The Vancouver Film School for being the first to integrate the first edition of the book in their program of excellence. My many superb Assistants over the years for their dedication, hard work, and good humor.

My team of readers and critics for their invaluable input: Paul Bernard, Charles Braive, Trish Brown, Mark Callow, Carrie Chase, Brian de Paoli, Alex Downie, Laura Fisher, Lon Hall, Barb Harwood, Danny McCoy, Leslie Padorr, Marian Elliott, Richard Patz, Joan Pearce, Eva Schmieg, Barbara Selkirk, Jim Sternberg, Cesar from Packair, Clive from Renown Freight Limited, and Melissa from O'Reilly, Dean & Power.

Special thanks must also go to Scott Baker for buying me the book that got the ball rolling; to Francis Fougere and his flying f-stops for the lovely photograph; to Nick DeMunnik for security of "plan B"; to Victoria Ridout at the Writer's Union of Canada for her work beyond the call of duty; to Sue Phillips for seeing my abilities before I did; and to Ann Marie Fleming for never letting me forget them.

Also, heartfelt thanks go to my mother for teaching me how to reach for my dreams, and to my father, in loving memory, for teaching me how to live them.

Finally, my deepest thanks go to Mo Patz and Kathryn Emslie, without whose help the first edition could never have been completed — and to Ken Elliott, without whose gentle encouragement, patience, and caring this second edition could never have been completed.

PRODUCTION MANAGEMENT 101

TABLE OF CONTENTS

III. PRODUCTION

IV. MORE MONEY & MANAGEMENT ISSUES

V. MORE CONTRACTING ISSUES

VI. MORE PRODUCTION & COORDINATION ISSUES

VII. ONGOING SPECIAL ISSUES

VIII. POSTPRODUCTION

IX. APPENDIX

The sample forms in the Appendix can be downloaded in full size (8.5" x 11") at
www.mwp.com/pages/booksfilmprod101.html

Production Manager & Coordinator links at
http://www.goldenarrowproductions.com

INTRODUCTION

A film production explodes from paper agreement into life as a thriving expanse of business. Propelling itself forward in a frantic race against time, it captures on tape or celluloid a collaboration of ideas — entertaining, thrilling, and educating. Long before audiences see the final product, production has vanished, and crews are working with different people on other projects. Yet in that brief existence of time and under such frenetic circumstances, a film has been made.

There is glamour to working behind the scenes on a film production. The lifestyle is exotic. It is no regular nine-to-five job. Where do you begin this fabulous journey? Here! This book is a hands-on "how to" guide for the management and the coordination of a film or television shoot. A two-for-one book, it is told through the eyes of both the Production Manager and the Production Coordinator, as they are the team in the production office who budgets it all, arranges it all, does it all, reports it all, and double-checks that it all gets done... on time and on budget.

The Production Manager (or "PM") is the person who is basically handed all the money to make the film and is responsible to bring it in for the Producer on time and on budget. If you think this sounds like a weighty job, it is. Good Production Managers are hailed as people who know how to keep the money "on the screen" to make the final product look like it cost more than the sum of the budget.

The Production Coordinator (or "PC") deals with everyone during the course of making a film, implementing and coordinating everything from preproduction to postproduction, at head office and on set. If you think it sounds like an enormous job, it is. Good Production Coordinators are hailed as people who "keep the show running."

Together, the PM and the PC form a dynamic producing team. They have secrets on how to do their jobs effectively that tend to remain just that — secrets. This book is written to share those secrets.

This book is designed to be open on your desk at work as you work. Forms, checklists, and samples are abundant for your daily use. True production stories are interspersed with the straightforward how-to directions. Beyond entertaining, the stories are intended to balance out the simplicity of managing and organizing in the sterile environment of the pages of a book. See how real-life situations happen. You do not have to be perfect. Though their daily accomplishments may make them appear super-human, Managers and Coordinators are just like you and me.

The book is written for Executives, Producers, Production Managers, and Production Coordinators. Knowledge and understanding of the management team and its expanse of responsibilities can only help production to proceed with trust, good humor, and a sense of teamwork. Together you are responsible for everything in this book.

Production Accountants, Location Managers, Assistant Directors, Production Secretaries, Office P.A.s, and Receptionists will also deem this book invaluable. With it, you will gain a familiarity of the scope of duties that you accomplish together in the production office, and bring meaning to and put into perspective the work that you do.

Those entering the film industry will learn about the business side of filmmaking from this book. Not only is there entry-level advice, but also detailed information as you move up the ladder to management. Since the PM and the PC deal with everyone from prep to post, you can acquaint yourself with an overview of the entire film production process in this book.

Finally, this book is for those in and interested in the film industry who are baffled by what the PM and the PC are doing all day long while the set is shooting. It is those people who ask: "How can the Coordinator be that busy?" and "What is it like to be the Manager responsible for all the money on production?"

So, absorb and enjoy! Use this book as a daily reference. Over time, be inspired to develop your own style of management or coordination. All sorts of unpredictable events on a production are about to come your way. They will test your ability to think on your feet. So you need to know the basics of the job. You are in the right place.

Whether you read the entire book at once or skip over chapters until you are ready for them, enter the world of production management and coordination. Grasp the full production experience, from the perspective of the dynamic team of the Production Manager and the Production Coordinator. No other jobs can compare!

I.

PROJECT DEVELOPMENT

Hire the right people and let them do their jobs.

Interview Novices

Going for my first interview to become a Production Coordinator, I was very nervous. I had jotted down in tiny writing on a cue card all the questions I could muster about the show and my prospective role in production. What I didn't know at the time was that I was being interviewed by a relatively new Production Manager.

He asked me a few general questions. I sputtered out a few answers. Silences and uncomfortable moments crept into the interview. Now and then I referred to my cue card and asked a question myself. The Production Manager was intrigued by the card in my hand. He leaned forward to get a glimpse of its contents, then said: "You seem more prepared for this than I. Why don't you take over the interview?"

I realized then that he was as nervous as I was. So I blatantly referred to my cue card and continued with my questions, jotting down answers as we discussed the different topics. Soon conversation was lively, direct, and informative. He leaned back in comfort and we lost track of time chatting about film, the project, and the workings of a production office.

By the next day I was working in that office. But it occurred to me that the only question I didn't ask him at the time was: Did I get the job?

CHAPTER 1

GETTING HIRED

Before thinking about working as a Production Manager or Coordinator, you first think about getting hired as one. You have exhausted all your contacts and their contacts and have finally made it to an interview for just that job. Your C.V. is short, to the point, and shows off your experience and education related to this particular job. If it is your first interview as a PM or a PC, you have worked hard to get here and you are pretty sure you can do the job. You just need the chance to prove yourself. You are trying your best to show how relevant your experience is, how professional you are, and basically emanate all your best working qualities. But what are "they" looking for from you?

YOU AS THE PRODUCTION MANAGER

BEFORE THE INTERVIEW
You have probably already had a telephone interview. You have an idea of what the film is about. You may know some of the key people involved, the overall size of the budget, and when and how long the shoot is planned. You need to know more.

The Internet is a fabulous place to start your research. Surf by the company's Web site and read up on them prior to arriving at the interview. Surf by the Web sites of their previous productions. Research the Producer, the Director, and other key members of the team with whom you are already familiar. How professional are their presentations? Do you want to be associated with these people in your career?

You may also have the opportunity to read the script prior to attending the interview. Take the chance if you can. As PM, or as PC, you will be selling how wonderful the script is to many other people and companies along the production process. You better love it — or something about it — now.

You may also have the chance to read the budget prior to attending the interview. Take this opportunity if you can. You are going to be hired to keep to this budget. You want to know it as soon as possible, both inside and out. Read the script first, then the budget, making notes and questions. How were the key decisions made? You are going to be hired to follow up on these decisions during production. Can you do it?

Call industry people you know and trust to find out what they know about these Producers or this production company. You are checking their references. You want this job to be a good fit for both you and them. Remember, when checking references, you want information closest to the source. People who have heard rumors, rather than having had direct experience working with those you are checking on, can give you dangerously misleading information. Also remember that personality clashes can give you biased feedback. Just store up the reference information you collect, go to the interview, and make a decision for yourself. It is your career, after all, and your prospective employer is calling your references right now, too.

WHAT TO BRING TO THE INTERVIEW
Take notes during your research. You will have questions to ask the Producer(s) about the production. Prepare now so you don't end up leaving the interview saying to yourself, "If only I'd asked…" Use a small note pad or index cards you can refer to. Bring a pen or a pencil so you can jot down answers or names you collect. You are not being hired to memorize. Reference material is okay. A scripted book of notes would be excessive.

Also bring another copy of your C.V. The Producers should already have a copy, but it may only be an illegible fax, or they may forget to bring it. Be prepared.

AT THE INTERVIEW
The interview could be in a production office, a head office, or even in a restaurant. It depends on the people, their style and situation… and where they can get a private space away from telephones to talk with you. You will be interviewed by the Line Producer, the Producer, the Executive or VP in Charge of Production, or perhaps a combination of them all. It will depend on the circumstances.

Ease in with chitchat. Chitchat is an opportunity to find out something personal about the people you may be working with. You can use chitchat as your opportunity to show off your attitude toward life and work and how you balance the two.

WHO ARE THE PRODUCERS?
There are always a number of Producers on a production. They can be: Executive Producers, Co-Producers, Producers, Associate Producers, Line Producers, Creative Producers, etc. Find the complete list of who is on board the production and how involved they are. Some may have worked on the initial assembling of the development package; you may never see them during the course of production. Some may be very "hands-on," showing up daily on set, and attending all meetings. Some Producers work in-house at a production company, while others are freelance and hired, just like you. Take all of the Producers' names on your notes. You can research these new names later when you get home. Confirm to whom you, as a PM, will be reporting. You should be reporting to the Line Producer or the Producer, who will in turn report to the Executives. You will not have time to report to several people. <u>Determine if there is a clear chain of command in place.</u>

WHAT "THEY" ARE LOOKING FOR

The job of the Production Manager is a hugely responsible position. The Producers have been raising money for years to make this production. They have expended a lot of effort developing this project to where it is today. You, as a PM, are being hired to spend the money they have assembled in a superbly short time frame to move this project from script to screen. You better be able to spend the money wisely — on time and on budget. A Producer is not looking to train you as a PM. A Producer wants you for your expertise and professionalism. The company is going to put a lot of trust in you and the team you hire. How wisely do you spend the budget? How well do you track the money as it is being spent? How fast and how accurately do you create cost reports? Can you handle the stress of it all?

KNOW YOUR EXPERTISE

Now, of course, no two productions are identical. Just because you production-managed one show does not mean you can manage any production. Some projects are much larger scale than others. Some involve several countries. Some involve shooting with kids, animals, and special effects. Some are shot on film, others on video. Some specialize in doing everything for "food and favors," while others can pay some of the crew overscale. Do you have experience in production with any of these specialties? Is your background experience compatible with this budget, this script, and this company? Maybe you were working on a production, but not as the Production Manager, and you were the one who negotiated all the rights for the pre-recorded music — and this production is all about music. Though not PM-experience specifically, your knowledge may be superbly relevant to this particular production. You may know more about music clearances than the Producers, so that they will need your expertise. You must understand what you can do. Then you can demonstrate how useful your experience is to this production.

WHAT IS THE VISION?

The Producer wants to hire people who are all moving in the same direction, making the same film. Take time to discuss the "vision" of the final film and the budgetary choices already made in the development budget. If the Producer at the interview has created the current production budget, this is fortunate for you. Bring out your budget questions and start asking. Where does the Producer want the money to be spent? Is the shot with 1,000 extras integral to the story, or can it be cheated with 100 extras or moved to another location with no extras at all? Now is the time to <u>find out what has to stay in the</u> story and what is expendable. While asking the questions, ask yourself if you can make this vision for this budget. This responsibility will be yours.

KNOW YOUR STYLE

Are you a "paper person" who loves to analyze numbers and report them? Or are you a "people person" who prefers to be on set, physically overseeing production and discussing and observing the status? You will need to balance both abilities. For example, if the producer you are about to work with is a people person, be prepared to compliment his style as a paper person to work most effectively. Also know if you prefer to rule a set in almost military efficiency, or if you prefer a quiet approach to earn the crew's respect. Are you an organizer, or do you need an organizer to get through the day? Know yourself. You will be working in close quarters with the Producer and the Line Producer. Be prepared to admit if your work style is compatible or not with theirs.

DIFFICULT DECISIONS
Have you ever fired someone? Have you dealt with difficult people or bruised egos? How do you inspire people? Are you confident enough to advise the Producer or the Line Producer how to cut costs? Have you ever analyzed a situation and decided that, for the best of the project, someone key needs to be fired? Can you make these difficult decisions? Look into your career history. What have been your most difficult decisions? Share these. The Producer needs someone who can make such decisions. The Producer also needs someone who can deal with widely varied issues both delicately and confidentially.

WHO DO YOU KNOW?
The Producer or the production company may have preferred suppliers they already use. They may have names of people they want in key roles or suggest to be in key roles. Others will be looking to you to bring your contacts and crews. Your experience with crews will grow over time, but you should know some reliable crew already. How do these people work? How do they work together? Do they have your respect? A Producer needs a PM who has the crew's respect. As PM, you will often be the "no" person, informing the crew that they cannot have or rent something because of budgetary restrictions. You have to inspire them to think of creative alternatives. Do you have an office team of a Production Coordinator, Secretary, and Assistant ready to go? If preproduction is fast approaching, it will be good for you to have these people on standby already. You may be starting tomorrow.

WHAT YOU ARE LOOKING FOR
You are part of this interview, too. The fit has to work both ways. Here are some things to consider and to ask yourself during the interview to ensure a good fit. Your questions and participation in the interview will generate further questions and discussions from the Producer, and show the Producer how involved you will be on the production. You will win some trust and assurance with the questions you choose to ask. Notice if the Producer evades some of your questions or is open about the answers. This interview will set the tone for your working relationship.

WHAT'S THE FILM ABOUT?
Have the Producer(s) tell you about the film. Find out both the creative and the financial aspects of the production. Find out the development history of the project. Now is a perfect opportunity for the Producers to show their excitement about the project and sell it to you. If you are to become the PM, you will have to sell the project over and over again to many others. Find out what magic the Producers see in the project.

IS THE BUDGET LOCKED?

Find out how "locked" the budget is. At a certain stage, the Producer has to lock the budget for the financiers and begin cost reporting to the locked budget, showing the overages and saves on a line-by-line basis. Hopefully, you will have the opportunity as PM to take a final pass at the budget before locking it, adding your budgeting expertise to it, bringing the estimates per line as close to reality as possible. With all the variables that happen during the course of production, you will never be exact about each line item, but from working on show after show, you will have a better sense each time where money is actually spent instead of just budgeted to be spent. This pass at the budget will also help you become intimately familiar with each budget line and what it is intended to purchase. Ask yourself: Can I hire the crew I need on these wages? Can I rent the equipment I need with this budget?

IS ANYTHING SPENT ALREADY?

Sometimes a Producer will have pre-allocated costs to contingency. Find out immediately if such is the case. Do not wait until you are hired before you find out that the contingency money in your budget is already spoken for and will not be there for emergencies.

WHAT COST REPORTING IS NEEDED?

Usually you generate a cost report weekly during production, monthly during post-production, and either bi-weekly or monthly during preproduction. If you are working on a co-production, are you reporting on all the costs of production or just this country's costs, leaving the other costs for the other country's accounting people? How soon in the next week does the Producer expect to see a completed cost report? What will your production office be audited on after the end of production? Ask yourself if you and your Accounting team can generate cost reports this soon. Remember that cost reporting is all geared toward the final audit. Plan for the end of the process from the beginning. Is your office going to audit all the costs of production or just the local costs of production?

WHAT IS THE SCHEDULE?

Find out what the production schedule is. How flexible is the delivery date? Does the Producer think the schedule is tight already? Have you shot films this fast before? How fast does the director shoot? Discuss the possibilities and ask yourself if you can bring the project in on time under these circumstances and with these people.

MORE ABOUT THE VISION

You have already discussed the vision of the film with the Producer. Get a sense, if you can, whether the Director and the Producer have the same vision or not. Is the Director known for wide-sweeping expensive vista shots, yet the Producer is planning an intimate, close, personal story? How do the Director and the Producer communicate? How long have they been working together? Are they making the same film? Any sense you get about their communication abilities will give you a foreshadowing of how difficult or seamless the production will be.

WHO IS THE TEAM?

You have already found out about the list of Producers attached to the project. Who else is on board? Find out how involved you are expected to be when it comes to hiring the key crew. Ask yourself if you know of qualified people to fill these roles.

IS THE OFFICE READY?

Find out if the Producer has a production office or a studio already, or if you are expected to find them. More than likely, finding a production office will be your first task.

ANY PREFERRED SUPPLIERS?

Find out if the Producer has preferred suppliers. Is there a computer graphics company already on board? If they have quoted on CGI (computer-graphic imagery) costs for the development budget, there will be one on board already. If the Producer has a track record, he will likely already have a post house he prefers to use, and an insurance company. Find out and note these names. It will be time to introduce yourself soon, should the job be yours.

WHAT DO YOU GET OUT OF THE FILM?

Finally, ask yourself what you get out of this production should you be offered and take the job. Do you like the project and the people? Are you comfortable with the pay and confident you can do the work? Maybe you are being offered this job for less pay than you would rather earn. In that case, evaluate how this show will further your career. Will you be working with someone with whom you want to develop a career contact? Will you be working in a medium with which you have little experience? Does this job fit nicely into your calendar to fill in the space before the high production season begins? Are you particularly passionate about this script or this story? On super-low-budget productions, remember that you have to be getting something out of the production, too. You are about to work extremely long and hard hours, face difficult decisions, and defy all sorts of odds to bring the production in on time and on budget, allowing the creative vision to be realized. Whatever you are paid, you have to be totally dedicated to the project. If you do your job badly, you will hurt your career. You have to find the passion to do it well. Ask yourself: Am I passionate about this project?

THINK ABOUT IT

There is no need to accept a job on the spot if you are offered the position. Thank the Producer or the Line Producer for his or her* time, and leave the interview to at least have a cup of coffee and evaluate what you have just learned. It is more likely you will want to sleep on the decision. You are making a career choice. It is a big decision. Take the night before answering.

Once hired, you will be changing seats and first hiring a Production Coordinator to be your right hand during production. This person will put the office together and keep it all running for you. You need an organizer. Have a look over the coordinator interview questions

---

* This is the last time you will read "his or her"; from this point on, I will use one or the other pronoun and assume you understand that at any single time, either sex could apply.

below, and get the answers from the Producer before you are faced with these questions yourself. You will be answering them over and over again with all crew interviews.

YOU AS THE PRODUCTION COORDINATOR

BEFORE THE INTERVIEW
As a Production Coordinator, just like the PM, do your research prior to the interview. The Internet is a fabulous source of information about companies and people.

Bring a pen, paper, and cue cards into the interview. Assemble some questions on them. As a Production Coordinator, you are being hired to organize not to memorize. This is your opportunity to be organized in the interview. On the job you will be walking around with pen and paper anyway, so get into the habit now.

THE INTERVIEW
Relax and enjoy, if you can. The Coordinator and the Manager need to develop an easy communication and working relationship. Here are some questions to start the conversation rolling. Do not be afraid, however, of interview tangents. If these questions spark further conversation and further questions, that is okay. The Coordinator and the Manager will be spending a lot of time together, so you are expected to be able to communicate well. The only warning about interview tangents is to be aware of any time restrictions. Too much chat can warn the Manager that more conversation than work will get done during the shoot.

WHAT ARE THE SHOOTING START AND END DATES?
This will be the first question the crew will ask you.

DO YOU EXPECT TO HAVE WEEKEND SHOOTS OR 6-DAY WORK WEEKS?
Some films schedule their work week to include shooting on Saturdays, Sundays, and holidays to take advantage of reduced traffic or greater location availability. If you will be dealing with a 6-day work week, consider and adjust your fee accordingly.

DO YOU EXPECT TO HAVE LONG SHOOTING DAYS?
The film will be budgeted to shoot a certain minimum number of hours per day. Is it planned to be a 9-hour day or a 12-hour day? Note that lunch hour is not included in describing the day's length, so a 9-hour day plus lunch is actually 10 hours long.

HOW DO YOU LIKE THE OFFICE RUN?
Some Production Managers insist that the office be open at least 30 minutes prior to call time until 30 minutes after wrap, with prep and wrap days being a minimum of 9:00 a.m. to 6:00 p.m. Some Production Managers will leave the office-opening schedule up to the Coordinator.

WILL THE FILM HAVE "DAY SHOOTS" AND/OR "NIGHT SHOOTS"?

On night shoots, some Production Managers prefer to have the office open both business hours (9:00 a.m. to 6:00 p.m.) and set hours (all night long). If this is the case, you will need extra office crew to make it happen. Discuss this now. What is budgeted?

HOW ELABORATE IS THE SHOOT?

Will there be a lot of extras, locations, special effects, music clearances? The Production Manager may ask what you mean by this question, which is designed to help you determine how complex your job is going to be.

WILL THERE BE ANY ACTORS OR CREW FROM OUT OF TOWN?

This question will determine how much you will need to deal with travel agents and immigration.

WHO IS THE FILM FOR?

Another question the crew will have for you right away — in order to find out who is broadcasting the show or which distributor is handling the feature.

WHO ARE THE PRODUCERS? HOW MANY ARE THERE? HOW INVOLVED ARE THEY?

Executives from many different companies and countries can be listed as the Producers for a film. There can be Executive Producers, Supervising Producers, Associate Producers, Creative Producers, Producers, Co-Producers, Line Producers, or any other "Producer" title newly invented. Since the titles are not standard for describing the duties of each position, you need to find out how each Producer is involved and in what order (often a political decision) to put them on the crew list. As subtext, you will also learn how big a job your paperwork distribution to the various companies will be, and you may get an idea of how long head-office decisions take by determining how active each of the various Producers intend to be.

WHAT IS THE COMPANY NAME FOR THIS FILM PRODUCTION?

For legal and accounting purposes, film companies set up separate incorporated companies for each production. You need to know this name to conduct any business, from making letterhead to setting up accounts and contracts.

WHERE ARE THE PRODUCTION OFFICES? HOW SET UP ARE THEY?

Some offices are simply empty rooms that you have to furnish from scratch. Others are fully furnished right down to telephone systems and photocopiers. This question will determine how busy you will be in your first few days.

DO YOU HAVE A COMPUTER SYSTEM ALREADY? WHAT KIND IS IT?

Often the Production Coordinator comes to a production with a computer. If you do, negotiate a kit-rental fee and find out if your system or training is compatible with the company's.

DO YOU HAVE CORPORATE ACCOUNTS ALREADY ESTABLISHED?

Some companies prefer that you use their head-office courier, photocopier, office stationery accounts, etc., whereas others encourage you to bring in your own contacts.

WHAT PRODUCTION PAPERWORK DO YOU REQUIRE? ANY PREFERRED FORMS?

These questions are merely confirmation that the Production Manager wants completed production reports, call sheets, production schedules, and so on. Though redundant, the queries should spark further discussion about any existing forms the company prefers to use, and who, between the Assistant Directors and you, will be responsible for certain paperwork. You will also learn how easy it is to talk to the Production Manager and how much the PM will rely on you for the correct paperwork on the show.

HOW MUCH OF THE CREW HAS BEEN HIRED?

Here is where your pen and paper prove useful. Write down all names and positions the Production Manager mentions. Also note the status of each person. Often names will be chosen for the various positions, but not yet confirmed. Be aware of who may come on board, but never publish any unconfirmed information on a crew list. This is your opportunity to show how you deal with confidential information.

HOW MANY STAFF WILL BE IN THE OFFICE?

Find out how much the budget allows for a Production Secretary and Assistants. Also find out if you will be hiring the Assistants or if they will be appointed for you. Some Assistant roles may be already hired or promised by Producers, Managers, or Executives prior to your arrival.

HOW SOON DO YOU WANT THE PRODUCTION COORDINATOR TO START?

This will be a budgetary concern for the Production Manager. Be prepared if the date is tomorrow.

WHAT IS IN THE BUDGET FOR THE PRODUCTION COORDINATOR?

This is the dance of the numbers. You ask the Production Manager how much is in the budget, the Production Manager asks you how much you expect to make. If the coordinator job is union, the dance can be short, as you can look up the scale rate to start; but if the job is non-union, the price range is enormous. If you intend to jump in with the first number, consider the scale and the budget of the film together with your research from other coordinators to determine a starting price. Remember to negotiate your computer and equipment kit rental separately.

You may not be able to get all the answers to your questions right away. That is okay. You can leave some of the questions for the first day of the job. As mentioned in the Production Manager section, you as the Production Coordinator do not have to decide to take the job at the interview. The Production Manager may be interviewing other candidates and will want to make a decision later. You are welcome to think about the possible job overnight, too. Later, review your cue cards and notes. Do you want to get involved with this job? It will be a huge commitment. Long, hard hours. Think about it seriously. Sleep on it. Then follow up with the Production Manager the next day.

ABOUT THE PRODUCTION MANAGER & THE PRODUCTION COORDINATOR

The Production Manager oversees everything the Production Coordinator does. This process may seem slow at first, but as the PM and the PC develop a relationship of trust, the Coordinator can be given room to initiate more duties unsupervised. The production office is a very busy place, and everything eventually makes it past the Coordinator's desk. A Production Coordinator should never forget to inform the Production Manager of what is happening. The PM needs to know as much as the PC does about all that is going on in the making of the film. At its best, the PM and the PC will become friends and trust each other with secrets that will help both in excelling at their jobs. At its worst, the PM and the PC will neither inform nor help each other, and the production will stumble along with great problems as everyone finds out crucial information after the fact. Communication is a two-way street, so start off your side as best as you can. Work at it. Invest in it.

Congratulations! You made it to the end of the interview as a Production Manager or a Production Coordinator! You have been hired! Celebrate. Take yourself out for dinner and a movie. After today, you are going to give an awful lot of your time and effort to the production. The real adventure is about to begin. You are about to turn an empty set of rooms into a running, thriving film production office. Armed with all the answers you acquired during the interview, you are ready for the adventure.

The Person To Know

Film festival parties are nothing less than schmooze fests. Schmoozing. Not only is it a game, it is an art. But then again, a little luck can help, too.

The goal of schmoozing is to be the Person To Know, or know the Person To Know, or be talking to the Person To Know, or be the person to introduce the Person To Know to others at the party.

Thick in a crowded festival party, I ended up in a circle with an Executive, a Distributor, a Producer, and a Director — all schmoozing at their very best. Not being perceived as being the Person To Know, I was actively ignored, which was rather uncomfortable. And being in a corner, I was unfortunately trapped from leaving the group gracefully.

The Director was the Person To Know. The Executive had his arm around the Director and was schmoozing away. The Producer input some schmooze trying to introduce some of the Director's little known facts to the Executive. The Distributor contributed, too. The Director bathed in the attention. He was the Person To Know. I just watched from my corner, for I did not know the Person To Know. On and on they went. On and on. I was getting thirsty. My drink was long gone.

Then a Big Financier walked by the group. Roles immediately shifted. The Big Financier was perceived by all to be more of a Person To Know than the Director was. The Executive leapt from the Director over to the Big Financier to be the one to introduce him to the group. The Big Financier took in the group's dynamic in a second. Then he waved off the Executive with a "not now" and stepped forward into the middle of the group to greet me... for as luck would have it, I knew him personally. "Hi, Deb. How are you doing?" After exchanging brief pleasantries, he excused himself again with a simple "Sorry, I have to go," and did not stay for any of the schmooze competition.

All eyes swung toward me. In an instant I had become the Person To Know. And they had no idea who I was.

The Executive was first to capitalize on it. He put his arm around me to introduce himself, and more importantly to find out who I was.

I held up my empty glass and answered cryptically, "He's a friend of mine. Now, if you'll excuse me, I need a refill. Cheers!" And I left gracefully... thanks to a little schmoozing luck.

14

CHAPTER 2

BEFORE OFFICIAL PREP

Okay, you have the job, but the production office will not be opening for another week or so. Official preproduction has not really started yet, since it begins when the production office opens. Life before "official prep" is actually the tail end of "development." The Production Coordinator rarely starts prior to the first day of official prep — the day the production office opens — so this chapter is primarily for the Production Manager. If the Producer can afford it, the PM will start in late development. As a PM, here is what you can start accomplishing.

FROM DEVELOPMENT TO PREPRODUCTION

You may be starting work at a desk with a telephone at head office, or, if space is at a premium, you may be starting from your own home. Basically, you need a telephone and your contact lists.

PRIORITY MEETING WITH THE PRODUCER(S)

Meet with the Producer(s) again after the interview. You will have many more questions now that you are working toward production instead of working toward getting a job. What is going to be hard to find for this production? The Producers may have insight from their past experiences. You will have insight from yours. Share. Is it hockey season, and you need to rent an ice rink for three weeks? Is the busy summer season approaching when studio rental space will be at a premium? It is time to prioritize what you first need to find and secure.

BEWARE WHAT YOU PROMISE

The reason so few people are hired during development is because the financing of the production is likely still being assembled by the Producer(s). Not all sources of financing may have committed to paper their financial participation to the project. Because of this uncertainty, there is always the possibility the project could go under before it is made. Keep in daily conversation with the Producer on the status of the financing structure, and get approvals on any plans you have for spending preproduction monies at this stage. Remember that every time you make a promise to someone or some company on the telephone, you are spending the Producer's money. If the project happens to fall through at this early date, the Producer is responsible to pay for all your promises. You do not want to over-commit what the Producer is willing to risk. You will spend much of your time "holding" rental spaces and "checking availability," confirming that you are not ordering or booking at this stage.

SINGLE-PURPOSE COMPANY STATUS

Film companies set up a single-purpose company to produce each film they make. It keeps the accounting totally separate from both head office accounting and taxation and all the other films the company happens to be making. You will find that each season of a series will be produced by a different single-purpose company. For example, Film Company Inc. may be the parent company producing a series, but the first season of the series was actually made by Season One Productions Ltd., and the second season made by Season Two Productions Ltd. Both Season One Productions and Season Two Productions will be companies owned 100% by Film Company Inc. It makes business sense. If head office or legal counsel has not set up the single-purpose company yet, now is a good time to remind the Producer to do so.

THE PRODUCTION-OFFICE TEAM

Your support team is the staff of the production office: the Production Coordinator (your right hand) with the office staff (the Production Secretary or Assistant to the Coordinator and Office Production Assistant or Office P.A.), and the Production Accountant (your left hand) with the accounting staff. The sooner you can hire these people, the more you will be able to accomplish. A Producer or an Executive may already have someone in mind for the Office P.A. position. You may have a team you have worked with before waiting in the wings. Decide on these people early. These positions will be discussed in more depth in later chapters.

PRODUCTION OFFICE

If official prep starts the day the production office opens, one of your first jobs will be to find that office. Consider parking: How many trucks and crew vehicles can you park there? Will you be parking the unit there every night and on weekends? Consider location: Is it accessible to highways and convenient to potential locations or equipment rental facilities? Consider office space: Will the Art Department and all their drafting tables fit alongside Wardrobe and all their storage, and do you have to house the Writer(s) too? Consider security: Is there a system built-in already, or will it be easy to install one? Consider your budget: Can you afford a deluxe office space attached to a high-end studio or are you budgeted for using the basement of a church? Consider the extra costs: Will you have to pay for the existing security, the telephone system, the fax and copier, or set up your own? If the office space has a fax and a copier for you to assume, is the equipment reliable and powerful enough to handle the heavy load you are about to inflict on it? Film commissions know of office space used for previous productions. Location Managers and other Production Managers are other sources for finding appropriate space. You can also find out what companies are wrapping about the time you want to start official prep, to possibly assume their space.

KEY CREW

While you are waiting for calls back regarding office space, start assembling the key crew. Who is already committed to come on board the project? Start a crew list of your own. A list of key crew positions to get you started is in Chapter 7. In a race for the top of the list, the first jobs you will want to fill are: the Location Manager, the First Assistant Director, the Director of Photography, the Production Designer, and the Construction Manager. The Producer and the Director will be involved in these decisions, too. Key crew are critical to the realization of the project. A lot is at stake with every crew choice for key positions. The Production Designer may be on board already and drafting up designs for sets. A Storyboard Artist may be on board already penciling shots designed by the Director. The First Assistant Director, though it sounds like a Director's Assistant, is actually the Producer's or PM's representative on set. The First A.D. keeps the set running smoothly and efficiently, allowing the Director to concentrate on the creative aspects of her job. This person is the scheduling expert. You will be involved in the choice of First A.D. As your job is to bring the show in on time as well as on budget, choose the First A.D. carefully. The keys will be discussed in more detail in Chapter 7.

STUDIO

Even if you are shooting many scenes on location, chances are that part of your shoot will be in a studio. You may have budgeted for a warehouse space or for a high-end studio. No matter which, you are likely competing with other production companies for the same spaces around town. Book as early as you can for studio space. Meet with the Production Designer and the Producer to discuss the size of space actually needed — both floor space and ceiling height. As with the production office space, consider parking: Will the unit fit in the space allowed, and are the entry points convenient for equipment loading? Consider location: Is the studio close to the office, or have you found a studio with an acceptable office space attached? Consider dressing rooms: Are they decent, or will you be in studio and on location so much that you will be using the mobile units anyway; or can you schedule in such a way so as to stop renting the mobile unit when you move to the studio? Consider hair/makeup rooms: Are they acceptable in the building, or do you have to build a workable space? Consider construction space: Is there enough room for a construction shop on site? Consider multiple studios: Can you rent two studio spaces in the same building, allowing construction or set decoration to be working in one studio while the main unit is filming in the other, and does soundproofing allow such a plan? Consider sound: If you are looking at a non-professional studio space, are you on an airport landing path, or is the space so large that the sound recordings will echo so much that you will have to replace the entire soundtrack in post?

HIDDEN COSTS

Remember that when you get something for free or next to free, there are bound to be hidden costs. Find out the hidden costs for this studio space. They could be transparent costs like the place has no power to tap into, so you have to rent a generator. They could be not so transparent costs like the place has skylights that you cannot afford to cover, causing you to shoot at night — so you find you cannot hire the crew you want due to your all-nights shooting schedule. They could also affect other not so immediate costs: The daily rain on the tin roof makes the soundtrack so unacceptable you have to bring in all the actors and dub their voices expensively in post. Always find out how much the "free" space costs you. You may be spending more on hidden extras than if you were to rent a professional studio space. Your job is not about not spending money… it is about spending it wisely.

Film commissions and your local city/town reference books will have listings of many acceptable studio spaces. Again, you can speak with Location Managers and other Production Managers or people wrapping productions for their experiences at certain spaces. Find out what worked for them, and what drove them crazy. They will give you a sense of where you may have to spend money to make the space workable.

LOCATION SCOUTING

If you do not have a Location Manager on board, you will obviously need a Location Scout until you can hire the Location Manager. You need to come up with potential locations as well as studio spaces and office spaces. You cannot do this alone. The Location Scout or Manager will visit potential locations and photograph them for review at the office with you, the Producer, and the Director. This person will save you hours of searching. Film commissions have location libraries filled with pictures of various locations that have been used for filming or would like to be used for filming. This is only a starting point. You need a Scout who can research beyond these files. A smart Scout will consider the locations you need and come up with potential places where locations can be linked. For example, you can look one way down the street for a certain part of the script. And inside one of the houses on that street there is a room that can be used as a boardroom for elsewhere in the script. And in the backyard of another place is a potential location for another part of the script. Driving the unit across town to various locations during the shoot is an expensive waste of time. A smart Scout will also ensure the owner of the location is amenable to a production filming there before you consider the place. Scouting is not just about taking pictures of beautiful places. You do not want the Director to fall in love with a location, and then have the Scout mention that the owner has no idea you were looking at the space, only later to find the owner does not want a film crew there at any cost. Do not waste precious prep time chasing unattainable locations. As PM, do not miss any location meetings. Many decisions are made that radically affect production at these meetings. You have to know about every one of those decisions.

CASTING

The Producer, the Director, and the Casting Director are taking care of casting the stars and the leads. You just need to know it is happening, and if any promises are being made that will affect the budget. You will spend more time dealing with locations issues than casting session issues.

PRODUCTION INSURANCE

Arrange for production insurance as soon as you can. There are various insurance brokers who specialize in the film industry. You can get quotes from different brokers before committing to use one. Since some departments (like Art and Construction) may already be working, and since some of the insurance covers delays related to key cast illness, you will need insurance coverage as soon as possible. Insurance will be discussed in more detail in Chapter 17.

EQUIPMENT HOUSE

Camera, Lighting, and Grip equipment houses book packages of equipment like studios book space for a shoot. There is a finite amount of equipment in their stock, and each equipment house will be able to equip a finite number of productions. You will want to book your equipment package, or at least pencil in a booking regarding equipment for your production. If you book too late, you may end up with a smaller package of equipment, and be forced to pay for many daily (read "expensive") rentals to make up for what is lacking. Get more than one quote for comparison. Decide on a supplier by both its price and its service. When a piece of equipment breaks down on set during filming, you will need service to replace it more than you will need rock-bottom prices.

POST HOUSE

If you think it is too early to be thinking about postproduction, you are wrong. It is true that on day one of principal photography you are shooting, but on day two, you have begun editing the footage from day one. You need to assemble quotations from a production lab for processing and printing or transferring your film, and from a post house for editing facilities.

OTHER SUPPLIERS & SPECIAL NEEDS

Other suppliers to whom you can make initial calls for quotations are: film stock or tape stock suppliers, special effects companies, and computer graphic imagery companies ("CGI"). Basically, evaluate what will be the most difficult or the most complex to achieve. Start assembling quotations on those items. If initial quotations are showing to be over budget, now is the time to address your concerns to the Producer. The earlier you can warn of potential budget problems, the more thought that can go into the solution. A script revision or a different way of shooting may solve the problem. With early warnings, you can have time to work out the difficulty the best way for all concerned.

READ THE SCRIPT AGAIN

You read the script before starting. Read it again. Find out what the revision schedule is. Talk to the Producer about what revisions are planned for the script but are not currently reflected. There is no sense in chasing quotations for a location or an effect that does not exist in the revised script.

BUDGET & CASH FLOW

Budgeting is detailed in the next chapter, but you need to be working on this budget during late development. As you assemble the many quotations from various sources, you will want to reflect these savings and overages in the budget. Find out when the budget has to be locked for the Financiers. Make changes until you have to lock it. Read the budget over and over again. You are the budget expert. You are going to report all costs in comparison to this budget. In which lines is there potential extra money? Which lines are tight? Is the budget structured well enough for easy cost reporting? Are the fringes in one easy-to-report account or are they attached to each person throughout the budget? Make any reallocations now so that the budget is easier to read. A first cost report filled with reallocations is not only messy, but makes you look like you did not know how to write a budget in the first place. Also, start a cash flow to find out how much money you may need from a bank to interim finance the bills during production. The Producer will arrange for the interim financing, but will be relying on you to say how much of a loan is needed and for how long.

GET LISTED

Inform the film commission of your production and its contact information and shooting dates. Most film commissions publish a weekly list to the industry reporting on who is shooting what and when. If you do not want to receive unsolicited resumes or calls, ask the film commission to note on their list that you do not want such resumes or calls. You can wait until you open the production office before calling the commission to get on this listing; if you do that, you can have the Production Coordinator make the call.

You may not have a production office yet, but you've chosen one, and you will move in shortly. You have been contacting people and suppliers and assembling a plethora of quotations. Even if you are not listed with the film commission yet, the rumor mill has begun. People will find out about your production any second now. Are you ready for official prep? You bet you are.

The Writers' Joke

When you work on a series, you have to deal with the issue of the crew's boredom. It is a different story, but it's the same set, the same cast, the same premise, the same crew, the same camera angles week in, week out.

So challenges arise to keep the crew's interest up. How can we push the envelope a little farther becomes the challenge. One time, the Writers got in on the fun. They wrote a shot into the script that involved moving the camera through every single room in the house... without cutting... from the point of view of a housefly. Yeah, right. Cute joke. Now what are they really going to film?

Well, the crew was up for the challenge. Grips and Electrics figured out how to light the shot so that the camera could travel through all the rooms of the house set without seeing a light, a grip stand, or a flag in shot. Camera and Grips figured out how to move the camera through all the sets and keep framing and focus in and the crew out of the shot.

The day came. A rig and harness was set up for the camera operator to start on the balcony, "fly" down to the floor, be unhooked by a grip in hiding on the set, then move through the living room, the kitchen, the dining room, back through the living room, and into the den. And what a shot it was!

So watch out for those "joke shots" the Writers write into scripts. They just might happen!

CHAPTER 3

BUDGETING & BREAKDOWNS

There are good books on the market that walk Production Managers through a budget line-by-line in much detail. This chapter will not try to replace those books. Nor will this chapter teach you how to create a budget in record time or even create one for you. The first budget you create will take you plenty of time to do because you will have to look up every calculation and double-check all your numbers against quotations and price lists. That is okay. It is normal. In time you will become faster in creating budgets, because you will have old budgets and cost reports to refer to and the memory of creating them to aid you. For now, expect that the learning process will take time. What you do need to know now is what specific issues and questions will help you to understand how to read and write budgets effectively. That is what this chapter is about.

The Production Coordinator will not be nearly as hands-on when it comes to a budget, so the PC can either read this chapter to be informed of the budgeting process or skip to Chapter 4.

OVERALL BUDGETING ISSUES

WHEN TO WRITE A BUDGET
The Producer may make the first budget or hire a Production Manager during development to create one. A budget is required during the process of assembling the financing, months or years before shooting begins. It makes sense to hire a budgeting specialist, like a Production Manager, to create the initial budget. Hiring this individual is the best way to create a realistic cost plan early in the process. Production Managers know the costs of production from being on set and tracking the costs on a day-to-day basis. If you have experience, you may be hired to create a preliminary production budget early in development. You may be hired to create a budget for less than your usual rate in exchange for the promise of being the Production Manager when and if the film makes it to production. If you are new to budgeting, you may offer to write a free budget for a Producer to demonstrate and hone your untried skills.

This preliminary budget, however, will not be the final, locked budget. Some line items will certainly be locked at their cost allocations and the bottom line of the budget will not change (because the financing being raised will be defined), but the script is developing and changing along the way to preproduction. The budget has to change to reflect those script changes. At some point, though, the budget must be locked, and the Production Manager has to know this locked budget inside and out. He must "own" it and report all costs in comparison to it. Just prior to locking the budget is most likely the time when you as a Production Manager will come on board the project. In development the Producer and Financiers needed a budget to give them an overview of the feasibility of the project, to comfort them that the budget size would be adequate to complete the production. Now, closer to first day of principal photography, you need to ensure the budget is being prepared for the details of production and for the reporting of those costs in the audit. If the budget is not locked when you come on board, prepare to revise the budget allocations for ease of reporting during production and audit.

BUDGETING IS ABOUT MAKING DECISIONS

How big is a budget? How long is a piece of string? Both questions have the same answer: It can be anything. Budgeting is about making decisions. Whether you are writing a budget in development or revising one just prior to locking the budget, with every cost allocation you choose, you are making decisions that production will have to follow. The number of extras you choose for a day will affect the lens size the Camera Department will need to capture the shot. The amount of overtime you budget will determine the number of set hours you shoot on a daily basis. The money you allocate to film stock will determine how many takes the Director can have. Needless to say, you cannot make all these decisions alone, and you will be discussing many questions with the Producer and the Director, but during the budgeting process, you will be surprised how many of these "production decisions" you will have to make in isolation. Be prepared to know the ramifications of the money you allocate to each budget line. Be prepared to advise the Producer on areas in the production where money may be saved if certain production decisions are effected.

AUDIT-LOGICAL BUDGET LINES

The audit happens long after you as the Production Manager have left the production. Why do you want to think about it at the beginning of preproduction? Producers must account for every penny they spend of the Financiers' money. You have seen the budget. The Financiers have given a lot of money to the Producer to make this film. The production costs must be viable, accountable costs. The Financiers want to know that they financed the cost of making the film and nothing else. If the production ends up under budget, the Financiers will ask for some of their money back from the Producer. If the production goes over budget, the Financiers will either give more money to the Producer to finish the film or — more likely — require the Producer to cover the budget overage. The audit is a report from an outside source that the costs of production were true and accurate. It will report costs compared to the locked budget. If the locked budget is poorly structured — so that during production many cost allocations were changed to reflect where the money was actually spent, showing huge variances throughout the budget — this problem will come out in the audit and make its interpretation more difficult and therefore more expensive. Allocate costs to lines of the budget logically. Anticipate where you are really going to report on the money being spent. Fringes, for example, are easier to account for in one budget line instead of in each crew member's budget line, as Production Accountants will need only one budgetary code to report on fringes paid instead of fifty budgetary codes — one for each crew member.

DEVELOPMENT BUDGETS VS. PRODUCTION BUDGETS
Development costs are very different from production costs. In development, Producers finance costs with development money. Development money is always a loan until the first day of principal photography. In nearly all cases, if a project never makes it to camera, the loan is never paid back. Yes, that means that financing the development of a script is a very risky investment, and there is no opportunity for profit, only for recoupment of the initial investment. Development loans are to assist Producers moving a project from script to screen; the first day of principal photography is the first day a script is no longer just a script, hence this is why you pay back these loans on the first day of shooting.

As a Production Manager, you will likely never write a development budget. Producers do it. Development costs can include: story rights (so the Producer has the right to develop the project), Writer's fees and fringes, Story Editor's fees and fringes, Researcher's fees and expenses, options or holding fees for stars, legal start-up costs, travel for Writer's meetings, Producer's fees and overhead. In later stages of development, costs can also include: pre-casting costs, pre-location scouting costs, costs for the creation of a production budget and breakdown, storyboard costs, and possibly a pre-shoot. There is a catch-22 when it comes to development costs: The Producer needs money to develop the project, but the more money spent on development, the higher the budget is required for production to pay the development costs back and still have enough money to make the film.

DEVELOPMENT MONEY IS DEVELOPMENT LOANS
Since development loans are paid back on the first day of principal photography, all the development costs are included and itemized in the production budget. Ensure to get a proper breakdown of the development costs and receipts from the Producer. In effect, the production is "buying the development receipts" from the Producer on the first day of principal photography. The Production Accountant will need these original receipts to cost report effectively and to prepare for the final audit.

INCORPORATE DEVELOPMENT COSTS INTO THE PRODUCTION BUDGET
There are two ways of incorporating development costs into a production budget. If you do not incorporate the costs carefully, you may be double-booking the development costs and robbing yourself of production money you can spend wisely elsewhere... or worse, you may be paying somebody twice for the same job due to a poorly structured budget!

INCORPORATING THE DEVELOPMENT COSTS – SYSTEM #1

Insert a detail breakdown of the development budget into the development line of the budget "above the line." Remember when you are noting these costs, you will have to deduct some of these costs elsewhere in the budget; for example, you paid the Writer $25,000 during development to write the script, but her production script fee is $75,000 less any amounts payable in development. In the development line, you budget $25,000 paid to the Writer. In the Writer's line, you budget $75,000 paid to the Writer and you also report "-$25,000" for amounts paid in development. In effect, the Writer's line in the budget will add up to $50,000, and the Writer will also be reported in the development line for the $25,000 balance. The only difficulty of this system is that the Production Accountant will be writing checks on the first day of principal photography to Financiers, not to the line items of the development budget (like to the Writer).

INCORPORATING THE DEVELOPMENT COSTS – SYSTEM #2

This system is remarkably like the first system, but addresses the problem of to whom the checks are payable (the Financiers) on the first day of principal photography. Itemize in the development line of the budget the list of Financiers to be paid back and the amount each check needs to be; for example, Financier #1: $10,000; Financier #2: $35,000; Financier #3: $5,000. Also note in the development section of the budget the itemized costs of development, but do not add these numbers to the budget — just note what the costs breakdown is for development. Then, as in the first system, ensure that you deduct double-booked lines of the budget, like Writer's fees paid in development against a future production fee, Performer's options paid in development toward their production fee, and possible Producer fees and corporate overhead fees which may have a cap on allowable levels in the production budget. If you do not take the time to show the breakdown of development costs in this system, you will no doubt double-book items unknowingly. (See samples on pages 387 and 388.)

THE FIRST READ OR PREPARING FOR THE FIRST PASS

THE PHYSICAL STRUCTURE OF A BUDGET

A budget is made up of a top sheet, detail pages, and an assumption page or memo that details assumptions on which the budget was made (the "production decisions" made during the budgeting process). (See samples on pages 389-391.)

BUDGET TOP SHEET

The top sheet summarizes the entire budget by category in one or two pages. You never do any budgeting calculations on this page; just summarize the attached budget in a short form. It is the top sheet alone, rather than the complete budget with detail pages and assumption memo, that Financiers require attached to their agreements and signed by the Producer. Few people need ever see the entire budget. The budget is not a public document.

BUDGET DETAIL PAGES

The budget itself is all the detail pages of the budget. Each category from the top sheet is expanded into showing the complete calculations of each cost. The more detail you show on the detail pages, the more you will understand and remember how you achieved these cost estimates when you are in the midst of shooting. You will require this detail when you need to move costs to show savings and to cover overages as you start spending.

HEADER INFORMATION

The top sheet and the first page of the detail portion of the budget have some of these "assumption" notes in the header by the title. These header notes are of global importance to the budget and include at least the following information: how many shoot days, how many weeks in post, when in the year is this to be filmed, what format is the shoot and the post, which unions are or are not being used, how much is location versus studio shooting, what is the general location (city) of the shoot, what currency is being used at which exchange rate, what are the names of the production company and the Producer, and who wrote this budget and on what date and what version. This header information gives you a quick glance to note if this budget version is the most current or the most accurate. With a notation on a Christmas Special of "Shoot: Summer 2004" in the header, you will know this is the budget that requires a lot of snow special effects instead of the budget that has "Shoot: February 2005" in the header.

BUDGET ASSUMPTION PAGE OR MEMO

The assumption page is a separate page or memo attached to the budget, detailing further why some of the noteworthy calculations in the budget are what they are. Assumptions may mention a global cost for special effects that was not based on a quotation, but based on an allocation as instructed by the Producer to you — or be a notation of any other production decision you have made during the course of budgeting. It is wise to draw these noteworthy calculations and production decisions to the attention of the reader (especially the Producer), as all these notes make it clear what restrictions you have imposed on the production during the course of budgeting.

BUDGET FORMS

There are many budget forms available. Studios each have their own form of preference for budget structure, each with their own accounting codes. Each format may vary about which categories are above and below the line, or whether the departmental labor costs are budgeted separately from the departmental rentals and purchases, but the differences are minimal. They are all designed to be logical for the purposes of audit. If you budget a non-union production, you will probably want to use a studio-friendly budget format anyway, since the form itself will remind you to budget for categories you may otherwise forget by simply listing all the possible categories you could apply money to. It is also good to get into the habit of using studio budget formats, as this is an accounting language that works well already. In all cases you can remove empty categories you will not be using, and therefore amend the form for your own personal use. In all of Canada, for example, Producers tend to use the Telefilm Canada budget format whether the production is being funded by Telefilm or not, because the separation of labor costs from all other departmental costs simplifies the process of calculating and reporting on labor costs for labor tax credit purposes.

BUDGETING SOFTWARE

Budgeting software is discussed further in the next chapter, but know that if you are planning to budget more than once, you will need budgeting software. There are a host of shortcuts imbedded in the software that will save you the time of re-calculating employee fringes and other amounts every time you modify the budget. Movie Magic Budgeting, the most popular software for production budgeting, is excellent. Take time to become familiar with some of its features, like globals and fringes; if you are just starting, don't worry about the other features for now. There are other key-typing short cuts in the program, but when you are learning to budget, you need the repetition of entries to teach yourself about the act of budgeting. When you have developed a skill in budgeting (you will know when), then you should learn about the other timesaving features of the program. Besides, when you learn the timesaving features later on, you will appreciate them more fully.

SCRIPT BREAKDOWN FOR BUDGETING

If you have the time and the energy, you can do an entire scheduling breakdown and create a production ("strip") board to give yourself a detailed look at the schedule of the production before starting to budget. It is more likely that you will not have the time to do a full breakdown. What you need to do, however, is a "budget breakdown" to assist you in making production decisions when creating the budget. There are two systems I have used as budget breakdown. Neither of these two systems replaces the quality of information you can get from doing a full breakdown, but they will assist you in starting the initial budget to determine a production's feasibility at a certain budget level.

BUDGET BREAKDOWN #1 – "THE LISTS"

Have several sheets of paper handy when reading the script, and on each one, create a separate breakdown: a list of locations, noting beside each location how many scenes per location using one tick mark for each scene; a cast list, noting beside each character, the same way, how many scenes each is in; a list of each special item that costs money (like a list of vehicles, animals, children, extras, special effects, CGI, stunts, special locations, songs, etc.). If a scene is hugely long, note it on your breakdowns as more than one scene to account for the extra work that might be involved. Also note with an "N" if a scene is required to be a night shoot. This system gives you a rough idea of the contents of the script, and a rough balance of where the money might be spent. You can look, for example, at the list of locations and determine if you can reasonably achieve a shoot at 35 different locations in a 25-day shoot or not. (See sample on page 392.)

BUDGET BREAKDOWN #2 – "THE SPREADSHEET"
If you prefer to be at a computer screen, this system may work for you. Open a new spreadsheet and make columns for Scene Number, Set Description, D/N, # of Pages, Cast, Extras, Special Notes. If you have a large number of stunts or animals, you could create a column just for that item, too. Any special item (like vehicles, animals, children, special effects, CGI, stunts, songs, special locations, etc.) that does not warrant its own column, will be included in the Special Notes column. The information on this spreadsheet is rather similar to that on a one-line schedule, but adds special notes. As you read the script, you need to fill in each line with the appropriate information. Each entry needs to be so brief that it is in code in order to include the information and not to end up with pages and pages of notes afterward. Cast characters, for example, may appear as initials instead of spelling out their entire names. Be rough on page counts. You do not need the detail of counting in eighths of pages at this stage, as you are looking at the global picture and the proportional size of the scene to the script. You may want to round out page counts to half pages to enable this process. (See sample on page 393.)

MAKE DECISIONS, MAKE NOTES
While making your breakdowns, and while creating the budget, always have paper and pen or pencil next to you. Jot down questions you need to ask the Producer or the Director before making a production decision for them. Note anything unusual for your assumption notes later. If a thought crosses your mind that something has to be shot in a certain way to film the scene on this budget, make a note of it. When someone else reads your budget, they must understand the restrictions you place on them, agreeing to shoot the show using this particular budget. You are making decisions every time you write a budget.

HOW TO READ AND WRITE A BUDGET — THE DETAILS
Perhaps you have not written the preliminary budget. How do you read someone else's budget to understand where the money is allocated beyond a cursory glance? Look at the calculations. If there are no calculations, and only "allowances" for each category, the validity of the final budgeted numbers is questionable. Even on flat weekly rate salaries, it is easy to enter a calculation for how many weeks of prep, shoot, and wrap is assigned to each person. When it comes to postproduction, you know how much footage was shot by how much was purchased, so it is possible to estimate, to the foot, how much the processing will cost at the lab. Also look for entire sections of the budget encompassed by one budget estimate; for example, picture and sound post being allocated a single budget figure. There are many, many steps to picture and sound post that can be itemized in the budget. By encompassing a huge number of steps into one budget number, there is a danger some or many of these steps have been omitted in estimating the cost. Replace these "allowances" with more accurate estimates based on calculations, and detail the breakdown of costs as much as possible. Review the sample budget detail page to see how much detail you can include in one line of the budget. This detail will help you immensely when cost reporting during production. (See sample on page 394.)

MORE SPECIFIC BUDGETING ISSUES

WHAT IS THE LINE?

"Line" Producer. Above-The-"Line." Below-The-"Line." What is that darned "Line" anyway and do you want to be above or below it? The Line's placement varies moderately from budget form to budget form, but in general, consider that Above-The-Line costs are all the costs associated with the people who made up the creative package that was assembled in development to put this production together: the Producer, the Director, the Writer and story rights, the Star, the other development costs. Costs associated with these people include not only their pay, but also their travel and living, Assistants, and offices. Everything else in the budget is Below-The-Line — starting with the Production Manager. Above-The-Line costs are sometimes called the "fixed costs," because by the time you get to production, these costs have been negotiated. Costs like contingency and the completion bond are often based on a percentage of the budget. They tend to remove the Above-The-Line costs from their percentage calculation because Above-The-Line costs are often above union scale rates, and sometimes are so high they artificially inflate the size of the budget, thereby artificially inflating the costs based on a percentage of the budget.

BUDGET SIZES

How many days can you shoot if you have $1 million to make the film? What kind of crew can you hire if you have $1.2 million per episode to shoot the series? Where in the budget will you be spending the most money in a $500,000 feature film? After you have written a number of budgets, you will be able to picture the answers to these questions. Each answer is dependent, too, on the complexity of the script and the production. You may have $1 million to make a film, but you are planning to shoot out of town, so you will have extraordinary costs for travel and living for the crew; you will have to reduce the number of shoot days you had planned to pay for the costs of moving to a distant location. The series may sound simple, but the CGI budget is so high, you may have a tough time finding enough money left in the budget to hire a union crew. The $500,000 feature will undoubtedly be spending most of its money on postproduction costs, unless, of course, something goes wrong during the shoot.

Yet, still oversimplifying, I will give you an idea of what overall budget size means to a production:

- A "$1.2M per episode series" means a union crew, a significant studio build, and great catering.

- A "$1M feature" means a below union-scale crew or non-union crew, a superbly tight budget for all departments, and great catering.

- A "$250,000 feature" means a crew working on deferral or for free, everyone cashing in favors in every department to obtain what is needed, insurance costs to enable cheaper equipment rentals, and great catering.

On a big budget it is expected you feed the crew well. They are working long, hard hours on the production, so it is only respectful that you do so. As the overall budget gets smaller, the catering must be excellent on the production, too; since you are probably not giving the crew enough time or money to buy their own groceries, you need to feed them well to fuel them through production and keep them healthy for their work.

BUDGET PROPORTIONS

If you like to budget where you take the bottom-line budget figure then subdivide it into rough allocations or targets for Above-The-Line, Below-The-Line production, and Below-The-Line postproduction costs, then you like to budget to budget proportions. You will therefore need to be aware of the overall proportions of where you will spend the money in a budget. This depends on the overall size of your budget. A "big" budget has incredibly high ATL costs, high production costs, and less high postproduction costs. For a "medium-sized budget," you will have medium ATL costs, medium production costs, and medium to high postproduction costs. For a "low-budget" film, you will find low ATL costs, low production costs, and high postproduction costs. And finally, for a "micro-budget" film, you will find the ATL costs are negligible, the production costs are incredibly low, and the postproduction costs are high. Though you may be able to get crew on deferrals, and incredibly cheap equipment rentals or borrowed equipment during production, you will find that postproduction has hard costs you cannot ignore. There are chemicals in the lab that have to be paid for. There are film stock and sound stock that have to be purchased. You have to mix the sound at a facility, ousting paying customers to get the time. Be prepared for the costs of postproduction.

QUESTIONS TO ASK BEFORE WRITING A BUDGET

You may have the answers to many of these questions already from your interview, but just in case you are writing the budget early in development and have not yet been hired to production-manage the show, here are questions you need to ask to get started: (For a short checklist-format form of these questions, see page 395.)

- What is the project title?
- What is the type of production (i.e., a feature film, a TV series, a Movie of the Week)? If a TV series, how many episodes?
- What is the overall budget size? Is the figure locked?
- When is the shoot planned for? Summer? Winter?
- How many days is the shoot planned for?
- When is the production's delivery date to the Distributor or Broadcaster? (This will tell you how long postproduction may last.) Is the date flexible?

- What format is preferred for the shoot? 70mm? 35mm? Super 16? Digi-Beta? Betacam SP?
- What format(s) is/are being delivered? Film finish? Video finish only? NTSC and PAL video finish?
- What language versions need to be created?

START BUDGETING BTL

You can start to budget Below-The-Line instead of Above-The-Line. Above-The-Line costs will generate a host of questions for you that only the Producer can answer. Rather than be stalled so early in the budgeting process, start Below-the-Line. You should already know how big a crew you are planning and how many days you are planning to shoot (as noted above), and since a number of costs — even Above-The-Line costs — are based on a percentage of the Below-The-Line costs, you might as well start budgeting there anyway.

ATL (ABOVE THE LINE) – "THE PACKAGE"

Though you may be starting the budget Below-The-Line for simplicity and order, here are questions you need to answer about the budget while finalizing it: (The Producer may know most of these answers, or may defer to you to make a production decision on them.)

ATL – SCRIPT RIGHTS

How much did they cost? What is the nationality of the original work? (Nationality may affect funding sources.)

ATL – WRITER & SCRIPT COSTS

Is the Writer union or not? What rights are being purchased up front? Does the Writer need to travel? If so, what for, where, and for how long? What is the nationality of the Writer?

ATL – PRODUCER

Who are all the Producers and how much do they make? Is there a restriction to the overall size of Producer fees (some funding sources impose, for example, a 10% of production plus postproduction costs maximum for the total sum of all Producer fees)? Who needs to travel where and for how long? What are the nationalities of the Producers? Do the Producers have Assistants to be included in the budget?

ATL – STARS

Who is/are the Star(s) of the film and what is/are their negotiated deals? What rights are being purchased up front? Which union has jurisdiction? Are travel, rehearsals, makeup tests, wardrobe fittings, overtime, and ADR/looping included in their deals? Do they need to travel? If so, from where? Are there other extras in their deal, specifying type of on-set dressing room, etc.? What is the nationality of the Star?

ATL – DIRECTOR
Who is the Director and what is the deal? What rights are being purchased up front? Is this person union or not? Does the Director need to travel? If so, from where and when? Will the Director need to travel for postproduction as well as for production? What nationality is the Director?

ATL – OTHER DEVELOPMENT COSTS
What costs have been attached to the project already? Is a breakdown of these costs available, as well as a list of the funding sources from development (i.e., Writer's costs, Star options or holding fees, travel, budget/breakdown costs, Producer costs, Location Scout, etc.)?

BTL (BELOW-THE-LINE) PRODUCTION – "PRODUCTION COSTS"
Production ends when you have processed the film, either struck a workprint or transferred to video, and you have viewed the rushes (also known as dailies). Sometimes this section is called Section "B" of the budget. These are questions and notes to ask yourself — or the Producer — while writing the budget:

BTL PRODUCTION – OVERALL QUESTIONS
Are you shooting union or non-union? Can you pay the keys above scale? What rights do you need to buy from the cast? Who of the crew is on board already, like the Director of Photography or the Production Designer? Is the show a period piece or is there a period piece sequence? Are there night shoots? Are there special effects? CGI? Trained animals? How much is planned to be on location versus in a studio? Are there children in the script? Is there money for a B-Camera? For second unit? For cranes? For camera cars? Any other special notes that will cost the production money?

BTL PRODUCTION – CAST
What rights are you purchasing? Refer to your budget breakdown to determine how many days per character you are going to budget. Detail out each character name on a separate budget line, no matter how small. Each actor costs money. It is best to see that money clearly detailed, in case a script revision can help ease the cost of production by removing some of the minor talking characters. Create separate lines for rights purchases or advances against royalties, rehearsals, wardrobe fittings, ADR/looping, hair/makeup time, and overtime. They all cost money and add up quickly, whether budgeted or not. If someone has a flat picture fee, still calculate all the scale costs of that person in the budget, so that you can compare the rate with the flat picture rate. Sometimes flat rates sound high until you back-out the numbers; once Accounting calculates the actual working cost of that actor after all the overtime is worked, you may still owe him money. Prepare to find out before this situation happens in wrap.

BTL PRODUCTION – CREW
Detail each crew member in the budget with at least three lines of budgetary calculations. Mention how many weeks you are hiring this person for preproduction, how

much for production, and how much for wrap. By detailing out each line separately, you can see clearly in the budget what week before shooting you planned to hire this person. Three lines noting "Prep 5 weeks, Shoot 4 weeks, and Wrap 2 weeks" is much clearer than reading: "Work 11 weeks." You can even detail an extra line for how much overtime you are budgeting for that person. The more detail now, the easier it will be to cost report to this budget.

BTL PRODUCTION – NON-UNION LABOR RATE PATTERNS

There are no rules to budgeting for non-union. In union shoots, you can negotiate crew labor rates at scale, and there is a pattern as to how much each person makes depending on their hierarchy in their department. On non-union shoots, there are no rules to how each person must be paid, and each crew member could effectively have a very different rate from another. It is wise to create a "labor rate pattern" for low-budget productions. The key crew in each department gets the same rate, the second in charges get a lower rate, and the thirds or Assistants get an even lower rate, but each department is structured the same. All keys get the same. This creates equality on set, and crew will develop a sense of "we're all in this together" rather than looking at each other with suspicion over who got the best deal. Another way to create pay equity is to pay everyone the same rate per day and defer the balance of their paychecks. Be sure the deferral language is clear in the crew deal memos, and that it works in synch with the other financing sources of the production.

BTL PRODUCTION – KIT RENTALS

Are you going to hire crew with kit rentals? Crew can augment their paychecks by bringing and using their "kit" on the production and charging a rental fee. Consider this possibility, especially for heads of departments or construction and grips and electrics.

BTL PRODUCTION – EQUIPMENT RENTALS

Equipment houses rent equipment at regular rates, but will likely only charge you three days for a weekly rental. This is known as a 3-day week. You can negotiate the number of days in a week for the rental cost, for example, maybe to a 2-day week, and affect a terrific savings. How much you can negotiate will depend on your track record with the equipment rental house, the track record of the technical crew you hire, and the track record of the head office production for paying their bills. It is best to start budgeting at a 3-day week. Extra daily rentals during production may take up the savings you affect by negotiating a short week anyway.

BTL POST – "POSTPRODUCTION COSTS"

Sometimes this section is called Section "C" of the budget. Again, the questions are for you, and for you to ask the Producer while budgeting:

BTL POST – OVERALL QUESTIONS

What are all the versions (film and video) required for delivery? What are all the language versions required for delivery? What are all the deliverables required (like M&E [Music and Effects track], a transcription, a closed-captioned master, 100 publicity stills, an EPK [Electronic Press Kit], etc.)? What union, if any, are you using for the postproduction crew? How fancy are the titles/credits planned to be? How much stock footage might be used? What other effects or CGI is planned?

BTL POST – MUSIC
Is the Composer's fee a flat rate which includes the studio and music rights? What songs are in the budget for which you will need to secure music rights?

BLT POST – FACILITIES DEALS
Are there any facilities deals with postproduction houses that include labor costs as an investment to the production? If a post house is investing in the production, it may provide you with equipment rentals and labor costs instead of a cash contribution to the budget. You must determine the value of the facilities deal and include and lock those costs in the budget. It is good to make a note in brackets that this is a facilities cost. You will have to account for the cost as it happens to, in effect, "drawdown" the investment. In some cases you can negotiate a flat rate with the facility. Remember to negotiate both time and money. If you can afford to transfer your rushes in the afternoon instead of during the lab's prime and busy morning transfer slots, you will get a better rate.

OTHER COSTS
Sometimes this section is called Section "D." A funny title: "Other." The costs here do not really fit into any other category, but are hugely essential in the making of a production. Such items include insurance costs, legal costs, publicity costs, financing costs, and the all-essential audit. Ask yourself or the Producer these questions:

OTHER – OVERALL QUESTIONS
What is planned for publicity costs? How many years of E&O insurance need to be purchased? How much money needs to be set aside for legal costs? Is an allocation necessary for a Post Accountant as well as for an audit? Is corporate overhead to be included in the budget? When are the Financiers planning to drawdown money to the production, so you can calculate how much of the budget will need to be interim financed at a bank? Are foreign currencies involved and costs of currency exchange? If there is to be a completion bond on the production, what is the production company's history with previous bonders? Is any treaty office involved in the production that may affect the budget's requirements?

CONTINGENCY
You may hear of contingency as a percentage of B plus C. Since ATL costs can vary incredibly, and Other costs can also vary hugely and are not directly related to production costs, you often calculate costs based on the "production costs" of B and C. The bigger the contingency, the more you are unsure how much the production will cost. If it

35

is too small, it will not be effective enough to cover any unplanned costs. 5-10% of B plus C is considered fair.

Check with the Producer if any of the contingency has already been allocated to overages that the Producer is aware of. Contingency should really be spent on unexpected costs in production, not from development. These types of costs might be the deductible on an insurance claim; you never budget for an insurance claim, but you have to pay a deductible if you have one. If some of the contingency is already allocated, try to revise the budget to reflect what is really there, and therefore not give anyone reading the budget a false sense of security that there is a pot of money ready for emergencies. If you leave it allocated, but do not indicate so on the cost report, the contingency can end up being spent several times over, pushing you way over budget. Due to unforeseen circumstances, you can easily end up spending 40-50% of contingency in postproduction, so whatever is pre-allocated now, is robbing you from production costs.

SERIES & CO-PRODUCTION BUDGETS

AMORTIZATION (AMORT) & PATTERN BUDGETS

A series is best budgeted with two budgets that work together: one amortization budget and one pattern budget. The pattern budget multiplied by the number of episodes of the series will add up to the overall budget amount of the show. Here is how both budgets work together:

You have a series of 22 episodes. Just prior to shooting Episode #1 you build a set and it costs you $220,000. You do not want to allocate all the costs of building the set to Episode #1, because all 22 episodes will be shot on that set. You want to amortize the costs of that set over 22 episodes, each episode taking $10,000 of the costs. We believe in equality. Now when you are analyzing the costs from episode to episode, there is some common ground on which to do so. Costs you can put into an amort budget include: all prep costs, wrap costs, any hiatus costs during the series, set build, legal costs, audit, and other costs that affect all the episodes equally or seem to affect none of the episodes at all.

In budgeting you create one pattern budget that ends up being a template for each episode being shot. When you cost report, you will have a separate cost report for each episode, matching costs to this template. One line at the end of the pattern budget (template) near the contingency will be the amort line. This is the amort budget price divided by the number of episodes in the series. Costs included in the pattern budget are: the crew, Writers, cast, locations, catering, equipment rentals, film stock, etc. — all production costs, all post costs. Think of the things that cost money during production, or rather during the particular week(s) the show is being shot and edited.

You need to write both these amort and pattern budgets at the same time, remembering to incorporate the amort costs into the pattern budget.

COLUMNAR BUDGETS

Co-productions offer another layer of complexity to budgeting. You will need to prepare for two audits, not one. You want to know how much the whole show costs, as well as each country's costs separately. Therefore, you need a budget with three total columns: my town costs, the Co-Producer's town costs, total costs. Yes, that means three cost reports each period when in production: my town, the Co-Producer's town, and the consolidated costs. Keep track of any dual costs (like dual citizens). They can help you later when you are going over budget in certain categories and are jeopardizing the cost split balance.

Sub-groups are an advanced feature in the Movie Magic Budgeting software that works well to help create columnar budgets. To do so properly, you need to allocate each line of the budget to one subgroup or another: my town, the Co-Producer's town, dual/either country costs.

Ensure that no line of the budget (and therefore no one accounting code) is shared by two different countries. By separating each line — even separating the Producers by country to individual budget lines — you will make reporting these costs much easier. If all the lines have been separated and marked so early, it will be clear which country is to account for which lines of the budget. You will notice that all budget forms have large leaps in account codes for the specific purpose of your being able to add extra new accounts within a budget without renumbering the entire accounting code system.

A FEW MORE OVERALL BUDGETING ISSUES

THE CONFIDENTIALITY OF THE BUDGET

The Producer, the Production Manager, and the Financiers of course need to see the budget. Unions will ask for a copy of the top sheet, too. But do you show the crew their budget lines? Their departmental budgets? Budgets are confidential documents, not public documents. On some productions you will find you have to sign confidentiality agreements if you work with the budget, so that you do not share the information with just anyone. Besides that, what you decided when writing the budget will modify as you head into production. As you spend money or promise deals, you may be moving money from one line to another to make that deal happen, so the budget line items become stale very quickly, and the budget itself is no longer telling the whole truth that the cost report is. Nevertheless, do not show the budget to anyone who does not absolutely have to see it.

HOW TO CATCH OVERSPENDING

You will be working closely with the Production Accountant, tracking and predicting costs all the way through production. For more on this relationship, see Chapters 19-22. Beyond that, you need to attend all meetings with Location Scouts. Find out what is being promised, especially by the Producer. Have discussions with department heads regarding their departmental budgets and status spending them. Make the crew accountable for their spending. If they do not report to you, you do not know what they are spending. If something new is mentioned in meetings, speak up and ask how it is being paid for — what is being removed to make it happen? Be vocal. Be sure the Director and the Producer and the AD are behind you and the budget. You are the crew's reminder of money being spent.

ABOUT WRITING BUDGETS FOR FREE

When Producers know you are writing budgets, they will ask you to write budgets for free. If you are new to writing budgets, go ahead. The practice is good. Each budget you create will be another you can use for reference in future budgeting work. The practice will be invaluable. Be sure to do an excellent job each time. Your work must be as thorough and accurate as if you were being paid. If not, the final budget will not be worth the effort — for you or for the Producer. Budgets take a lot of work and sweat to create. If you cannot afford the time and the energy, or do not need the practice, you do not need to make budgets for free. Like any voluntary work... if you are not getting something out of it, you will end up resenting the time you lose in working for nothing. You have to enjoy even the "free" work.

So, now you have a locked budget, and it is time to spend the money. The production office is about to open. Let's consider what you need in that office to work effectively.

The Locked Room

There was a time when fax machines were considered such valued equipment that they were stored in locked rooms. This is a locked-room story.

Script revisions came in from Los Angeles about 8:00 p.m. the night before each voice-recording session. These changes had to be incorporated into the script, and the incorporation process was a lengthy one. Now 8:00 p.m. Los Angeles time is 11:00 p.m. Toronto time. Since waiting until 11:00 p.m. in the office for one fax was rather silly, my co-worker and I would go out for dinner preceding this regular event.

One night we returned to the office to find the room to the fax machine closed and locked. Not good. We had about 10 minutes to figure out how to get in. Finding someone who might have a key was not an option so late at night. The fax bell rang. We were out of time. Then we noticed the air vent.

We knew there was another air vent in the general neighborhood of the fax machine. It was our answer. We had to work fast. So, with a yardstick decked out with sticky tape on one end, my co-worker climbed onto a desk then onto my shoulders so she could stuff herself through the air vent above the fax machine. One by one she snagged the pages as they came off the machine and stuffed them back through the vent to me.

Then I with sore shoulders, and she with sore neck and arms, incorporated the changes into the script. The voice-recording session proceeded the next day as planned, and we once again recognized the glamour of working in film.

CHAPTER 4

YOUR KIT & THE WEB

Though a desk and a telephone will suffice for you to start work, it hardly ends there — or rather, it hardly begins there — to work effectively. You probably already have a computer and a printer you will be using on the production. If so, you have already begun to assemble your kit. It is time to think about the rest of that kit: key reference items and material you can bring to the office to start working more quickly and efficiently.

YOUR REFERENCE BOOKS

A key part of the kit you bring to a production is your reference books. I will not mention this book, because you obviously already have it. Let's have a look at the Production Manager's reference books compared with the Production Coordinator's.

THE COORDINATOR'S REFERENCE BOOKS CHECKLIST
- ❑ Your Own Binder of Old Crew & Contact Lists
- ❑ Telephone Book (White Pages & Yellow Pages)
- ❑ City/Area Film Reference Book
- ❑ Other City Film Reference Book
- ❑ More Reference Books
- ❑ Who's Who Books
- ❑ Zip Code/Postal Code Book
- ❑ Map Book of The City
- ❑ Union Information (Crew)
- ❑ Union Information (Cast)

THE MANAGER'S REFERENCE BOOKS CHECKLIST
The Production Manager may have a copy of all the reference books the Production Coordinator has, plus a few extras:
- ❑ Budget Reference Material
- ❑ Your Files of Old Crew Resumes and Flyers

YOUR OWN BINDER OF OLD CREW & CONTACT LISTS
Over time, you will collect a wealth of reference paperwork (such as contact lists, crew lists, and crew resumes) from every film you complete. Assemble them into a binder for future reference. Since the information in this binder will be most relevant to producing films, it will end up being your first and foremost research tool.

TELEPHONE BOOK (WHITE PAGES & YELLOW PAGES)

Next to your own binder of crew lists and contact lists, this is your first and foremost research tool. Never underestimate its value in helping you find something or someone.

CITY/AREA FILM REFERENCE BOOKS

Your local bookstore with film books will have reference guides to the local city or area. In Los Angeles you can use the *BlueBook* or *LA 411*; in New York, the *Madison Avenue Handbook*; in Toronto, the *Toronto Film And Video Guide*; or in Vancouver, *Reel West*. The list goes on. Government Liaison Offices also have publications for your reference library. All these guides are valuable in that they categorize companies and individuals in film-related sections.

OTHER CITY FILM REFERENCE BOOK

If you deal with another city repeatedly, you would do well to buy the guide to that area, too. From these books you can find, for example, that limousine company or costume shop you need.

MORE REFERENCE BOOKS

Your local bookstore or your local Government Film Liaison Office will have a wealth of other reference books. How much you want to spend will be the deciding factor on how many books is enough.

WHO'S WHO BOOKS

Optional perhaps for the PC, but the PM will find these hugely useful when crewing. Who's Who books regarding the film industry are also very handy for Producers and Director when crewing and casting, and especially when you cannot obtain the Guest Star's list of credits from the Agent or the Manager fast enough.

ZIP CODE/POSTAL CODE BOOK

Companies can order this from the post office if you do not have easy access to the Web for this information. The PC will find this book more useful than the PM will.

MAPS & MAP BOOK OF THE CITY

Have detailed maps and/or map books of the city and the area. You can even post one of them on the wall at the office, indicating the office and the studio location(s). These are superbly helpful as references during the location-scouting period. They are also useful for the Office Production Assistant. Besides that, they will become essential reference when the Production Coordinator must make location maps while the Locations Department cannot.

UNION INFORMATION (CREW)

All unions and guilds (from technical to Directors to Writers) have agreements and membership lists worth acquiring. The Production Manager will refer to these lists when looking for crew; the Production Coordinator will refer to them both when looking for daily crew and when completing the crew deal memos.

UNION INFORMATION (CAST)
Actors' unions have agreements and forms you will need in completing cast contracts. The union's membership list is in the form of a book or a series of books that depicts actors by photograph. These books are extraordinarily useful to Producers and Director for casting.

BUDGET REFERENCE MATERIAL
As a Production Manager, you will not only be collecting old crew lists and contact lists, you will also be collecting rate sheets and flyers from various suppliers over time. Assemble these into another binder or set of files and bring this information from show to show. These will help you in estimating quotations and therefore determining the feasibility of acquiring a specialty item before committing time to looking for it. Government Liaison Offices may also publish a "budgeting book" as a quick reference guide to pricing just about anything to do with producing films, sometimes including floorplans and dimensions of all the studio spaces in your city. Use these guides as rough initial reference, and remember to get proper quotations to obtain the best price.

YOUR FILES OF OLD CREW RESUMES & FLYERS
As a Production Manager, you will collect a lot of resumes over the years for every possible department you can imagine. These will be unique and useful reference material to you, even though many of them will likely be irrelevant to your current production. Assemble them into a set of binders, or use a set of files in a paper file box for storage. Due to the volume of resumes and flyers you will accumulate, I suggest the file box method. You will not want to spend the time punching holes into all the paper and inserting each resume into a binder. With files, you just pop it in, and if you keep "the latest on top," the files will stay more organized than you can imagine. If the resume or flyer comes in without a date, write the date on it, so that when you do refer to the document, you will be aware of how stale it might be.

YOUR START-UP SUPPLIES

Every time you start up a new production office, you find that production has to buy over and over again all sorts of the same supplies, from the rental computer all the way down to the paper and the pen to write down the first telephone message. The Production Manager may do well to add photos and a calendar to the PM kit to feel more at home, but the Production Coordinator would do well to add a number of office supplies to the PC kit to get the office up and running swiftly.

THE COORDINATOR'S DETAILED START-UP SUPPLIES CHECKLIST
Upon first arriving at the production office, here is what the Production Coordinator will need: (For items that are "expendable," bring them with you in your kit, then top them up to the same starting level at the end of production, preparing for the next office you will need to start-up.)

❑ Date Stamp and Pad (for date-stamping the mail)
❑ Three-Hole Punch
❑ Stapler and Staples
❑ Heavy-Duty Stapler (for thick scripts — depends on your funds)
❑ Box of Pens and Pencils
❑ Fat Permanent Marker (for labeling courier packages)
❑ Eraser
❑ Electric Pencil Sharpener
❑ Manual Pencil Sharpener (for backup when electric one fails)
❑ In-trays
❑ Scissors
❑ Glue Stick
❑ Dull Clear Tape (shiny clear tape gets tacky in time)
❑ Packing Tape
❑ Telephone Message Pad ("duplicates" so you retain a record)
❑ Paper Clips and Dispenser
❑ Ruler
❑ Pad of Lined Paper
❑ Desk or Wall Calendar
❑ Manila Envelopes
❑ Letter-Sized Envelopes (for before letterhead is printed)
❑ Some File Folders (to furnish the files on your desk)
❑ File Folder Labels
❑ Plastic or Tin Box for Storing Copies of Keys
❑ Extra Typewriter or Printer Ribbon
❑ Some of Your Usual Courier Waybills and Packaging
❑ Pictures and Knick-Knacks to Make You Feel at Home

YOUR OFFICE & COMPUTER EQUIPMENT

Not all of the following equipment is necessary to complete your kit. You decide how big a kit you would like to maintain.

THE COORDINATOR'S OFFICE & COMPUTER EQUIPMENT CHECKLIST
❑ Typewriter
❑ Paper-Cutting Board
❑ Computer with Word-Processing & Spreadsheet Software
❑ Computer Printer
❑ Web Software & Connection Software
❑ Other Computer Software

THE MANAGER'S OFFICE & COMPUTER EQUIPMENT CHECKLIST
The Production Manager will not likely have the typewriter or the cutting board, but

will have the rest of the items the Production Coordinator has, plus a few extras:
- ❑ Telephone Headset
- ❑ Computer with Budgeting Software

TYPEWRITER

Computers have not replaced typewriters entirely. Typewriters are still useful — especially for the Production Coordinator — for typing up forms (like cast contracts), envelopes, and checks. Crew members will use a typewriter if it is accessible for them to share. With the onslaught of computers throughout the working world, typewriters are now cheap to buy. Include one in the PC kit.

PAPER-CUTTING BOARD

After reduce-photocopying script sides, you will need to cut them. A cutting board makes this job much easier and faster than using scissors. It is not necessary for the PC kit, but advisable.

COMPUTER WITH WORD-PROCESSING & SPREADSHEET SOFTWARE

Computers are so prevalent today that it is pretty much expected for you to have your own to use during the course of production. If you need to build a network of computers, renting might still be the way to go to ensure full computer compatibility around the office. In your own computer, you can collect all sorts of information that you have gathered from production to production. This information will always be at your fingertips. Your growing familiarity with one machine will also allow you to become expert in its use. Just about all functions needed to run a production office can be done on word-processing software (like Word) or on spreadsheet software (like Excel). Take the time to learn these two software programs to fluency.

COMPUTER PRINTER

You have choices between laser printers, bubble-jet or ink-jet printers, and perhaps the old dot-matrix printers. Laser printers offer the best quality, but are large and expensive, and require expensive replacement toner cartridges. Bubble-jet or ink-jet printers offer good quality, can be large or very compact, and can be much less expensive to buy and maintain. Dot-matrix printers are very old now, so it is doubtful this item will be a purchasing option for you. Also, their quality and affordability have been far exceeded by bubble-jet and ink-jet printers.

WEB SOFTWARE & CONNECTION

More and more communications are done by email. You will need Web-connection software, email software, and browser software on your computer to hook up to the Internet. You may also need file transfer software if your computer is the one uploading the production's Web site to the Internet.

OTHER COMPUTER SOFTWARE

Other software you may wish to include on your computer are: anti-virus software, utility software like zip programs, or database software for your contact lists. As the

Production Coordinator, you may wish to also include some publishing software to create beautiful letterhead. The world of software is open to you. How much you wish to purchase is up to you.

TELEPHONE HEADSET
Since the Production Manager spends so much time on the telephone, it is wise to have a headset to hook up to the telephone to save neck and back trouble.

COMPUTER WITH BUDGETING SOFTWARE
The Production Manager, too, will no doubt need budgeting software on the computer. Since it is the PM who has likely written the budget, this software will probably already be there.

ABOUT BUYING COMPUTER EQUIPMENT
Being aware that the state-of-the-art of computers changes and improves every few months, consider the following when deciding to purchase:

PC VS. MACINTOSH
The film industry uses both systems. If you work with one or a few companies most often, find out what computer systems they use. The answer may sway your decision. Talk to people who own both types and try both systems out. Though software grows more sophisticated and can read many documents on either system, not all programs have this ability. You are still choosing between two very separate systems.

NEW OR USED EQUIPMENT
New computers change all the time. What was top-of-the-line yesterday is ordinary today and outdated tomorrow. Buy the latest equipment you can afford. Used equipment may seem very affordable at the time, but too soon you may find out that you cannot upgrade your system to accommodate the latest standard software.

LIKE THE PHYSICALNESS OF THE COMPUTER
Before purchase, try out the keyboard to make sure it is the right size for your hands. Do you like the way the mouse fits into your hand? Is the screen big enough and bright enough? Do you have to peer or hunch over to look at it? Can you find the "Page Up" and "Page Down" buttons with your eyes closed? How about the arrow keys? You are buying a computer and it will belong to you. You will use it constantly. If there is something that you find annoying about the computer when you first look at it, that something will grow into a major aggravation, guaranteed. Love your computer from the very first moment.

PORTABILITY
The nature of a freelance life is to work at a job for a period of time, then move home, then move to another job, then move home, then move to another job, and so on. If it

takes you four trips to the car just to move your computer parts — (1) the CPU, (2) the monitor, (3) the printer, and (4) the keyboard and the accessories — the frequency of your jobs should make you consider laptop computers and portable printers.

OPTIONS & EXPANDIBILITY

The options available on a new computer are seemingly limitless. As computers upgrade month after month, today's new option is tomorrow's standard equipment. Good features to have are: a fast fax modem, the ability to add memory, the ability to add features, and long battery-power time.

PRICE

As options and equipment skyrocket in quality and availability, so the prices plummet. Know that as soon as you buy a computer, a new one will be invented and yours will be marked down. Though the longer you wait, the better a computer you can buy for your money, the longer you wait, the longer you do not have a computer. Buy a computer at the last possible moment that you need one, then buy the best computer you can afford and close your eyes to what comes onto the market next. The computer you choose will be just fine.

ABOUT COMPUTER SOFTWARE

The list of programs available to install on your computer seems endless. The choices are mind-boggling. No two people or companies appear to use the same software. As first priority, buy programs that have the capability of translating from other programs, if possible. Since you are freelance, you will be dealing with many different people and computers from many different cities or countries. Compatibility is key.

Though addressing a list of all the programs available is an impossible and ever-changing task, here is a category list of some of the types of programs appropriate to you. Educate yourself about your computer. Take a course, read manuals, ask friends how... do whatever it takes to learn. Your computer is to be your right hand; you are not its slave.

OPERATING SOFTWARE

PC computers (also known as IBM-compatible computers) often operate on DOS. DOS stands for "Disk Operating System." Basically, DOS is a computer language that tells the computer how to read other programs. Without it, the computer is just a series of mechanical parts. PC computers are sold with DOS included.

ASCII (pronounced "askey") is the language that DOS uses to talk to the computer and to other programs. It is also known as "ASCII text" or "DOS text." ASCII can only be a series of letters, numbers, or spaces. It is the most basic language to which a computer can reduce a document. Because it is so basic, modems can easily send and receive ASCII text on telephone lines, and all computers (no matter what software they have) can read the file. If you are having compatibility problems, try saving the file as an ASCII text file before sending it.

SHELL OR ENVIRONMENT SOFTWARE
Windows is the most well-known "shell" program. It creates a picture environment where you can access your programs with the click of a mouse button, instead of using a DOS command. Windows does not replace DOS. It creates all its icons and graphics using DOS, but just does not display on the screen all the DOS commands it takes to create such a show. For that reason, it is called a shell or "environment" program.

UTILITIES SOFTWARE
Both Microsoft and Norton are known for their utilities programs. Programs to unerase files you deleted by accident, or disk-fixing programs to diagnose and fix problems in your computer, are truly handy to have and know how to use.

ANTI-VIRUS SOFTWARE
This type of program is specifically made for searching for known computer viruses and fixing them. Like catching a regular virus, you can get a computer virus from contact with another computer, or another computer's programs or files. Anti-virus software is preventative medicine, well worth its cost, and essential if you are connected to the Internet.

WORD-PROCESSING SOFTWARE
Very appropriately, word-processing programs process words. You type in words, and through the program, you will be able to make certain letters bold, underlined, centered, in different fonts, and so on. You can cut and paste sections of words without scissors and tape, join documents together, let the program number the pages, and do a host of other features. Basically this software makes your computer a very intelligent typewriter. As a Production Coordinator, this will be your most-used software. Love this program. Invest the time and the money to take a course and learn how to use this program thoroughly. Ask other users what they like and dislike about their word processors. Get all the features you want, and be able to use all the ones you need quickly and with little effort. Two popular word-processing programs are Word and WordPerfect.

SPECIALITY WORD-PROCESSING SOFTWARE – SCRIPT-FORMATTING SOFTWARE
Though you can format a script to look like a script on a word-processing program, there is script-formatting software designed specifically for the film industry. Writers tend to use this software to aid them with script formatting as they write the story happily thinking more about story than about script format. What these programs can do for you is number your scenes (even A and B scenes), number your pages (even A and B pages), and print the script in script format. When you lock the script and revise it, these programs will show you the changes you made with asterisks on the right hand side of the page. If you have the time to get familiar with this program, it can be useful. If you find the program's use too complex to make speedy production-ready script

revisions, output the file to a word processor and make the changes on the word processor, where your expertise lies. Do note that when you move to the word processor, you will not be able to go back to the script-formatting software.

DATABASE SOFTWARE

Database programs let you input lists (like mailing lists) and reorganize those lists any way you would prefer (like alphabetically by street name). Many word processors have information-sorting features that make a separate database program unnecessary for you.

SPECIALITY DATABASE SOFTWARE – FILM PRODUCTION SCHEDULING SOFTWARE

This type of software is simply a database program written specifically to schedule film productions. Movie Magic Scheduling is most noted for this ability. The program takes the input of A.D. breakdowns of each scene and creates a production schedule for manipulation and printing. Assistant Directors likely have this software on their computers. It is expensive, and as PM or a PC, you will rarely use it. Still, it is wise for the Production Coordinator to be familiar with this program should you have to revise the schedule in the A.D.'s absence; and it is wise for the Production Manager to be familiar with this program should you have to generate a detailed schedule for budgeting purposes, or because you are on a super-low-budget film and you need to be the one creating the shooting schedule.

SPREADSHEET SOFTWARE

Spreadsheet software is basically the blend of putting a calculator into graph paper. With the right codes in the right boxes, the program can add, subtract, multiply, divide, and average numbers for you. As you change the source numbers, the program will automatically change the totals accordingly. You can create graphs and lists with this program. Lotus and Excel are known for their spreadsheet programs.

SPECIALITY SPREADSHEET SOFTWARE – FILM-BUDGETING SOFTWARE

Movie Magic Budgeting is the most known specialty program written specifically to aid Producers and Managers in creating budgets for film productions. It is basically a specialty spreadsheet program. As a Production Coordinator, you will not need this program, but it is good to know what it is. As a Production Manager, it behooves you to learn all the shortcuts the program offers to write budgets efficiently, with integrity, and with the ability to do easy modifications.

FAX MODEM SOFTWARE

Fax modem software is a type of communications software that tells the computer how to use the modem that is attached to your machine to either connect to another computer for sending/receiving information and files, or to connect to a fax machine for sending/receiving faxes. Instead of printing documents to your printer, you can telephone a fax machine and print out the documents like faxes.

INTERNET SOFTWARE

To hook up to a provider or an online service, you need a collection of software that the connector will likely provide. The Internet is blossoming and growing daily, so it is difficult to predict with accuracy where it is going and how it is going to evolve. To discuss the systems of today, you can choose between a dial-up service or a high-speed connection to the Internet. Dial-up services are portable, in that you only need a telephone line to call up the Internet, but the service ties up that line while you are connected. You can choose a connection package designed for the number of hours you expect to be surfing or picking up and mailing your email each month. High-speed connections by telephone line or cable modem are much faster but restrict your computer to be next to wherever the hardwire connection is.

INTERNET SOFTWARE – CONNECTION SOFTWARE

Connection software does just that. It connects your computer through a telephone line or a cable to the computer at your provider — your entry point to the Internet — and keeps you connected for the time you are surfing.

INTERNET SOFTWARE – BROWSERS

Another required software is Internet-surfing software called browsers (like Netscape Navigator or Internet Explorer). These allow you to view the vast numbers of word and graphic Web pages available on the Internet. Web pages are a great place for all sorts of local and international research. Learn how to use search engines effectively to find what you are looking for more efficiently. You can start by surfing the Golden Arrow Web site for links that I have specifically designed for Production Managers and Coordinators: *http://www.goldenarrowproductions.com*.

INTERNET SOFTWARE – EMAIL-READING SOFTWARE

Another required Internet software is email-reading software, which sometimes is packaged with the browser and sometimes comes separately (like Outlook Express or Eudora). These allow you to send and receive email messages, not unlike real mail but in electronic format. You can also attach document files, pictures files, or programs to your email messages. Note, however, that most computer viruses arrive into a computer through attachments sent with email messages; once you open the infected attachment, you invite that virus onto your computer. To prevent such infection, have anti-virus software on your computer, and do not open attachments from people you do not know or trust.

INTERNET SOFTWARE — OTHER TYPES

Other Internet software include chat software to allow you to type-chat online with other people currently online (this is more entertainment than resourceful), newsgroup-reading software that allow you to post and read messages on a given subject as you would be able to do on a bulletin board (also more entertainment than resourceful), file transfer protocol (FTP) software to allow you to upload Web pages to the Internet if you are publishing a Web page, and Web-page building software to help you create a Web page simply and easily (in case you plan to set up a preliminary Web site for your production). There are also other add-on software that will aid you in reading files, watching video clips, or listening to audio clips while surfing the Internet. As you surf, you will be notified of these programs on an as-needed basis. Most often you may choose to download a free version of the add-on software or purchase a deluxe version of the same. Note that software programs change often, so the free version will often serve you fine. As the Internet continues to blossom and grow, more specialty software will be invented to make your life online more user-friendly. Join the wave and learn along the way.

IDENTIFY & INSURE YOUR KIT

Mark all the equipment of your kit with your name and address. A simple file-folder label with your name can be attached to almost anything in your kit for identity. This system will help you collect all your equipment at the end of production. As for insurance, your kit belongs to you. Get the expensive equipment properly insured. If the software you have purchased is hugely expensive and comes with a serial number, you can insure the software, too.

You have boxes or milk crates of reference material standing by. You are prepared to start work in the production office. Get set to enter the empty office and turn it into a functional, living, breathing production office. You are ready.

II.

PREPRODUCTION

Fail to prepare… prepare to fail.

.

Sweaty, the Burglar

Most break-ins are memorable for the grief they cause. Critical office equipment is stolen, yet you must continue on with production at the same frantic pace. You feel your privacy has been invaded, knowing that someone was in the office routing through your things in your absence. You are not alone.

Well, my most memorable break-in was by a fellow we never caught. We didn't even know this guy broke into the office four times, until a month after he'd done so! He left no trace of his presence and took no office equipment of any kind. Yet a month after his first deed we had an exact record of his movements and written proof. At this point, I dubbed him "Sweaty," because this is what he was up to:

Sweaty broke into the production office every Thursday morning precisely at 2:00 a.m. Each time he came in, he used our office for a solid three hours. He spent his time dialing and re-dialing "1-900" phone-sex numbers.

We never discovered the way Sweaty got into the office, and by the second month, he was gone and never returned. His signature? He left us his $750 telephone bill.

CHAPTER 5

SETTING UP THE PRODUCTION OFFICE

The Production Manager has found the production office. An empty office. The Production Coordinator is about to bring it alive, setting up the physical office. The Production Manager is about to bring it alive, setting up its financial backbone. After production wraps, the production office is to become empty again. But where do you start now? Turn to your bedside table. Put a pen and paper beside the bed. This is for when you wake up in the middle of the night panicked that you have to remember to do something in the office the next day. Next, set up two alarm clocks (one battery-operated) so that no matter how tired you are, and no matter what power outage may happen, you can wake up on time. Finally, go into the office, open the book to this chapter, and begin.

THE COORDINATOR SETS UP THE PHYSICAL PRODUCTION OFFICE

Though it is the Production Coordinator who actually ensures this setup happens and does most of the hands-on work, the Production Manager needs to know the answers to the Coordinator's questions before they are asked. Both should read about setting up the physical production office.

You have an empty office and a group of people that will be using it. Your first order of business is to place everyone logically in that office. Draw a rough sketch of the office floor plan. Your artistic skills are not being tested here, so have fun with it.

THE OFFICE FLOOR PLAN
The office likely will have a large open area and several offices with doors and locks. Do not worry about creating a drawing of exceptional quality or even a floor plan to scale, but do note which offices are larger than others and which ones have windows. You will use this floor plan extensively in this chapter, and again for marking the placement of telephone extensions, so *legible* is the key word.

LIST CREW WHO WILL NEED OFFICES AND/OR DESKS
Make a list of who will be using the office, who needs a desk, who needs a lockable room, and who has already been assigned a desk or a room. The Production Manager's input will increase accuracy.

PLACE NAMES ON THE FLOOR PLAN
With pencil and eraser, or with names marked on sticky (post-it) notes, place the crew on the floor plan. Talk to each department for their wish list regarding office placement.

55

Move the names around and around until you achieve an appropriate compromise for all wishes. Using a modest film as an example, here are some likely initial minimum concerns about crew placement:

- Producer   Private office

- Director   Private office

- Production Manager   Private office, near Production Coordinator for frequent access

- Production Accountant   Private office that locks

- Production Secretary   Near entrance door to act as reception

- Production Coordinator   Near the entrance if there is no Secretary — in a place of high traffic, so that crew and Coordinator have frequent access to each other

- Office Production Assistant   Desk

- Assistant Director Department   Desk and telephone, near Director

- Locations Department   Room for maps on walls and room for storage of tables, chairs, and other locations purchases

- Art Department   Room for drafting tables and large filing cabinets

- Set Dressing Department   Room for storage of purchases

- Wardrobe Department   Room for wardrobe racks and wardrobe purchases, dressing rooms and fitting room for studio shoot, laundry room

- Hair/Makeup Department   Room with makeup mirror for studio shoot

- Transportation Department   Desk and telephone

OFFICE FURNITURE & EQUIPMENT

Once the crew is placed on the floor plan, make a list of required furniture to be rented or purchased. Have the Production Manager approve the list, then order the furniture immediately. While you wait for the furniture to show up, use pencil and eraser or more sticky notes to add further decorating concerns to your office map. Some items are too small to be drawn on the map, but can hardly be called insignificant, so arrange for them too, imagining them on the map.

THE FURNITURE & EQUIPMENT CHECKLIST

- ❏ Photocopier
- ❏ Facsimile Machine
- ❏ Telephones
- ❏ Computer & Printer Equipment
- ❏ Typewriter
- ❏ Photocopier & Facsimile Machine Supplies
- ❏ Office Supplies - Photocopier Paper Storage Shelf
- ❏ Office Supplies - Stationery Shelf/Cabinet
- ❏ Filing Cabinets
- ❏ Television & VCR (Office)
- ❏ VCR (Producer or Director)
- ❏ Office Craft Service Area
- ❏ Water Cooler
- ❏ Washer/Dryer
- ❏ Distribution Table
- ❏ Wall Envelopes (Crew)
- ❏ Wall Envelopes (Companies)
- ❏ Wall Envelopes (Forms)
- ❏ "To Set" Box
- ❏ "To Head Office" Box
- ❏ "P.A." Box
- ❏ "Mail" Box
- ❏ Rushes/Dailies Sign

PHOTOCOPIER

You will be making up to 10,000 copies per week. Honestly. Rent the best high-volume and fastest machine you can. This means you will be getting a loud machine, so do not place the photocopier next to the Reception telephone. Put it in its own room, or at least in the most remote place in the office with dividers around it for sound containment. You will be double-sided copying the call sheet, collating masses of scripts, copying on letter-size, legal-size, 11"x17" size (for the Art Department), enlarging and shrinking, and clearing out paper jams with great frequency. Some companies will loan you a second machine at no charge to have on hand in case the main photocopier breaks down (which it usually does on Fridays after 5:00 p.m.). Get a service contract.

FACSIMILE MACHINE

This is the second most popular machine in the office. If you can afford a plain paper fax, it is worth the money. (Imagine getting a 120-page script by fax minutes before shooting, and having to photocopy every curly, non-plain paper page for the 75 crew and cast members.) This machine is not loud. Keep it accessible so that you and/or the Secretary can monitor it from your desks.

TELEPHONES

Make a list of who needs a telephone before you approach the telephone company. Note that you will need a fax line. Do you also need a modem line? Note, too, who really needs to have access to long distance on their telephone sets and who would just like to have it. You can restrict long distance and directory assistance on individual sets. It is amazing how many long distance calls happen on a telephone that is on an unmanned desk in an open-concept office. It is also amazing how many times you will pay for directory assistance no matter how many telephone books are stacked by each telephone set. (More on choosing a telephone system is in Chapter 9.)

COMPUTER & PRINTER EQUIPMENT

Are you using Mac or PC? Laser or ink-jet? Are you bringing in your own equipment or renting? How many people need a computer? Which ones need to be hooked up to the Web? Is the Accounting computer and printer updated and fast enough to run the payroll software and print all the checks? Keep the name of a repair company handy. When you look at the price difference between renting and purchasing, does purchasing make more sense? Check if head office will want to buy back the purchased computer equipment at the end of production before committing to renting versus purchasing.

TYPEWRITER

The old-fashioned typewriter is still handy for typing envelopes and checks. It is also great when you cannot afford a computer. And it is especially useful when you have a repair company name nearby.

PHOTOCOPIER & FACSIMILE MACHINE SUPPLIES

Both machines need toner and paper. Store these supplies near each machine for efficiency of replacement and for frequency of monitoring them. Supplies can come from your office supplies source, from an independent source, or be included in your service contract. Check around for best rates and accessibility. Most places deliver.

OFFICE SUPPLIES – PHOTOCOPIER PAPER STORAGE SHELVES

Have plenty of shelving available for the various colors of paper you will need for script revisions. Store the paper near the photocopier for ease of access. Label each shelf for each color and stack the reams of paper so that at a glance you can see which colored paper is running low.

OFFICE SUPPLIES – STATIONERY SHELF/CABINET

Place a cabinet or a shelf in a visible area of the office for storage of all the supplies. Have a pen and paper (preferably attached to each other) on hand for crew requests. Make sure there is a space on that paper for crew to note their requests and their names, so that the right supplies get to the right people. To prevent crew overindulgence, the Production Manager needs to approve the requests before ordering. Many companies deliver office supplies. Delivery is a great way to cut down on the Office Production Assistant's runs. Check how long the turnaround for an order is, what conditions are inflicted on the order, and if the price makes it worthwhile.

FILING CABINETS

Note who will require them, from the Producer to the Production Accountant to the Production Manager and Coordinator. The top of a two-drawer lateral filing cabinet can serve a great second purpose as a shelf for the facsimile machine or a set of binders. An empty filing cabinet drawer can serve as a locking drawer for supplies you or the Accountant will need hidden and secure.

TELEVISION & VCR (OFFICE)

If production is going to have video rushes, a VCR and a television for the office are essential. Discuss with the Production Manager which VCR features you will need and how long you will need the machine. Shop around, because depending on the term, renting or buying will be the better option. Remember to get a stand with or without wheels for the equipment, and decide if the unit is going to be kept in the Producer's or the Director's office, or in the main office (for everyone's access). Remember to get plenty of extension cords and patch cords. Does head office want to buy back the equipment after production?

VCR (PRODUCER OR DIRECTOR)

Visiting Producers or Director may need a VCR in their hotel rooms. The Production Manager should know if this is necessary, or find out. A second VCR in the office (when not at the hotel) can be used to dub rushes and final shows.

OFFICE CRAFT SERVICE AREA

Often this area is where the office television and the VCR are kept. Impromptu meetings happen here as people talk over a cup of coffee. Place a couch or a few chairs in this area to make the area more like a lounge or waiting area. Use a coffee table, end tables, lamps, and posters as other decorating ideas. Be creative. Set up the food and drink section with some or all of the following:

- Coffee Machine: So mandatory, the coffee machine could be a union requirement; keep in mind you'll be ordering a second one for use on set.

- Tea Kettle: Good for instant soup, hot chocolate, and, of course, tea.

- Refrigerator: To store milk, cream, brown bag lunches, and, of course, after-work beer.

- Other Equipment: Cappuccino maker, toaster, toaster oven, microwave oven, hot plate, and any other equipment your heart desires and the budget allows.

- First Aid Kit: When shooting, the set will need one, so get one early for use around the office; when shooting begins, you can scale down the size of the office First Aid Kit and give the big one to set.

WATER COOLER
The water cooler is just about as necessary as the coffee machine. You can choose from cold water only to hot-and cold-water machines. Either way, water and coffee machines have a love-hate relationship. It is not a good idea to have them next to each other. The high mineral content of bottled water creates a build up and plugs the coffee machine in such a way that water will pour out its side cracks. You can check with your coffee company and find out if your machine is designed, like most, for tap water. If the crew does not like the taste of the coffee, try a new coffee bean. Also note that you will likely be ordering a second water machine for use on set.

WASHER/DRYER
The Wardrobe Department will need these. Louder and hotter than the photocopier, this duo needs its own room. Check whether renting or buying makes more sense. You will need a plumber for installation.

DISTRIBUTION TABLE
Place a folding table in the highest traffic area of the office. Position it so that everyone will trip over it. You want them to do just that, because on the distribution table you will be putting all the latest paperwork that the crew wants and needs (copies of scripts, crew lists, call sheets, and so on). Make sure that you (the Coordinator), the Secretary, and/or the Office Production Assistant can see the distribution table so that you all can keep the paper topped as the hoards of crew descend on this table daily.

WALL ENVELOPES (CREW)
Assign wall space for the wall envelopes near the Secretary's or the Coordinator's desk. Use heavy-duty envelopes, mark them for each department, and use them to gather paperwork for those departments that are currently not in the office. A paperclip on front can also serve to gather each department's telephone messages. (A list of possible departments for wall envelopes is in Chapter 30.)

WALL ENVELOPES (COMPANIES)
Assign wall space for these, too. Similar to the crew wall envelopes, these are used to gather paperwork for the various producing and outside companies involved. Collect paperwork over the course of the week and send these packages at week's end. (A list of possible companies for wall envelopes is in Chapter 30.)

WALL ENVELOPES (FORMS)
Assign more wall space for these envelopes. These are blank forms that crew will ask you for constantly, from letterhead to time sheets. (A list of forms for wall envelopes is in Chapter 30.)

"TO SET" BOX

This box can be made out of a wonderfully big paper box top and can be placed on the distribution table or near the entrance door. Use it to collect paper, notes, and all those various items that must go to set on the next run. Everyone (such as the Drivers and the Office Production Assistant) on route to set should check this box before leaving the office. Make it convenient for them to stumble across and check.

"TO HEAD OFFICE" BOX

Like the To Set box, place this box so that it becomes the last place to check before going to the head office. This box can be made redundant if all items to go to head office are put into the P.A. box.

"P.A." BOX

This is the in-tray for the Office Production Assistant. Place it on the P.A.'s desk, and make sure it is big enough to hold parcels as well as paperwork.

"MAIL" BOX

Place this in the office to gather mail to be posted (near the P.A. box or the To Set box). Ensure that each night someone takes the contents to a real mailbox. Set a policy about buying stamps so that crew do not get in the habit of leaving you their unstamped mail for production to mail.

RUSHES/DAILIES SIGN

Some call them "rushes," others call them "dailies." Since dailies can sometimes take several days to ship and process, and dailies also means those crew that are only working today, rushes is the better term. So, whatever you call the film that has just been processed and is ready for first viewing, be familiar with both terms and make and place a sign by your desk that reads: "Rushes Tonight Will Be At _____" — and leave a space for the time and the location. The time will change daily and even hourly. Having it posted saves you remembering the latest change and informs people around you without their having to interrupt you.

INVISIBLE OFFICE REQUIREMENTS

Your handy office map can take a break. "Invisible" office requirements are services that you must have on hand to complete the office setup. Over time you will have a contact list of these companies that you use from show to show. On your first show, take the time to start this list early... before something happens and you need a plumber at midnight.

THE INVISIBLE OFFICE REQUIREMENTS CHECKLIST

- ❏ Web Access & Domain Name Registration
- ❏ Security (Office Alarm System)
- ❏ Security (Locations & Studio)
- ❏ Cleaners

❑ Plumber
❑ Production Assistant Car
❑ Keys
❑ Circuits & Electrician

WEB ACCESS & DOMAIN NAME REGISTRATION

More and more, Internet access and email are becoming essential to a functioning production office. You may decide on a high-speed connection or a cheaper dial-up service and a modem line. Set up a generic email address for the production office and discuss with the Production Manager who really needs email on the crew to do their jobs. Who is going to check the email regularly? Regarding domain name registration for the production, check with the Producer to see if it has been registered yet. If not, now is the time register it. Domain names get snapped up quickly. Since the Internet is constantly changing and growing, I am not going to supply a list of links for you here; I have set up useful Web links at the Golden Arrow Productions Web site (links such as a list of terrific search engines, weather information sites, budgeting information sites, industry news sites, currency exchange sites, and tons of other informational links): *www.goldenarrowproductions.com*. Surf by. These links will change and evolve with the Internet to stay useful to you now and in the future.

SECURITY (OFFICE ALARM SYSTEM)

An alarm system in the production office is very wise indeed. Though film shoots are transient, unprotected computer equipment is asking for trouble no matter how short a time you intend to be there. The cost of an alarm system makes sense. You may think that replacement through insurance is adequate, but imagine working for weeks without any computer equipment until the insurance company completes the claim.

SECURITY (LOCATIONS & STUDIO)

If there is no Locations Department, you will be arranging for a security company to watch the set after hours. You can find names and references in your film reference books or from your Location Manager friend.

CLEANERS

It is usually best to arrange for them to clean the office at least twice a week.

PLUMBER

Have a plumber's name on hand. It could be the same plumber you use to install the washer/dryer. Know what hours she is accessible — especially for those after-hours bathroom jobs in old buildings.

PRODUCTION ASSISTANT CAR

The sooner you get this car, the sooner the Office Production Assistant can run wildly around the city taking care of business. Well, not too wildly, you hope. Check if the Production Manager already arranged for an account for the production vehicles with a car rental company, so that you can get the office car from the same agency. Know that you may arrange for the office car to be the Secretary's, the Office Production Assistant's, or your car after hours.

KEYS

The Production Manager may want to change the locks when you first move in. Arrange this procedure as soon as possible. As for how many copies you will need, start a list for one key per department head as a rough estimate. Keep a log of who gets which keys. Keys will get lost, so keep a master set for yourself.

CIRCUITS & ELECTRICIAN

Pull out the office map again. Mark on it where each wall plug is. Take the time to do a circuit check and label each wall plug, the breaker panel, and the map. This is a great job to delegate to the Office Production Assistant when few people are using the office (and therefore few using the electricity). Have an electrician's name on hand for after hours. Heavy drains on a circuit are:

- Photocopier: Most high volume, fast photocopiers require a dedicated circuit, i.e., a single wall plug that is connected to a single breaker. Have an electrician install one.

- Craft Service: Any electric appliance that prepares food is a big drain on the circuit. (This includes coffee machines, tea kettles, microwave ovens, refrigerators, toasters, etc.) Have an electrician install a few dedicated plugs in the craft service area.

Though this project sounds like a lot of work, it will be time well spent. When you turn on the coffee machine and blow a circuit someday, you do not want to find out that the Accountant's computer is sharing that same circuit.

SUPPLIER ACCOUNTS & CONTACTS

The office map aside again, it is time to set up supplier accounts. Armed with the corporate name of the film company and help from the Production Accountant in filling out account applications, you are ready. Before committing to a new company right away, do a price check on three competing companies. From this process you will be able to judge how suppliers are to deal with, and how affordable they are.

THE SUPPLIER ACCOUNTS & CONTACTS CHECKLIST

- ❑ Courier Account
- ❑ Stationery Account
- ❑ Taxi Account
- ❑ Walkie-Talkie Account
- ❑ Pager Account
- ❑ Cellular Phone Account

❑ Travel Agent
❑ Limousine Account
❑ Hotel Account
❑ Research Company
❑ Customs Broker
❑ Credit Card Number

COURIER ACCOUNT

You will need three couriers: a local courier, a national courier, and an international courier. Some couriers can cover more than one of these needs, but beware that the price differences can be excessive in the overlapping territories.

STATIONERY ACCOUNT

Set up an account with an office-supplies company that delivers, or a discount store of your choice. An account will save the Office Production Assistant from keeping copious amounts of cash on hand.

TAXI ACCOUNT

Taxi account chits are simple, convenient, and often misused. But there is an administrative cost involved in using an account, so the taxi charges are usually higher than if you pay cash. Decide with the Production Manager whether or not to go with a taxi account.

WALKIE-TALKIE ACCOUNT

The Assistant Directors will have their preferences about who should have walkies and accessories such as headsets, speaker mics, and holsters. Make a list of who needs what on set and approve that list with the Production Manager before contacting walkie-talkie suppliers. When negotiating the account, you will often be able to get an extra walkie-talkie or two rent-free to cover yourself for inevitable equipment breakdowns. Maintain excellent records of who has which walkie-talkie equipment (including serial numbers), so that none are lost by the end of production. Walkie-talkie equipment is very expensive and very portable. Know the replacement value.

PAGER ACCOUNT

The crew will have various preferences from the three types of pagers available. Approve your list with the Production Manager to ensure the budget can cover the requests:

• Numeric: These are the least expensive, but note that generally you need a touchtone telephone to leave a message. Only telephone numbers can be left as messages.

• Voice: Still inexpensive, these pagers do not need a touchtone telephone to leave a message, but voice messages are often fuzzy. These pagers are never used on set because they are very loud.

- <u>Alpha-Numeric</u>: Expensive. A monitoring station turns your voice message into a brief written message and sends it to the pager. Often the messages are cryptic because the spelling is very poor and possibly phonetic.

CELLULAR PHONE ACCOUNT

Note that people who use cellular phones tend not to know how much airtime costs. Since cellular phone companies have after-hours and weekend rates, take advantage of discounts. Be cautious about locking into long-term contracts.

TRAVEL AGENT

This is one of the Coordinator's best friends. Producers, Guest Stars, and Directors are very busy people who usually change their travel plans at least 100 times before boarding an aircraft. Booking the cheapest flight is rarely the way to go with all the restrictions attached to cheap flights. Make your travel agent work for you — and obtain a home number if you can.

LIMOUSINE ACCOUNT

Either you or the travel agent can arrange for limousines. Since spellings of names and specific directions can become muddled when several people are involved in the chain of communication, arranging for limousines yourself is the best way to ensure accuracy. It is also wise to have the name of a limousine company in any other city that you deal with repeatedly.

HOTEL ACCOUNT

Go to see the hotel rooms in early preproduction. Visit their facilities. As production nears, you will not have the time. Take your camera and take pictures like a Location Scout. You will find it easier to talk about the hotel when you have actually been there and have photographs to remind you and to show guests.

RESEARCH COMPANY

Check with the Production Manager to determine if you will be clearing the script for legal purposes, then find a company best able to serve you. Clearance companies read the script and note potential trademark infringements, for example. You will find names of companies in your reference books. (More about script clearances is in Chapter 32.)

CUSTOMS BROKER

This is one more of the Coordinator's best friends, helping you to bring all sorts of items across the border. Find a broker and prepare a letter giving him power of authority to clear packages through customs for you, and get a home number if you can. (More about customs is in Chapter 31.)

CREDIT CARD NUMBER

The Production Manager may furnish you with the company's credit card number for use, with discretion, in emergencies when only a credit card will get the job done. Keep this number well protected.

THE MANAGER SETS UP THE FINANCIAL BACKBONE TO THE OFFICE

With the physical office in good shape thanks to the Production Coordinator, the Production Manager is busy setting up the financial backbone to production. Here is some of the information you will need, as the Manager, to ensure this setup:

- ❑ Incorporation Documentation
- ❑ Financing Structure, Status & Agreements
- ❑ Recoupment Schedule (optional)
- ❑ Locked Budget
- ❑ Cash Flow
- ❑ Audit Discussions

INCORPORATION DOCUMENTATION

Find out from the Producer if the production company has been incorporated yet or not. If not, arrange with Legal Counsel to do this immediately. Have a copy of the incorporation documents on hand. Though the whole crew needs to know the legal name of the company, you and Accounting need to have proof of that legal name in your hands and files.

FINANCING STRUCTURE, STATUS & AGREEMENTS

If you have not received the one-page financing structure summary from the Producer, listing all the financing sources participating in production, obtain it immediately. You need to know to whom you are reporting, and which paperwork each Financier needs during the course of production. The financial structure should also detail the type of money being supplied: equity participation, a grant, a distribution advance, a Broadcaster pre-sale, a Producer investment or deferral, etc. Get a copy of all the financial agreements, too. Accounting will need them. You will need them. The agreements detail when the money is paid out to production and on what conditions or triggers. Since the Financiers are basically investing in a product that does not exist yet, they will have a payment schedule for their participation. Some payments may be triggered, for example, by production reaching the first day of principal photography plus delivering the latest cost report to the Financier, or by reaching wrap of production plus delivering the latest cost report to the Financier. You need this information to generate an accurate cash flow. Find out (from the Producer) the status of each of these financial contracts. It often takes plenty of time to bring all sources to signed contract to get the money flowing to production in a speedy manner. You may have drafts of these contracts to start your work, but whatever you obtain, you need this paperwork to know how soon the money will be flowing.

RECOUPMENT SCHEDULE (OPTIONAL)

This document details, in the form of a chart, a list of the equity partners and Distributor(s) with advances, along with who need to get paid back their investment from monies earned during distribution (in proportion and in position compared to other investors). Since recoupment happens long after production, this schedule is not necessarily relevant to you on a daily basis. It is still good to have a copy of the final, approved recoupment schedule in the Production Manager's and/or the Production Accountant's files for completeness. The Producer will be negotiating the Financier's placement on the recoupment schedule.

LOCKED BUDGET
As mentioned in Chapter 3, you should be trying to lock the budget as soon as possible, so you can move onto cost reporting in comparison to the budget. Going to production without a locked budget is like going to camera without a script. Meet with the Producer to finalize the budget allocations.

CASH FLOW
With information from the financing documents, the Producer, and the locked budget, it is time to create a cash flow to see when you might need to arrange for interim financing from a bank to get you through the monetary demands of production. Sometimes Accountants create this document on their own, but usually it is the Production Manager who is heavily involved in its creation. (More on creating cash flows is in Chapter 20.)

AUDIT DISCUSSIONS
Discuss the plan for audit with the Producer. Prepare now to set up the accounting system for an easy, clear audit. These discussions are especially important if you are on a co-production involving two or more Accountants and audits in two or more cities or countries. (More on audits is in Chapter 35.)

WHEN INFORMATION IS CONFIDENTIAL

Realizing that you talk to all the departments of the production, you will often be trusted with confidential information from everyone. Some information will need to be forwarded on to others under the cloak of continued confidentiality, other information you will wish you never heard because you cannot tell anyone even though it drastically affects everyone. Some information the Production Manager should not tell the Production Coordinator, even though the Coordinator is the Manager's right hand. Everyone should be very, very careful about confidential information. When confidential information gets shared among the office staff, consider the following advice:

USE A CODE WORD OR PHRASE
With your closest staff, use a code word or a phrase (like "you didn't really hear that") to inform them that the information they just heard, whether on purpose or by mistake, is strictly confidential, and they should not pursue the subject. Have the staff respond with another phrase to let you know they understand.

USE ENVELOPES OR FILE FOLDERS

Never have confidential information left face up on your desk. Use sealable envelopes, or put such paperwork into file folders to hide from view, thereby quelling people's curiosity as they pass by your desk or enter your office. If there is no time to use an envelope or a file folder, place the document face down on the desk. Make sure all the office staff understands and uses this system.

BE CAREFUL WHEN FAXING & PHOTOCOPYING

Avoid faxing confidential information, if at all possible. If necessary, do not fax anything else at the same time, and do not use speed dial. A confidential fax going to the wrong recipient by attaching it to the back of another fax, or by pressing the wrong button, is inexcusable. When photocopying a confidential document, take the same care. Take the time to copy it on its own. Without distraction, chances are you will not leave the original in the photocopy machine. Make sure the office staff understands and abides by this system, too.

As a house becomes a home, so these empty rooms are becoming a production office. Be proud. In essence, you have a production office ready to function already! Over time, you will find that each office has slightly different needs — not all offices will require a full setup from bare floors and walls. Revise this chapter to suit each production's needs and your own personal style as it develops. But now is the time to add people to the office and stir.

Lost & Found

When the Office P.A. calls in sick, you have to hire a Daily P.A. very quickly. There is no time to review qualifications or check references. In such an instance I hired a fellow who had been begging me for his chance to "break into the film industry." And as with many such P.A.s, I'm sure he embellished his merits in order to get the job. Embellishing is okay. Lying is a bad career move. He said he was a very experienced driver and knew the city well.

Run #1: First up in the day, I sent him to our payroll company to drop off the payroll. The company was right downtown. The trip normally takes fifteen minutes to get there from the office in the east end and fifteen minutes back. We didn't hear from the Daily P.A. for over four hours. He never called. He never wrote. I was confused, then concerned, then worried. The PM needed him for another important run and, in the P.A.'s absence, I had to send the Production Secretary.

When the P.A. finally called, he was at a telephone booth in an industrial area of the west end. He was lost. Didn't have a map. Didn't know the city at all. Didn't know that downtown was a small collection of very tall office buildings, and when he wasn't driving in that vicinity, he wasn't downtown. I directed him back downtown and asked him to buy a map en route. He returned to the office — run completed — another three hours later. That was seven hours for a 30-minute run. I hoped he was just having a bad day and decided I would schedule the next run for him closer to the office.

Run #2: I asked him to pick up some stamps at the drugstore one block away from the office. He borrowed the Production Manager's car and took forty-five minutes to get there and back. He could have walked faster. Another important run came up in his absence. It had to be delayed. Upon the P.A.'s return, he broke the key in the ignition thereby making the PM's car undrivable. He finally admitted that his driver's license was considerably newer than he had originally let on and that he didn't know the city at all. At this point, the PM asked me to send him home.

We've never seen him since. We just hope he got home all right.

CHAPTER 6

HIRING CREW

The roles are now reversed. You are sitting in the chair across from the seat you occupied a short time ago. You are about to hire crew and support staff. You may not be sure how to hire and manage staff. You may not be sure how to be a good boss. It may seem daunting to have the responsibility of hiring, managing, and sometimes even firing people, but it is not as difficult as it first appears. Whether you are hiring experienced department heads or someone green to the industry applying for his first Production Assistant position, the essence is the same: Hire a good team and let them do the job.

WHO HIRES WHOM

The Production Manager will tend to hire the Production Accountant, other departmental heads, and key creative crew alongside the Producer, and may also have a voice in the staffing within the departments. Though Chapter 7 details all the departments, here is a list of the first priorities in hiring for the Production Manager, presuming these people are not on board already: the Production Designer or the Art Director, the Construction Coordinator, the Director of Photography, the First Assistant Director, the Casting Director, the Location Manager, the Editor, the Set Decorator, the Property Master, the Wardrobe Designer, the Hair and Makeup Artists, the Continuity Supervisor, the Gaffer, the Key Grip, the Transportation Coordinator, and the Post Sound team or facility.

The Production Coordinator will tend to hire the Production Secretary, the Office Production Assistant, and perhaps the Craft Service Person — usually in consultation with the Production Manager, since both of you are, after all, a team working together. The Production Manager has the budget that the Production Coordinator is trying to spend and honor.

REGARDING RESUMES & COVER LETTERS

Resumes and cover letters are the first step in finding crew. You want to read them to narrow down your search so that you bring in only selected qualified people to interview for the job. This is a paring-down process. Naturally, a discussion about resumes and cover letters may lead you to review and revise your own, but this chapter deals with what you need to know about how to *read* resumes and cover letters. What are you looking for in the pages that come in? Do Production Assistant and other entry-level resumes differ hugely from First Assistant Director and other department head resumes? How do you read a resume?

RESUMES

When you read resumes, especially lots of them at one time, your attention cannot help but wane. Resumes in general should not exceed one page; however, if there are huge numbers of relevant film credits to list, they can be two pages long. You want to read resumes that are short, to the point, and perhaps demonstrate a little of the person's personality. Every crew resume is basically structured the same way.

CONTACT INFORMATION & PROFESSIONAL ASSOCIATIONS

Near the name and contact information (address, telephone number, email address, pager, fax number, etc.), you want to see professional associations, or the crew position this person most associates herself with. This is especially important if the person has a diverse resume. With a resume that notes a huge variety of film positions in past experience, you need to know for which position or department this person is applying.

MOST RELEVANT EXPERIENCE AT THE TOP

You want to read resumes that are structured so that the most relevant (and therefore hopefully the most recent) film-related information is at the top, just after name and contact information. This way, as your attention wanes, you will have read the most relevant experience to this job without having to search for it. If education is noted at the top, this person is likely to be a recent graduate. If education is noted at the bottom, just above references, this person's recent experience is more likely earned working in the industry than in a school environment.

DIFFERENT RESUMES & SKILLS FOR DIFFERENT JOBS

Because of this structure, crew members will have different resumes for different jobs. That is okay. For certain jobs you need to see certain skills stressed. You do not want to read a notation and description of every single position this person has ever held — especially if much of it is irrelevant to this job. For Office Production Assistants, you would like to know if they can drive standard should the production car have a standard transmission. For First Assistant Directors, you would like to know with which Directors they have worked, and which shows were completed on time. For Production Accountants, you would like to know if they are fluent in the payroll software you are intending to use. Different skills are for different jobs. You want to see these skills on the resume. Other skills of use might be: safety training, fluency in a language, fluency using a specific software, knowledge of certain production paperwork, typing speed, certification to use a certain piece of equipment, a license to drive a certain type of vehicle, and so on. Know what you need from each department skill-wise, and read the resume looking for that type of experience.

THE FILMOGRAPHY

The majority of the page will be taken up with a filmography: a list of film credits, the production titles, the year produced, the production company names, the key supervisors, and any other key, short relevant information regarding each production (like awards). You, as a Production Manager, are looking for names you recognize in this list of supervisors. You will tend to call these people for references over the list of references at the bottom (if there is a list at the bottom).

HOBBIES OR INTERESTS
After the list of experience and a notation of skills, you may see a line noting hobbies or interests. This is a good line to use for conversation starters at the interview.

REFERENCES
Finally, if there is room, about three references may be listed at the bottom. More likely, however, references will be noted as "supplied on request." With a well-structured resume, you will not need to ask for extra references. There will be enough names and companies on the resume for you to do your due diligence.

PORTFOLIOS OR REELS
Art Department staff and Set Photographers may note there is a portfolio on request. Directors of Photography and Second Unit Directors will have a reel available on request, whether noted on the resume or not. As you narrow your search, you must review these support materials, too. This type of creative experience cannot be demonstrated in the resume format.

COVER LETTERS
Cover letters give the opportunity for applicants to demonstrate their style, their awareness of the demands of the job ahead, their preparation to put in the hours it takes to make a film, and to basically tell you what is not on the resume due to format restrictions. Read the cover letter and ask yourself if this person is professional enough and prepared enough for the complexities of this particular film production.

If resumes do not have cover letters, toss them — well, certainly for people applying to P.A. positions. You will learn more about a P.A. by the cover letter than by the fact that the resume says he delivered a newspaper at age 16. The P.A. position is an entry-level position, so chances are the resume will not have any Office P.A. credits on it yet. You must look to the resume to determine the person's working style and attitude. As crew members work up the ranks, cover letters become somewhat less frequent. This situation is okay, as the resume is now more clearly demonstrating skill level with a growing number of credits in the filmography.

QUESTIONABLE RESUMES
It is always easy to remember the questionable — or bad — resumes first... but you will not remember them as people you wanted to hire, but as people you want to avoid. Still, you may be mildly entertained by some of the resumes that come to you, like the resume that was sent in a shoe in order for the prospective Production Assistant to get a "foot in the door." Maybe you like this kind of humor and would consider hiring this person

to keep you laughing in this manner, or then again, maybe you prefer to find crew who work first and play second. It all depends on your management style. But be sure they can do the job. Is there substance in the resume alongside the humor? Having someone keep you laughing is fine unless you have to make up for his slack at doing a bad job. Remember you are building a team to work together. You are producing a film together. This work is not play. It is an industry and you first have to do a job. Consider how each member of the team will fit and do his part. What is his working style versus yours? Though we work in a creative industry, a resume typed all in italics stating why that person was fired from every single job in his life might seem funny at first, but do you really want someone to be that much of a rebel? If hired, maybe that person will be rebellious of authority or of the hierarchy on the set, thinking he is being funny. If so, this is not a team player, and most certainly someone you do not want on the crew. Think about the barely-out-of-adolescence Production Assistant that sends you a student's directing reel as a P.A. resume. Do you think this person will be happy enough and therefore do a good job of photocopying and driving when it is obvious he would rather be directing your production? Very unlikely.

REGARDING CREW INTERVIEWS

After reading all the resumes and the cover letters, and calling some references, you have narrowed down the search to a few people for each position. It is time to bring them in for interviews.

DUE DILIGENCE BEFORE THE INTERVIEW

Will this person, her skills and contacts, complement the team you are assembling? Call to check with former employers, even if the credentials are incredible. The resume may seem impressive, but this person may have been fired from all those fabulous previous jobs. If you recognize names of people you know and trust on the resume, call them. But call other people, too. Try to get a rounded view of this person. Be aware that you may learn about bad experiences that came from personality conflicts due to working style, so some bad references may be misleading.

THE TELEPHONE INTERVIEW

Before committing to an interview time and date, find out if the potential crew member is pleasant on the telephone, and ask her if she is available for the term. No sense in wasting your time and hers in coming in for an interview if your schedules do not mesh. If there is a specific skill that is required for the job (like use of certain computer software or of certain equipment), ask now for proficiency to see if this person is qualified.

CONDUCTING THE INTERVIEW

You need to structure this interview the same way yours was structured: (1) ice-breaking conversation, (2) questions relevant to production asked and answered, (3) conclusion and thanks.

The ice-breaker gets the conversation flowing. You are both likely to be nervous at this interview. You are looking for the right person to fill the role, and this person is hoping for the right job to suit her experience and career. Look for any notation of hobbies or interests on the resume to help you get started. If not, invent a starter. Weather is a boring subject, unless, of course, you have just experienced an earthquake or a heat wave. As conversation flows, you can begin to discuss the production's needs in more detail and the team you are assembling.

Here are questions to ask yourself during the course of the interview. You will get some of these answers from asking outright questions, and others will come from your own observations:

- Team Player: Who is this person? What is this person like? Will this person fit into the team? How has this person worked in a team environment previously? What is not on her resume?

- Part of a Team Already: Is this person part of a team that moves from production to production, or does this person need help in finding a team of Assistants?

- Resume Value: Are the credits on the resume overstated or are there more credits omitted? Are the past work experiences relevant to working on this production?

- Job Requirements: Can this person fill the requirements of the job? For example, can this First Assistant Director schedule a show? Does this Production Secretary enjoy answering the telephone and is she familiar with production paperwork? What does this person think is key to be able to do this job? (See more about job requirements below and in Chapter 7.)

- Skills: If there is no list of skills on the resume, ask what relevant skills this person has for this job, like language fluency, software or equipment proficiency, and so on.

- Stress & Long Hours: How does this person deal with the stress of a film production? Does this person think a long day is eight or eighteen hours? How does this person deal with difficult people?

- Ambition: What direction is this person's career going? If this person were to get a better offer one week into filming, might she leave your production?

- Price: How much does this person expect to make? Can the budget support this person? Is there a kit rental to augment the fee?

Take your own mental notes during the interview. Learn about this person's manner, attitude, honesty, and maturity. Can you work with this person? Will she put forth the type of professionalism you expect? Do not be afraid to take notes. A word scribbled here and there on the resume during the interview will aid you later in evaluating the people you have met.

AFTER THE INTERVIEW

Make written notes about each person after the interview and review them later. Before making a decision, the Production Coordinator can discuss these notes with the Production Manager, and the Production Manager can discuss these notes with the Producer.

Also, do not be afraid to do more due diligence by calling references for more information after the interview. The more responsible the job you are trying to fill, the more due diligence is necessary.

REGARDING THE OFFICE STAFF & CRAFT SERVICE

The Production Coordinator is the Production Manager's right hand. Therefore, the Production Accountant must be the Production Manager's left hand. The Coordinator's right and left hands are the Production Secretary and the Production Assistant. As these people are so critical a team together, it is worthy to look at them in more detail. Because Craft Service is a unique entry-level job, it is worth a further look at this position, too.

If any or all of these positions are unionized in your city, go to the union as a source for a potential crew for your production. If they are not unionized, there will likely be a list of such non-union personnel at the local film commission. It is also wise to speak with other Production Managers, Producers, and contacts at film organizations and clubs for recommendations.

THE PRODUCTION ACCOUNTANT

For a Production Accountant, you are looking for someone to track the money being spent during production even more closely than you! This person has to understand the budget, payroll, petty cash, cash flow, financing inflows, and cost reporting in great detail. The less you know about any of these issues, the more the Accountant needs to be the expert. You want someone who is: organized, a good communicator, detail-oriented, fast, accurate, and understanding of the nuances of film production budgeting and accounting.

When interviewing and doing your due diligence on the Production Accountant, find out if this person:

- <u>Payroll Issues:</u> Understands the complexity of payroll and knows the computerized payroll system inside and out.

- <u>Budget Issues:</u> Knows when and why it is required to lock a budget, and understands columnar budgets if your production is a co-production, or pattern and amortization budgets if your production is a series.

- <u>Communication Issues:</u> Knows how to communicate often and effectively with you regarding all accounting issues, including budget savings and overages, both actual and predicted.

- <u>Petty-Cash Issues:</u> Understands that petty cash is not petty at all (the first time you approve $5,000 cash to be handed to a crew member to go shopping for the production, you will understand how petty it is not), and knows how much to hand out to which departments to keep them functioning efficiently, but not keep them in excessive cash — thereby putting an unnecessary drain on your cash flow.

- <u>Cost-Reporting Issues:</u> Knows how to report on actual costs as they are incurred during production, both efficiently and accurately.

- <u>Cash-Flow Issues:</u> Understands how Financiers pay out money on triggers; knows how to read and write a cash flow; knows which bills can be pushed and for how long if cash flow is tight; and both knows and uses the purchase order system right through to the cost report.

- <u>Reporting & Filing Issues:</u> Knows how to keep impeccable books to affect a seamless transfer of the accounting files to the Post Accountant and/or the Auditor (allowing the Producer to trigger all financial drawdowns as fast as possible).

- <u>Prioritizing Issues:</u> Knows how to say "no" to the crew or to the Producers or to you for the good of the production, and can prioritize effectively.

- <u>Stress Issues:</u> Knows how to handle a lot of stress. (The Accountant is often harassed by crew and Producers for various money and reporting demands.)

- <u>Working-Team Issues:</u> Has an accounting team or can pull together a team if the project is large enough to warrant. Has worked together with any of the keys already on the production.

THE PRODUCTION SECRETARY

For a Production Secretary, you are looking for someone to work with the Production Coordinator effectively and effortlessly, easing the huge workload of running the production office. How that workload is divided is rather hazy and very personal between the Coordinator and the Secretary. Often the Production Secretary is responsible for: telephone reception; paperwork distribution to all crew, cast, and related companies; shipping and receiving; organizing the P.A. runs (to be sure the P.A.

does not get overloaded by too many input sources from Coordinator, Production Manager, Producers, and various crew departments). This person may also be the one to type up the call sheet every day. But no matter what the Secretary does, he should constantly report to the Coordinator what jobs are in progress, so the Coordinator can be informed, aware, and able to prioritize those jobs. You want someone who is: organized, a good communicator, a team player, good at answering the telephone while doing much other work, and understanding of the running of a film production office.

When interviewing and doing your due diligence on the Production Secretary, find out if this person:

- <u>Telephone Issues:</u> Enjoys answering the reception telephone (you will be surprised how many hate answering the telephone and will tell you so) and can figure out how to use all those many features that now come with telephone systems. Remember this person will give the first impression about your company to anyone who calls in.

- <u>Communication Issues:</u> Will communicate with the Coordinator often and clearly, be able to take direction, and fit into the team.

- <u>Production Paperwork Issues:</u> Is familiar with production paperwork like production reports and call sheets, etc. — because you will not have time to teach this person from scratch on the job.

- <u>Organizational & Filing Issues:</u> Knows how to file, track paperwork distribution as it happens, and can deal with the reams of paperwork that flow through the production office.

- <u>Computer System Issues:</u> Is fluent on the computer system and the various software programs you are using on production. (If you can test this person, all the better, as a number of people will over-estimate their computer skills in order to get a job.)

- <u>Handwriting Issues:</u> Has legible handwriting for telephone messages.

- <u>Boredom Issues:</u> Understands this industry has always been a "hurry-up-and-wait" industry.

- <u>Stress Issues:</u> Knows how to deal with stress and work with difficult people.

- <u>Work-Day Issues:</u> Understands that a long day is closer to sixteen hours rather than eight, and prepared to work it if scheduled so.

- <u>Career Issues:</u> Is prepared to perform this job, not taking this job only until a better offer comes along, and is expecting a paycheck in line with what is budgeted.

THE ASSISTANT PRODUCTION COORDINATOR

When there are two Assistants to the Coordinator, the main Assistant is the Assistant Production Coordinator and the second Assistant is the Production Secretary. In some cases, people are tending away from any titles that include "Secretary" in the description and moving toward titles that include "Assistant." When there is one main Assistant who is inexperienced, it is wise to call that person a Production Secretary, leaving the Assistant Production Coordinator title for an experienced person. This scenario gives the former room to grow within the position, and therefore earn recognition for that growth.

THE OFFICE PRODUCTION ASSISTANT

You will probably hire a variety of more Office P.A.s than Production Secretaries in your time, because the Office P.A. is the entry-level job that everyone who wants to break into the film business covets. Unfortunately, many are disillusioned when they discover the job — once achieved — is not a creative position after all. They take orders all day long, drive around the city like a courier, make coffee, and learn how to remove paper jams from the photocopier. At this point they get bored, feel unimportant in the making of the film, lose interest, and so do the job badly. They were looking for that mythical creative job that comes with great pay and lots of responsibility, because they think film work is easy and film pay enormous. You are looking for a team player, not a self-imagined leader. You are looking for Assistants. And Assistants do just that... they assist. On a crew of ten people, it is true that each person has great responsibility and a varied set of tasks to do. That is the beauty (and the nightmare) of low budget. On a crew of 50 or 75 or 120, the same set of tasks has to be divided between many people; on individual analysis, each person's job may seem small and pointless. You need people who can see themselves as an integral part of the whole picture, because that is exactly what they are.

Here is information you need to know prior to and during the interview to narrow down the search for genuine workers. The requirements may not sound like much, but you will be surprised who is out there looking to break into the film industry. You will interview P.A.s who think they deserve your wage and more per week, P.A.s who think they have to be hired because they know someone on the show, P.A.s who are ready to start their own production company but want to make a quick buck before doing so, and even P.A.s who think that answering phones, making coffee, and fixing the photocopier is beneath them. Remember: attitude, attitude, attitude — then choose accordingly.

- <u>Read the Cover Letter:</u> Read the cover letter to learn the most about this person. There are bound to be next to no relevant film credits on the resume to tell you about this person and what she is like. If there is no cover letter, this person has not spent much time, if any, applying to work with you. Do you want this kind of person as a P.A.?

- <u>Attitude & Work Day Issues:</u> Does this person have a good attitude towards working long, demanding hours?

- <u>Workload Issues:</u> Does this person have some idea about what an Office P.A. does?

- <u>Memory Issues:</u> Does this person have some intelligence and remembering ability?

- <u>Boredom Issues:</u> Will this person enjoy the job and atmosphere, not growing bored within two weeks? Is this person prepared to work in this hurry-up-and-wait industry?

- <u>Driving Issues:</u> Does this person have a license to drive the production car you have, or does she own a car you can rent from her? What is this person's driving record?

- <u>Stress Issues:</u> Can this person deal with stress and be able to work with difficult people?

- <u>Teamwork Issues:</u> Can this person deal with the many sources of requests for runs (from Producers, Manager, Coordinator, and other crew departments) and work with the Coordinator and the Secretary as a team to ensure the jobs are prioritized together?

- <u>Career Issues:</u> Is this person prepared to perform this job, not taking this job only until a better offer comes along, and expecting a paycheck in line with what is budgeted for the P.A. position?

Since the P.A. position is entry-level, there will be teaching required for this person during the course of the job; therefore, here are tips for working with the P.A. *on the job* to ensure her efficiency and responsibility. Though the Production Secretary may be the one monitoring the P.A. runs in detail, the Production Coordinator is responsible for the whole office team, so I have used only Coordinator references below:

- <u>The P.A. should write everything down:</u> First things first. Make sure the Office P.A. has a notebook and pen at all times. The Coordinator will give this person lists and lists of things to do, and each task may sound simple, but the sheer number of them dictates that something will be forgotten if not written down.

- <u>The P.A. should keep in constant contact with the Coordinator:</u> Ensure that the Office P.A. has a pager at all times, or make sure she calls the office from every location traveled to in case there is a change in plans for the office runs. An Office P.A. out of touch for hours at a time is a gamble that nothing will change in this ever-changing business.

- <u>Double-check the P.A. did the tasks:</u> Take nothing for granted. Tell the Office P.A. a task and explain why it has to be done in a certain way, have her re-tell it back to you so that you know she understands. In time, such double-checking may not be necessary, but at the beginning of a show, it helps to teach the P.A. how things are done and why. If you tell half a tale, expect half a job.

• <u>Check the detail of the P.A.'s paperwork</u>: Teach the Office P.A. about purchase orders and petty cash reports. Teach her detail.

• <u>The P.A. should know who to report to/take orders from</u>: The Office P.A. takes orders primarily from the Coordinator. Do not let the P.A. do runs for any other crew member, including the Producers and the Production Manager, without talking to the Coordinator first. The Coordinator is responsible for prioritizing the P.A.'s runs, even if it is the Secretary that is listing and tracking these jobs. Sometimes the P.A. must sit waiting in the office until the next task is ready. But that is the true nature of film... hurry up, then wait.

• <u>The P.A. should have things to do when waiting</u>: Give the P.A. some responsibilities. This way you can learn if she is indeed responsible or not. Put the P.A. in charge of the weekly photocopier paper count (so you never run out of any color), and let her monitor the Polaroid film stock, fax supplies, coffee and water supplies, the status of the distribution table, and so on. She can make more coffee during a "wait" period, help with answering busy telephones, or ask the Secretary and the Accountant if they need help. Get her to report back to you on these responsibilities. If all else fails, there are still plenty of learning opportunities for the P.A. who wants to succeed, like learning how to read a production board instead of reading the comics section of the daily newspaper.

• <u>The P.A. should know which runs happen on a regular basis</u>: The responsible P.A. can anticipate runs that happen on a regular basis and help you manage her time, like: delivery and pickup of the payroll for Accounting, weekly runs to the companies that have wall envelopes, petty-cash runs, cast-contract runs, script-package runs, grocery runs for office craft service, and lunch runs for office people too busy to leave their posts.

Since many P.A.s dream about that mythical creative job, you can dream about that mythical perfect Office P.A. Let me paint one for you now:

Always has a map book of the city. Knows the nearest liquor store, beer store, and post office — and their hours of operation. Knows how to fix a jammed photocopier and fax machine. Knows how to use the telephone, fax machine, photocopier, coffee, and water machines. Makes coffee first thing in the morning and when the coffee is low. Buys a few snacks for the office as allowed by petty cash and the Production Manager and the Coordinator. Never lets the car run out of gas or windshield-washer fluid, especially if borrowing the car from another crew member. Never lets petty cash run too low. Never leaves the building or the room without letting the Coordinator know where she is going and for how long. Anticipates what runs happen on a regular basis. Knows how to open the office or close it by herself, in case she has to on a weekend. Treats original scripts with great respect so that the paper will not get chewed up in the photocopier. Always looks for something to do to help pass the time — because there always is something to do.

THE CRAFT SERVICE PERSON

Though the Craft Service Person works on set making food available to the crew and the cast between meals, the Coordinator can be the one to hire this person. Often a non-union position, the Craft Service assignment is another entry-level job, and the only true entry-level position that gets to work on set. If attitude is key in hiring the Office P.A., it is double-key in hiring the Craft Service Person.

Many craft service companies save you the trouble of hiring crew for this position and possibly teaching someone from scratch. Their staff is usually prepared and knowledgeable about the job and their role on set. Make sure you meet and introduce yourself to this person.

When interviewing the Craft Service Person, discuss the following:

- Work-Day Issues: Coffee must be hot and ready on set fifteen minutes prior to the first pre-call. That means that the Craft Service Person is on set about a half hour before call time, and it also means she is the person on set with some of the longest hours of all the crew.

- Entry-Level & Paycheck Issues: If the job is paid a flat rate, tell this person not to calculate the hourly wage. You can tell her right now, as an entry-level position on set, Craft Service is paid the least and works the most hours of any crew member. It is a fact. But know that the position is excellent for observing many jobs on a working film crew, so when the Craft Service job is well done, the crew will help that person move into any department she wishes.

- Food Issues: Imagine feeding fifty different people with fifty different tastes in food. No one can ever satisfy them all, so do not exhaust yourself trying. Present fresh food to the crew to renew their energy throughout the day. Address food allergies. Serve the food in a pleasant manner. Picture how much food the number of crew will eat, double it, and double it again. Crews eat a lot.

- Craft Service Budget Issues: It is very easy to go over budget in this department, so you need someone who can monitor a budget responsibly.

- Driving Issues: The Craft Service Person needs to be able to drive a cube van (or not be afraid of driving one), unless the production budget only allows a panel van. Does this person have a license to drive the production vehicle you have, and what is this person's driving record?

- <u>Responsibility Issues:</u> If the Craft Service job is done well and professionally, you will find yourself treating this person more like a department head than an entry-level worker. The job is as responsible as the Craft Service person wants to make it.

- <u>Stress Issues:</u> Can this person deal with stress and be able to work with difficult people?

- <u>Attitude & Career Issues:</u> If someone is always looking to do the next job up the ladder, that person will never fully enjoy the work she is doing at the moment, since when she moves up to the next job, there is always another rung to look toward. Enjoy the steps along the way. This is advice for any job, including Craft Service's. The bonus of the Craft Service role is the opportunity to watch what happens on set and learn like a fly on the wall. The weight of the position is that the Craft Service person can set the mood of the set with her attitude, just like a morale officer.

UNION & NON-UNION CREWS

It is the Production Manager more than the Production Coordinator who will deal with the various crew and cast unions, if applicable, but it is essential that you both know and understand them. Is production going to hire a union or a non-union crew? If the choice is to go with a union crew, the production company has to become signatory to the appropriate union(s) and guild(s) when the hiring is about to begin.

If you choose a union crew, you will find that unions are terrific for helping you when hiring crew. They are especially able to find people with specialized skills, as they have banks of resumes and lists of qualified workers. Unions are also wonderfully helpful in the budgeting process, since they have scale rates from which you can start budgeting. There are unions and guilds that represent technical crew, camera crew, accounting and coordination crew, directors and production staff, and so on. Some unions compete with other unions in the same city, so you may find an arena of competitiveness for union negotiations.

UNION AGREEMENTS & NEGOTIATIONS

Though union agreements may be boring to read, the Production Manager has to know them. You must understand the many terms and conditions these agreements encompass, and how those terms and conditions affect the production. For example, how many hours is a minimum requirement for crew turnaround (the hours a crew is required to have between going home at night one day and starting work the next day) without monetary penalty? It is therefore most wise to read and to understand these agreements prior to initial budgeting, to ensure you address all the money triggers of the decisions you are about to make during the budgeting process. Also know that not all the terms in these agreements are carved in stone; some are negotiable to address the specific needs of each production.

BECOME SIGNATORY
Find out if head office has already become signatory to one or more of the unions or the guilds. Some unions and guilds will ask you to sign up the head office of the production company as signatory to their agreement for all future productions. Head office may not want to commit to this type of agreement when it reviews all the various types of productions the company produces. Beware. You may want to ensure only the single-purpose production company is signatory to the unions or the guilds.

UNION NEGOTIATIONS
Most union or guild agreements have an enabling clause in them to allow you to modify some of the terms of the master agreement to suit the specific needs of your production after you become signatory. If there is no enabling clause, be sure to ask for any concessions you need prior to becoming signatory. Imagine your production has two days of its shoot five miles outside of the allowed free-travel zone; if you used the master agreement as written, production would be required to house the entire crew and pay travel time and per diems for those two days, but with the enabling clause, you ask for a concession to allow this travel outside the zone for only the cost of travel time. When you read the agreements, you will find other clauses that hinder your production unreasonably. List them all and discuss them with the union to negotiate which modifications can be made. There will be some give and take, so be prepared. Have some things on your list you can give up. Amend the union agreement early in preproduction to make it work for your production.

AFTER UNION NEGOTIATIONS
After negotiations, the Production Coordinator should be the one to keep in touch with the union, sending them informational paperwork about production as it proceeds. (More on this paperwork is in Chapter 30.)

NON-UNION
There are no rules when you shoot non-union, but remember you need to respect the crew whether it is a union or a non-union crew. You do not want to burnout the crew. Once tired, they will perform badly. This performance will show onscreen, and/or worse, will cause crew to have accidents due to tiredness: accidents where people get hurt, accidents that production has to pay for. If you are shooting non-union, become familiar with the union structure. It works. Emulate it. Being non-union you do not have to be heavy-handed about union-type rules, but you can schedule regular meal breaks. You can schedule the availability of substantial snacks three hours into the day to keep the crew's energy up until lunchtime. You can wrap at a reasonable hour so the crew will have enough turn-around to go home, get rested, and return to work the next day. Respect is the key.

NON-UNION DOUBLING UP ON JOBS
The size of a crew can vary enormously from production to production, depending on

the budget size. On some films the budget is so restrictive and the production simple enough so that the Production Coordinator is also the Production Secretary and the Receptionist, while the Production Manager doubles as Line Producer, Location Manager, and Production Accountant. On other films, you will have the luxury (or the necessity) of having people report to you in these other positions. The Production Manager can sometimes double for the First Assistant Director, but only on very short shoots, since someone has to be doing the Manager's job in the office while the Assistant Director is running the set. On union shoots there is less flexibility about crew doubling up on jobs. If you are going to double-up jobs, be sure the jobs are compatible and you are not asking someone to be in two places at the same time. This suggestion may sound obvious, but remember: Sometimes you have to spend money, like hiring an extra crew member, in order to save money, like saving time.

HIRING UNION CREW ON A NON-UNION SHOOT

Any union crew or cast working on a non-union shoot require special dispensation from the union. It is the crew's or cast's responsibility to arrange for this. If they do not receive dispensation, there will be a penalty; if the penalty is money, it may even become your production's expense. Other penalties can include that crew member being thrown out of the union, so be cautious — this is dangerous territory. Crew members, however, are generally eager to upgrade their skills, and can often do so on non-union shoots, with the union's permission. The union primarily wants to know that you are not going to abuse this member. Since you are not a signatory, they cannot legally step in to protect their member from your production, should you treat the crew member unfairly, like refusing to pay him after work is done. Respect, again, is key. Structuring your production to work similar to a union shoot structure is helpful. Doing so, you may have an incredible crew available to you. Look for crew members that are experienced enough to move up to the next union level, and let them try their wings on your shoot at that higher level. Your production gets fabulous crew for less money, and the crew member gets the experience he needs to boost his career.

FIRING STAFF

Sometimes you will have to fire someone for poor job performance or poor attitude. There is nothing easy about doing so. Imagine that someone falling down on her knees and begging for you not to fire her. Imagine firing someone and not realizing it is her birthday tomorrow. If you think firing has to be done, consider the following:

WEIGH THE PROS AND THE CONS AND DO DUE DILIGENCE

Film production contracts are basically short, so you have very little time to teach someone the job she has been hired to do. In some positions you cannot expect to need to teach the person the job she has been hired to do. Have you given this person the chance to improve? Have you talked to her about the seriousness of the situation? Is this person's poor performance or attitude creating other problems on the set or in the office? Do your due diligence in giving her space to improve, and preferably document your steps and discussions. If this person is with a union, you will need this documentation to prove the firing was justified. If you weighed the pros and the cons, have done your due diligence, and there is no change, you cannot keep covering for this person.

DECIDE WITHOUT EMOTIONAL INVOLVEMENT

Never fire someone out of an emotional reaction, like anger or frustration. Cool off and decide logically if firing is the right solution. Talk this situation over with your superior.

IS THERE ENOUGH TIME TO HIRE SOMEONE NEW?

If there is only a week or two to the end of the production, firing the person may not be worthwhile. Flying in someone to fill-in for the final two weeks may be more work for you than putting up with a poor worker. Evaluate how much damage this person has caused or is causing. If you replace this person now, can the damage be repaired or at least stopped? If you do not replace this person, will the damage become greater or remain stable? You may feel that replacing a person at such a late date does not make sense. It is for this reason that you should always check references with previous employers before hiring someone.

HOW TO FIRE SOMEONE

After all your consideration, if the decision is to fire the person, pull her aside, explain why, and fire her. It is not easy, but know that you have done all you can. If your reason is valid, the next person you hire will excel at the job, and the person fired will go on to excel in the next job she achieves.

The crew is now coming together. You are no longer alone in the office preparing for the shoot. Give positive feedback to the crew when you see them excelling at their work. Do not make a habit of private talks only being critical. Managing staff will always have its ups and downs, since both managers and staff are, after all, human. You will all make mistakes, but realize that your Assistant today may be your boss tomorrow. Together you must create a team that works together to prepare for production.

Dollies, Redheads, and Best Boys

The film industry... it's the only place where...

You can play with dollies as an adult.

You can put pancakes on the floor.

You won't find any fruit in an apple box.

You know the similarity between a giraffe and a tulip.

You can use cookies, but not eat them.

You can have babies, juniors, seniors, redheads, or blondes on set — but none of them are people.

You can work alongside Gaffers, Best Boys, Gennie Ops, and TADs — and know what that means.

You can open two barn doors with one hand.

You can hire a Greensperson to bring in and set up trees in a forest.

And... you can hire a wrangler for bugs.

What an industry!

CHAPTER 7

CREW DEPARTMENTS

You run into someone in the hallway and exchange information. You have just had a meeting. Meetings in production can be casual or even accidental get-togethers. As the Production Manager or the Coordinator, you will talk to everyone on the crew in order to do your job. Talk as much as possible to keep your finger on the pulse of the production: Find out what is going on and what is being spent.

Let's look at these departments in more detail, and how you interact with each of them:

OFFICE PEOPLE

"Office People" are the people with offices in the production office or in head office, who retain those offices actively throughout production, and are associated with overall production issues rather than specific departmental ones.

PRODUCER
The Producer, who answers to the Executives, is responsible for the whole production, and is involved in balancing both creative and financial decisions to ensure the project is completed, maximizing the creative vision within the financial restrictions of the budget. The Producer, therefore, is your source of information about big production issues, plus the casting status of actors and the revision status of the script. Producers come in many forms: Line Producer, Executive Producer, Supervising Producer, Co-Producer, Associate Producer, Producer, Creative Producer, and Consulting Producer. In general, the Line Producer is usually heavily involved in the budget and can be seen as an experienced Production Manager ready to move into producing, and the Executive Producer is usually key to the financing of the production, but most producer titles vary from production to production. Some Producers are attached to the project because they were key in setting up the initial deal to make the project happen; you will never hear from them. Other Producers are heavily hands-on during production, overseeing every day on set personally. Still other Producers supervise the series postproduction process closely, because the Producer on set will not have time to devote to the needs and the decisions of postproduction. Find out the list of Producers that are on your production, and identify what roles each will play; determine whom you need to meet regarding, and whom you must keep informed of, various production issues.

PRODUCTION MANAGER & PRODUCTION COORDINATOR
As this entire book is about the Production Manager and the Production Coordinator, there is not much to say here. You work hand-in-hand together. Meet every day for

approvals, direction, and to keep each other informed. The Production Manager is responsible to ensure the film is made on time and on budget, and oversees everything the Production Coordinator does.

DIRECTOR
The Director has the overall creative vision of the project and meets with each department to realize that vision (within the restrictions of the budget). The Director will be involved in location choice, set design, casting, and script revisions early in prepro-duction, and will be involved at least until the first cut (known as the "Director's Cut") of the production in the picture-editing phase. He knows what script revisions and cast-ing choices he wants, though the Producer must confirm these choices before the Production Coordinator can proceed with publishing script changes or issuing cast lists. If the project is director-driven, like a feature film, the Director may also be a Producer. If the project is a series, the Director will be hired by the Producer. If the Director has no Personal Assistant, the Production Coordinator will be covering such needs for him.

WRITING DEPARTMENT
In the Writing Department, there may be a Creative Producer, Executive Story Editor, Story Editor, and Story Consultants, along with a team of Writers — depending upon how complex a production or series you have. Since the Writing team has a handle on the official script revisions that may affect the budget, the Production Manager needs to be in communication with this team often. The Production Coordinator may be typing up the script revisions into script format for this team; if so, they will likely want to know the page count of the typed script as soon as possible. It is wise to ensure that both the Writing team and the PC use the same software. As PC, you may have to correct their grammar, too. Make sure the Producer approves each draft you get directly from them.

PRODUCTION ACCOUNTANT
As discussed previously, the Production Accountant is key to the Production Manager, and they meet more than daily with each other. This person can output cost reports, cash flows, and basically track real costs and promises (purchase orders) as they happen. As with the Coordinator, the Production Manager needs to work hand-in-hand with the Accountant too, for accuracy of cost reporting and estimates. The Production Coordinator discusses with the Accountant which individual will track purchase orders. The Coordinator may have the Accountant arrange to complete an exemption from sales tax form, and help determine how much petty cash the office will need, and which person from your team is going to keep and monitor it.

PRODUCTION SECRETARY
The Production Coordinator, more than the Manager, tends to hire the Production Secretary, as this person is the Coordinator's right hand. As mentioned previously, the Coordinator and the Secretary need to keep up a constant conversation, meeting at least daily to give direction and approvals and to keep each other informed.

OFFICE PRODUCTION ASSISTANT

The Production Coordinator also tends to hire the Office P.A. — or at least highly recommend this person to the PM for hiring — as this individual is the other critical person in helping the Coordinator manage the production office. Be clear who in the office gives direction to the Office P.A., so the latter will not be confused with having multiple bosses. As discussed previously, there needs to be a constant flow of communication between the Coordinator and the Office P.A. to keep the office and the office team running smoothly.

HEAD OFFICE/CO-PRODUCTION OFFICE PEOPLE

There may be Executive Producers, Co-Producers, Legal Counsels, and Controllers at head office who need to be kept abreast of the goings-on of production. The Producer should be the point person to keep head office informed, but there may be times when the Production Manager is brought into these conversations. Discuss with the Producer. Head office Legal Counsel may be a source of advice for production decision-making, and that office may be the place where long form actor contracts are generated. Most meetings with head office are done by telephone, often conference calls. Find out what paperwork and reports these people need and when. The Production Coordinator can ensure the paperwork is sent to them regularly.

CAST & CASTING PEOPLE

The only reason that "casting" has anything to do with "fishing" is because casting people are always fishing for the right talent to fill all the acting roles in a film.

CASTING DIRECTOR

The Production Manager needs to keep atop who is being hired for how much, and what bonuses the actors want that will no doubt affect the budget (dressing room requirements like a Winnebago, and transportation needs like number and class of flights, type of car rental, etc.). The Producer tends to hire the Casting Director(s); you may have one for the guest star-type leads and a different one for the main cast, but you should have at least one per city where you are shooting or casting. The Production Coordinator needs to keep the Casting Director apprised of the latest script revision and she will keep you apprised of the latest status of actors chosen. Casting Directors make the deal with the actors' agents, and then send the deal memos to the Coordinator. The Production Manager needs to keep in the loop prior to the commitment of the deal letter, since once the deal is on paper the money is as good as spent. The Coordinator turns these deal memos into cast contracts, and may also be involved in helping the Casting Director set up audition sessions, and in making and distributing audition sides to be read at the auditions.

CAST

Though the Production Manager may not actually meet the cast until they are on set, or when they visit the office looking for their per diem, the PM signs the cast contracts. Go figure. The Production Coordinator, however, may be the first person to deal with the actors, and therefore give them their first impression about the company. The Coordinator is responsible for sending them all the paperwork necessary for them to act in the show. Keep them updated on all script revisions immediately. They are the ones who have to memorize the lines. You may also have to arrange for immigration, travel, and living for them.

EXTRAS & EXTRAS CASTING DIRECTOR

The Production Manager never really interacts with the Extras (also known as Background Performers). The Extras Casting Director tends to be hired by the PM on strong recommendation by the First Assistant Director. The A.D. Department keeps up the communication with this person, and the First A.D. directs the background action on the set. Extras are non-speaking cast to fill the background of scenes. On film, they can pass by, walk dogs, or comprise crowds. Special Skills Extras (or Special Business Extras) are paid slightly higher rates because they have a special skill to perform on set; for example, they play hockey, ride horses, and do other things on film that require a special skill. The Production Coordinator will, however, deal with the Extras Casting Director in order to coordinate the Extras' arrival on set.

SET PEOPLE – ASSISTANT DIRECTORS

Both Production Manager and Coordinator deal with Assistant Directors several times each day, funneling any information you have for set through them; therefore, they warrant having their own section. A.D.s are in charge of running the set, so that the Director can be creative without worrying about the time or gathering the people and props together. That is why Assistant Directors seem to do an awful lot of running around.

ASSISTANT DIRECTORS

While the Production Manager is overseeing the budget, the Assistant Directors are overseeing the schedule. Between the two of you, you cover it all: time and money. Work together. Together you report on the daily activities of the set on the Daily Production Report, both signing the official, completed form. Discuss the schedule. How flexible is it? The First A.D. is running the set, trying to keep it to schedule, so he is the source of information on how fast (or not) set is moving through the day's work. The Production Manager may hire the First A.D., but the Director may have approval or choice of this person, depending on the Director's agreement. The Director and the First A.D. work hand-in-hand. Some A.D.s prefer a military style of running the set, but others have a softer approach. Some use screaming to keep people on their toes, and some find other ways of earning the crew's respect and focus. Some can be considered "production-hostile." There are many different styles of Assistant Directing. This person will be key in determining the mood of the working set, so find out what style you are in for before hiring your First A.D. Discuss working styles with the Director and the Producer to be sure all are looking for the same style. Assistant Directors tend to own their own scheduling software and have their own computer equipment. Often the First A.D. comes with a full team of Seconds and Thirds. Is this a long-running team, or is this A.D. constantly replacing his A.D. team? Does the Director have a history with the First A.D.? Sometimes the First A.D. will pick up the Director in the morning on the way to set to discuss the day prior to shooting. No matter how they do it, the First A.D. and the Director need to be a team, so the First A.D. can worry about moving the schedule along, leaving the Director to worry about the creative issues of each shot.

For the Production Coordinator, the A.D.s have the lowdown on the schedule. They make it. You have the lowdown on casting status. You can swap information. Inform them of special agreements in the cast contracts that affect the set (like private dressing rooms that have been promised for the length of production, and driver pickups promised daily). Decide together which call-sheet form, schedule form, day-out-of-days form, and production-report form to use. Find out if you have compatible computer equipment. Discuss the shoot day responsibilities in detail: Who is to call crew with the next day's call times, who is to inform actors of change of dates, who is to inform the crew when the call time gets pushed or pulled in the middle of the night. Before the shoot, the A.D.s will come to you to stock up on all the paperwork from the distribution table and forms from the wall envelopes for their portable office on set. Give them a hand and work as a team.

OTHER SET PEOPLE

Many of these people float from office to set, but their primary responsibility is to set.

LOCATIONS DEPARTMENT

Briefly, these people scout and survey potential locations, then once chosen, make the location deal with the owners and secure permits for permissions. They also ensure that the location remains protected and clean during the shoot day, that lunch arrangements are made, that the unit trucks have accessible space to park, and that there is parking available for the crew, too. If owners have had a bad experience with a film crew, the location may become burned from any film crew ever going back there to film. Burning locations must be avoided at all costs, as it has a domino effect on the entire industry. Respect is key. When it comes to hiring the Location Manager, ask yourself, or the interviewee, how does this person deal with the public? How has she protected locations from being burned? Has she ever had access to film in a burned location and turned the public's attitude around regarding filming? How well does this person know the city? Can she creatively find and use locations, like finding one location that links two different sets from the script in one place, cutting down on unit moves? During preproduction, the Production Manager needs to look over the location contract and approve it. If it is complex, you may even want Legal Counsel to review the document.

As Production Manager, you should attend at least all major location scouts and surveys to learn about costs being planned. For the Production Coordinator, the Location Manager will often ask you to type up the agreement letter or the contract, and arrange for insurance certificates for each location. She will usually need these documents hurriedly. She will also give you location maps to attach to the call sheets. Ask for the maps early, unless you enjoy making maps at the last moment. (More on Locations is in Chapter 16.)

CONTINUITY SUPERVISOR

This person is basically the Editor's representative on set to make sure that each shot will be able to cut to the next without faults, like arm movements that do not match and burning cigarettes that change length. Continuity, therefore, makes many, many notes about and photographs each and every shot during the course of the shoot day. The Production Manager needs to hire someone who is incredibly organized, diligent, and detail-oriented. The Production Coordinator will deal with this person in prep, making sure that the Continuity Supervisor and the Editor meet. Find out what forms need to be printed, have them made, and arrange for the purchase of the correct Polaroid film for his camera. Also discuss the most efficient way for that paperwork to flow from set to the editing department and back to set.

TRANSPORTATION DEPARTMENT

The Transportation Department basically arranges for truck, car, and picture vehicle rentals, then drives and parks the units. But wow, what a unit it is, made up of numerous huge trucks and trailers that Locations has asked to be parked into the most incredibly tight spaces! It is an amazing feat. They also courier items and make purchases throughout the day, ensure the vehicles are working properly throughout the day, and take the film to the lab nightly. Since the Transportation team is on set first in the morning and last at night, they work some of the longest hours. The Production Manager needs to keep a conversation going with the Transportation Coordinator to minimize overtime and keep the Drivers fresh and functional for the daily work. The Production Coordinator will see Drivers every day in the office during the course of their many runs. Talk to them often, because you can usually help them out with use of the Office Production Assistant, just as they can help you out with use of a Driver.

CRAFT SERVICE

As already discussed, Craft Service supplies snack foods to the crew all day to keep them energized between meals. Since it is the Production Manager who receives all the complaints about food from the crew and the cast, ensure you hire a fabulous Craft Service person or company. If the person is new to the industry, he will have a lot of questions that the Production Coordinator can field. Help by discussing the accounts you have with coffee and water companies. Make sure Craft Service has the first-aid kit handy for the set.

CATERER

The Caterer brings a hot lunch to set for the crew. If not Craft Service, they may also be the one to supply substantial snacks three hours into the day to keep everyone energized until lunchtime. The Locations Department will help set up the lunch, including chairs and garbage cans. You may hire a Caterer who can supply craft service, too. As mentioned, the Production Manager will have to deal with any and all complaints about food. Be sure the Caterer can address food allergies. The caterer must be reliable and serve good, healthy food with lots of variety. On long shoots, it can be a good idea to alternate between two Caterers on a weekly basis to keep variety in the diet. The Production Coordinator will be calling the Caterer every day with the time for lunch the next day, along with the particulars for where, when, and how many. Find out from the crew if there are any special needs (not requests) for catering, like those food allergies.

DESIGN, BUILDING & DECORATING PEOPLE

Depending on the needs of the production, these people may have been hired before you begin and are already working when you start.

ART DEPARTMENT

This department can be made up of the Production Designer, the Art Director, the Assistant Art Directors, and the Art Department Coordinator, or any combination thereof. They design the whole physical look of the film, especially the sets. The Production Manager needs to discuss the art budget with the head of the Art Department. Since a Production Designer can be involved not only in the creative design and building of the sets, but also in overseeing the set dressing, props, and greens — and may even be involved in overseeing wardrobe and makeup — the art budget is a sizable chunk of the entire budget. Keep in conversation with the head of the Art Department on the status of this budget being spent. Find out, too, how big a studio space is required for the set plan. As you find locations, modifications may need to be made to each location so that the place works for filming. Be sure the Art Department is preparing for these modifications, by allocating time or planning to hire more people to cover these needs. For the Production Coordinator, the Art Department can make beautiful, artistic letterhead for you. They will need items couriered by you and cleared through customs. They also need you to arrange for a speedy script clearance so that once the names in the script are legally approved, the correct signs can be made.

SETS DEPARTMENT

These people buy and rent the set furnishings, from lamps to furnish a house set to fake garbage to furnish a location alley set. The Set Decorator is hired in consultation with the Production Designer. The Production Manager may deal more with the Production Designer than directly with the Set Decorator, but should be no stranger to either in order to keep atop production spending promises. The Sets Department may arrange for a set sale (along with wardrobe and props) at the end of production, or for set storage, as needed. You need to discuss these details. The Production Coordinator primarily interacts with the Sets Department to arrange for couriers and customs clearances for them. This department also needs pagers to keep in touch with each other.

PROPS DEPARTMENT

Props are anything the actors handle as written in the script, from cigarettes to food to suitcases to clothing they carry, and so on. The Production Manager will likely deal with the Production Designer, rather than with the Property Master directly, to oversee the spending in this department — but again, the PM should be no stranger to this department. The Production Coordinator will arrange for couriers, customs clearances, and pager rentals for these people, too.

CONSTRUCTION DEPARTMENT

As the name suggests, these people build the sets. The department can be made up of a Construction Manager, a Construction Coordinator, various Carpenters, Scenic Painters, and Laborers. Hiring of the Construction Manager is done in consultation with the Production Designer, then the Construction Manager tends to bring together his entire team. As time draws short to complete sets prior to shooting, taking all set and location modifications into account, this department often goes over budget in overtime. No matter what the set design, it always seems to take longer to build than originally planned. Be prepared for this situation. Ensure you have hired a Construction Manager who can deliver what the Production Designer plans in a timely manner, so that you are not lighting while the last coat of paint is still being applied. The Production Coordinator does not have to deal with this department very much, as they are usually working before the Coordinator is on board and have their own system of organization in place. It is still worthy to talk to them now and then to keep in touch with the progress of production.

GREENS DEPARTMENT

If you shoot in a forest, no doubt the trees will be in the wrong place for the camera, and you will have to hire Greenspeople to place trees and shrubs to augment the forest location. The same rings true for gardens, and Greenspeople are especially needed for studio sets that must show a bit of the "outside." If production is small and simple enough, the Props or Sets Departments may cover greens work. Since this is another team under the Production Designer, the Production Manager and Coordinator may not deal directly with these people often.

TECHNICAL PEOPLE

Technical crew is hired toward the end of preproduction and report directly to set. If they are not in the production meeting, you will have to visit set to meet them.

CAMERA DEPARTMENT

The Director of Photography (also known as "DOP" or "DP") designs the technical look of the production. As the Production Designer oversees all the Art Departments, the Director of Photography will oversee all the technical departments — Camera, Sound, Electric, Grip — and will be heavily involved in issues relating to Special Effects and CGI. The camera team can be made up of the DP; the Camera Operator; the Focus Puller (since focus is measured with a tape measure, not by eye), who is also known as the First Assistant Cameraperson or "1st AC"; the Clapper/Loader, who is also known as the Second Assistant Cameraperson or "2nd AC"; and the Camera Trainee. On smaller shoots, the DP may also operate the camera. The Production Manager will interact with this department regarding choice of film stock, size and nature of equipment package rental, and will listen to the DP's design of shots. Are they expensive? Do you need second camera, second unit, cranes, steadicams, jimmy jibs, camera cars, scaffolding, and are these wishes in the budget already? In prep, the Production Coordinator needs to find out what film stock is being used, as it is the Coordinator who will do the ordering. Keep informed, too, when the camera equipment and the stock tests are scheduled, because you will likely be asked to help in those arrangements. From the Camera Department, you can get a battery order and an expendable order (like camera tape and lens tissues).

SOUND DEPARTMENT

Another obvious department, the Sound Department is made up of the Sound Mixer (or Sound Recordist), the Boom Operator (who holds the microphone at great heights and for inhumanly long hours), and sometimes includes a third member, the Cableperson. Because sound recording is essentially much cheaper than filming (camera), the sound team is often placed second or forgotten on set when it comes to production issues. The Locations Department may have found a fabulous location, but not considered the flight path that will ruin your location sound recording at regular intervals. As a Production Manager, be sure you hire a production team that considers sound issues, and also a sound team that is excellent at capturing location sound — a very difficult job. If you manage to achieve good location sound, you will save production loads of money in postproduction as they try to rebuild the soundtrack. Research your sound team's past projects. Discuss the merits of radio mics versus booming. Sound Mixers often have their own equipment. When you visit a set, the Sound Mixer is a great person to visit... he hears everything the microphone is pointed at! For the Production Coordinator, find out and order which sound stock the Sound Department intends to use, unless the Sound Mixer is planning to arrange for purchase of the stock himself. Sound always has an extensive battery order for production.

ELECTRIC DEPARTMENT

The Gaffer is the head electrician, and the Best Boy is next in charge. The rest of the team are called Electrics. These people, obviously, are in charge of the lights on the set. The Production Manager may be the one hiring the Gaffer in consultation with the DP. Discuss the wish list for the rental package with the Gaffer. You may need to negotiate the list down, depending on your budget. Be sure you have enough crew for the equipment. Renting a huge equipment package and being short on crew will cost you time on set. The Production Coordinator will address the order of expendables, i.e., for gels (colored-gelatin sheets or rolls to color the lights), black wrap, and clothes pegs (to hold the gels onto the lights).

GRIP DEPARTMENT
Grips move all sorts of things around on the set, and create the most beautiful rigs to enable the camera to dolly around, in, and through just about anything. They also set up flags to block or pattern some of the lights. The Key Grip heads the department, the Dolly Grip pushes the camera dolly, and there can be a Best Boy Grip who is second in charge. Again, the Production Manager may hire the Key Grip in consultation with the DP or the Gaffer, and you need to discuss the wish list and the crew list to make the beauty happen. The Production Coordinator needs to get the expendable order for tape and sash, etc. Grips may also have specialty rentals they will ask you to arrange, like scaffolding and cranes. Get necessary approvals from the Production Manager.

HAIR, MAKEUP & WARDROBE PEOPLE

Affectionately known as the Pretty Department, its members dress and makeup the actors into character for on screen.

WARDROBE DEPARTMENT
Obviously, this department designs the wardrobe (or costumes), shops for wardrobe, makes wardrobe, does laundry of wardrobe, dresses the actors, and keeps notes of who wore what for which scene (using Polaroid film). Knowing the retail price of clothing, you must be aware that it is hugely easy to go over budget in this department. As Production Manager, discuss the wardrobe budget with the Wardrobe Designer and determine how the department plans to keep to the budget. Can any of the wardrobe be sold after filming, or must it all be stored? Be sure you hire a wardrobe team that has designed similar costumes: Period wardrobe differs radically from contemporary glamour or grunge. As Production Coordinator, find out which type of Polaroid film they use. Keep them abreast of the casting status as soon as possible, because these people never seem to get enough time to fit the cast.

HAIR & MAKEUP DEPARTMENT
Again, the job of this department is obvious. The Hair Designer and Makeup Artist should be budgeted to come to some preproduction meetings to meet the Director, the cast, and possibly to do screen tests. As Production Manager, find out if these people have worked with any of the Actors you are planning to cast. From their previous projects, find out how fast (or slow) they are in doing their work on the day. An entire crew waiting for an Actor to come out of hair/makeup is an expensive wait. Do you need any special needs makeup for this shoot, like glamour makeup or wounds? How adept are these people at production's special needs? For the Production Coordinator,

these people also need to be kept informed of the casting status, but not quite so hurriedly as the Wardrobe Department.

SPECIAL DEPARTMENTS PEOPLE

Depending on the scale of the production, you could have any, all, or none of the following departments to create the magic of movies.

STUNTS DEPARTMENT
When the script calls for someone to walk through fire, the script calls for a stunt double — and you need a stunt coordinator. The Production Manager must consider safety as a first priority when hiring the Stunt Coordinator. Naturally, you want to see a track record of stunts performed that look good for the camera too, but safety is always your primary goal. Also, when looking for a Stunt Coordinator (or company), does he (or they) have access to people who will double for your Actors? Stunt adjustments in the budget are bonuses beyond the stunt price for particularly difficult stunts. As Production Coordinator, you need to know from the Stunt Coordinator who is going to play which role, so that you can inform Wardrobe and also can whip up the appropriate stunt contracts. Discuss the nature of the stunt with the Stunt Coordinator and the Assistant Director to determine if a Nurse or an Ambulance Attendant is required on the day. If so, order one.

SPECIAL EFFECTS DEPARTMENT
Special Effects can be fires, snow, rain, and more — created on set. These effects are sometimes known as Physical Effects, to differentiate them from computerized special effects. This is another department where the Production Manager has to be concerned with safety first. Special Effects people need to work hand-in-hand with at least the Art and the Locations Departments initially; larger effects require lots of planning to do them cost effectively. In order to ensure accuracy, be specific about your needs when you ask for quotations from Special Effects companies. Keep updated on the quotations to keep the spending in line. For the Production Coordinator, these people often come from a supplier that does not work in the production office with you, so it is your job to keep them informed of meetings and script changes that affect them. Find out the nature of the effect, and how you can help. You can arrange, for example, for a representative from the fire department to be on set or for someone to have a fire extinguisher handy. Discuss all arrangements with the Assistant Directors.

COMPUTER GRAPHICS IMAGERY (CGI) OR VISUAL EFFECTS & ANIMATION
Different from set special effects, visual effects or CGI are usually computer effects or motion-controlled camera equipment (to enable computerized matching of camera movements). You may have one department creating 3D computer effects and another creating 2D computer effects. This team has to work hand-in-hand with at least the Art Department. Again, the more planning time, the more cost effective the effects will be.

Beware on set, as it is easy for crew to say "fix it in post" and do a sloppy job on set to rush forward. Imagine if a tether is left on a bird for the shot to save the crew five minutes in removing it (because the bird was trained for this action already). You save the five minutes of shooting, but find that to remove the tether in CGI, the cost equals that of one of your fancy effects; so you have to remove a fancy effect from the script to cover the cost of the tether removal — leaving you with a CGI effect that is in effect, invisible. "Fixing it in post" is expensive. Avoid it. As Production Manager, keep an eye on CGI quotations and the changes that affect the original quotations at all production meetings and in all script revisions. Keep an eye on crew that likes to shift responsibility from set to CGI, too. For the Production Coordinator, the CGI people are rarely in your office fulltime, though they may have a representative on set for all effects shots. Keep them informed of meetings and script changes that affect them.

SECOND UNIT
Second Unit may be dedicated to being the Special Effects Unit, the Stunt Unit, the Action Unit, or the Animal Unit. Whichever unit they are, whatever shots they are achieving, they do not require the lead cast nor any meaty dialogue scenes, so they can be a reduced-size unit capturing shots that would be expensive for the entire Main Unit to be standing around waiting to capture (like an establishing shot of the sunrise or a dog fetching a stick). They take direction from the Main Unit Director and the DP to ensure their shots will match seamlessly in style into the whole picture. They can also work closely with the Editor for the same reason. Have Second Unit start after Main Unit begins, to be sure that Second Unit is capturing shots that Main Unit did not get — instead of getting ahead of the Main Unit shooting schedule and locking Main Unit in to Second Unit's choice of camera angles for matching. If both units schedule to finish on the same day as wrap, this situation will be a bit tricky. Try to schedule so that Second Unit finishes a few days into wrap to ensure they are available to get last minute pickup shots that Main Unit could not. When Editors ask for shots to help with transitions that did not work as originally planned, they often create a videotape reference for Second Unit's playback reference on set. As the Production Coordinator, keep Second Unit informed of meetings and script changes that affect them.

POSTPRODUCTION PEOPLE

The term "postproduction" sounds like "after production," but the process actually starts long before the end. The Editor is usually aboard cutting the film together while the film is still being shot — from the second day of principal photography!

EDITING DEPARTMENT
There may be a Postproduction Supervisor, a Postproduction Coordinator, Editors, and Assistant Editors in postproduction. The Supervisor is hired by the Production Manager or the Producer, and it is to this person you hand over the running of production after wrap. The Supervisor will manage the post budget; if not, the

Producer will. Supervisors know how postproduction works. They have contacts with post facilities. They are responsible for monitoring the budget. They are highly organized. The Editor, being a key creative on the production, may have already been chosen prior to your arrival in preproduction. On a series you may alternate Editors on each episode to more efficiently move postproduction along. Though production has managed to film shots on set, it is in the editing room where the film is actually created. This is the reason many Editors make a transition to Directors. As the Production Coordinator, you have already made sure that the Continuity Supervisor and the Editor connected during preproduction to discuss the continuity paperwork flow. Other things to discuss with the editing team are: a system for the information flow regarding the arranging for and screening of rushes, and who is to call the lab for the daily negative check.

MUSIC DEPARTMENT

Another key creative, the Music Composer is often part of the team assembled by the Producer in development. This person often negotiates a flat fee to include her work and music rights, studio rental, musicians hired, and their rights. If the Production Manager is still on board in postproduction, he should ensure that a music-spotting session happens where the Director and/or the Producer sits with the Music Composer and a cut of the film to decide when music is required and what it might sound like. If production's plan is to fill the soundtrack with pre-recorded music instead of original music created by a Composer, beware of music rights. They are expensive. (More on Music Rights is in Chapter 32.) As the Production Coordinator, you likely will not need to deal with the Music Composer very often. She will tend to deal with the Producer directly. If a piece of music is to be played back on set for filming, you need to arrange for a transfer of the music — in the appropriate format — to get to the Sound Mixer on set. Make sure you have an extra copy of this music in the office in case of emergency on the shoot day.

POSTPRODUCTION LABORATORY

If you are shooting on film, the lab receives your negative at night and processes the film overnight, workprinting it in the morning or transferring it to video for you to watch. If you are shooting on video, you still need a lab to transfer viewing copies and work copies of the original videotape for reference and postproduction. As Production Manager, you need to set up the lab deal and book processing and transfer timeslots for production. You will also want to store your negative at the lab for safekeeping. The Producer may have set up a facilities deal with the lab, trading some facilities costs for investment participation in the production. Discuss with the lab which costs are associated with the facilities deal and which costs are to be paid for with cash; then discuss with the Accountant how to track those non-cash expenses. Decide how rushes are to be viewed: on film at the lab or only on video, and if only video, which format for best quality screening. Ensure a film-stock test happens before shooting, and be sure you are informed of the negative check or "neg report" daily (stating if the negative was processed okay with no scratches). If there are negative problems, address them urgently. How big is the problem? How expensive the fix? Investigate the severity of the problem before committing to re-shooting all of yesterday's film and filing an insurance claim. There may be ways to cut around much of the troubled footage. (More on insurance claims is in Chapter 17.) The lab is also required to sign a letter for the Completion Bond, granting access to the negative should production be taken over by the Completion Bond.

Because of the Postproduction Supervisor, the Production Coordinator may not have to deal directly with the lab very often. The Coordinator, though, may be the one to call the lab first thing every morning for a neg report, and pass on that information to the Production Manager and the Producer. Another reason to be in touch with the lab is to arrange to screen rushes at their facility, as you need to make plans for the screenings to happen following the shoot day's wrap to allow the key crew to attend.

POST SOUND FACILITY

You may have a Sound Designer, Sound Editors, Dialogue Editors, Sound Effects Editors, Music Editors, a Mixer, and a Foley Artist. The work of the Sound Editors is obvious, as it involves cutting the sound into separate tracks so the quality of each sound can be treated separately in the mix. The Mixer is different from the Location Sound Mixer, in that he sits at the Sound Facility's control panel literally mixing all the numerous sound tracks (you can easily have over 100 different tracks of dialogue, sound effects, foley, music, and atmosphere) down to a mere few tracks for marrying with the print for playback (in mono or stereo). This person will also ensure you mix a separate music and effects (M&E) track to allow for dubbing the film into foreign languages. The Foley Artist is that cool person who watches the film from a sound studio and recreates sounds live to tape to add richness to the soundtrack — sounds like footsteps (on various surfaces), clothing rustles, door slams, kisses, and so on. As this happens far in postproduction, only on a series might you as a Production Manager or Coordinator still be on board when sound post is happening. The Coordinator may still be around to assist in setting up ADR sessions (Additional Dialogue Recording, also known as Looping) with the Actors. Make sure that the Actor's work reports are filled out so that the Actor will be paid for this work. There will not be an A.D. around in post to do this task.

PUBLICITY PEOPLE

Though it may seem that publicity arrangements get in the way of filming, a film would have a hard time finding an audience if publicity people failed to do, or were not allowed to do, their job.

PUBLICITY DEPARTMENT

The Unit Publicist and the Publicity Department conduct interviews, arrange for publicity shots (action shots on set), arrange for gallery shoots (the Actors in character in a studio setting), create one-sheets and other promotional materials, arrange for or make an EPK (electronic press kit or behind-the-scenes video), arrange for press to visit the set, and issue press releases, too. The Producer or the Production Manager hires the Unit Publicist, but it is the Producer who is key in deciding how much publicity needs to be assembled for the production. Be sure that the A.D.s schedule time for publicity shots and interviews. The Production Coordinator can be involved in arranging for the Publicity Department to visit and work on set. Keep them informed of the shooting schedule, and keep them in contact with the Producer to discuss the best days to be there. Keep the Assistant Directors in the loop with these communications also.

STILLS PHOTOGRAPHER

As this person is likely to be on set a lot more often than the Unit Publicist, it is worth dealing with her separately. When hiring the Stills Photographer, consult with the Unit Publicist and review the portfolio. Note that both the Stills Photographer and the EPK Cameraperson will be covered under the Camera union if you are using a union crew, and also note you may require Executive approval in the hiring process of either or both of these positions. As Production Manager or Coordinator, be sure that stills are both scheduled and captured. Make sure, too, the Producer and the Director are involved in the choice of what is most interesting to shoot. Be sure the Assistant Director is in the loop to give input concerning the lighter workload days (to schedule a gallery shoot). Keep the Stills Photographer aware of the shooting schedule and stills time windows.

This chapter has been a micro look at the whole crew. Okay, so I am leaving lawyers and bankers and auditors to be dealt with in the money section of the book. I know you know what they do! The more you deal with each department, the more you will understand the nuances of what everyone does and respect them for their work. You earn their trust and they give you trust in return. Keep talking to everyone on the crew. The constant input will be helpful and educational. There is always something to learn from the professionals you hire.

Midnight Creations

An excerpt from notes from the Production Coordinator to the Production Secretary, penned during one of those late-night shoots:

1. *1:28 a.m. The call sheet is done and faxed. Office P.A. is on his way to set with it.*
2. *1:34 a.m. A ginger ale is opened.*
3. *Please call the female lead with call time change: It's now 5:30 p.m., not 3:30 p.m.*
4. *Office P.A. will be in at noon; I'll work at 2:00 or 2:30 p.m.*
5. *Office P.A. needs to return the standard picture vehicle at 2:00 p.m.*
6. *Only after having cleaned both vehicles. With a toothbrush.*
7. *Just kidding! About the toothbrush, that is.*
8. *I'm returning your script pages used for "siding."*
9. *Oh, and one more thing for Office P.A. Camera is sending back the 2nd unit equipment tonight and having it put in the PM's room. Please have him take it back to the equipment house first thing.*

A little later...

17. *A production report to distribute... really.*
18. *And some lovely state-of-the-art deal memos for that "distrib thing."*
19. *1:54 a.m. Heart failure. I've been all alone since the Office P.A. left. Then I heard a voice. Of course I knew that someone was trying to make their presence known, but who? It's pretty dark and scary here sometimes... the Office P.A. came back for the craft service water.*
20. *1:57 a.m. Heart resumes, and I'm alone again.*
21. *Please find out from the Location Manager, or whomever, when the A.L.M. is coming back to visit the office. I need something from him.*
22. *No, only a signature.*
23. *2:36 a.m. And now what? Another ginger ale.*
24. *A note to the Daily 3rd Electric from the Gaffer: Please bring the other Daily Electric in with you.*
25. *An equipment house order and purchase order: 200 amp 3-phase disconnect for today.*
26. *2:57 a.m. I realized the Art Department copier was still on.*
27. *3:03 a.m. Found the off switch.*
28. *3:12 a.m. I get my second wind. Or is it the third?*
29. *3:14 a.m. False alarm.*
30. *You might as well send the Office P.A. out to post the mail. It keeps getting forgotten.*
31. *5:14 a.m. A slew of call time changes. Please call all the actors with changes in their times.*
32. *As for them editors: I didn't call the Post Coordinator at night and just as well. At 1 a.m. they didn't want rushes on Thursday. At 5 a.m. they want RUSHES AT 7:00 P.M. Let the Post Coordinator know.*
33. *Please note the call sheet is pink. The Location Manager and the Set Decorator know. Everyone else is to find out in the morning.*
34. *Gotta run to take pink call sheets to set. I've only faxed pink to head office and technical union...*

CHAPTER 8

WORKSPACE ORGANIZATION

You are sitting at your desk. If you are the Production Manager, you will likely be in an office, as nearly all the issues you deal with are highly confidential. If you are the Production Coordinator, you could be in your own office or working in open concept, as you need to be near the traffic of the active production office. In either case, this is your personal space. Set it up to work best for you.

How you organize your workspace is most certainly up to you and your own personal style. Yet, are you ready for the reams of paper that will flow onto and off your desk? Will you be able to find every single piece of paper or information with lightning speed or will it all get lost? Will passing crew members be able to read Actor contracts left face up on top of one of the great many piles? What you want are tips on handling your workspace before it handles you. Since even the Production Manager relies on the Production Coordinator's organization, the Coordinator's workspace is more structured than that of the Production Manager's.

THE PM'S WORKSPACE

THE PM'S DESK
Basically the Production Manager needs to keep on top of tons of issues and deal memos and long form contracts without dragging paper in and out from files in a cabinet, because all issues in preproduction are current and immediate. You also want to be organized enough to find anything quickly and for the Coordinator to be able to come into your office to find something if you need her to do so while you are on set. Your workspace organization cannot be too complex.

Here are two systems that work well:

LATERAL FILING ON THE DESK
If you like to spread paper out over a wide, lateral surface, this system is for you. Since you have an office where you can close the door, you do not need to enclose every bit of paper in file folders for confidentiality. Flag sticky notes dry side up atop each stack of paper and offset the piles in a column down one side of your desk. You can now view many differing stacks of papers at once by their sticky note labels. Though this system uses up maximum desk space, it is good for hiding confidential information lower down on the stacks of paper — a bit like hiding documents in plain sight. If you want to organize further, you can use colored highlighters to code the sticky notes by subject,

departmental matter, or level of urgency. The only downside is that if you have so much paper in this system, the piles can slide off the desk.

IN-TRAY FILING
If you prefer a vertical look to your organizational system, tuck stacks of paper away in in-trays. This system works for keeping similar issues together, as you will no doubt have a limited number of in-trays stacked on your desk, each labeled with a different subject or department: Locations, Casting, Cost Reports, and so on. Since you cannot see everything at once, you may find that you lose track of an item or two, or at least spend a little time looking for it. This system, however, does keep your desk surface relatively clear of stray paper.

THE PM'S FILING PILE
In both cases, you can allocate a space or a box to a filing pile. As you finish dealing with issues, put the related paper in the filing pile for filing at a later time or date. (To keep on top of filing, it is advisable to do this once a day.) Determine between you and the Coordinator who will be maintaining the Production Manager's files. Do you want the PM files to be folded into the production files? Also, when filing into your filing pile, if you want to keep a draft of a document only until a certain date, use a sticky note to mark a "trash date" on the document; that way, when the files are being purged at a later date, no review is necessary to remove this document from the files.

THE PC'S WORKSPACE

On to the much more structured environment of the Production Coordinator's workspace. It is wise for the Production Manager to read this section too, to gleam hints of organization that may prove useful to his own organizational style.

The surface of the Production Coordinator's desk looks like a sea of paper. A big sea. Paper will be constantly moving to and from your desk. Not only that, but at any given time, you will need to be able to find any one sheet of paper from that mess. Separate your desk surface into sections.

THE "TO-DO" LIST
The to-do list is not actually a section of your desk because it should be portable, but when you are at your desk, it should sit center stage. There are many styles of to-do lists, from calendar books, to steno pads, even to scraps of paper. Choose a method that best suits you:

CALENDAR BOOK
Choose a calendar book that shows one week for every two pages. Though it gives you the illusion you can plan one week in advance, you will probably be thinking one day at

a time anyway. Still, this is my favorite method. It keeps a history of what you have done, as well as allowing you to plan for future events. If you write small, each day has enough space or lines to jot down the sometimes fifty-odd things to do for that day. Use the margins to note important names and numbers you may want to add to your contact list. Prep the calendar, labeling the days of the shooting schedule with day number, set name, and approximate call time. During production you can correct the call times and add the wrap times. This will be a handy reference when you are completing the production reports. Always write in a pencil dark enough to read and hard enough to not smudge. You will make lots of changes.

LEGAL-SIZED LINED PAD OF PAPER
Letter-sized pads of paper will not have enough lines for the number of jobs you will do in a day. Legal-sized pads are big, and hard to lose on the desk. Use one page per day, and one line per job. You will not have to write as small as you would in the calendar book, but you also cannot glance at the full week to see what is approaching. If you find one day of stress at a time is the best for you, this is your system. Tear off the pages that are done and file them in case you need to refer to them again.

LINED NOTEBOOK
A combination of the legal-sized pad of paper and the calendar book, a notebook works best if you want to refer back to recent days without having to dip into the filing cabinet, and you do not worry too much about the future. Since this system is not in a calendar format, you will not have the same feeling of schedule that comes with a calendar — and it is hard to plan too far in advance, since you do not know how many pages in advance you need to write about a triggering event.

STENO PAD
The portability of a steno pad cannot be matched. The drawback is that you will be constantly flipping pages back and forth, as the pages are much too small to hold all your jobs for one day. You can use this drawback to your advantage, however: It is a fine way to look organized but a little frantic at the same time, thereby letting the frantic crew members relate to you.

ONE STICKY NOTE PER JOB
If you love to put sticky notes all over your desk, the telephone, and the walls around you, this method is for you. This is a good system to make people think you are totally disorganized and totally busy. When things get done, you come across as a miracle worker. When you delegate something, just hand your Assistant the note. Drawbacks are: losing sticky notes that have lost their stickiness and have fallen behind furniture, and having no record of what is completed — since you throw out the notes as the jobs are finished.

DESK CALENDAR
A blotting paper desk calendar is not recommended. The squares are too small to list even a portion of what you have to do, and it will spend most of the time on your desk covered by the reams of other paperwork that your desk supports.

TYPED NOTES

This is another method that is not recommended, but mentioned only because on my first coordinating job, I actually typed myself a list of things to do every night for the next day. Call me crazy. I have never had the time or the inclination to do it again. The Production Manager from that show still shakes his head in remembrance.

GENERAL NOTES FOR ANY TO-DO SYSTEM

Remember that you will need to refer to your to-do list daily, and may reference it later in production. Take the advice you gave the Office Production Assistant and note absolutely every task you need to do, no matter how simple each may seem. Do not try to remember fifty different things to do without the aid of written notes. With a list you can check off each item as it is completed, so that you will be able to see both what is left to be done and what you have already accomplished.

THE "IMMEDIATE" NOTES

Always carry around sticky notes and pen for when you do not have your to-do list handy. These are your "immediate" notes. As people ask you to do something, write it down on a note for transposing onto your to-do list as soon as you have time. If it is a job that requires a question of someone on set, you can put it into the "Set Square."

THE SET SQUARE OR BIG STICKY MEETING NOTES

Mark off an area on your desk near the telephone (about six inches by six inches) with any colored tape. Put all questions for the set on separate sticky notes for when you next talk to them. The set always calls when you are in the middle of doing something else, so with this system, all the questions are immediately handy; you will never have to waste time hemming and hawing trying to remember why you paged someone in the first place.

The Production Manager can adapt this system to have big sticky notes with different names on each for meetings or discussions to have with people like the Producer, the Executive Producer, the Production Coordinator, the First A.D., the Production Designer, and so on. When an issue comes up and you have to talk to someone — but now is not the time — note it on the big sticky notes (big, because you will need the size for all you need to write). Then, when you meet with that person, you have a collection of questions to ask at once, rather than returning to that person over and over again.

THE "DESK" FILE FOLDERS

These files hold ongoing issues that generate a lot of paper for themselves, and can take over the Coordinator's desk if you let them. Most of that paper is confidential, so by using file folders, you will never have contracts exposed on your desk for passing crew members to glimpse. By name, the desk file folders are:

❑ Cast Contracts
❑ Crew Deal Memos
❑ Credits
❑ Script Revisions
❑ Legal Clearances

One file folder per issue, they sit stacked to one side of the desk with all the most current information for each issue inside. More on each of these file folders will be dealt with in later chapters.

THE "MOVEMENT" FILE FOLDERS

Use a file-folder color that contrasts with the desk file folders. These files are used to move stacks of paper to and from the people you most deal with as the Coordinator. They should be placed so that passing crew can access them easily.

THE COORDINATOR-TO-COORDINATOR FILE

Okay, this may be stretching the topic of movement, but this folder holds all the backup to the items listed on your to-do list. It will become a really fat file, so paperclip groupings together and give each a label with a sticky note at the top. Then lay them in the file, one grouping slightly lower than the next, so you can see most of the grouping names as soon as you open the file folder.

THE COORDINATOR-TO-PM FILE

This file will get used and beat up the most, since you have daily meetings with the Production Manager. Inside put all the papers to be signed by, approved by, and discussed with the PM. Encourage the crew to put items in for signature so he can have a single signature session, instead of one for every member of the crew. Once this system is in place, the Production Manager may not want any other in-tray. Paper clip telephone messages to the front.

THE COORDINATOR-TO-PRODUCER FILE

Like the Coordinator-to-PM file, this file collects paperwork and telephone messages for the Producer. This one may not get as much usage as the Production Manager's, but it will probably be close.

THE COORDINATOR-TO-DIRECTOR FILE

As it sounds, this file works the same as the above crew files, but for the Director.

THE COORDINATOR-TO-PERFORMER FILE

If you have a visiting star or guest star, this is a great way to have a temporary in-tray for her. Do not let this file gather information until the performer comes to you. Deliver the contents. The personal treatment will be appreciated.

IN-TRAYS OR BOXES

With the movement file folders, you will find that you do not need a traditional in-tray. By not using an in-tray, people will have to hand you every item, thereby giving you the opportunity to quickly glance at each and determine its level of priority. But there are some in-trays or boxes that you should use. Place them on or near your desk for use by you and your Assistants only.

TO-BE-FILED TRAY

Dump all the paper to be filed into this tray for you or your Assistants to do the actual filing when convenient. Pencil in the file name where you would like the page to go at the top right hand corner (especially near the beginning of production), so that both you and your Assistants are on the same track filing-wise.

ORIGINAL SCRIPTS TRAY

The second tray houses the original white pages of each script revision that is current. These pages go through the photocopier many, many times, so make sure they are treated with respect so they can continue to do their job. Label each revision with a sticky note indicating what color the revision is (even though the title page will clearly say so). The more double-checks in the system, the less likely mistakes will get made.

ORIGINAL FORMS TRAY

Like the original scripts tray, this one houses the original white copies of all the types of paper on the distribution table (from crew lists to contact lists to schedules, and so on). Label the color of the respective item with sticky notes, and move outdated versions immediately to the to-be-filed tray to avoid confusion.

THE PC's HIDING PLACES

If the Coordinator's desk has a section underneath that is enclosed, celebrate. You likely are working in open concept and need space for hiding items. Under the desk is a perfect hiding spot. If you are not blessed with such a desk, the bottom drawer of a locking, lateral filing cabinet is good, too. The Production Manager's office may also prove useful for hiding spots. As for items worth hiding:

VHS TAPES OF RUSHES OR FINAL SHOWS

Copies of videotapes (like final shows) get borrowed for personal consumption, and therefore the inevitable loss. Copies of rushes will not disappear as fast as master copies of final shows. Even with a sign-out sheet, people forget to note which tapes they have borrowed. By "hiding" the tapes, you must be asked personally by crew members to borrow such tapes. You can keep the sign-out sheet accurate.

EXTRA CREW GIFTS

Hats, t-shirts, sweatshirts, jackets. Crew members love crew gifts, and many love having more than one per person. Keep any spares hidden.

THE PRODUCTION OFFICE WALLS

The Production Coordinator already has wall envelopes posted for crew and for companies. Add a regular wall calendar, displaying several months at a time. Mark down the production schedule, noting prep weeks, shoot weeks, hiatus weeks (if applicable), and wrap weeks. Crew will often come to look at this calendar. So will you.

THE DOORS

Decide with the Production Manager what is the wording needed for the sign on the front door. Production may want a sign as simple as a photocopied sheet of paper naming the production company or as fancy as a professionally engraved door plaque. Should the sign list the show title along with the production company name?

Next, choose the most artistically inclined person in your department and have him make paper door signs for all the doors in the company (every department and every door, including dressing rooms). Note the company or the show name (ask the Production Manager) and the description of the room. Door signs are great for looks, to help when you describe to someone how to find a certain room, and to teach you why wardrobe tells you they need seven different rooms for storage.

YOUR RELATIONSHIP TO PAPER

To the Production Manager and Coordinator, there is nothing like having information down on paper. Be paper-friendly. When you do something and there is no one to memo about the task done — but it seems an important bit of information — send a memo "To File." You may be teased for the thoroughness, but those around you will soon learn that if you have dealt with a matter, you have completed it and recorded it. This system is very comforting in such a transient way of conducting business.

Imagine that you have been looking for the owner of a certain piece of music to negotiate a legal clearance, and you have talked to thirty different people in five different countries over three weeks — all to no avail. When the Producer and the Legal Counsel ask for a report on your research, you can remember only three contacts. You are advised to continue searching. The search takes up a lot of your time and production's time. Write down what you need to do, what you are doing, and what you have done. You will never know what piece of information you will need to access in the future, but you will not be sorry if you are thorough.

Some people think organization is hereditary; okay, my mother is hugely organized too. But systems can be learned, and now you have a system of dealing with the everyday information and paper flow that will cross your desk during the course of production. You are already well on your way to developing your own working style.

Manners, Manners

When several telephone lines light up at the same time, I help the Production Secretary by answering a few myself. We work as a team.

One day an Office P.A. Hopeful called in and I happened to answer the phone. He asked some detailed questions about production before introducing himself. When I asked who was calling, he insisted that he needed to talk to the Production Manager or the Producer to apply for work. I explained that as Production Coordinator, I handle all the incoming resumes and hire the Office P.A. position, since the position reports to me. I would be happy to talk to him more about it. He became very insistent about speaking to the PM or the Producer, and, shall I say, got very irate about the matter, insulting me and my position very pointedly along the way. I pleasantly put him on hold, then explained the situation to the Production Secretary. She took the call.

The Office P.A. Hopeful was as sweet as pie to her. He was happy to be passed along to whom he thought was the Production Manager. Never questioning her identity, he just presumed that his ranting would get him results. She asked him to send in a resume, and he agreed to do that right away. Then she asked for his name so that she would recognize the resume when it came in.

We did.

CHAPTER 9

TELEPHONE ETIQUETTE

It is in your office, it is in your home, and it haunts you long after production has finished. It is the telephone ring. There are many particular rings of differing telephone systems nowadays. You will be haunted for years by the ring of whatever system you intend to use, because the production office telephone will ring incessantly. Hope it is not the same ring as your house phone. Now, talking about telephone etiquette may seem overly basic, but it is through the telephone where the public gains first contact with — and a first impression of — your company. Executives call the production office. So do crew, cast, suppliers, and the general public. Are you portraying a professional image?

CHOOSING A TELEPHONE SYSTEM

If there is a telephone system already in place when you start, you are fortunate. If not, make it one of the Production Coordinator's many first priorities. Know the features you need before you start looking.

HOW MANY EXTENSIONS (TELEPHONE SETS) WILL YOU NEED?
You will never have enough for all the crew that will request one — especially for the week before filming, when everyone is in the office — so review the list with the Production Manager.

HOW MANY TELEPHONE LINES WILL YOU NEED?
Twenty-four extensions and three lines will not work. Also keep in mind you will need a fax line and perhaps a modem line or two at the same time.

WHAT FEATURES DO YOU NEED AND HOW EASY ARE THEY TO USE?
You will want the ability to do conference calling without calling the conference operator, the ability to restrict long distance and directory assistance on some extensions, and some sets to be speakerphones. Do you want direct dialing to extensions and/or voice mail? Can you plug a telephone headset into any of the sets?

List your requirements and get delivery as soon as humanly possible.

RECEPTION: THE JOB

Reception has got to be the most underrated job on the film production. Good Receptionists know who wants the calls screened and who wants certain calls to interrupt any meeting. They recognize people's voices, are pleasant and professional, and do not lose their cool when eight lines light up at the same time. They never volunteer information to any unnamed person who calls, and on and on. They basically have a mature attitude.

These are further specifics about what the person who answers your telephone should know:

WHO WILL ANSWER THE TELEPHONE
On small productions, the Coordinator is the Coordinator, the Production Secretary, and the Receptionist all rolled into one. On large productions, you could have enough support staff to cover each job separately. Though hard to judge accurately, know that answering the telephone will likely take up about 30-40% of your workday.

"HELLO, PRODUCTION"
This is the best way to answer the telephone if you are working on multiple productions out of the same office, or if you do not want to advertise what production you are at this phone number. Other options are: "HELLO, SHOWNAME" or "HELLO, PRO-DUCTION-COMPANY NAME." Find out which the Production Manager or the Producer prefers.

"HELLO, PRODUCTION. HOLD PLEASE"
When the telephones become extraordinarily busy, you will have to put people on hold as soon as you answer. That is okay. Just get back to each one as soon as humanly possible. Imagine all the calls coming in might be long distance.

ANSWER BY HOW MANY RINGS?
Some people get angry if you cannot answer by the first or the second ring. If eight lines light up at the same time, we all know that is impossible. Answer as soon as possible. With the frequency of voice mail, callers expect you to answer within three rings.

TELEPHONE EXTENSION MAP OR LIST
You have two choices here: (1) the map. Retrieve that floor-plan map you made of the office. Write the people and the telephone extensions on the map, and copy (or reduce-copy) the map for reference at each telephone set. Or, if you prefer lists: (2) the list. Type up a list of crew (alphabetical by first or last name) and their telephone extensions. The map often works best because with the speed that crew is hired on a production, people tend to identify where someone is located in the office first and their name second. Another feature of the map is speedy access to alternative extensions in the same department, if you have trouble finding someone.

KNOW HOW TO USE THE FEATURES OF THE TELEPHONE
The Coordinator and the Secretary should know how to do conference calling, last number redial, and any other useful feature. Read the telephone manual because the crew members will not; they will come to you for lessons in how to use the telephone.

DO NOT HAND OUT INFORMATION FREELY

Some productions are more confidential than others. Often callers will not identify themselves and ask a fair amount about the production. These people could be anyone, including reporters getting information that the Publicity Department wants to keep secret for some reason. Do not let the staff (Secretary or Office P.A.) hand out any information. Depending on how confidential the information might seem, have the Production Coordinator or the Production Manager take the call. Find out who is calling. If you are still uncomfortable with the call, hand it over to the Producer.

SCREENING CALLS

The Receptionist should find out who on the crew wants to have their calls screened. Chances are it will be Producers, Director, Production Manager, Production Accountant, and the Actors.

TAKING MESSAGES – WHEN SOMEONE CAN'T TAKE THE CALL

Generally, if someone cannot come to the telephone, do not volunteer information as to where that person is and when she is expected back. Occasionally you will find that certain crew members are avoiding certain phone calls until a certain time.

TAKING MESSAGES – SPELLING

This may sound basic, but get the correct spelling of the caller's name, where he is calling from, the phone number, the reason for the call, and note the time and the date. Thoroughness is essential. Imagine getting a phonetic message with no phone number or time, like "Gerie called" — and you know a Jerry, Gerry, Geraldine, and Jahri. Who do you call back?

TELEPHONE MANNER

It is absolutely essential to be pleasant and professional every time you and your staff answer the telephone. If you do not ensure this approach each and every time, it will come back to haunt you. The old saying still rings true: You only have one chance to leave a first impression. When you answer the telephone, you are representing the company.

TO VOICE MAIL OR NOT TO VOICE MAIL

Voice mail is a terrific invention that allows Receptionists to go to the bathroom, to handle extremely busy telephones, and to gain time to complete the other tasks now swamping them. The negative side effect is that voice mail is not personal. Machines cannot tell how important the call is (and so cannot interrupt someone on another call because this call is more important), cannot tell if you are calling long distance, cannot tell that it is the one person you have been trying to reach for days, cannot tell that it is the set calling and it is also the last coin in the pay phone. Consider the importance of a person as a Receptionist. Use voice mail as a tool, not a crutch.

HOW TO LEAVE A MESSAGE

Imagine the A.D.s have charged you with informing the crew of a revised call time for the next day because wrap happened in the middle of the night and you are the one in the office first thing in the morning. Be responsible. When you leave a message on an answering machine, leave the following critical information:

1) The time you called
2) Why you are calling
3) A request to return the call for confirmation

You need to know each person got the message. Do not presume that because the message is on the answering machine that the person received the message. Machines are not perfect. People do not always check them. Make a list of the people you called, when you called them, and if you talked to them or left a message on the answering machine. Try to reach them hourly until you get through personally. If you do not get through, you will have proof in your notes of how hard you tried to reach these people. If they do not show up to set on time, and happen to cause an expensive set delay because of their absence, you want to prove how hard you tried to reach them.

Telephones are becoming more complex every day. Even with voice mail and direct-extension calling, do not forget the importance of the person that answers the telephones. If you have never answered a system telephone that rings wildly every day while trying to do your daily work, try it. You will learn a new appreciation for the brave soul who does.

Any Files At All

I love two-drawer lateral filing cabinets. Filing boxes are great for those low-budget we-have-to-be-portable shows, but you can't beat a solid two-drawer lateral filing cabinet to double as a TV stand, a fax machine table, or even a distribution table. And the big drawers? Well!

The Production Manager came up to one of the filing cabinets one day deciding to look for a specific file himself. Knowing that I am an organized person, he was confidant that he could find the file he needed without a problem and wouldn't have to interrupt me on the telephone.

The first filing cabinet drawer he opened was stacked with Polaroid film and a sign-out sheet on a clipboard. The second drawer he tried housed VHS copies of all the episodes to date and a few patch cables. He paused. There were only two drawers to this filing cabinet.

When I was off the phone, he asked me: "Do you keep any files at all?" He told me which file he needed, and I produced it right away from a filing box behind my desk. He looked from the filing box to the filing cabinet one more time. Then he shook his head and took the file into his office.

CHAPTER 10

SETTING UP A FILING SYSTEM

When all the dust is settled, the sets all broken down, and the crew gone home to live their lives again, the production files are some of the only source material depicting what happened during the making of the film. When you set up the filing system, you are making it up for more than just yourself. Rather than waste busy production time creating new files one by one and chance making too many duplicate or similar files, you can prepare the filing cabinet early in prep.

THE PRODUCTION COORDINATOR'S FILES

The Production Coordinator and the Secretary will keep the bulk of the files, but the Production Manager needs files, too.

THE PC'S PRODUCTION SERIES FILES
For a television series or a mini-series, divide the filing cabinet into four sections as follows:

A-Z FILES
These alphabetically-labeled files do not refer to any specific episode of the series. A more specific list of file names for this section is noted below.

EPISODE BY EPISODE FILES
Make a section for each episode, labeled by episode number and title. In this section, file cast lists, schedules, credits, locations, memos, and any other information specific to that episode. These file names are marked by an asterisk (*) in the file list below.

PRODUCTION REPORT FILES
Mark this section for production reports. Each shooting day gets a separate file. In these files, put all the production report backup information and both the pencil and typed copies of the production report. Note the shooting day as well as the date on the file folder label for future reference.

FORMS
Since you will be making numerous forms, store them in their own section.

THE PC'S PRODUCTION FEATURE FILM FILES
Feature films or single-episode productions require files simpler than the series files, in that you can include the episodic files section in the A-Z files section.

THE PC'S PRODUCTION A-Z FILES

Use this list to start your filing cabinet. You can substitute actual names for general descriptions — like "John Doe" can replace "Lead Performer" — and re-alphabetize accordingly.

Accounts & Credit Applications
Actor Union or Guild
Accommodation
Animals
Art Department
Breakdowns – A.D.s
Breakdowns – Continuity
Broadcaster
Call Sheets (one complete set)
* Cast
* Cast Contracts
Catalogs
Catering Menus
Clearances – Script Research Reports
Clearances – Music Rights
Contact List
Correspondence
Correspondence – Fan Mail
* Credits
Courier Waybills/Acct
Crew List
Crew Deal Memos
Crew Union or Guild
Customs
Distributor
Director
Director Union or Guild
Equipment – Set (e.g., cell phones, walkie-talkies, pagers)
Equipment – Office (e.g., photocopier, fax machine)
Fax Top Sheets
Funding Agency
Immigration
Internet (email accounts, Web page)
Insurance
Insurance – Accidents
Lead Performer
* Locations & Agreements
* Memos
Music & Cue Sheets

Paperwork Distribution
Parent Production Company
Postproduction
Postproduction – ADR
Postproduction – Schedule
Production Reports (one complete set without Production Report backup)
Publicity
Publicity – News Clippings
Resumes – Crew
Resumes – P.A.s
Resumes – Other
Second Unit
* Script – White Draft
* Script – Pink Draft (etc.)
* Script – As-Produced
* Schedule – Preproduction
* Schedule – One-Line
* Schedule – Shooting
Special Effects Company
Stock Footage
* Storyboard
Studio
Synopsis
Technical Specifications
Travel
Vehicles
Visual Effects Company (CGI)
Wardrobe Department
Wrap Party
Wrap – Inventory

THE PRODUCTION MANAGER'S FILES

The Production Manager or Coordinator may set these files up, but the Production Manager will use them. Most of the documentation in these files is more confidential than the Coordinator's production files, as they include more financial and accounting-type paperwork. You can combine both sets of files in wrap, throwing out duplicates for less storage space and more efficient information retrieval after production is completed. Here is a starter list:

Actor Union or Guild
Art Department
Audit Preparation

Auditor
Breakdowns
Broadcaster
Budget – Early Drafts
Budget – Locked and Signed by Producer
Call Sheets
Cash Flow
Cast
Cast – Leads or Stars
Casting
Chain of Title & Writer's Agreements
Clearances – Script Research Report
Clearances – Title Search
Completion Guarantor (or Completion Bond)
Conference Calls
Correspondence
Cost Reports
Cost Split (between companies or countries)
Credits
Crew
Crew – Key Creatives
Crew Union or Guild
Currency Exchange
Director
Director Union Guild
Distributor
Financing Plan
Financing Agreements
Incorporation Documentation – Production Company
Incorporation Documentation – Parent Company
Insurance – Entertainment Package
Insurance – Production Liability
Insurance – E&O (Errors & Omissions)
Interim Financing
Interparty Agreement
Legal
Legal – Corporate Opinion
Marketing
Memos
Parent Production Company or Head Office
Personal
Production Reports
Postproduction
Postproduction – Schedule

Recoupment
Schedule (per episode)
Script (per episode)
Studio
Synopsis
Treaty
Writer Guild

Now you have cabinets of file folders waiting for the paper to fill them. It will not take long for you to do just that. You may find it useful to print a list of these file names at your desk to remind you what your options are. Revise these starter lists as you develop your style of filing. As you do, remember to keep in mind the question: "Where would I look for this information if I were looking for it?" Also ask yourself: "In a year from now, where would someone look for this information if I were not around?" When you can answer that question, you will file the information in the right place.

Balcony Paperwork

For one low-budget show, the entire crew and cast were housed in three cottages by a lake. Breakfasts, meetings, dinners, and social time were usually held in the big cottage's living room. I had the room with a balcony that overlooked this room. On that balcony, I set up my "office." While I was completing the production paperwork, I could also participate in the meetings and the social activities.

I was known for keeping up with all the paperwork in spite of the surrounding diversions, and the crew got used to looking up at the balcony if they wanted to find me. Time slipped away on that picturesque balcony. I never knew how much until the day that the crew bombarded me with paper airplanes made from old call sheets.

I got the hint and came down for dinner.

CHAPTER 11

FORMS, MEMOS, LOGS, CHECKLISTS

You are in a forest — not of trees, but of paper. Reports, sign-outs, requisitions, logs, and checklists flow back and forth across the production-office desks creating the paper trail of production. There is a form for every purpose and new forms are being made constantly to keep up with the speed and the complexity of production. Where do you begin finding or designing all these forms? And where do you begin to decide which forms and paperwork go on the distribution table?

The answers are right here. Checklists are provided so you can mark your progress. Samples and blanks of many of the following forms are in the Appendix, which begins on page 385. They can also be downloaded from the Web at www.mwp.com/pages/booksfilmprod101.html

FORMS & MEMOS TO ALL CONCERNED

There are a host of different forms to create. I have divided them into the following categories to make it easier to tackle: Letterhead & Office Forms, Accounting-Related Forms, Schedule & On Set-Related Forms, Memos to All Concerned, Sign-Out Forms, Log Forms, Weekly Office Checklists, and the Inventory List.

LETTERHEAD & OFFICE FORMS CHECKLIST
The Production Coordinator arranges for or creates each of the following forms, then should store the original of each in an "Original Forms" file; that way each form remains as pristine as possible, photocopy after photocopy.

- ❑ Letterhead
- ❑ Letterhead Envelopes
- ❑ Address Rubber Stamp
- ❑ Business Cards
- ❑ Big Letterhead Labels
- ❑ Memorandum Form
- ❑ Fax Top Sheet

LETTERHEAD
First up, make letterhead for the company. If the Art Department is too busy to aid you, design it yourself. Include: film title, company name, address, telephone, fax, and any

other appropriate numbers. Even if the Art Department does the design, review the design and the information with the Production Manager and the Producer before printing. The design may be made with the production company's Web site in mind, or be adaptable to creating a simple Web site. Find out if the budget allows printed, colorful letterhead, or if you need to design letterhead that uses the computer fonts and prints directly from file each time.

LETTERHEAD ENVELOPES
If production has the money, make letterhead envelopes at the same time as letterhead. Check if Accounting needs window envelopes.

ADDRESS RUBBER STAMP
Make a rubber stamp with the company name and address. It is a functional, affordable, multi-purpose labeling device that can be used to label purchase orders, or even to create very cheap letterhead envelopes. Consider the amount of mail you will be sending out and get a self-inking stamp.

BUSINESS CARDS
Some productions arrange for business cards, and some prefer not to. Locations, Sets, and Art Departments use them constantly. Considering how quickly productions set up, shoot, and wrap up, business cards validate the professionalism of the company. Make blank cards (i.e., those not identifying any employee by name) to give you the option of typing any crew name on them. This tactic will avoid your having hundreds of useless named cards left over midway through the show, while you run out of other named cards.

BIG LETTERHEAD LABELS
These labels are about 3" x 5". They have the letterhead information printed on them, and are great for addressing script packages, other courier packages, and for labeling videocassettes (unless you plan to make custom videocassette labels, too).

MEMORANDUM FORM
Once you have letterhead, use part of it by removing the address and the contact numbers to make a memorandum form. Include in the heading:

> Memorandum
> Date
> To
> Cc (carbon copy to)
> From
> Subject

FAX OR FACSIMILE TOP SHEET
Take another piece of letterhead to make a fax top sheet. Leave the address and the contact numbers on the form. Be sure you leave spaces large enough for people who write big. Include in the heading:

Fax Cover Sheet
Date
To
Company
Fax Number
From
Number of Pages (including cover sheet)
Subject
Notes
Confidentiality Note (optional)

If you are working on a series and know the air date, include this information on the fax cover sheet too, as a way of informing every single person you fax when to catch your show on television.

ACCOUNTING-RELATED FORMS

Often Production Accountants come with their own forms. If not, they and head office will have definite preferences about the design of forms that relate to them. The Production Coordinator needs to talk to them before designing the following forms:

- ❑ Crew Deal Memo – Union
- ❑ Crew Deal Memo – Non-Union (sample on p.433)
- ❑ Time Sheet (sample on p.397)
- ❑ Check Requisition (sample on p.425)
- ❑ Petty Cash Report (sample on p.421)
- ❑ Sales Tax Form
- ❑ Accounting Procedures Memo

CREW DEAL MEMO – UNION
These forms are available from each union directly and become part of the start pack. (More on start packs is in Chapter 23.)

CREW DEAL MEMO – NON-UNION
Accounting, the Payroll Company, or Legal Counsel has a form or specific requirements for this form. Be sure you leave enough space for the crew member and the production company to sign and date. There will be different forms designed for "employee" crew and "corporate" crew. (More about employee versus corporations is in Chapter 23.)

TIME SHEET
Flat weekly rates make for easier time sheet forms than hourly rates and their many calculations. Design a form that works for both. Always have plenty of these forms on hand. Payroll companies often have their own forms and will supply them to you.

CHECK REQUISITION
This is another form that Accountants use all the time. They will have very specific preferences about design — because they will be coding the costs to the cost report based on the information presented. Make sure there is space for the appropriate approvals necessary for the check and contact information of the company, in case this form becomes the only backup paperwork Accounting will ever receive for this purchase.

PETTY CASH REPORT
It is best to design this form and have it printed onto 8½" x 11" envelopes. When crew submit their expenses, the envelope serves to collect all the receipts applicable to the report on the front of the envelope. Be sure there is a column for splitting out any refundable tax that is paid, and columns for Accounting to code the receipts to cost report/budget accounts. If you cannot afford envelopes, just photocopies of the form will do fine. (More on Petty Cash is in Chapter 19.)

SALES TAX FORM
If production's purchases can be exempt from sales tax, get the appropriate form from the tax office, and have the Accountant or the Production Manager assist you in completing it. Sometimes you will be able to apply for a tax number to use for the exemption, and other times you need to have a "blanket" tax form that crew must attach to each purchase to effect the exemption. In either case, you will need plenty of copies of the number or the form for the crew's usage when purchasing.

ACCOUNTING PROCEDURES MEMO
Some Accountants will spell out in a memo to all crew exactly how to fill in a purchase order, how to complete a check requisition, and so on. If your Accountant does not do this, find out the procedures anyway and write it down for yourself, the Coordinator. Each Accountant has a different style, and you will be explaining that style to crew, including the office staff and dailies, over and over again throughout production. (More about money issues is in Chapter 19.)

SCHEDULE & ON SET-RELATED FORMS
Though the use of these forms overlaps many departments, the following forms are to be designed or acquired with the help of the Production Manager, the Assistant Directors, and the Accountants. The Production Coordinator usually designs them with the Production Manager's input. Think about what information you might want to refer to later when looking back at and analyzing production.

- ❑ Call Sheet Form (samples on p.412-415)
- ❑ Daily Production Report Form (the DPR) (samples on p.416-418)
- ❑ One-Line Schedule Form (sample on p.445)
- ❑ Shooting Schedule Form (sample on p.446)
- ❑ Actor's Union Forms
- ❑ Accident Report Forms (sample on p.398)

CALL SHEET FORM

Simply put, the call sheet tells the crew what is being filmed on the day, where set is, when everyone is to report there, and what the forecasted weather is. There is no one single format for making a call sheet. Collect versions from past productions, get input from the Assistant Directors, then the PC can design a form. The First or Second Assistant Director will probably have the most input in the design of this form. Second Unit call sheets are separate from Main Unit call sheets. It is best to print them on different-colored paper to differentiate them from each other at a glance. All call sheets tend to be printed (double-sided) on legal-sized paper to be obvious from all the other production paperwork on the day. All call sheets are required to have a map-to-location attached (describing, in both pictures and words, how to get to location from the production office). Also included on the map should be directions and contact information for the nearest hospital. (More on call sheets and location maps is in Chapter 13.)

DAILY PRODUCTION REPORT FORM

At the end of every shooting day, the Production Manager and the Assistant Director must report to the Executives and to Accounting what transpired that day (so the Accountant can give an estimate of how much the day cost to the Executives and the Production Manager). Executives are rarely on set and must keep abreast of the running of production: Is it on schedule? What scenes were shot? What is the updated timing of the entire script? What events happened that caused delays? Accounting needs to know what was spent daily to keep atop costs as they happen: How much film and sound stock was used? What hours did the cast and crew work? What daily crew was working? The A.D.s and Production Coordinator are in charge of completing the form daily with input from all departments, then the First A.D. and the Production Manager give their approval to the document (by signing it) before it is distributed. It is expected the completed report is approved and distributed by the end of the next day's shoot. The Production Coordinator should design this form with the Production Manager and the Assistant Director. Just as Second Unit requires a separate call sheet, the PM and the A.D. also require a separate production report. It is wise to print Second Unit production reports on a different-colored paper to differentiate them from Main Unit's reports. Treat completed production reports as confidential information. They are. (More on production reports is in Chapter 14.)

ONE-LINE SCHEDULE FORM

Assistant Directors often have their own computers equipped with scheduling programs, and they often make one-line schedule forms themselves. If this is not the case, design a one-line schedule to show the schedule of scenes to be shot during the entire production, with, naturally, one line of text per scene. Include: scene number and description (including interior/exterior and day/night), cast (by number code), script day, and script page count. This form is the shortest way of expressing the entire schedule to the crew. The A.D.s will give you their scene breakdown pages, shuffled into shooting order, to create this schedule. (More about schedules is in Chapter 28.)

SHOOTING SCHEDULE FORM

This is also a form that Assistant Directors tend to generate themselves. If not, design a shooting schedule as an expanded version of the one-line schedule. Also include the character names and the various set requirements of each department, as indicated on each scene breakdown page. Due to the detail of this schedule, when completed it may be as thick as the script.

ACTOR'S UNION FORMS

Contact the actor's union, find out who your representative is, and get the following forms for the Assistant Directors to use on set — and for you, the PC, to use in post-production:

- <u>Performer Work Reports</u>: These are for the A.D.s to report which hours the Performers worked each day, and you (production) to report which hours the Performers worked for postproduction looping.

- <u>Performer Contracts</u>: There are likely several versions of Performer contracts to address various genres, so get the correct one for your production.

- <u>Extra Vouchers</u>: These are like contracts for Extras and often too for Stand-Ins; make sure you get enough copies for production.

- <u>Permit Forms</u>: You may need permit forms for non-union Actors.

- <u>Union Agreement</u>: This is the agreement that the Production Manager signs to make the production company signatory to the union. It is filled with details and requirements you must know when hiring Actors. Get several copies of this agreement for your reference, as they are invaluable to the PM when budgeting and cost-tracking, the PC when typing contracts, the A.D.s when working with the Performers on set, and the Accountant when calculating meal penalties.

MEMOS TO ALL CONCERNED

Most paperwork the Production Coordinator generates is approved by the Production Manager and is, in essence, from the Production Manager. You two are a team. But, here are two things the Coordinator may generate alone:

- ❑ Color Revision Order Memo
- ❑ Episode List & Synopses

COLOR REVISION ORDER MEMO

As the script is revised, you will copy the new pages on another color paper for clarity and speed of recognition. Make a memo to "All Concerned" what the colored-paper order is of the script revisions. Know that some head offices have preferences. Here is a suggested order:

White
Blue
Pink
Green
Yellow
Any other pastel-colored paper of your choice, until...
White again
(etc.)

Remember that non-pastel-colored paper does not photocopy well, and you need the ability to re-photocopy pages over and over again (i.e., do not use cherry-colored paper).

EPISODE LIST & SYNOPSES
When you work on a series, after several episodes, it is difficult for anyone, Writers included, to remember all the episode numbers, episode titles, and stories. Make a list of the episodes, noting episode number, title, former titles, and a one- or two-line synopsis for each. You will be surprised how useful the entire crew and head office finds this list. And Publicity. If it goes to Publicity, be sure the Producer is okay with the wordings, as the content may be published somewhere.

SIGN-OUT FORMS
Track all equipment rented or even exchanged when broken. Many people during the course of production will handle a lot of equipment, and it is very easy to misplace an expensive piece or two if you do not know who had the equipment last. Production is responsible to return all that is rented. The Production Coordinator needs tools to help track the use of these items by whom. Sign-out sheets work wonderfully. Completed, the Production Manager and the Accountant will also find them useful reference tools.

- ❏ Walkie-Talkie Sign-Out Form (sample on p.399)
- ❏ Pager List
- ❏ Scripts (By Label)

WALKIE-TALKIE SIGN-OUT FORM
Walkie-talkies are essential on set, very expensive, and very portable. Track serial numbers and each accessory alongside each crew name. The Assistant Directors are primarily responsible for these forms on set, but a double-check tracking system in the office is also wise. When you rent a large number of walkie-talkies, you should expect a large number of parts constantly being exchanged for repair. Know where all the pieces are at all times.

PAGER LIST
Pagers are not quite as expensive as walkie-talkies, and do not break down as quickly, but you should track them nonetheless. Make a memo to "All Concerned" noting crew

names, pager numbers, and serial numbers. This single sheet is handy reference during production for identifying a found but unlabeled pager, and for collecting the equipment during wrap.

KEYS SIGN-OUT FORM

Either use a crew list to list the keys each person gets beside their names, or make a simple log form for people to sign out copies of keys. Using a crew list, you have to transpose all the information each time the crew list gets updated, but it is an easy reference by department of who has access to the office. The act of using a sign-out form hopefully makes crew realize that there are a select number of keys, and therefore they will try not to lose them. Either way, label each key copy with indelible ink for future identification, then cover the inked label with clear tape to prevent the ink from being rubbed off. There should also be one master set of every key kept safely away in a locked space. The Production Coordinator should have the key to that locked space.

SCRIPTS (BY LABEL)

Though scripts do not fall under the heading of "equipment" when it comes to signing equipment out, signing out scripts is a terrific way of cutting down on over-photocopying the long document, and thereby saving a few trees. Put each crew member's name on file folder labels for marking each script: one sticker, one script. When crew sees that the scripts are specifically named, they will realize that the copies are limited in number, and will likely take better care of the one given to them. It is heartbreaking to see piles of discarded scripts tossed in the garbage. Discuss the names for this scripts-by-label list with the Assistant Directors.

LOG FORMS

Using log forms is another tool for the Production Coordinator. Keeping logs inspires people to put a higher value on the item(s) being tracked. Since all items indeed do cost money and do add up rapidly if left unchecked, the use of log forms will keep costs down. Also, logs report on where money is currently being spent, and this process enables Accounting to keep updated with the "spending status" of production.

- ❑ P.O. Log (sample on p.424)
- ❑ Equipment Rental Log (sample on p.401)
- ❑ Long Distance Log (sample on p.403)
- ❑ Photocopy Log
- ❑ Polaroid Film Sign-Out Form (sample on p.404)

P.O. LOG

If you keep no other log, keep a log of every purchase order you handle! A purchase order is a promise to pay for the item ordered. Blank purchase orders are like blank checks. With enough detail, your P.O. log can assist your listing everything that has been rented when it comes time to do the returns during wrap. (More on Purchase Orders is in Chapter 19.) Include the following columns:

> Purchase Order Number
> To Whom
> For What
> Episode Number
> Department
> Date
> Price

EQUIPMENT RENTAL LOG

If you keep a detailed P.O. log, you will not need this log. If not, note the following each time production rents an item, whether on a daily basis or for the length of production:

> Date
> Rental Company
> Equipment
> Department Ordered By
> Episode Number
> Rental Start/End Dates
> Price

COURIER LOG

If you have an efficient Office Production Assistant, you will not need a courier around town very often, but when you do, track couriered packages. Fill out detailed waybills or keep a separate log including the information below. The person in charge of shipping and receiving should be in charge of this log. You may need proof that an item was sent to someone. You may have to report who received a certain piece of paper on which date and when. There is no sense in trying to tax your memory for this information when you have incomplete waybills or the absence of a courier log. You may not refer to this log often, but when you do, the work you put into it will be invaluable.

> Date
> To Whom
> What Sent
> Courier Company
> Waybill Number

LONG DISTANCE LOG

Though it is nearly impossible to track all long distance charges, make a miniature log form to attach to each telephone set. Encourage the crew to complete it, especially when making personal calls. Long distance on all sets in the office can get out of hand. You may find you will need to restrict long distance on certain sets to keep the situation under control. This log is particularly handy when you are working on two different productions simultaneously; it also helps the Accountant code the long distance incurred to the appropriate productions.

        Date/Time
        Phone Number
        Your Name
        Personal/Business

PHOTOCOPY LOG

If you have several companies using the same photocopy machine, have a log by the photocopy machine (with pen attached) to fill out each time the machine is used. If you have a code system built-in to the photocopier's hardware, you may not need this log.

        Date
        Company or Film Title
        Department
        Number of Copies

POLAROID FILM SIGN-OUT FORM

Have a log, with pen attached, by the Polaroid film stock to track who is using which film stock and how often. Reviewing this log will be invaluable for you to anticipate how much more film is needed to complete the last few weeks or days of production.

        Date
        600/Spectra Taken
        Department

WEEKLY OFFICE CHECKLISTS

As the variety of supplies gets used, few people will tell you it is time to order more until the shelf is absolutely empty. Check supplies on a weekly basis. Give the Office Production Assistant the opportunity to show you if she can be responsible by taking charge of the weekly checks, keeping track of that information, and reporting the results to you, the Coordinator, regularly. These checklists will also help you both learn how much of these items are being consumed — information you will use on future orders or your next production.

        ❑ Craft Service Supplies
        ❑ Coffee Supplies
        ❑ Water Supplies
        ❑ Photocopy Supplies
        ❑ Copier Paper Count Form (sample on p.405)
        ❑ Fax Supplies
        ❑ Office Stationery Supplies

❑ Polaroid Film Supplies
❑ Cleaning/Paper Supplies

CRAFT SERVICE SUPPLIES

If Craft Service is ordering coffee and water through the office supplier, talk to set weekly about Craft Service's supply needs.

COFFEE SUPPLIES

Check supplies a day before the coffee company is scheduled to call you for an order.

WATER SUPPLIES

Like the coffee supplies, check before the company calls you for an order or before the company's automatic delivery. Water companies tend to put all companies on an automatic delivery. Beware if you make a one-time order of 27 bottles; the water company may automatically send you 27 bottles every two weeks until you tell them otherwise.

PHOTOCOPY SUPPLIES

Keeping in mind which colored revision is due next, check the amount of colored paper and toner you have. There is little worse than running out of toner on a Friday night of a weekend shoot.

COPIER PAPER COUNT FORM

When checking the paper supplies, jot down the number of copies used to-date on the machine. You will need this number for your photocopy service agreement, for Accounting, and if you have several companies using the same machine. It is also enlightening to discover how many thousands of copies you actually do on a weekly basis. Have an office lottery, if you like.

FAX SUPPLIES

Check fax paper supplies and toner.

OFFICE STATIONERY SUPPLIES

Have an order form hanging by the office supply cabinet with a pen attached to it. Check the general supplies, such as pens, on a regular basis also.

POLAROID FILM SUPPLIES

Even though you have a log form to sign out Polaroid film, crew may not tell you that they just took the last box of film. Check weekly.

CLEANING/PAPER SUPPLIES

Does the office have enough paper towels, cleaners, bathroom tissue, and first-aid supplies?

THE INVENTORY LIST
The Production Coordinator should start making an inventory list as production acquires items during preproduction. You will find out this information quickly from the P.O. log. The chance of your remembering everything that was rented or purchased throughout the entire film after the fact is slim... or, rather, impossible. The Coordinator already has a file in the cabinet labeled "Wrap," so both Manager and Coordinator can use this file to collect notes to trigger you both later to address certain things. The work you do now leaving notes for future reference will save you hours of searching after the film is done and any crew that could help you has gone home. If your P.O. log is very detailed, it can double as your inventory list. Make and use the P.O. log! Did I say that already?

THE DISTRIBUTION TABLE & OTHER PLACES TO PUT PAPER

Basically, where do you put all this paper so it is used efficiently? You have a distribution table, wall envelopes, and your desk drawer. Here is a recap of the forms mentioned in this and other chapters, and where to put them for appropriate access.

WHAT'S ON THE DISTRIBUTION TABLE
    Script & Script Revisions
    Crew List
    Cast List
    Pager List
    Contact List
    Telephone Extension List
    Episode List & Synopses
    Schedules (all kinds)
    A.D. Breakdowns
    Accounting Procedures Memo
    Crew Deal Memo Start Packs
    Color Revision Order Memo

WHAT'S IN THE "FORMS" WALL ENVELOPES
    Letterhead
    Fax Top Sheets
    Memorandum Forms
    Check Requisitions
    Exemption From Sales Tax Forms/Proof
    Time Sheets
    Petty Cash Reports

WHAT'S IN PC'S DESK DRAWER
    Everything Else (logs, checklists, accident reports...)

If not before, you probably now have the sense that the Production Coordinator's desk is quite a hub of paper activity. It is. The Coordinator has lists to jog the memory about what is going to happen, forms to take care of all that is, and logs to keep track of all that was. Store these forms for future use. Assemble more from every production you know. Create your own collection and preferences. You are ready to anticipate, analyze, and organize. You are ready to record it all on paper. And you can sleep at night too, because you are not trying to keep it all in your head. Being part of a team with the Production Manager, the information can be shared. You are ready to move forward.

Hot Copies

Yes, a photocopier does have a mind of its own. It is only trying to be an artist when it jams and folds fifty sheets of paper into tiny little accordions in the duplexer. It wants to be fed when it runs out of paper or toner. And its favorite pastime will always be complaining about the weather by feeding multiple sheets of paper through at the same time. By understanding the mind of the photocopier, you are on your way to a mutually beneficial relationship.

The Production Manager decided that no production office needs air conditioning in the summer. Summer is too short. Even heat waves last only a few days. He simply had to put up with the office staff's complaining and all would be well sooner than later.

Heat wave day #1: The office temperature started in the morning at 115 degrees Fahrenheit. The air was thick with humidity. Even a sauna would have been more refreshing. People moved slowly and the photocopier decided enough was enough and stopped working. It refused to feed any less than five humid stuck-together sheets of paper at any one time. No production information could be copied to anyone on the crew. No scripts. No schedules. No deal memos. We went home early.

Heat wave day #2: 113 degrees. We bought and rented fans to cool off the copier. It appreciated our attention and copied about three sheets of paper before shutting down. Tempers quickened. Work pace slowed. No information got to the crew this day either.

Heat wave day #3: 115 degrees. A balmy 110 outside. We tried to trade in the photocopier for a more hardy machine, but no copier would submit itself to this working environment. Added more fans. Kept holding on to tempers. How long can humans or machines put up with this heat? Five copies today. Not even a dent in a full script.

Heat wave day #4: PM arranges for air conditioning. Copier is happy and starts to work again. Coordinator decides that a photocopier has the power to save human lives.

CHAPTER 12

COUNTDOWN TO PRODUCTION

You have an office. You have a crew. You are in preproduction. Go. This chapter will help you to do just that. Far in preproduction, the pace of work seems easy throughout the crew, but as the date of first day of principal photography nears, stress heightens and nerves tighten. There is nothing like a deadline to change the feel of the workplace. Rather like preparing for a wedding, these checklists will count you down to the first day of shooting as a team, flagging what you need to work on each week.

THREE WEEKS OR MORE BEFORE PRODUCTION

The Production Manager is busy closing out development and assembling the framework for production, while the Production Coordinator is busy dressing the distribution table as soon as possible with informative paperwork (approved by the PM for distribution). Go through this list every day to check if you can revise, update, or do something on it.

THREE WEEKS OR MORE BEFORE PRODUCTION – PM CHECKLIST
- ❑ Locked Budget Matches Cost Report Accounts
- ❑ Development Cost Report (sample on p.406)
- ❑ Start the PM-Only Cost Report (sample on p.430)
- ❑ Accounting Procedures
- ❑ Payroll Services
- ❑ Cash Flow & Interim Financing
- ❑ Union Negotiations
- ❑ Crewing Keys & Rest of Crew
- ❑ Casting – Stars & Support Cast
- ❑ Studio
- ❑ Locations Scouting & Surveying
- ❑ Completion Bond

THREE WEEKS OR MORE BEFORE PRODUCTION – PM & PC CHECKLIST
- ❑ Crew List (sample on p.407,408)
- ❑ Cast List (sample on p.409)
- ❑ Catering Choice
- ❑ Script-Research Report
- ❑ Shooting Schedule (sample on p.446)
- ❑ Production Schedule (samples on p.416-418)
- ❑ Preproduction (Prep) Schedule
- ❑ Insurance

- ❏ Customs
- ❏ Equipment Orders
- ❏ Film Stock
- ❏ Audio Tape Stock
- ❏ Other Suppliers (Animals, Stunts, CGI, SPFX...)
- ❏ Post House

THREE OR MORE WEEKS BEFORE PRODUCTION – PC CHECKLIST
- ❏ Set Up Office & Files
- ❏ Contact List (sample on p.410,411)
- ❏ Crew Deal Memos (Start Packs) (sample on p.437)
- ❏ Script Revisions (samples on p.437-441)
- ❏ Director Medical
- ❏ A.D. Breakdowns (samples on p.443,444)
- ❏ Continuity Breakdowns
- ❏ Cast Contracts
- ❏ Nurse/Ambulance Attendants
- ❏ Cast Packages
- ❏ Travel for Crew/Cast
- ❏ Immigration
- ❏ Cast Medicals
- ❏ Polaroid Film Stock

THREE OR MORE WEEKS BEFORE PRODUCTION – PM DETAIL
LOCKED BUDGET MATCHES COST REPORT ACCOUNTS

Ensure the budget is locked and check with the Producer to be certain all the Financiers have the same budget. Prior to locking it, ensure all the fringes are coded in one line item in the budget for easy reporting in accounting. Discuss with the Accountant any other reallocations that will make cost reporting easier prior to locking the budget. Now is the time; the two of you are going to be working with that budget a lot from now on. Double-check, too, that the Production Accountant is using the account codes from the locked budget. A cost report with totally different code numbers from the budget defeats the purpose of writing a budget in the first place. No revised budgets may happen any more. From now on, you take savings and show overages on the various budget lines on the cost report. The budget is locked. Time will show how well the budget was made... by you or whoever wrote it.

DEVELOPMENT COST REPORT

It is time also to find out where you are, cost-wise. What has been spent so far? The next cost report you do after the development cost report will probably be the end of preproduction cost report, so you need to know what has been spent up until now — especially since you have to pay back all the development loans acquired on the first day of principal photography. Better know now in which line items the money was spent.

Closing out the development costs may also trigger the last development money inflows from Financiers. You can use this money now, so report it soon. Even though development money is only a loan until the first day of principal photography, at least it is money in your bank providing cash flow to you through preproduction. You will need it. (See sample on page 406.)

START THE PM-ONLY COST REPORT

Yes, the Production Accountant is monitoring and accounting all the costs. Accountants are accurate and detail-oriented, reporting on purchase orders, check requisitions, and actual money inflows and outflows. You, however, may need to monitor costs before they happen — when the costs are still words and ideas exchanged between people and are only estimates of the future. You need a "work-in-progress" or PM-only cost report to track down all the promises as you spend them and before the Accountant reports them. The DP has agreed to come on for a flat rate that is lower than the budget amount; note it in your PM-only cost report and note the savings you can take for this. The Production Designer is worried that a certain set may cost an extra $5,000 because of the initial supplier quotes for materials. You note the suspected overage in your PM-only cost report. You may mention the DP savings on the official cost report the Accountant creates, but you may not report the suspected overage on the official cost report yet — because the overage is not yet confirmed, and the Production Designer is working on other suppliers or finding other ways to build the set and avoid or minimize the overage. Two weeks later the Production Designer finds a different supplier, and the overage will only be $150. You approve the purchase order, and change the overage in the PM-only cost report to a $150 overage. The Accountant notes it in the official cost report because now the cost is official — the amount is on a signed purchase order, and you have not worried anyone about a suspected overage that never happened anyway. (More on PM-only cost reports is in Chapter 22.)

ACCOUNTING PROCEDURES

Identify with the Production Accountant what the accounting procedures are. Which Producers and Executives are you reporting to? How often will you be publishing official cost reports? Ensure the purchase-order system is explained to the crew in a memo, and ensure that you use the system. What else might you add in a memo to the crew regarding accounting procedures — rules about per diems, about receipts, about petty cash reporting? What day and by what time each week must payroll be paid? Review the inflow schedule from the Financiers' agreements, and review the requirements that trigger each inflow. Is interim financing involved? Are you working on a co-production that requires two audits? Set up the accounting system now to prepare for it.

PAYROLL SERVICE

If the Accountant is more closely related to payroll service than you, she may set up the deal for you. If not, contact a few payroll companies to discuss your production. Basically, production pays these companies a percentage of the payroll, and they write the payroll checks (doing all the fringe and union calculations) and generate proper tax forms in wrap, loaning you the accounting software to create cost reports. When you consider fringes, union dues, retirement payments, cast buyouts, overtime, meal penalty calculations, and so on, a payroll company is worth every penny — especially with frequency of weekly payroll.

CASH FLOW & INTERIM FINANCING

Start the cash flow soon. If the Accountant is too busy to start it, you do it. You need to know when interim financing is needed, which will probably be sooner than later. When is the money flowing in, and when is it flowing out? Arrange interim financing as needed with the Producer. (More on cash flows and interim financing is in Chapters 20 and 21.)

UNION NEGOTIATIONS

Are you shooting union or non-union? It has already been decided in the budget, and issues regarding the union have been covered previously (Chapter 6). Call up the unions now and negotiate any concessions you need with them right away. You are already assembling the key creative crew. By next week you will want the union's help in finding support crew.

CREWING KEYS & REST OF CREW

Look over the empty crew list and discuss crewing with the Producer and the Director. Do you have a DP and a Production Designer on board already? Do these people have teams? Start finding the rest of the heads of departments and lock up a great crew. How solidly you can offer a job to someone may be contingent on the financing closing, so keep in close conversation with the Producer so you can turn availability checks into job offers. Note all deals made on the PM-only cost report.

CASTING – STARS & SUPPORT CAST

Again, how solid is the financing to allow the cast to be confirmed, instead of your checking their availability and interest only? Find out what bonuses the cast may be asking for, like private dressing rooms, motor homes, drivers to and from set, and so on. Can the budget cover it? Do you have the crew to cover these extras? Note all deals on the PM-only cost report.

STUDIO

Get a studio. Be sure it is large enough for the sets that the Production Designer is designing. Is there construction space on site or do you need to rent another space nearby and have the crew travel the partially-built sets from the shop to the studio? What is included in the studio cost and what is extra? How much insurance do you need?

LOCATIONS SCOUTING & SURVEYING

Attend location scouts and surveys. Learn what is being promised during the discussions that occur while walking around the potential sites. Script changes happen. New items to build happen. All sorts of ideas that cost money happen. Discuss the potential changes with the Producer, along with their cost ramifications.

COMPLETION BOND

Are you purchasing a completion bond? Start getting the paperwork prepared now: lab access letters, locked budget, schedule, director letters, and so on. The Producer will likely do most of this work, but the Bonder will want updates on the running of production from you. They will need daily production reports and cost reports at the very least. (More on completion bonds is in Chapter 18.)

THREE OR MORE WEEKS BEFORE PRODUCTION – PM & PC DETAIL

CREW LIST

Get a crew list onto the distribution table as soon as possible. On page one list the addresses of all the production companies involved, then start the crew list itself with all the Producers in order of importance. The Production Manager needs to approve the crew list being published. You only want to publish names of confirmed crew on the list. Do not publish names of people with whom you are still negotiating.

CAST LIST

This list includes the character names; Performer names, home addresses, and telephone numbers; respective agent names, addresses, telephone and fax numbers. Do not identify any Performer on the cast list who has not been approved, or until you have a deal memo in your hand to prove he is on the film. Some Performers prefer not to list their home addresses and telephone numbers. Often they will let you and the A.D.s have the information for emergency use only. Honor their wish for confidentiality.

CATERING CHOICE

The Production Manager can choose the caterer from a list of choices the Coordinator generates from experience or film reference books.

SCRIPT-RESEARCH REPORT

If it is in the budget, send off the script to a script research company as soon as the Producer says the draft is ready for clearing. Keep the research company informed of all script changes after that draft. In order to get speedy results, it is wise to telephone first to warn them about impending changes. Art Departments wait with bated breath for these reports, so they can make signs with "clear" names for set. (More on clearances is in Chapter 32.)

SHOOTING SCHEDULE

With more and more A.D.s using computers, the Coordinator rarely has to type up a shooting schedule, just copy it. The only downside to this situation: You must keep making sure that the present schedule you have is the current one. If the A.D.s do not have a computer, type up this form from their breakdown notes. Get the information onto the distribution table as soon as possible. (More on schedules is in Chapter 28.)

PRODUCTION SCHEDULE
Simpler than a shooting schedule, this schedule lists the production's plan on a weekly basis. Identify which weeks are prep weeks, which are shoot weeks, which are wrap weeks, and which weeks production is on hiatus. Put all this information onto one page. This form is very useful to all sorts of departments in production and in head office.

PREPRODUCTION (PREP) SCHEDULE
The A.D.s will have a list daily of what is going to happen tomorrow and for the rest of the week. The Prep Schedule is another item for typing, copying, distributing around the office, and putting on the distribution table very quickly. Confirm with the A.D.s if anyone affected by the schedule needs to be called with the information. (More on Prep Schedules is in Chapter 28.)

INSURANCE
Are all the insurance certificates in to cover production and the Financiers? Most Financiers have particular wording for each of their certificates. Are the insurance certificates typed correctly and does the coverage indeed cover the cost of production or the needs of the locations you will be using? Also, keep blank accident reports in the Coordinator's filing cabinet. Get even the most reluctant crew member to fill them out for any type of accident or injury. You never know when a small accident is going to develop into a larger problem. Memory fades with time. Fill out the forms immediately. The Production Manager can decide which reports need to be forwarded to the insurance company.

CUSTOMS
Appoint a customs broker. Brokers help you with moving equipment, clothing, or basically anything across the borders of the world. They alone know what reams of paper need to be filled out each time. Be aware that clothing has to win the award for "most difficult to cross a border," so when Wardrobe starts shipping clothing in, get as much lead time as you can for customs clearances. (More on Customs Clearances & Brokers is in Chapter 31.)

EQUIPMENT ORDERS
The Production Manager will deal with the basic equipment packages; if the Coordinator is tracking the purchase orders, the Coordinator can be responsible for the specialty equipment orders, like cranes, man lifts, and jib arms. The Production Manager should approve all special requests (so they can also be noted on the PM-only cost report).

FILM STOCK
When you know what the Camera Department needs, the Coordinator can order the film with a purchase order. Know that the Camera Department will be doing camera and film tests before first day of shooting.

AUDIO TAPE STOCK

Get this for the Sound Department when you know what stock and how much. Some Sound Mixers supply this stock themselves.

OTHER SUPPLIERS (ANIMALS, STUNTS, CGI, SPFX...)

If you need any of these specialty suppliers, it is time to look for them now. Identify what exactly you will be requiring from these suppliers with the Producer, the Director, and whomever else you need to ask. Suppliers cannot quote effectively if you give them generalities. Be sure you get quotations from at least three sources, and do your due diligence researching them with previous Producers before committing to one. Track all your research on memo for ease of reference and comparison later.

POST HOUSE

Find a post house and negotiate the deal for postproduction facilities and services. On which formats do you need to deliver the final production: film, video, PAL, NTSC, and so on? What is the specialty and the expertise of this post house? How is their service? You will no doubt be asking them for favors later on.

THREE OR MORE WEEKS BEFORE PRODUCTION – PC DETAIL
SET UP OFFICE & FILES

Setting up the office, files, distribution table, and so on, has been covered by all the previous chapters, so I will not recap any of the detail here.

CONTACT LIST

Once you start generating accounts, you can put this list onto the distribution table, too.

CREW DEAL MEMOS (START PACKS)

Have blank union and non-union deal memo forms ready. Approve the forms with the Production Manager. The head office Legal Counsel may have blank forms that office prefers. Make sure crew members fill out the correct forms. Rather than tackle crew members several times for several different forms, make a start pack all stapled together to include all you need: crew deal memo, payroll company information page, tax forms, corporate forms, citizenship forms, permit forms, confidentiality forms. (More on start packs is in Chapter 23.) Once signed by the crew member, each deal memo can be gathered in the Production Manager's file on your desk for countersignature by the Production Manager at one of your daily meetings. Keep an extra crew list as a checklist as deal memos get completed. Chase down missing deal memos and keep in touch with Accounting in case the missing forms end up there before they come to you for countersignature.

SCRIPT REVISIONS

Trying to keep up with script revisions is like trying to hold onto a waterfall. In time, you will learn who is affected most by what change, and you will be able to inform the appropriate department before the typed revision comes out. Until then, keep in touch with the Producer about the estimated arrival of the next wave of revisions, and publish the changes as fast as possible. Hand them out to each department and place them on the distribution table.

DIRECTOR MEDICAL

Check with the Production Manager if the Director is to be covered in the insurance policy. If so, arrange for a medical with a doctor approved by the insurance company. Note that some Directors have a kind of illness called "Gosh-I-forgot-the-appointment-again."

A.D. BREAKDOWNS

A.D.s basically generate a lot of paperwork to get out to the crew. If it is in the script, they break it down. You distribute it to the crew.

CONTINUITY BREAKDOWNS

The Continuity Supervisor cannot come close to the A.D.s in the amount of paper generated in prep, but the day/night breakdown and script timings are memos you will need to distribute right away.

CAST CONTRACTS

The deal memos come from the Casting Director. Know the actor's union agreement before typing memos up. The agreement may not be the best for late-night reading, but you will find it incredibly useful before working with cast contracts. Get permits as needed. If the Actor is young enough, check with the Production Manager about arrangements for a Tutor.

NURSE/AMBULANCE ATTENDANTS

Check with the A.D.s if a Nurse or an Ambulance Attendant is required on set for any specific days. If so, arrange one. Nurses are on set for minor stunts, Ambulance Attendants for major ones.

CAST PACKAGES

As the cast gets contracted, send the Office P.A. to each one with a "Welcome Aboard" package including: script, schedule, cast list, crew list, call sheet (if available), and a personalized welcome letter. Keep track of which version of each item you sent to each Actor.

TRAVEL FOR CREW/CAST

For visiting Performers or crew, the Coordinator is a travel agent. Once a visitor is confirmed, you will need: flights, limousines (both ends), hotel, flowers in hotel room, per diem from Accounting, script package (sent by courier), and possibly an immigration permit.

IMMIGRATION
Inform the Immigration Department early! Warn them that you are going to use a Foreign Performer or crew even if you do not yet have a name. Then keep them abreast of the information as it unfolds.

CAST MEDICALS
Like the Director, most Lead Performers are insured and need medicals. If Performers live out of the city, your insurance agent can furnish you with approved doctors closer to where they live. The sooner these medicals get done, the sooner the Performers are fully insured. Be speedy.

POLAROID FILM STOCK
Wardrobe uses it on set and in fittings; Continuity uses it for each shot; Hair and Makeup Department uses it, too. Polaroid film is very expensive, so get a good supplier, buy it by the case, and hide the film in an office drawer so that the stock gets used, not abused.

TWO WEEKS BEFORE PRODUCTION

Review your list for three weeks before, plus address these issues:

TWO WEEKS BEFORE PRODUCTION – PM CHECKLIST
- ❑ Pre-Calculate Extra Day Costs, Extra O/T Costs
- ❑ Hot Costs Prep
- ❑ Daily Production Report Evaluation Prep

TWO WEEKS BEFORE PRODUCTION – PM & PC CHECKLIST
- ❑ Script-Research Report In
- ❑ Cast Medicals In
- ❑ Forms for Call Sheet & Production Report Chosen
- ❑ Rehearsal Room
- ❑ Arrange Preproduction Party

TWO WEEKS BEFORE PRODUCTION – PC CHECKLIST
- ❑ Film Stock In
- ❑ Audio Stock In
- ❑ Craft Service Order
- ❑ Continuity Forms
- ❑ Battery Stock
- ❑ Expendables Order
- ❑ Catering Deal Memo
- ❑ Stunt Contracts

TWO WEEKS BEFORE PRODUCTION – PM DETAIL
PRE-CALCULATE EXTRA DAY COSTS, EXTRA O/T (OVERTIME) COSTS

You must prepare now to answer questions on set during shooting like: "Can we afford to shoot an extra hour or two today?" or "How much will it cost if we stop shooting now and rent this location again tomorrow to finish up at straight time?" You should have hired most of the crew by now, so you can estimate these scenarios. Prepare an estimate sheet on a spreadsheet program, like Excel, so you can revise it as more confirmed crew costs come in. Pre-calculate the cost of an extra hour shooting after wrap time. How much is two hours? How much is an extra day? What if that extra day were a Saturday (or sixth day)? Run through some scenarios and estimate costs now, so that you can con-fidently — at a moment's notice — say that overtime tonight makes more financial sense than returning to this location tomorrow or not. You need to be able to advise the Producer on the day. You need to know the budget and costs inside and out.

HOT COSTS PREP

Do you need to generate "Hot Costs" for Producers and Executives on a daily basis to keep them in touch with the daily cost of production? Find out what costs need to be tracked. Usually the costs that fluctuate the most on a daily basis warrant a close eye, costs like: hours of overtime, amount of film stock and processing, and so on. These cost report estimates are fast, dirty, and therefore not always terribly helpful, plus they keep the Accounting staff busier than ever. If you manage to output official and accu-rate cost reports in a timely manner, hot costs may not be necessary.

DAILY PRODUCTION REPORT EVALUATION PREP

It is worthwhile for you to pre-calculate the daily average for things like film stock usage, to find out if production is on budget or not when you evaluate even the first daily production report (DPR). Review the DPR and decide which items you need to track for this production. What is budgeted? How much is used on day one? Prepare your budgeted daily averages as a template now.

TWO WEEKS BEFORE PRODUCTION – PM & PC DETAIL
SCRIPT-RESEARCH REPORT IN

The research report for the script should be back and distributed. Keep the research com-pany informed of any script changes, especially any changes to character or company names.

CAST MEDICALS IN

Depending on casting status, this process should be done, too.

FORMS FOR CALL SHEET & PRODUCTION REPORT CHOSEN

Choose or design a set of forms that suit both the A.D.s and the Production Manager. Once chosen, give plenty of blank forms to the A.D.s. (More on Call Sheets and DPRs is in Chapters 13 and 14.)

REHEARSAL ROOM
If there are going to be extensive rehearsals, book an appropriate room.

ARRANGE PREPRODUCTION PARTY
Is there a budget for a preproduction party for the crew? If so, commit to a date, decide on a budget for it, and let the Coordinator start planning it now.

TWO WEEKS BEFORE PRODUCTION – PC DETAIL
FILM STOCK IN
Depending on the Camera Department, the film stock should be in by now.

AUDIO STOCK IN
Some Sound Mixers arrange to pick the audio stock up themselves. Check that it has been done.

CRAFT SERVICE ORDER
If Craft Service is using any of your accounts (like coffee and water), the orders should be in with enough time for delivery before the first day of shooting.

CONTINUITY FORMS
Review the forms that the Continuity Supervisor is going to use. You may need to arrange for printing of NCR ("no carbon required") forms by the hundreds before shooting.

BATTERY STOCK
Get orders from the Camera and Sound Departments, then use your battery supplier.

EXPENDABLES ORDER
Grips, Electrics, Camera, and Sound will have orders. Expendables are everything from sticky tape to gels to black wrap to clothes pegs. Try to get all the orders in together. One call to your supplier is better than four. Approve the extensive request list with the Production Manager.

CATERING DEAL MEMO
When the Production Manager has struck a deal with a caterer, make sure a deal memo gets done.

STUNT CONTRACTS
Check with the A.D.s when Stunt Performers are being used and make the contracts. These daredevils tend not to be booked through Casting Directors, so their deal memos can be forgotten.

ONE WEEK BEFORE PRODUCTION

Review your previous lists for completion, plus address these items:

ONE WEEK BEFORE PRODUCTION – PM CHECKLIST
- ❏ Preproduction Cost Report

ONE WEEK BEFORE PRODUCTION – PM & PC CHECKLIST
- ❏ Final Production Meeting
- ❏ Final Location Survey
- ❏ Prep Production Report
- ❏ First Call Sheet
- ❏ Camera Test

ONE WEEK BEFORE PRODUCTION – PC CHECKLIST
- ❏ Who Is The Crew Representative?
- ❏ Who Is The Safety Representative?
- ❏ Crew Deal Memos Done

ONE WEEK BEFORE PRODUCTION – PM DETAIL
PREPRODUCTION COST REPORT

The end of preproduction (start of principal photography) is a trigger for financing inflows. Your final prep cost report ends at the end of this week. Are you and the Accountant prepared to generate it quickly? Meet with the Accountant, reviewing the PM-only cost report against the actual costs incurred to date. You are a team.

ONE WEEK BEFORE PRODUCTION – PM & PC DETAIL
FINAL PRODUCTION MEETING

Usually done a few days before shooting, the final production meeting often takes place on the same day as the final location survey. The Coordinator arranges for an appropriate table or room for this meeting, with plenty of chairs and coffee. Both of you should attend the meeting. The Coordinator needs to arrange for clean-up afterwards.

FINAL LOCATION SURVEY

Usually the Locations Department, Transport Department, and the A.D.s take care arranging for this procedure. The Production Manager needs to attend. The Coordinator needs to keep in touch.

PREP PRODUCTION REPORTS

Production reports in prep are for the day of the final production meeting and location survey, and for all rehearsal days. Are there any other days for which you would like production reports completed? The A.D.s can help the Coordinator complete them, but the Production Manager needs to approve and sign them before distribution.

FIRST CALL SHEET
In the ideal world, the first call sheet — complete with location map — will be generated in time to distribute at the final production meeting. Not so ideally, a scribbled, handwritten version will be given to the Coordinator a few hours after the meeting for deciphering, typing, and distributing. Work with the A.D.s to get the necessary information to all the cast and the crew.

CAMERA TEST
The Camera Department tends to arrange the camera test a few days to a week before shooting. The Coordinator should ensure the film stock is ready. After the camera test, the Camera Department should give the Coordinator a final film stock order. Make sure it arrives before shooting.

ONE WEEK BEFORE PRODUCTION – PC DETAIL
WHO IS THE CREW REPRESENTATIVE?
The Crew Representative needs to be named at the bottom of each call sheet. Get the name.

WHO IS THE SET SAFETY REPRESENTATIVE?
Someone from the set crew will volunteer or be appointed the Safety Representative, and then needs to be named at the bottom of each call sheet. Find out who it is.

CREW DEAL MEMOS DONE
Except for the crew that starts on the first day of shooting, you should have all the deal memos completed. Let people know that a time sheet is useless without a deal memo, and chase down the stragglers.

That is it. On different production teams, you will find differing expectations of a Production Manager and a Production Coordinator. No matter how much work you take on, someone will always be surprised that you take care of certain matters and do not take care of others. Leave that to style. You cannot do everything for everybody. But right now, it is the night before shooting. You have a crew, cast, script, equipment, film and sound stock, vehicles, lab, location and/or studio, and a call sheet. You can go to camera tomorrow morning. Relax.

III.

PRODUCTION

Spending money during principal photography is like standing on a street corner throwing $100 bills into the wind.

The Daily Chuckle

I'm proud of the fact that I have never published a call sheet without a joke on the back. It's an incentive. Crew make sure they get a call sheet at the end of the day when they know they are going to get their daily chuckle. Then one day the hydro building across the street from the production office blew up.

The office power went out and we were left with one emergency telephone in a darkened, silent place of work. Without a telephone system and computers, there was little to do but watch the black smoke billow out of the remains of the building across the street. Our front step afforded us a picture-perfect view. The wind was blowing the smoke away from us.

The emergency crew arrived quickly and got to work breaking windows and, I suppose, drawing straws for who was to go inside. The police soon noticed us, came over to give us ten minutes to leave the building and area. If not, they would seal us in. Several blocks already had been closed off for the crisis. Oh boy.

We could only grab what was portable and absolutely necessary. The Production Manager took the budget, the Accountant took the crew deal memos and cost report, and the Production Secretary grabbed a selection of office supplies. I looked at my computer. It was a desk-top model. Too big. I still had the call sheet to do today, so I grabbed a copy of the shooting schedule, a type-writer, and... the joke file.

Later, in a makeshift space at head office, the call sheet was completed, the evacuation was lifted, and my reputation for supplying the daily chuckle remained intact.

CHAPTER 13

THE SHOOT DAY & CALL SHEETS

Filming has begun. Most of the daily action happens on set now. There is a different routine. You have to adapt to a new daily schedule. The set runs on time that does not really exist on a clock. Times like morning and afternoon are all relative to the start of your set day and set lunchtime. 11:00 a.m. falls in your morning if the set started at 8:00 a.m., but it falls in the afternoon if set started at 2:00 a.m. Keep this in mind as you walk through the following explanation of a set day.

THE SHOOT-DAY FORMAT

The set's shoot day is basically structured into four phases that repeat over and over again: blocking, lighting, rehearsal, and shooting — all orchestrated by the Assistant Directors. Because of this structure, not everyone is active at all times and it appears there is a large number of people standing around doing nothing; in fact, some people are preparing for their jobs, and others are on standby to do their jobs. Because of the structure, too, there will be time to speak with nearly anyone on set should you need to.

BLOCKING
Everyone on set — especially the keys — watch the Director walk the Performers through the scene. This may be the first time the Performers have walked through this location, so it is an orientation for them, too. The Camera Department finalizes where the camera positions are going to be. Everyone makes note of the action and where and when it is planned to happen; for example, a Camera Assistant will put markers on the floor during blocking to mark the Performers' positions for various lines to prepare for focus points. At the end of blocking, the Director and the Performers leave the set (where they can discuss the scene, or the Performers can finish in Hair, Makeup, and Wardrobe) and the technical team can move on to the next phase.

LIGHTING
With Stand-Ins on the set instead of the cast, the technical team (Camera, Lighting, Grip) prepares for the shot. Depending on the complexity of the shot and the planned movement of the camera, this phase can take a very long time.

REHEARSAL
Once the shot has been lit, the Director and the Performers come back to set for rehearsal. The Sound team has their first opportunity to practice, too. They have to find a spot or two to record the sound where they create no shadows — always a challenge — and they can get an idea of the recording level from the Performers' run

through the lines. Everyone, Camera and Focus included, has a chance to practice before committing the shot to film. The Lighting and Grip team are on standby in case lighting needs to be tweaked for perfection.

SHOOTING

Finally the camera rolls... or rather, sound rolls then camera rolls, because sound is cheaper. The A.D.s will "lock up the set" to keep it quiet like they did for rehearsal and even more so than they did for blocking. All work on set, save the action related directly to the shot, ceases and the magic is captured. After the take, if the shot is wanting in any way, they will shoot again; if it is okay, they move back to blocking for the next shot.

EARLY MORNING

"Early morning" for the office usually starts about thirty minutes before unit call time or 9:00 a.m., whichever is earlier.

WHAT THE PM IS UP TO...

The Production Manager usually starts the day on set, but will not be the first person there, guaranteed. Unit call time is the "default" time for crew and cast to show up for set. There are usually so many pre-calls you will wonder if having a unit call time makes any sense. Makeup, Hair, and Wardrobe are busy prior to unit call, dressing and making up the Cast. Drivers are already on set, having parked the unit, some having driven Performers to set. A.D.s and Locations people are already opening up the location for use. Electrics and Grips are already pre-lighting for the day's work. Craft service beat them all to set to ensure that a steaming cup of coffee awaits the early risers. You will find you can meet anyone and everyone at craft service this early in the morning.

OVERSEE PRODUCTION

Oversee how the team works together. Oversee how fast they prepare for the first shot. The faster a first shot gets off, the higher energy the crew has for the pace and the tone of the day. The A.D.s are doing much more hands-on overseeing than you. You are here in case there is any trouble to be fixed... with money. If you have just moved in to a new location, set may discover that a certain piece of equipment does not fit as originally planned and a specialized piece of equipment has to be rented. You are there to approve it, or to encourage a different line of problem-solving. Who knows what the trouble will be? Time to test how you think on your feet. How fast can you calculate the extra money being spent? Is weather holding you up? Are you reliant on sunrise and sunset to get the shots needed this day? You may need to do nothing at all. Relax, if you can.

PROBLEM-SOLVE

Hopefully nothing goes wrong, and you can just have an enjoyable visit to set. Chat with crew as you can, without preventing them from doing their jobs. If you have hired the right people, then you have hired the right people. Let them do their jobs. In a good scenario, you can primarily watch the magic unfold. If it is falling to pieces and horrible things are happening, do not panic. It is merely time to evaluate the size of the problem. Will the problem grow bigger in time? How much will it cost to change (for example, to fire someone)? During principal photography, you are at the stage of filmmaking that costs the very most per minute. You do not have the time to be leisurely about fixing problems on set. Evaluate quickly and thoroughly. Act fast to stop a problem, but do not act before thinking through the consequences. Talk over your concerns with the Producer. If the Producer wants to refrain from action at this stage, write a confidential memo documenting your observations and recommendations. It may seem drastic to be thinking about radical changes even on the first day of shooting, but you will recognize problems sooner when you have lived through a few nightmares; if you do not fix it early enough this time, you may at least be able to fix it next time. Do not cry wolf, either. It may be thin ice you step on, but that is the responsibility of the job. You are responsible for lots of money. You are responsible to complete the project on time and on budget. Remember the phrase "good, fast, cheap… pick any two," and you will realize that any money you spend during principal photography will be expensive money.

NEG REPORT
From day two onward, find out the report on the negative from the Production Coordinator (as noted below).

DAILY PRODUCTION REPORT EVALUATION
Evaluate the DPR's information daily against the averages you expected per day for film stock, number of scenes completed, and so on. How much overtime are you shooting daily? Especially for a series, have a look at the continuity top sheet — if the DPR is regularly late — to find out the estimated running timing for the entire show. If the show is estimated to come in too long, why shoot the extra footage that will have to be cut out of the final show? Cut scenes now and spend more time on what will end up in the show. If the show is coming in too short, maybe the Writers will have to add lines or a scene to fix the problem. Discuss with the Producer. (More on DPRs is in Chapter 14.)

GO BACK TO THE OFFICE
After a while, you can head back to the office to tackle all the urgent business sitting on your desk to be completed.

WHAT THE PC IS UP TO...
Back at the ranch, uh, office, the Production Coordinator and the office staff are busy opening the production office.

PUT COFFEE ON
The first person in the office makes the first pot of coffee; like any other crew member, you will probably want a cup to start your day. Most people come to set or office before

having had breakfast at home, and need a jolt of caffeine. Put a sign on or near the machine asking people to clean up after themselves, but expect to do the job anyway. Ceramic mugs are preferred to save trees and garbage dumps, but do have some Styrofoam cups on hand for times when all the ceramic mugs are dirty and guests come to visit.

HIRE DAILY STAFF
Have a list of Production Assistants and Secretaries handy so that you can call one in when a member of your office staff calls in sick first thing in the morning. The A.D.s may also call from set to ask you to hire daily crew for other departments. For union positions, start with the union office. For non-union positions, get preferred names from the departmental heads. It is for this purpose that you should meet and interview Production Assistants and Secretaries even when you have no job to offer. You will have no time to interview crew you call in on a daily basis. Note all of these daily crew names on your copy of the call sheet or to-do list so that you can send each one the correct deal memo start pack, and you can be accurate in completing today's production report later.

CALL FOR A NEG REPORT
As mentioned before, call the lab (or have Postproduction call the lab) to get a report on the negative as soon as possible after processing. Forward the information, good or bad, to the Production Manager.

FORWARD EXTRAS LIST TO SET
Extras Casting Directors often fax a list of Extras and at what times they will be reporting to set in the morning. Send this list to set with the first run, but keep a copy for yourself in case the original gets lost or delayed.

FIRST RUN (FROM SET)
The A.D.s should send you the draft copy of the production report with all its backup paperwork, usually by a Driver. If you do not have it by now, call set to ask for it. Review the entire package while the Driver is waiting, in case there are items that must be copied and returned to set immediately.

FIRST RUN (TO SET)
You likely already have items to return to set in the To Set box. Some of those items are the draft call sheet (explained later in this chapter) and the Extras list. Have the Driver wait for you to address the immediate requests that just came in the envelope from set. Ask Accounting if there is anything from their department that needs sending to set. Send all office/set packages to the A.D.s for distribution on set.

DAILY PRODUCTION REPORT (DPR)
You get a draft from the A.D.s first thing in the morning. Check it over for accuracy and completion. Add to it any notes you made on your copy of the call sheet or to-do list. Accounting will be grateful if you make sure daily crew names are listed.

Photocopy the "corrected" draft copy for the A.D.s and Accounting. They need the form immediately. If you are new to production reports, review the report with the Production Manager at this point. Then type it up for approval signatures by the First A.D. and the Production Manager. Once approved, you can finally distribute it to all who need it.

MORNING

"Morning" is an hour to a few hours after call time.

WHAT THE PM & THE PC ARE UP TO...
You may both be back at the office, or the Production Manager may still be on set.

SET CALLS THE OFFICE WHEN FIRST SHOT HAPPENS
One of the A.D.s will call the Production Coordinator when set has rolled film on the first shot of the day. The Coordinator needs to note this information on your copy of today's call sheet. You will need this information to keep Producers and Executives informed, and to complete the production report tomorrow. Before hanging up: Always ask the Production Manager, the Producer, and the Accountant if they need to talk to set.

MORNING AND/OR AFTERNOON

These events can happen in the "set" morning and/or the "set" afternoon. The timing of some items is up to your discretion, or some will be dictated for you.

WHAT THE PM IS UP TO...
Review ongoing issues mentioned in the Countdowns, because issues like interim financing are never solved quickly. Make notes in whatever you use for a Set Square of any questions you may have for the A.D.s or others on set when they call.

COST REPORT & DAILY PRODUCTION REPORT STATUS
Review how much yesterday cost. Read and evaluate the production report. Calculate figures on the PM-only cost report. How does the PM-only cost report match (or not) the official cost report? Meet with your buddy, the Production Accountant, if need be. Keep the Producer informed of the spending status. Depending on the time of the week, you may have a full-out cost report meeting with the Accountant today.

WHAT THE PM & THE PC ARE UP TO...
The Production Coordinator may initiate most of these issues, but the Production Manager is heavily involved in them, too.

MAIL DELIVERY

When the mail comes in, the Production Coordinator can open it, stamp it with the date received, and distribute it to the rightful recipients. Leave confidential mail sealed. Some people prefer their mail to be opened for them, others not. Check with Producers, Production Manager, Accountants, Director, and Stars before doing so. Some productions will open fan mail for some Performers (like children) to edit out any pieces that might be upsetting. Find out.

RUSHES TIME & PLACE

The Coordinator needs to discuss with the postproduction team when and where yesterday's rushes will be screened. Keep the A.D.s informed of the changes as they happen throughout the day. Are there any people in head office you have to keep informed? Depending on the arrival time of the rushes, the Manager and/or the Coordinator may be the first to see them and give feedback to Producer and to set. Hopefully, the Editor will see them this quickly also.

A.D.s CALL THE OFFICE

Whenever an Assistant Director calls the office to speak to anyone, the Production Coordinator is usually first to field the call. Ask where set is on the call sheet and write it down. Find out who (of the producing team) is presently on set. Refer to the notes you have been gathering in the Set Square by your telephone to make the conversation useful and brief. Chances are the A.D.s are calling from a cell phone, and they may be limited on battery time. Always check if the Producer, the Production Manager, or the Accountant needs to talk to set before hanging up.

When the A.D. calls from set, the Production Manager should always get the latest update on the status of set. What is happening? Find out the schedule of shots. Did they stop for lunch on time or generate a meal penalty? How far ahead or behind are they on the day's schedule? How much time might they need tonight to complete the day? Can shots be carried over until tomorrow because this scene needs lots of attention, or do you have to leave this location tonight and therefore have to finish the slate of scenes no matter what — because a few hours of overtime is cheaper (or is the only possibility) compared to returning for another day to this location and adding a day to the end of the shooting schedule? Will set be able to catch up if they get behind schedule? How decisive is the Director? Does the DP take forever to light? Does the Director ever stop the DP from tweaking lights to over-perfection? Note on your copy of the call sheet when the latest setup date was, with details about it. You may need to relay updates to head office frequently, or you may just need to be prepared to update head office when they call you to ask what is happening on set.

HEAD OFFICE CALLS

Someone from head office, parent production company, or co-production company may call — even on a daily basis — to keep in touch with the production. The Production Manager will likely be the person of contact, but if he is not there, the Production

Coordinator should have some information to give. The Coordinator talks to the A.D.s as constantly as the Manager does, knows when first shot happened, and knows if set has broken for lunch yet.

PUBLICITY EVENTS & VISITORS TO SET

As the Production Coordinator sets up events with Publicity or visitors to set, remember to discuss with and keep the A.D.s informed. Regarding publicity events, the A.D.s need to know about these early so that they can arrange for time during the shoot day for the Performers and/or the Director to be available for interviews. A.D.s will also help identify which locations and days are most appropriate to fit publicity into the schedule. Gallery shoots may end up being on a weekend, incurring sixth-day overtime fees for the crew needed, like Makeup and Hair.

The Production Manager and the Producer need to decide who can approve visitors to set, and how closed a set it will be. Some sets like to shoot on a set closed entirely from the public, while others do not mind the odd family or friend visiting set and staying out of the way. All sets welcome visitors from the financing companies. Make your "set visitor" policy clear to the crew before they bring visitors to set to enjoy free lunches on the production budget. You may find you will have to be host to a visitor or two for the first day that the Publicist is on set, as she may need an introductory tour. Be ready to play host.

OFFICE PETTY CASH

The Office P.A. may need to do a petty cash report daily to avoid a float getting too low. The Coordinator should review the report for enough detail before the Production Manager does, so you can answer any questions the PM may have about it later. The Coordinator needs to know what is happening with the office team.

UNUSUAL TELEPHONE REQUESTS

The Producer may call the office with unusual requests, like finding a monkey that can retrieve things on command, or finding fluorescent-colored contact lenses. These are requests that do not seem to fit into any department on the crew, so they tend to fall into the lap of the Production Coordinator and team. Here is where you can get creative in researching the oddest of things. Refer to your kit of reference books and you can find pretty much anything. If not, ask fellow Production Coordinators. Have fun!

VISIT THE SET

The Production Manager will visit the set on a daily basis. If the Production Coordinator can do the same, do so. There is no better way of keeping in touch with what is happening on set than being there yourself. Use your visits to maintain contact with the crew, to gather information first hand to aid you in completing the production report, or to get the latest production report signed very quickly.

REVIEW OTHER CHAPTERS

A number of chapters are worth reviewing daily. Chapter 7 has lots of information about how to deal with each department. Review this chapter from time to time.

Chapter 11 has a list of supplies the office team can check on a weekly basis. Use these checklists when the day allows. Chapter 15 is the countdown through production to identify events before they are about to happen. Chapter 22 deals with ongoing accounting issues for the Production Manager.

LUNCHTIME

"Lunchtime" means the crew is being catered a buffet lunch. The office staff often has to purchase their own lunch, unless unionized. If set is nearby, ask nicely for take-out.

WHAT THE PM & THE PC ARE UP TO...
SET CALLS IN LUNCH BREAK

The A.D.s will call when the set has stopped for lunch. Even if neither of you has any more news than that, talk to each other — set and office. You may remember something during the course of a conversation. How many lunches were served (since lunch is usually charged to production by the number of plates used)?

The Production Manager often has lunch on set. Lunchtime is an ideal occasion to meet with crew and to discuss with the A.D., the Director, and the Producer the morning's achievements (or not) and the afternoon's plan (often to catch up). What is the target for wrap time tonight? The A.D.s are committing to tomorrow's call sheet over lunch. Is the plan to carry any shots over to tomorrow or to another time? Depending on the day's schedule, the A.D.s may even create two different call sheets so they can commit to the call sheet later in the afternoon.

AFTERNOON (INCLUDING CALL SHEETS & LOCATION MAPS)

How soon the draft call sheet comes to the office will determine how busy the Production Coordinator's afternoon will be. The Production Manager looks more and more toward "are they getting their day?"

WHAT THE PM & PC ARE UP TO...
THE FIVE O'CLOCK REPORT

This report rarely happens exactly at 5:00 p.m., but does occur after lunch and before wrap. An A.D. calls the Production Manager to report on the present filming status and what is expected to be completed by the end of the day. This is the Coordinator's opportunity to get an estimated wrap time or an approval to copy and distribute the call sheet. The Production Manager and the Coordinator should share information regarding potential wrap time.

CALL SHEET

After lunch, the A.D.s send the Production Coordinator a draft "pencil" copy of the call sheet for typing and copying. The Production Coordinator needs the Production Manager's approval, and the A.D.s' "go-ahead," before copying and distributing the call sheet to the many people who need it every day. As the Production Manager has already had discussion on set regarding this call sheet (likely at lunchtime), its information should not be news.

WHAT IS A CALL SHEET?

The call sheet tells the cast and the crew what time and where to show up on set the next morning, along with the weather forecast. It also informs everyone of which scenes are to be shot, and what special requirements (like specific props, wardrobe, lighting effects, etc.) or daily crew each department must have arranged for to accomplish the day. An advance schedule of what is planned for the following day ends the call sheet. All call sheets need to have a location map attached to be complete. (See samples of call sheets on pages 412-415.)

A WORD ABOUT PRE-CALLS ON THE CALL SHEET

There is a unit call time for everyone to arrive on set in the morning, plus there are specific call times prior to unit call (pre-calls) for certain departments to arrive earlier to ensure the most efficient start to the shooting day. Having a crew wait around for one department to finish their on-set preparation is an expensive wait, so pre-calls work. Experienced A.D.s are superb at giving the minimum number of crew pre-calls and still ensuring a fast start to the day. Though the PM reviews and approves the call sheet anyway, if the A.D. team is inexperienced, the PM has to review the call sheet very closely, and ensure a good look at the pre-calls. Are 90% of the crew being called prior to unit call time? Question the need for each pre-call. Are they truly necessary and efficient, or are you just going to get into overtime earlier on the bulk of your crew for the sake of comforting a nervous A.D.?

WHAT THE PC IS UP TO...

Now that the call sheet is happening, the Coordinator and the office team are rushing through a sea of related paperwork.

LOCATION MAP

The Locations Department will create a map to location to attach to the call sheet. If they cannot do this, make a map from the production office to location, depicting instructions in both pictures and words. The easiest way is to start with the local map as reference, and trace out a route from the production office to the shooting location. Include all major streets and ensure that north is to the top of the page for customary orientation. If the location is so far away from the production office that creating a map detailed enough on one page is impossible, create two maps: one of large scale to show where the location is in reference to the production office, and one in small scale to show the detail as you approach location. At location, note where crew parking is and any loading instructions the crew or the cast need. The map should also include the location of the closest hospital, along with its address and emergency telephone number. Do not forget to have the actual address and contact number for the location itself. Finally, supply written instructions to location on the map for those people who under-stand directions by words more than by pictures. Though scale can be approximate instead of exact, be very clear about your instructions. Do not write small.

SIDES & SIDE COVER
Sides are selected pages from the script. For shooting on set, you need to reduce-photocopy sides to pocket-sized for portability. Make them at the same time as you make the call sheet. Pull the pages from the script that correspond to the scenes on the call sheet, and reduce-photocopy them to pocket size. Use the first page of the call sheet as a cover sheet. It informs the cast and the crew what the planned shooting order is. Because sides are small, they often get treated as dispensable and get lost with great fre-quency. Label each set to the people that you and the A.D.s deem require them on set.

CAST & CREW CALL FOR TOMORROW'S CALL TIME
Clear up with the A.D.s who is going to call whom with call times on a daily basis. You may call the Caterer and the Extras Casting Director, while they may call the Cast, the Stunt Performers, and the Specialty Daily Crew. Some crew will call the office for call times without identifying themselves. Find out to whom you are talking before handing out the unit call time. These people may have a special call different from the majority of the crew, and you may have to call these people back should the call time change later in the afternoon. Write down their names and numbers. Keep the A.D.s informed of whom you have given call-time information. Never give out the wrong call time.

LATE AFTERNOON

Call sheet and plan for tomorrow done, you are now waiting for wrap. If set gets into overtime, the wait could be very long.

WHAT THE PM & THE PC ARE UP TO...
As time grows closer to wrap, the Production Manager finds the time to go back to set.

PREPARE FOR TODAY'S WRAP ISSUES
Catch up on the status of set in readiness for wrap issues. How is the day's shooting going? Will you get the day? Do you need to approve overtime? Does call time tomorrow have to be pushed to avoid expensive turnaround costs and to give the crew enough time to go home and rest before tomorrow? You already know how much an hour or two will cost. Can you find the money in the budget to cover it? How does this day fit into

164

the whole schedule? What are the extenuating circumstances of today's shoot? Did weather hold you up? Is the crew becoming too tired to work the overtime effectively? Might accidents happen because they are tired? Weigh the odds. If all is going well, it will be another pleasant visit to set. If all is going superbly well and Producer is on set, you may stay in the office and complete more of that office work that is piling up on your desk.

WHAT THE PC IS UP TO...
The Production Coordinator is back at the office, holding fort.

DRAFT CALL SHEET (FOR THE FOLLOWING DAY)
After the call sheet is completed, type a draft copy (with no times on it) for the following day to send to the A.D.s on set for completion tomorrow. Create this from the information on both the advance schedule and the shooting schedule. The draft call sheet is a great timesaver for A.D.s who do not have the luxury of a stationary desk and predictable weather on location.

AT WRAP

When the A.D.s call the office with "We've wrapped," it is not always time to go home.

WHAT THE PM IS UP TO...
The Production Manager's part in wrap decisions is made by wrap time. There may be a quick meeting after wrap to plan for the future day's work, or to discuss a future location or a schedule need or issue, but if not, go home. Get rest for tomorrow. You will need to be able to think clearly then. A whole new set of decisions and challenges await you.

WHAT THE PC IS UP TO...
The Production Coordinator and the office staff are still in the production office. There may be more work to be done after wrap.

SET CALLS IN WRAP TIME
Note wrap time on your copy of the call sheet, for reference when completing the production report tomorrow. At this point, the A.D.s will also tell you if call time tomorrow is pushed or pulled or remains the same. If it stays the same, ask them how long they need someone to wait around the office (in case a person who does not have a key needs access to the building).

WHEN CALL TIME CHANGES
If tomorrow's call time has changed from the call sheet (e.g., to one hour later), use a big fat red marker to write boldly at the top of all call sheets in your possession: "ALL

CALLS +1HR" (of course, you could even have a self-inking stamp or two in your kit to serve this purpose); then re-distribute and re-fax the sheet to everyone necessary. Next, telephone all heads of departments that are not on set with the new information. If it is too late to make telephone calls, leave a list for the person opening the office to make the calls in the morning. Double-confirm with the A.D.s who is calling whom with the call time change. Find out from the A.D.s which crew were not on set at wrap or left set early and therefore need a telephone call about the call time change.

WHEN THE CALL SHEET REVISES TO PINK

Sometimes the changes to the call sheet at wrap are so extensive that you need to make a "pink revised" call sheet. This is the reason having two people in the office until wrap is useful. Get the changes from the A.D.s and type up the new call sheet as quickly as possible. Select and reduce-copy the new sides. Indicate in bold at the top of both sides and call sheet that this is "pink revised," so there is no confusion about which call sheet to use (even when faxed, or photocopied onto the wrong colored paper). If there is no Driver standing by, and if time permits, you or your Assistant may be charged with driving the new call sheet out to set.

You made it to the end of the day. That is cause for celebration in itself. Pat yourself on the back. Go home. Prepare two alarm clocks beside your bed (one on battery power, in case of power outages), and rest before you come back to tackle tomorrow. This routine is different than prep, and perhaps a little more predictable in its form, so you will get used to it very quickly. Just remember: Now that the cameras are rolling, you must be prepared for the unexpected.

Production Report Entertainment

The notes section of a daily production report can be its most informative section. In the shortest words, set has to report what happened yesterday, how long specific delays were on set, and what those delays were.

There is no room for humor on these reports. You are reporting to Producers, Executives, Accountants, and possibly Lawyers. If there ever is an insurance claim, these production reports are the legal representation of what happened on the set. Yet sometimes these reports cannot help but be entertaining, because naturally a day comes when it is difficult to sum up the day's events and delays on the production report and remain tactful.

My favorite day was... filming a family story. The star horse was in his stall and all was going fine. Heck, we had filmed scenes with him before with no problem. This day, however, no one noticed — well, until it was too late — that there was a mare in the next stall. A very attractive mare, apparently. So here we were making a family show, and the star horse was on screen in all his glorious maleness. I don't think so. Set incurred a delay, and the crew stood around doing nothing while the star horse — a feisty, enamored stallion — was given a cold shower.

Just write about that on the production report...

CHAPTER 14

DAILY PRODUCTION REPORTS

They are published daily. The information on them may make them seem dry, but they are essential. They become the record of what officially happened on a daily basis on set during the most expensive time of filmmaking: principal photography. They are the daily production reports, also known as the DPRs.

WHAT IS A DAILY PRODUCTION REPORT?

Nearly every department creates a daily report on set detailing what happened in that department that day. Continuity creates the continuity top sheet; the Camera Department creates a camera report summary; the Sound Department generates sound reports for each roll of sound used; and the A.D.s generate or collect the Actor's work report (time sheet), Extra vouchers, and various other reports. The king of all of these daily reports is the daily production report or DPR. It summarizes all the departmental reports in one place, reporting, quite naturally, an official daily report to Accounting and to the Executives of what transpired during that set day. It is important to be clear in reporting everything on the DPR — from how much film and sound stock was used, to how long the film's running time is estimated to be, to the hours of all crew and cast members, to general and specific notes about what happened on set. Note that the daily production reports are the first documents examined in great detail if production ever has a legal battle or an insurance claim, so fill them out professionally. (See samples of DPAs on pages 416-418.)

WHO GENERATES THE DPR?

The A.D.s on set collect the departmental information and generate the draft report in pencil. They send the report and all its backup paperwork to the Production Coordinator.

The Coordinator distributes the backup information to the appropriate departments (Continuity information to Editing, and so on — see Chapter 30), keeps a copy of all production report backup paperwork in the production files, and checks the integrity of the information on the draft production report while typing it up for clearer reference. Accounting may need a copy of the draft production report in pencil to get even incomplete information immediately in order to estimate the cost of yesterday's shoot. This protocol is not unusual. While typing up the report, the Coordinator can also add notes to the notes section from her observations; once the report is typed, she gives it to the Production Manager.

The PM reviews the report, includes more notes, or revises notes as needed. The PM can evaluate the report in detail to garner information about the daily cost of production for the PM-only cost report. How many hours of overtime did the crew work? How many daily crew were hired? For more on how to read and evaluate a DPR, see below.

Both the PM and the First A.D. need to sign the official report to approve it for distribution. The Production Coordinator takes care of arranging for the signatures and for the distribution of the final, official report.

WHO ELSE READS THE DPR?

The Producers, the Executives, the Financiers, and the bonding company read the DPR to see how production is moving along. What is set achieving during the day? Is the shoot on schedule and on budget?

The Production Accountant uses the DPR to estimate how much the shoot day cost so that he can set aside money to pay for these costs when the bills come in or payroll is due.

If there is an insurance claim, the claim adjusters refer to these reports as the official word for what happened on set that day. Because of this procedure, there is no place for humor on the reports.

HOW TO READ A DPR

As mentioned, the DPR is made up of a variety of departmental reports. Here is a look at how to read those mini-reports (and who generates the information for them). Update the PM-only cost report as needed with what you learn from the DPR.

THE GENERAL DAILY INFORMATION (FROM THE A.D.s)
The header information of the DPR notes the day and the date of the shoot and the production title and key crew. Just beneath this is a notation reporting actual call time, time of first shot, lunchtime, first shot after lunchtime, wrap time, and last-man-out time. There should also be a notation of what the weather was like, which sets were used, and on which locations the scenes were filmed.

How fast is the crew getting the first shot off? Are the days regularly starting slowly? Is there a way to speed this up, like using a pre-call for Electrics and Grips to do some pre-lighting prior to the main unit's arrival? How much main unit overtime is being done per day? How long does last person take to leave set after wrap? Is this on budget? What are the extenuating circumstances of today? Might weather have held you up?

THE CONTINUITY REPORT
Just under the header information is usually a chart that reports the information from the Continuity top sheet. This mini-report details what scenes were planned versus shot, how many pages of the script were planned versus shot, how much screen time was planned versus shot, what is the running time of the whole show estimated to be now, which specific scenes were shot, and which wild lines were recorded.

Review this section to determine: How many setups (camera placements) are you achieving? Is the Director planning an unreasonable shot list of 45 setups per day, but the main unit is working at top speed and achieving only 18-25? Is estimated timing of each scene similar to final timing of master scenes? Are you getting lots of scenes but little page count? As long as you are achieving something, that will be okay, because lots of setups take time. Heavy dialogue scenes will be low on scene count and high on page count to balance these days. What are the average scenes and screen minutes you are achieving per day? How many scenes were not shot and are carried forward to be added to future days' work? Can you move them later into the schedule without adding a day to your shoot? Did you achieve any target shots (unplanned bonus shots) from the call sheet? You are formulating good questions to discuss with the First A.D., the Producer, and the Director when next you meet or talk.

Especially for television series, look at and track estimated final show timing. If the show is coming in too long, why shoot the extra footage that will end up on the cutting room floor? Cut scenes now. If the timing is too short, maybe the Writers have to write more scenes or more lines. Find out the plan. If the timing is just right, it will be broadcast length plus some extra to edit out in post to punch up the pacing.

THE CAMERA REPORT
The Camera Department each day summarizes the film stock used and remaining in inventory on the camera report summary. The information that is translated onto the DPR includes: the type of film stock(s) used; the number of feet of film that has run through camera, detailing how much was exposed, printed, or wasted (unexposed and too short to be used again); how much film became short ends (unexposed partial rolls that may be used again); how much film remains in the inventory; and how much of the inventory has been used since you began. For video shoots, the camera report details how much tape stock was used of varying lengths, and how much unused tape stock remains in the inventory.

Film stock is expensive. Consider the following: Are you on budget for what you planned to use daily? Is a lot of film being wasted? Are short ends being used or just stockpiled? As you are getting closer to the end of production, is the inventory growing smaller?

THE SOUND REPORT
The only information that makes it to the DPR from the sound reports is how many sound rolls were used.

As film is more expensive than sound, the number of sound rolls tends not to be reviewed very closely. Still, it is wise to remember to check with Postproduction if the sound quality is good. It is very expensive to replace sound and re-create a complex soundtrack in postproduction. Ensure you are getting good sound now.

THE CAST REPORT (FROM THE A.D.s)
The A.D.s are in charge of making sure the work report (time sheet) for the Actors is completed. The information that is transferred to the DPR from this report includes: a list of all cast members and each Performer's call time, travel time, lunch time, and wrap time. Wardrobe fittings may happen for Performers at the production office (not on set), so the Production Coordinator can track this information and ensure it is included on the DPR, too.

When reviewing this section, ask yourself: How much overtime is the cast doing? Are you budgeted for this overtime? Are there any meal penalties payable? Any extra hours payable to the cast are hugely expensive.

THE EXTRAS REPORT (FROM THE A.D.s)
The A.D.s also ensure the Extras are all accounted for on vouchers or on a cash report form. On the DPR you will read how many Extras of which type were on set, their call time, lunch time, wrap time, and travel time. You will also learn the set times for the Stand-Ins.

Review this information. How many Extras were there? Did they work overtime? Is this information in line with what was budgeted?

THE CREW REPORT (FROM THE A.D.s)
The A.D.s report on the DPR the arrival to set time and wrap time of every crew member. They also include a listing of daily crew hired beyond the regular unit and their work times.

Check this information to see who is working how much overtime. Are some of the times unreasonably excessive? Is there a pattern as to who is working excessive overtime? How many daily crew were hired? Are they covered in the departmental budgets?

THE LUNCH REPORT (FROM THE A.D.s)
The A.D.s talk with the Caterer to discuss how many lunches were purchased that day (the plate count), and report this on the DPR. They will also note on the DPR how many substantial snacks were purchased (three hours into the morning), and — if set went to a second meal that day — how many second meals were purchased. This information will be near the crew work times.

Again, review this section to determine if the meals being purchased are in line with the number of meals budgeted. The call sheet will have a notation of how many meals were ordered. Is the Caterer serving many more meals than were ordered?

THE NOTES (FROM THE A.D.s, THE PC & THE PM)

And finally, the A.D.s have a large note section in which to detail a miscellany of information. What is the list of specialty daily equipment rented? Did set achieve the day? What delays occurred, how long were they, and why did they occur? What is the list of scenes to be rescheduled, and the plan for folding them into the schedule? The section also needs to report all accidents that happen, minor or not.

The notes section has to be the most-read section by Executives and Financiers. This is the section you as a Production Manager must review in detail, add your notes, and edit the notes that are there, as needed. There will be set delays. Mention them. Report the plan to address them. Mention if someone was late on set due to traffic and that caused a set delay of ten minutes. Whatever. What accidents happened? Even if it is only a finger that was caught in a piece of equipment and needed a bandage, mention it. As you read DPR after DPR, are you noticing that the minor accidents are becoming more frequent? If so, the crew is becoming exhausted. Address the source of the problem. Is a particular cast or crew member difficult to work with? Mention how so, but be tactful. If someone is to be rightfully fired later in production, the justification must be evident here in the production report notes. The Production Coordinator may add notes to this section before the Production Manager sees the report to review and approve it. This is terrific, as the Coordinator has a finger on the buzz of production, too. Just think of what might have cost money, and report it. Discuss with Producer if you are not sure if a note should be included, or how it should be worded because of its sensitivity. When you are ready to commit to the wording, sign the report... but be speedy, because you have to publish a new report each day.

PUBLISHING THE DPR

Some productions ensure the report is completed in legible ink instead of going to the bother of typing it up. Typing is the easiest and the clearest to read, and therefore most advisable. But whatever you choose, never complete and sign the official production report in pencil. It is a legal document. Be permanent.

The Coordinator will take care of distributing the official, signed DPR. (More on the distribution of the DPR is in Chapter 30.)

THE SECOND UNIT DPR

Should you have a Second Unit shooting as well as main unit, you need to create a separate DPR for Second Unit. Track the information from Second Unit separately. Print the DPR on colored paper to differentiate it from the main unit DPR. Second Unit has less information to report, anyway. They usually have no sound and a small crew, but are furnished with their own First A.D. and their own shooting schedule.

Beware that main unit may push shots to Second Unit and overload them. Second Unit is not a miracle unit. Keep both units talking to each other.

When reading daily production reports, remember the big picture, too. Day one takes longer to achieve than other days because new patterns are being forged. People are working together for the first time. Unforeseen problems are being ironed out. Some props or sets might be rushing to set completed just seconds before shooting has begun. In this hurry-up-and-wait industry, all of this is normal. You will find that overtime worked is probably greatest in week one. If the overtime becomes a pattern, though, you may not be able to afford to support it. Changes must happen. Discuss with the Producer a plan of action and put it into place.

The Customs Police

This is the story of how I nearly got arrested for carrying the wrong customs documents.

Enlisted to hand-carry a number of post elements to Los Angeles, I sat down in my plane seat — still on the tarmac in Toronto — and heard my named paged. The flight attendant told me that the company I worked for had just called the gate to tell me that I had the wrong elements. She asked if I knew what that meant. I said yes, thanked her for the message, and asked to de-plane. She said that it was too late and closed the door right in front of me. Since wrestling with her at this point would have been useless, I sat back down and resigned myself to a lovely, fruitless day of traveling to and from Los Angeles.

Upon my arrival at the Los Angeles airport, my contact examined the elements I brought and declared that all was well. I had the correct elements, I just had too many. He gave me four items to return to Canada. Fine, I agreed, and looked at the customs documents in my hand. Written in clear, bold, underlined, block capital letters was the phrase: "Not to be returned to Canada." My contact gone, I called head office for advice.

They consulted their experts and reported back to me with this simple procedure: "When you arrive in Canada at customs, the officer will examine the documents and arrest you." Arrest me? "Then he will take you to a holding room where we will have someone there to bail you out and clear the whole thing up." Arrest me? Great.

Fifty minutes later, I boarded the exact same plane to go back. For the next four and a half hours, I sat down and rehearsed over and over again what I might say to the customs officer.

At customs in the Toronto airport, I handed over the offending document and spewed out as fast as possible — and in way too many words — my case, along with an explanation of the events of my entire day. The Customs Officer interrupted me, returned the paperwork, and said he didn't want to hear my story. I should just go away. Speechless, I did just that.

Then I remembered that there was someone waiting for me in a holding room. I had to go back and ask in my sweetest, most innocent manner: "Uh, if you were to have arrested me, where might you have taken me?"

He paused before answering. I smiled. He told me. So I thanked him and trotted off to the holding room, entering it from the visitor's (not the prisoner's) side.

Upon my entrance, the promised contact was there. She belted out fast and loud, "It's not her fault!", accompanying her declaration with grand gestures. The officers on duty regarded her with curiosity. I jumped in to shut her up and dragged her out of the room to explain. I did not want the officers to change their minds about arresting me.

CHAPTER 15

COUNTDOWN THROUGH PRODUCTION

You think about work day by day now. You initiated a lot of happenings during pre-production and you are wondering what you can initiate during production. As a continuation of Chapter 12, this chapter will count you down through the shooting period.

FIRST DAY OF PRINCIPAL PHOTOGRAPHY

This is the first day that the project is a film instead of a script. The cameras are rolling — an event that triggers a number of requirements that the Production Manager must address.

FIRST DAY OF PRINCIPAL PHOTOGRAPHY – PM CHECKLIST
- ❏ Visit the Set
- ❏ Memo Financiers that Principal Photography Has Begun
- ❏ Repay Development Loans
- ❏ Pay Production Fees to Writers & Others
- ❏ Update Producers/Executives & Bond

FIRST DAY OF SHOOTING – PM DETAIL
VISIT THE SET
First of all, visit the set! You have helped prepare for this wonderful day, so show up and see how it is going. There may be a few problems to iron out, as this is the first day these people have worked together on set for this production, and first days always reveal something to be addressed that was not dealt with before. Be on standby to assist in solving these last-minute problems.

MEMO FINANCIERS THAT PRINCIPAL PHOTOGRAPHY HAS BEGUN
Make a memo or a letter to the Financiers informing them that principal photography has officially begun. This memo is likely part of the triggers for the next money inflow you need to receive. Have the Coordinator send the memo out to all Financiers and to head office immediately.

REPAY DEVELOPMENT LOANS
As mentioned before, development money is only loaned to you until the first day of principal photography. You must pay back the Financiers today for the money they

loaned to you, so that you do not start generating interest on the unpaid balance. Some Financiers will allow you to do a "check swap" between the repayment of the development loan and their next payment to you that is triggered on first day of principal photography. Find out if you can do this and preserve your bank balance.

PAY PRODUCTION FEES TO WRITERS & OTHERS

A number of people will have payments triggered on the first day of principal photography. Discuss these payments, and whom they are to be made to, with the Production Accountant. Writers, for example, are paid for their writing work in development, but they have a production fee payable on the first day of principal photography — because the script they wrote is technically now a film, no matter how short it is at this point! Directors often have a payment triggered on this day. As you will have created a cash flow in preproduction, none of these payments will be a surprise to your bank account. Just ensure they happen on time, and note what has been paid on the PM-only cost report.

UPDATE PRODUCERS/EXECUTIVES & BOND

The Producer and some Executives will likely be on set with you on this, the first day of principal photography. It is quite a celebration to get a film from development to production. For those who are not or cannot be on set, it is good to give them a telephone call to update them that you have begun shooting. Call Executives and the Completion Bond to keep them informed. They will appreciate the call.

FIRST WEEK OF PRINCIPAL PHOTOGRAPHY

This week the Production Manager will tend to be working very much in the present, while the Production Coordinator focuses on items for the future. You are both still meeting every day to touch base; soon you will be in the new routine of the more structured production days, instead of the less-so prep days. Even though you will still be tidying up issues from preproduction, there are other issues you need to address, starting now:

FIRST WEEK OF PRINCIPAL PHOTOGRAPHY – PM CHECKLIST
- ❏ Review Cash Flow
- ❏ Approve Payroll
- ❏ Approve Petty Cash
- ❏ End-of-Prep Cost Report

FIRST WEEK OF PRINCIPAL PHOTOGRAPHY – PM & PC CHECKLIST
- ❏ Credits
- ❏ Crew Gifts
- ❏ Wrap Reel

178

FIRST WEEK OF PRINCIPAL PHOTOGRAPHY – PM DETAIL
REVIEW CASH FLOW

Thinking of cash flow, this week is a good time to review it. How close are actual bills to the projected bills as noted in the cash flow? Review this alongside the PM-only cost report and with the Production Accountant to keep you updated on the financial health of the production.

APPROVE PAYROLL

Payroll will not be terribly big this week, as you will only be paying for the crew that was on the last week of prep, but it is getting bigger. Find a routine in the week to approve the payroll to keep the Production Accountant working efficiently. Note payroll amounts in the PM-only cost report.

APPROVE PETTY CASH

Crew have been spending, and spending. Keep on approving petty cash. You may find you have to teach people how to be detailed while filling out the form, or teach them what a valid receipt is. Be prepared for this situation. You can track petty cash in the PM-only cost report by monitoring floats as they go out, or spends as they come in. Whichever way you do it, keep track. Petty cash is far from being petty.

END-OF-PREP COST REPORT

You prepared for this cost report during the last week of prep. Meet with the Production Accountant, bring your PM-only cost report notes when you review the draft, and arrange to publish the official end-of-prep cost report as soon as possible to trigger your next inflow from the Financiers, updating your PM-only cost report as you do. Be ready, because by the end of this week, you will have to generate another cost report!

FIRST WEEK OF PRINCIPAL PHOTOGRAPHY – PM & PC DETAIL
CREDITS

Though you may initially believe this is too early to think about credits, know that credits will have to go through many drafts and approvals from many companies before they are final. The Coordinator can start the first "pre-draft" to show the Producer and the Production Manager only. Consult the crew deal memos, cast contracts, and any other information you have gathered in the credits file folder on your desk. Double-check all spellings. Call those people if you are at all unsure about the spelling of their names. Do not promise them a credit (you do not have the authority), just check the spellings. Everyone is happy to confirm the spelling of their names when credits are being discussed! Credits are very sensitive information. Treat them with the utmost confidence.

CREW GIFTS

Crew gifts can be t-shirts, jackets, hats, bags, or doormats imprinted with the production name. Delivery of ordered items can take four to six weeks, so consider what you might want now. The Coordinator, the Production Manager, and the Producer can discuss this procedure. Some productions will pay for the gifts, while others will sell them to the crew. Some productions want them to be a surprise, others not. Find out how crew gifts are to be treated on this production and order the items immediately. If the crew is to pay for all or part of the order, get payment in advance.

WRAP OR OUTTAKE REEL

The Production Manager, the Producer, and the Coordinator can discuss if production is going to create a wrap reel or outtake reel. If you are going to create one, bring the Editor and Continuity into the discussion to ensure they flag interesting or funny takes as production proceeds. Finding outtakes at the end of production is a time-consuming process.

DURING PRODUCTION

Much of what you do on a daily basis is covered in Chapter 13 about the shoot day, but there are issues that come up during production which do not come up regularly day after day.

DURING PRODUCTION – PM CHECKLIST
- ❑ Weekly Cost Report
- ❑ Weekly Payroll Approval
- ❑ Petty Cash Approvals
- ❑ Daily Production Report (DPR) Approval
- ❑ Extra Equipment or Crew Approvals
- ❑ Overtime Approvals
- ❑ Unexpected Problem-Solving

DURING PRODUCTION – PC CHECKLIST
- ❑ Call Sheet & Draft Call Sheet
- ❑ Daily Production Report & Backup
- ❑ Daily Equipment
- ❑ Daily Crew
- ❑ Stunt Contracts, Nurses, Ambulance Attendants

DURING PRODUCTION – PM DETAIL
WEEKLY COST REPORT

Every week you need to meet with the Accountant and publish the official cost report detailing how much has been spent. Update your PM-only cost report each time.

WEEKLY PAYROLL APPROVAL

Along with the weekly cost report — or rather prior to — you need to approve the payroll for the Accountant. Take this opportunity to update the PM-only cost report with the information.

PETTY CASH APPROVALS

Petty cash comes in when petty cash comes in. How well are the departments managing their money? Keep up discussions with them as you approve their petty cash reports. Update the PM-only cost report as needed.

DAILY PRODUCTION REPORT (DPR) APPROVALS

Though this does happen daily, I mention it here again, as it is another approval you have to schedule for your workday. Compare the DPR information to the estimated averages you pre-calculated during preproduction. How is production doing?

EXTRA EQUIPMENT OR CREW APPROVALS

Now and then, crew will ask for extra help or extra equipment for which you had not originally budgeted. These requests are natural. Because you are keeping current on the PM-only cost report of what may be the final cost picture for the entire production, you can decide if it is wise or not to approve such extra costs. The more you dip into contingency approving these extras, the more you must keep the Producer informed of the declining balance. Save at the very least 40-50% of the contingency for postproduction use.

OVERTIME APPROVALS

You may have budgeted for some overtime, but not for all of it. This is what contingency is used for. You have already pre-budgeted how much overtime will cost per hour. Use this information when advising if you can afford production to work overtime or not. Keep a close eye on how much overtime the set is working. The first week is bound to have the most overtime during the production as the team irons out how to work together. But if you keep the hours up, the crew will become tired and burnt out and not perform well, plus the budget will not be able to handle consistent over-spending. You will be robbing contingency from postproduction to pay for it. Not wise. Problem-solve too much overtime early with the Producer and the First A.D.

UNEXPECTED PROBLEM-SOLVING

Speaking of problem-solving, you will encounter other events too numerous and of too much variety to mention here. Most of these problems, if not all of them, will cost money. Be ready for the unexpected, and be ready to find a way out of it, minimizing the impact on the budget so that the maximum amount of money in the budget ends up onscreen for all to see.

DURING PRODUCTION – PC DETAIL
CALL SHEET & DRAFT CALL SHEET
In review, send the draft copy of the call sheet you created to the A.D.s on set in the morning. Receive the penciled-in copy after lunchtime. Type up the call sheet as soon as possible, get approvals, add the location map to it, make script sides, and distribute it.

DAILY PRODUCTION REPORT & BACKUP
The draft production report comes from the A.D.s in the first run of the morning. Check and complete it using the backup paperwork provided and the information you gathered yourself yesterday. Get approvals as necessary, type the form, get signatures, and distribute it. Treat it with confidentiality.

DAILY EQUIPMENT
Purchase order any special equipment requests, remembering to get approval from the Production Manager as you go.

DAILY CREW
Be prepared to call unions or suggested people first thing in the morning to replace absent crew members.

STUNT CONTRACTS, NURSES, AMBULANCE ATTENDANTS
If a Stunt Performer is scheduled for the next day, check that you have already completed his contract. Also check with the A.D.s if a Nurse or an Ambulance Attendant is needed. If so, order one.

TOWARD THE END OF PRINCIPAL PHOTOGRAPHY

As production draws to a close, you think more and more about completing the show, about getting it "in the can." Crew should not be buying much in the way of office supplies now, except perhaps for boxes to wrap up their files. Before wrap begins, plan for it now.

TOWARD THE END OF PRINCIPAL PHOTOGRAPHY – PM CHECKLIST
- ❑ Finishing on Time & on Budget
- ❑ Cost Report Savings & Overages
- ❑ "Pink Slip" End of Production Notification
- ❑ Wrap Plans Per Department
- ❑ Plan Wrap Sale or Set Storage
- ❑ Prepare Memo to Financiers That Principal Photography Has Ended

TOWARD THE END OF PRINCIPAL PHOTOGRAPHY – PC CHECKLIST
- ❏ ADR Sessions (Looping)
- ❏ Credits Continue
- ❏ Crew Gifts In
- ❏ Wrap List
- ❏ Wrap Party Prep

TOWARD THE END OF PRINCIPAL PHOTOGRAPHY – PM DETAIL
FINISHING ON TIME AND ON BUDGET
There will be lists of shots on the DPR that are being carried forward from one day to the next. You want to know these are addressed, and the list of shots being carried forward is rapidly diminishing. Have meetings with at least the Producer and the First A.D. to ensure you will be finishing on time and on budget. If there are any flags you are not going to finish on time or on budget, address those concerns now. Do you need a reduced unit for pick-up shots for a day in wrap? Do you need an extra shoot day for the entire unit? What will it take to finish principal photography? What ramifications do these decisions have on the budget — some cast or crew contracts will be very specific about a stop date, inflicting a high monetary penalty should you shoot beyond that date. Weigh the odds and prepare now.

COST REPORT SAVINGS & OVERAGES
As production nears the end of shooting, you will be closer to closing out a good portion of the budget lines in the cost report, and will have a more accurate idea of where you are saving money versus going over budget. Coming in heavily under budget is just about as bad as going over budget, since the Producer will have to give back any budget "under-ages" or savings to the Financiers. If being under budget is your problem, target now how production is going to spend any savings on valid production or postproduction costs.

"PINK SLIP" END OF PRODUCTION NOTIFICATION
This is a payroll issue. Using a memo or a letter, officially notify the crew of the end of principal photography and the end of their particular wrap on the show. Unions often require such notification, even if production is very short in duration. Whether you are required to do so or not, this is your opportunity to thank the crew for their hard work and dedication to the project.

WRAP PLANS PER DEPARTMENT
While the Production Coordinator plans for the wrap party, the Production Manager should meet with each department to discuss their plans for wrap. As crew is no longer needed, are the departments letting them go off the payroll? What are the actual last days of work needed for each department? You can use this information to update cost projections on the PM-only cost report.

PLAN WRAP SALE OR SET STORAGE

Are you going to sell the sets, dressing, props, and wardrobe, or are you going to put them in storage? If you are going to put them in storage, how long can you do so according to the budget? Research the cost ramifications now. If you are planning a sale, make sure the various departments synch their dates to sell at the same time to ensure the most profit. Monies that come in from the set sale go into the production bank account and can offset overages in the respective categories. Find out other productions that are starting up as you are wrapping. They may need to buy a number of your items, and selling to one source is very convenient for you.

PREPARE MEMO TO FINANCIERS THAT PRINCIPAL PHOTOGRAPHY HAS ENDED

Just as the first day of principal photography is a trigger for financing inflows, the last day is often also a trigger. Though you will still need a cost report for the period ending on the last day of shooting, you can at least prepare the memo to the Financiers that will inform them that principal photography is completed. For maximum speed the Coordinator can send this memo to all concerned on the morning of the first day of wrap.

TOWARD THE END OF PRINCIPAL PHOTOGRAPHY – PC DETAIL
ADR SESSIONS (LOOPING)

After a Performer has completed filming, expect the postproduction team to ask you to arrange an ADR session for that Performer. Postproduction may coordinate the studio; you are responsible for the Performer. Be sure that the proper time sheet or contract is completed at the session so the Performer can get paid. Distribute a memo announcing the session and the attendees.

CREDITS CONTINUE

Drafts and drafts of credits will continue to fill your files. If you do not get approvals from the people you need, call them to speed up the process.

CREW GIFTS IN

With luck, the crew gifts will be ready early. The easiest way to distribute them, whatever they are, is to label each gift with each crew member's name, and order them into alphabetical (but decorative) boxes. Imagine handing out one hundred black sweatshirts to a crew that is working all over set. Unlabeled, the sweatshirts are identical and unidentifiable when crew members put them down temporarily as they work. Some will get lost. Few crew, if any, will mark their gifts with their names as soon as they receive it. Also note that the Producer usually says a few words to the crew as the gifts are being handed out.

WRAP LIST

Make a list of everything you have rented, leased, and bought during the course of production. You will have to return and sell all of it come wrap. The earlier you do the list, the more accurate it will be. Start by reviewing the P.O. log. The Production Accountant can help add to your list with a look over the petty cash reports for purchased items. Review the list with the Production Manager.

WRAP PARTY PREP
Get a budget from the Production Manager for the event, and budget a party accordingly. Start to think about appropriate venues. (More about wrap parties is in Chapter 33.)

Now you can see the big picture of production and plan ahead. You find that it not as daunting as you once thought it was. But before you think too far into wrap and post-production, there are ongoing issues that you need to explore further during production.

IV.

MORE MANAGEMENT & MONEY ISSUES

Know how to spend money in order to save money (like saving time).

Grandmother on the Set

There was a day I brought my grandmother to visit the set. I don't normally bring visitors to set, but my mother, who had been once before, was insistent that my grandmother see filmmaking first hand. My mother, you see, sees roses in everything in life, and will always see the magic created on a film set. She wanted to share this magic with her mother.

My grandmother was predictably very silent and observant on her visit. The crew and the cast were very friendly to her and she saw a fair amount before going home.

Afterward she made only three comments about the day. About the crew: Nobody bothers to dress up for work, they're all in jeans. About the time when the cameras are rolling: Everyone seems to be standing around doing nothing. And about filmmaking in general: I don't know how the show comes out in order, everyone looks so disorganized.

To anyone in film that I have mentioned these three observations, I get the same response: how very astute of her.

CHAPTER 16

LOCATION MANAGEMENT

Traditionally, shooting on location was a cheaper alternative to building a set and shooting in a studio, but it is not always the case. You may choose to shoot on location for other reasons. On existing locations, you may find a richness of production values (all the detailed dressing of the location) that would cost too much time and money to reproduce in a studio environment. On existing locations you can film and have the cast interact with a real vista, not a painted backdrop. In any case, you will be renting locations at some time during a film shoot, and as Production Manager you need a good Location Manager and location team to ensure the logistics of the set are taken care of wherever you film.

LOCATION SCOUT VS. LOCATION MANAGER

The Location Scout or Manager is the liaison between the film company and the public. A Scout is generally new to the industry and, as expected, is hired to scout out possible locations for use on the production. A Location Manager should have many more years of experience not only looking for possible locations, but also managing the logistics of them — all the way through the production process, including managing the departmental location budget. For affordability, you may hire a Scout early for location research, then when the Location Manager of your choice is available, bring that person on to take over.

Choosing initial possibilities for locations is both a hugely creative and hugely logistical endeavor. The Location Scout or Manager has the responsibility for finding and presenting possibilities for the entire backdrop for the film by her choice of locations. In essence, she is painting the background. Is this person capable of finding the choices that are along the same lines as the Director's and the Production Designer's creative vision? Balanced with that creativity, does the Scout or the LM consider logistical shooting issues when presenting the location choices?

The Location Scout or Manager will be seeking out possible locations from industry files, from discussions with other industry contacts, and will be finding locations on her own. She will be making cold calls to the public introducing them to the production company, and may have to deal with members of the public who have had bad experiences with other film crews — because you may want to repair this burned bridge to allow production access to a particular (perfect) location. Without a doubt, you need someone who is unwaveringly professional to provide this first impression of the production company. Choose wisely.

WHERE TO FIND LOCATIONS

There are a number of sources to seek out locations for the script. Government Liaison offices often have a location library as a first stop for initial location research. The library has picture files with further logistical information on them to aid Scouts and LMs in finding locations that have either had a film shoot before, or who are interested in having a film shoot. You can use a Chamber of Commerce in a smaller town where there is no Government Liaison office. Real Estate companies are also of help. You will consider previous locations from previous shoots, and the Scout or the LM may also contact Co-Scouts and Co-LMs on other productions. Naturally, Scouts and LMs spend a lot of time driving around too, because they may find a location that will work for the script close to another location that you have already chosen. Proximity of locations is good to reduce the time it takes for company moves. You want to spend more of the shooting day shooting film, not moving the unit.

WHAT TO LOOK FOR IN A LOCATION

When initially looking for a location, there are a number of issues to consider beyond the site's match to the creative vision. Here is a look at the logistical needs of potential locations. You want the Scout or the LM to consider these items, but if you are on a budget that is low enough, as Production Manager you may be heading up these considerations yourself.

PRIOR TO LOCATION SCOUTS & SURVEYS

Before even showing up to have a preliminary look around the location, be sure the owners of the property (not just the renters) are willing to give permission to a film shoot at their place. Renters may be thrilled to learn of a film crew coming to shoot and may think they will be receiving the site rental money, but they do not own the property and do not have the right to grant a film crew such permission. Find out who the owners are.

While having initial conversations with the owners, fill them in with a nutshell explanation of film production. Tell them exactly what you intend to shoot at their property, and if you are considering redecoration (like repainting walls). Explain this process to the owners, assuring them that the crew will redecorate the property back to its original form on the production's departure. Find out how interested the owners are in allowing a film shoot, and what the owners might know or think they know about film shoots. There may be a lot of myths you will have to set straight about what a film crew is like on a location.

Consider, too, how big the unit is, how many vehicles. Is there enough space in the neighborhood to park all the vehicles and still provide access to the location? Is there space for the crew to set up? Is there space for a cast and an Extras holding area? Where might you set up for the cast and crew lunch?

ON THE LOCATION SCOUT

Once you have preliminary permission, scout the potential location, considering all the departmental questions that may come up when you get back to the office. You have to think for both the crew and the owners of the property. You are indeed a liaison between the two.

When you speak with the owners and ask them a myriad of questions, ease their worries by telling them that your questions are all preliminary. You are scouting the potential of this property to fit into a series of locations and sets that make up the film shoot, and this location may or may not be chosen for many reasons that have nothing to do with the location's beauty. Explain the location research process: You scout the location and take pictures, asking preliminary questions about the location; then the crew narrows down the choice of locations in the office for various reasons; then the crew needs to come and survey the location for themselves to prepare for the logistics of a film set — those surveys often consisting of a few people at a time for a few visits, then a big survey of everyone just before shooting. Reassure them that production will arrange for insurance coverage should anything go wrong, and you will minimize the location surveys as much as possible. Respect the owners. If they are entering new territory entertaining the idea of a film shoot at their property, it is your job to help them understand what it means to have a film crew shoot there.

LOCATION SCOUT CONSIDERATIONS

When scouting a potential location or studio (or considering a potential one that the Scout presents), you have to think for all the departments: the Director, Camera, Sound, Art, Transportation, Catering, and so on.

LOCATION PHOTOGRAPHS & FILES

Thanks to one-hour photo finishing, the Location Scouts or the LM can provide photographs of all locations seen. These photographs are panorama pictures that need to be shot with a good 35mm camera. You stand in one spot and take photographs from left to right (or vice versa), ensuring you overlap the pictures a little. After processing, you can tape the photographs together and paste them into a file folder for presentation. Because the photographs are presented in a file, you can jot down the address, the owner name, and other logistical restrictions regarding the photographs. It is also good to note the date and the time of day so that the DP can consider the direction of the light.

Polaroid cameras have even more speed, but not the quality of image to allow for location consideration in the production office later. Some crews use a video camera alongside the 35mm stills to show the look of a particular location, too. Pictures are still best because you can lay two locations side by side on a table to see if they match enough for the story.

LOOK OF LOCATION & REDECORATION
The look of the location will be the first and most obvious consideration. Can, however, the walls be repainted? Are there other redecorations that might need to be done to make this location work alongside other sets and locations? Might you need construction to bring in a flying wall from the set to match the exterior location here to an interior set at the studio? Have these types of temporary changes been considered in the budget? Will the owners allow redecoration, remembering that you have to redecorate back after the shoot is done?

COST OF LOCATION
To properly negotiate the cost of the location, you have to ask yourself and the owners a number of questions: How much access is needed — how much of the property and for how long? Do you need to move owners out of their property into a hotel for the duration of the shoot? Do you need to compensate the owner for loss of business during those days? Also consider the costs of permits, parking lots in the neighborhood, and compensation to other neighbors for disturbing access to their properties.

THE LOCATION & THE SCHEDULE
Are there any restrictions regarding the availability of the location? Are there prior bookings already to work around? Are the other bookings temporary, so that you can counter with a confirmed booking?

PERMITS, RESTRICTIONS & SENSITIVE ISSUES
Consider the permits you need and the time frame required to arrange for them. Also consider what restrictions the owner imposes, or sensitive issues the owner has about the property — like no smoking inside, reduced light level in certain rooms to preserve expensive paintings, no allowances for redecoration, and so on.

INSURANCE
What are the insurance needs for this location? Does the owner need to be listed as an additional insured on the production's policy? What is the minimum coverage required?

TIME OF SHOOT
How much access to sun does this particular location really receive? What direction is it facing? Consider the sunrise/sunset times, the tide schedule, or the traffic patterns and how any of these issues may affect the shoot on the day.

WEATHER
What is the weather like at this location? Is it predictable or not? Is the location at the base of a mountain during rainy season, where it is likely you will have rain every day? Is there a waterfall that is trickling now, but with spring runoff will be blasting water off the rock within a few weeks? If you have to move to weather cover on the day, is there the potential for an interior location nearby?

NOISE OF THE LOCATION

Do not forget sound. If you want to use the location sound that is being recorded, consider if you are under an airplane landing path at this location. Is there an active railway track nearby? Do the pipes clank and crack when the heating in the building is on? Take a moment to really listen to the location.

POWER AT LOCATION

Production probably has a generator already, but if your budget is very low, you may be looking for locations where you can tie-in to existing power and pay the owner's power bill later. If you are looking at potential studios, what is the power at this stage? There are different phases of power at different stages, and you need to be sure the studio space can handle all the equipment production is planning to load in. If you are bringing equipment from other countries, there is another factor to consider: different electricity cycles.

COMBINING LOCATIONS

What other locations are nearby that production may be able to use? Is there a room in this house, for example, that can be used as an office set for elsewhere in the script while the rest of the house is the house set? Combining locations in one place removes the need for some company moves and saves production a huge amount of time that can be spent preparing and shooting actual shots instead of driving around.

CREW & UNIT PARKING

How long is the unit? How many feet of curb space do all the trucks take up? Consider the location of the unit trucks and crew parking. Where will the hair/makeup/wardrobe and dressing room trucks be (also known as the "base camp" or the "circus")? Will you need to hire Drivers to shuttle the cast and the crew back and forth from base camp to set all day to minimize travel time walking? Think through the crew equipment load-in. Are there accessible doors and elevators at the location to ease this job?

ACCESS TO LOCATION & THE ZONE

How accessible is this location to major roads and to bus lines for crew who do not have cars? Is it close to other potential locations? Is it close to equipment rental houses? Is it in the union "zone" where production does not have to pay for travel time, hotels, and per diems to the cast and the crew?

TRAFFIC PATTERNS

Do you need to close a road to shoot at this location, even temporarily? What might you need to do this? Most places require permits and off-duty police paid for by production to allow you this permission, with daily A.D.s assisting by directing traffic. Some small towns may even allow you to take two road-closed signs, and off you go!

LUNCH LOCATION

Consider where you will have all the lunch tables and the lunch truck set up. Is there space for this?

SERVICES IN AREA

Note services in the area around this location: the closest hospital with emergency services, food services in case you break for second meal, hardware stores, photocopy or photo finishing stores, and fuel stations.

OTHER ISSUES & EXTRA COSTS

Also consider dressing space, equipment space, storage space, bathrooms, and security issues. Can you lock up and have security here overnight, or do you have to return the equipment to your secured studio every night? What hidden extras are being charged? Studios may charge you for the stage rental, but add on costs for use of the telephone, dressing rooms, and so on. Other hidden costs might be the need to rent a parking lot near the location because there is no access to parking.

PREP & WRAP TIME

How much prep and wrap time do the Art Department and technical departments need beyond the shooting time you need at this location? Negotiate a lower daily location fee on prep and wrap days. Who of the crew really must survey the location, so you can minimize multiple surveys and try not to annoy the owners? Are the owners informed of all the access requirements of production?

NEIGHBORS & THE COMMUNITY

What is the history of filming in this neighborhood? The Government Liaison office will know. Has production considered how to "give something to the community," as well as the location fee to the owner? Is there a beautifying project that the film company can take on to demonstrate to the community that the film industry is grateful for their support in the making of this film? A film shoot is a huge endeavor, and the neighbors are being very gracious putting up with the inconvenience of your being there. Think about how to thank them for it, to leave a good feeling behind when you depart.

CREW MEETINGS ABOUT LOCATIONS

The Location Scout or Manager needs to present location choices, not location decisions, at these meetings. She will present the photographs and the comments about the issues that have been thought through so far about each location. Certainly voice any restrictions and sensitive issues immediately. She has been anticipating the crew's questions, but there will be more. Write the questions down and collect them. You do not want to telephone the owners every few hours with another question; you want to contact them a few times, and be professional each time.

LOCATION SURVEYS

Mini-surveys happen during preproduction when the locations become confirmed and certain crew need to visit the location to design logistically how to capture the story on film at this place. The Production Manager needs to attend as many of these mini-surveys as possible, because many story changes happen and many "ideas" (read "costs") are created during these mini-surveys.

If the owners follow the crew around during the mini-surveys, the Location Manager needs to be the liaison. Crew will ask all sorts of questions about what they can and cannot do at this location. These questions can easily scare the owner from having the crew there at all. The Location Manager has to deal with this process. Many of the crew questions at this stage are ideas, not solid decisions. The owner always has a say in access and use of the property.

The big location survey is done during the week before the shoot. All department heads go on this survey, and production will need a mini-van or two to drive them all around to see all the possible locations. This survey is to confirm the decisions made during preproduction, and to refresh everyone's memory about what is going to happen on set. If big decisions are changed during this survey, there is much to worry about. Discuss your concerns with the Producer immediately. Big changes at this stage cost lots of money. Can production afford these changes?

PREPARING FOR THE SHOOT

During the location-decision process, the Location Manager needs to arrange for all those permits and permissions and road closures and location contracts and insurances. There will be much to follow up from all the crew meetings and from liaising with the owners of potential locations. Always follow up with the property owners, whether production chooses their location or not. Send a thank-you note to all who you considered but did not use.

There is a generic location release on page 419 that you can use as a starting base for a more detailed location agreement, but remember it is most wise to consult Legal Counsel when finalizing any and all agreements for your production.

The LM also has hired a Location Assistant team to help with the logistical management of the location on the day. He has to inform the neighbors that a film shoot will be happening in the area (see a sample letter on page 420), and will have a Location P.A. deliver the letters by hand to each neighbor.

Location maps must also be completed to attach to the call sheet, including how to find location both in pictures and in words, noting the closest hospital on the map. There is more on creating location maps in Chapter 13.

LOCATION MANAGEMENT DURING THE SHOOT

Briefly, the Location Department ensures the prep team has access to the location to prepare. The Department also makes certain there are signs to the location on the shoot day, prior to the crew's arrival, to aid in their finding the place and where to park. They assist transportation in parking the unit because they know the parking plan. They liaise with the owners and deal with any of their fears or worries. They ensure there are garbage cans and other cleaning materials available for the crew's use so the location is protected. They make sure the lunchroom is set up and ready on time for use. They ensure the place is clean at wrap and looks better than when the crew arrived that morning, and they make certain the wrap team coming in tomorrow has access and also leaves the place looking better than they found it. They may even have to shovel snow off the outdoor set because it was supposed to be spring, and it happened to snow last night. What a team!

BURNED LOCATIONS

Have respect for each location where you film. Never burn a location (leave such a bad feeling with the owners that they will never again rent their property to any film production). You are representing the entire film industry whenever you shoot somewhere. Consider yourself a guest at the location no matter what you are paying to be there, how small your production, or how short the shoot. Be sure the crew that you hire has the same respect toward each location.

Dealing with the logistics on set of all the vehicles, the equipment, the crew, the cast, the owners of the property and the public... it is no wonder that many Location Managers become Production Managers.

We Were So Covered – Or Were We?

We purchased all the right insurance. We reviewed all possible coverages with the Insurance Broker and were sure we were covered for any emergency or accident. We bought coverage...

... if the air conditioning leaked onto the set, causing water damage
... if a tree fell on the studio, causing damage and a power outage
... if a key cast member or the Director happened to die during production
... if someone in the lab turned the light on during negative processing, fogging all the footage
... if our production office was burgled and all the props and office contents were stolen
... if the generator just blew up for no particular reason
... if anything.

We were so covered.

Then an election happened in a foreign country wherein the sure-winner incumbent was defeated by a long shot candidate and the new government immediately cancelled the event wherein our film would be shown. No event. No funding. It was four days before principal photography.

Now, why didn't we anticipate that? I wonder if you can buy foreign-election-that-directly-affects-your-funding insurance...

CHAPTER 17

PRODUCTION INSURANCE

Insurance is something you hope you never have to use — on a film production more than anything. But the longer you are in this business, the chances grow that someday you will exercise one of the policies. This chapter introduces you to the myriad of insurance policies that you need to purchase for a film production, and why.

BUYING PRODUCTION INSURANCE

You buy insurance from a Broker who specializes in the film industry. The Broker will shop around from insurance company to insurance company to get good rates for you. Choose a Broker you trust, who provides you with good service, and whose rates are competitive. Do not be afraid to shop around. You will bring this Broker with you from production to production if you are happy with his service, so choose wisely the first time.

There are four basic policies you need to purchase for a film production: (1&2) Comprehensive General Liability Insurance & Workers' Compensation Insurance, (3) The Entertainment Package (or Production Package), and (4) E&O (Producer's Errors and Omissions) Insurance.

(1&2) COMPREHENSIVE GENERAL LIABILITY INSURANCE & WORKERS' COMPENSATION INSURANCE

Simply put, these policies are used if someone gets injured on the set or if you damage someone's property. They are truly, utterly, essential insurance for any and all film productions. Some Financiers will require a minimum amount for your Comprehensive General Liability coverage (like $2M to $5M). Most locations you shoot at will require minimum coverage, too. The law may require Workers' Compensation Insurance, so that you protect the cast and the crew working on the production against work-related injuries. In some jurisdictions, you may only be able to purchase this insurance through the Workers' Compensation Board itself.

(3) THE ENTERTAINMENT PACKAGE

The Entertainment Package (or Production Package) is a collection of several specific insurance policies that cover you during principal photography. You can negotiate which specific coverages, but as this is the most common collection, you will likely end up purchasing the entire package:

CAST COVERAGE

You need insurance should the critical lead cast (or critical lead crew, like Director) fall ill or be injured by accident during the shoot and you need to suspend production for her recovery. This coverage, you see, is not just for cast as the name may imply. Usually eight to ten cast (or crew) members can be covered. Choose the most important cast, the Director, and maybe also the DP. Should one of these covered people fall so ill as to be unable to finish the film (or die), this coverage kicks in to give you the money to redo the film with someone else. This coverage, therefore, must equal the size of your budget. The deductible is hefty, but if you ever have to use this coverage, it will be worth it. As soon as you call the insurance company with the names of people you wish to be insured, they will be covered under accident coverage immediately. Send each person for a medical (by an insurance-approved doctor) right away, because by forwarding the medical to the insurance company, each person will now fall under full coverage (both accident and illness coverage). The Production Coordinator can arrange for speedy medicals.

FAMILY BEREAVEMENT COVERAGE

Imagine if one of the key cast has a family member die, and you find you have to suspend production for a day to reschedule around the funeral. You need this insurance. It covers the costs associated with that type of interruption. You cannot claim the full budget price.

FAULTY STOCK, CAMERA & PROCESSING

Imagine the light going on in the lab during processing. It can happen. It has happened. Hope it does not happen to you. If the film stock, tape stock, camera equipment, or the processing is faulty, you may need to re-shoot up to the entire film. Again, this coverage needs to be equal to the size of your budget. In order for the coverage to be effective, it is required that the Camera Department shoot, process, and view a camera test using the equipment they will be shooting with during the shoot. You cannot just pick up a camera, shoot with it, and then complain to the insurance company it was not working properly if you have not taken the time and the effort to check it prior to renting.

NEGATIVE FILM/VIDEOTAPE

This coverage works basically in tandem with the Faulty Stock, Camera & Processing coverage, and is more general coverage for problems with the original negative or videotape. Exclusions from this coverage are the reason that Faulty Stock, Camera & Processing coverage was created.

PROPS, SETS, WARDROBE

Be sure this coverage exceeds the entire cost of your props, sets, and wardrobe rentals put together. Some set rentals, props rentals, and wardrobe rentals are so pricey on their own that the company you are renting from will require proof that your insurance coverage is adequate for them to allow the rental. In these cases, you need to call your Broker after the coverage is in place to arrange for a separate, personalized certificate of insurance.

PHYSICAL DAMAGE TO VEHICLES
When you set up a rental vehicle company account, you need to insure all the vehicles you are renting. Using the vehicle rental company's daily or weekly rental rates may be higher than this insurance, which you can arrange separately. Again, you will need to arrange with the Broker for a separate, personalized certificate of insurance for the rental company. With a mere telephone call, you can make these arrangements.

MISCELLANEOUS EQUIPMENT
"Miscellaneous equipment" is all the equipment you are renting, including the camera equipment. You will not be able to rent any camera, grip, electric, and sound equipment without this coverage. Note that office equipment for the production office is not considered "miscellaneous" and shows up on another coverage further down the list.

PROPERTY DAMAGE LIABILITY
When you rent a location or a studio, you may be taking "care, custody and control" of that location or studio. Imagine renting Studio #1. The comprehensive general liability insurance you have already purchased covers damages and injuries to property and people outside the building and in the hallways of the studio space, but inside Studio #1 itself you need this coverage — because the comprehensive general liability is not in effect inside Studio #1, due to your having "care, custody and control" of this space. Every location where you shoot you may be assuming "care, custody and control" of at least a portion of it, so you will need this insurance. Either you call your Broker for each location you contract, or your Broker will set you up with blank "location certificates." Fill out the location name, the address, the owner's name, and the shooting dates to arrange for speedy personalized certificates to prove coverage. Do not forget to send a copy of all the completed certificates to the Broker, along with the owner of the location.

EXTRA EXPENSE
This coverage works in conjunction with other coverages. If the miscellaneous equipment coverage ends up paying for the replacement of a piece of rented equipment, it will not pay for the flight or the ferry ride for the replacement equipment's trip to the set, nor the downtime or the overtime to production waiting for the replacement equipment. Extra expense coverage will take care of these costs.

CIVIL AUTHORITY
This coverage kicks in, for example, when a civil authority declares a hazard in the area or in the building, and you are prevented from filming because of that declaration.

DISRUPTION OF OUTSIDE POWER
This coverage kicks in when there is a disruption of power beyond your location's local control. Imagine the city generator breaking down, creating a power outage that lasts long enough for you to need to re-shoot the day's work. That is one example of when you may trigger this coverage.

MECHANICAL BREAKDOWN
This is another coverage that works in conjunction with other policies, especially the miscellaneous equipment coverage, to ensure full coverage when equipment breaks down.

OFFICE CONTENTS
Office contents could be rented computers, furniture, office televisions, and VCRs. All these are included under this coverage. This is useful to replace equipment when someone breaks into the production office and steals it all, but remember that in a few days all the equipment will be brand new, so the robber may return for a second visit. Such dual robberies are not uncommon. It goes without saying that you will need an office security system to minimize using this coverage, because even a few days without equipment in the office is horrific.

MONEY & SECURITIES
As long as the petty cash in the production office is locked in a safe and the safe is broken into — and you can prove without a doubt how much money was in there — then you can make a claim on this coverage.

ANIMAL MORTALITY
If you are renting animals and one of them happens to die, you will have to pay the rental company (or wrangler) for the value of that animal, plus look for another that looks exactly the same to "re-cast" and re-shoot accordingly. Use this coverage to ease the financial burden. Note, though, that this coverage does not cover your mistreatment or negligent use of any animals. It is even possible to include a particular animal on your cast coverage if the animal is very difficult to replace.

STUNTS, SPECIAL EFFECTS & OTHER COVERAGES
Discuss with your Broker other coverages that you may need or are available for your production. You can basically dream up anything else that could cost you money if it goes wrong, and you can buy insurance for it. The world of insurance is wide open.

(4) E & O INSURANCE (PRODUCER'S ERRORS & OMISSIONS INSURANCE)

The above three policies get you through production, but you will likely need limited E&O insurance during production, and definitely need a complete E&O policy prior to releasing or airing the completed project. Your exposure to the risks of E&O increases as you exhibit the production to a wide audience.

We all know of lawsuits when someone sues a Producer or a Writer, saying that the Producer or the Writer stole his idea. This is a job for E&O Insurance. Errors & Omissions Insurance, once you have the coverage in place, says that you — the Producer — have done all the research necessary to prove that this idea was original (or purchased rightfully from the Creator), that these fictional locations as portrayed onscreen truly do not exist, that the fictional character names are indeed fictional, that the music you hear on the soundtrack is original or courtesy of written permissions, and so on… but there is a chance the Producer made an error or an omission during all that research, and one of the legally "clear" items is not actually clear at all. E&O Insurance is a kind of "Producer malpractice" insurance.

Now you cannot fail to do all the research and then get E&O insurance to protect yourself against lawsuits. No one sells "Stupidity" insurance. You have to do the research and the preparation in order to qualify to buy E&O coverage. You have to buy all the necessary music rights. Also, for example, you have to research to be sure there is not an actual dentist called John Smith in the "script" city — because your production depicts the murderer as a dentist called John Smith from a particular city, and this inclusion alone insinuates that the real John Smith is a murderer and you are labeling him so, whether you intend to or not. The real John Smith probably will not like your portrayal of him on film, and you will have to do a name change on the character. Be sure to acquire all the written permissions for all the product names you show onscreen, or "greek" all the product names so that no one can read them. All this work makes sure your film is clear. Once clear, then you will qualify to buy E&O insurance. There are research companies to help you with all this research work (see Chapter 32), but you will also need a professional team in the Art Department to be mindful of "clear" and "not clear" logos all over the screen before the images are committed to a shot.

Why you do all the research and work and then buy the E&O policy is because no Broadcaster wants to air your show and no Festival wants to show your film and no Distributor wants to sell your film without legal proof that it is clear. If they do distribute or exhibit your film, and you do have questionable or unresearched legal clearance issues in it, not only you, but the Broadcaster, the Festival, and/or the Distributor can also be sued. People looking to sue in these cases are looking for companies with money, and they usually end up suing several people and companies at the same time to maximize the possibility of a settlement. You may be a poor Producer, but the rich Broadcaster or Distributor will also be a target. So do not think that because you have little to no money that you are above being sued and therefore do not need to do the research of a Producer with more money. In this case, you will have a hard time trying to sell your film without E&O coverage. Most companies who participate in the distribution of your film will need to be added as an Additional Insured on your policy to further secure their coverage.

During production you will have done some of the research, like script clearances, but not all of the research — because the music has not yet been added in postproduction, and filming is not yet complete, so logos showing up onscreen in the final cut are still uncertain. You can still buy the E&O policy during production. It will be a policy with exclusions (especially exclusions for music rights), and some Financiers may require such a limited policy in place during the shoot. Once the production is completed and just before delivery, the policy can be amended to remove the exclusions when you supply the rest of the research to your Legal Counsel, who will report to your insurance company. Don't be shy about talking to Legal Counsel about clearance issues.

CORPORATE POLICIES

If a company is planning to shoot several productions within the year, it may be cheaper to insure the parent company rather than buy separate policies for each production. Your Insurance Broker will be more than happy to discuss insuring several or future projects for you or the parent company.

ADDITIONAL INSUREDS

The production company is not the only one at risk in the making of a film. As mentioned, when it comes to lawsuits, "they" always look for the entity with money to sue, and "they" often end up suing several people or companies at the same time. If George Lucas is your Executive Producer, you can bet anyone suing you will also be suing your Executive Producer. Therefore, all the Financiers, Distributors, Broadcasters, Executives, and their personal companies, and the Director and his personal company will ask to be named as Additional Insureds on the production and E&O policies. These people and companies need assurance that if you are sued along with them, it is not their own private insurance policy that takes effect, but the production policies that you bought for this particular film. Certain locations owned by large companies and other big suppliers may also ask to be added as an Additional Insured to the entire policy. The Broker and the insurance company will expect this process, so you will find there is no extra charge to create these certificates.

INSURING MICRO-LOW-BUDGET SHOOTS

Micro-budget films cannot afford a full insurance package. If you only have $40,000 cash to get your film in the can (shot and processed), paying for a full insurance package will ensure you will not have enough money to make the film at all. What will you really need?

Equipment Insurance: You will need insurance on the equipment you are borrowing instead of renting, because at the micro-budget range, you cannot afford to replace any of the equipment. Find out the current replacement value for even one of your studio lights.

The cost is huge. No equipment house will let you borrow equipment, even on a favor, without insurance coverage.

Liability Insurance & Workers' Compensation: In case someone sues you, or in case an injury happens on set and someone sues you, you cannot afford to be without these coverages.

E&O Insurance: Do all your research to ensure a clear film, and get E&O insurance so that you can sell, distribute, and showcase your film after it is completed. This is an industry. You are not making films only to show to your friends in your basement.

INSURANCE CLAIMS

Hoping you never have an insurance claim will not help you prepare if you do have one. Insurance policies are for when something is out of your control; you may have to file a claim some day. When that day comes: Be honest, be clear, and be organized.

RESEARCH IT AND ACT ON IT
When an event that causes a possible insurance claim happens, the first thing you need to do is research it with the Producer and whoever else is required for the particular event. How much damage is caused? What is the nature of the damage? What will it take to repair the damage? When can you reschedule? Can you shoot around some of the damage? Set must continue working at the fast pace of principal photography, and you will find that you have to put into effect the repair plan long before the insurance claim is completed, and likely even before the insurance filing is completed. Research, decide on a course of action, and set it into motion. You have to finish the film.

REPORT IT
Report the "accident" to the Insurance Broker as soon as possible — even if you are not sure if this will be a true insurance claim. Soon the insurance company will need a full report of the accident event and damage. You are already completing production reports daily. The DPR notes need to summarize the accident concisely. Get supplementary written reports from all people related to the accident. The insurance company will need these, too. The insurance company needs to do research on the entire incident. The more you prevent information from getting to them, the more time they will take to conduct their research.

COST IT OUT
You need to account immediately what the costs were associated with the accident. How much will it take to repair the damage? Have you already rescheduled the lost day? The insurance company will analyze what the day cost that you lost, and give you that monetary amount to redo the day. They will not replace a lost cheap day with the cost of a new expensive day. You have to prove beyond a shadow of a doubt how much

money you lost with the incident. You will probably have to assign a person to be responsible for the accounting. Be sure the accounting report is clear to read and understand. Some people think they are being smart by padding an insurance claim by 60%, expecting to come out ahead after the insurance company slaps on a "standard" deduction. Well, insurance companies will only discount questionable or unproven costs; if they discover you have padded the insurance claim budget, they will (rightfully) treat you with much less respect, and you may find your insurance claim takes an extraordinary amount of time to be evaluated (as they evaluate which costs may indeed be fraudulent). It pays to be accurate and honest.

The deductible you pay to the insurance company will automatically reduce the contingency in the budget, of course. When you have estimated the cost of the claim, you can create a new line in the cost report, near the insurance line, to track the monies due from the insurance company to pay for the overages associated with the claim.

SUMMARIZE IT
Put together a package for the insurance company of all the documentation it needs, including the production reports, the call sheets, and a summary of costs related to the accident. The adjuster will have a list of documentation she needs to review, so include this information in an easy-to-read package to help speed up her review of your file.

CASH FLOW IT
Insurance companies will work as fast as they can, but they have a different set of work hours than those on a film set. Insurance claims take time. The larger the claim, the more due diligence the insurance company has to undertake during its research. You will have to cash flow all the overages (front the money) associated with the accident out of production. Meet with the Accountant and the Producer to discuss a strategy for cash flowing production through the insurance claim wait. The insurance deductible will be deducted off the amount the insurance company pays you on settlement, so at least you do not have to write a check!

FOLLOW UP ON IT
It is essential you follow up with the insurance company. You are working for a production company that has an end date or a wrap date close in sight. Insurance companies have no contractual end dates, so their linear working priorities differ from yours dramatically. You have to keep the claim alive to see it to resolution as soon as possible.

You are now insured. You are now covered. The myriad of policies is not such a mystery to you anymore. All you need to do now is hope you never have to use any of them. Still, you can rest at night, because you are prepared if you have to make a claim.

The Guy from the Bond

There was a day when the crew was most tired, and the indecision between the key creative personnel was most high. Shooting inched along and there was no end in sight. This was the day that would not end. This was the day the Guy From The Bond came to set. It was a fateful day.

We all knew that Bonders only really visit a set when there is a serious problem. He must be questioning if the production was going over-budget or may not be finished on time. Still, we put aside our initial worries and said to ourselves he must have been in the neighborhood and just dropped by for a visit. So what if the set was a mere 4-hour drive from the Bonder's office.

But then he came back the next day. That is when the worry really set it. You have to give credit to the whole crew, though. We bonded together in worry, and worry we did. Nerves were taut. Tension was thick in the air. I mean we knew all about the Guys From The Bond. They were wicked, evil people, who take over film productions and fire everyone from the Producer on down whenever they feel like it. They would fire you if you so much as blinked in their presence. They ate ground glass for breakfast, and they pulled wings off butterflies for pleasure. They were certainly not anyone you dare cross.

This Guy From The Bond had to be particularly evil because he wore the guise of a nice guy. He smiled all the time. He hung out and chatted with crew. He was friendly. He had good jokes and a great sense of humor. But we were not taken in. He had to be evil. We knew he was the Guy From The Bond and we knew why he was here. But, who would be first to go?

Daily he showed up on set. Nerves stayed as tight as bowstrings. Sweated brows were rampant, with the key creative personnel leading the sweating contest. Still, we kept on shooting and waiting for the Guy From The Bond's move. He kept on hanging out with us and telling us stories of his days on set when he was in production. Days turned into weeks. The last day of shooting was coming ever closer.

Within sight of the end of production it finally happened.

One of the crew whispered to another, "You know, I think that Guy From The Bond really is a nice guy." There was a pause. A thought. Another whisper. And another. Word started to go around. This Guy From The Bond was not here to fire an entire crew. He was here to lend his production expertise to the key creative personnel to make sure the film would be finished on time. He used to work in production. We knew all his stories. Maybe we should give him a chance.

The Guy From The Bond stayed with us to the end of shooting, and we said our goodbyes to him as if he were part of the crew just like us, which in a way he was. His presence alone was the pressure that made the key creative personnel decisive enough to finish the film on time. And we were saved from the production that would never end. What a nice guy!

208

CHAPTER 18

COMPLETION BONDS

Financiers, Distributors, and Broadcasters have given you lots of money to make your film through equity investments, advances, or presales. But they are not in the business of funding production companies for the fun of funding production companies. They are buying into a finished film product, even though prior to delivery of the film, the "product" does not even exist yet. This situation makes their investment hugely risky; therefore they will want insurance that you are indeed going to finish the film, so they will have a product to distribute and sell to make their investment back and put them into profit. You need "completion insurance." This type of insurance is very specialized and is called a "completion bond" or a "completion guarantee."

Now, there are a ton of things that can go wrong from preproduction to post and prevent you from finishing the film. You cannot just go back to the Financiers and say, "Sorry, we didn't do it." If you do not finish the film, the Financiers will want all their money back, and no doubt you will have spent a fair chunk of it prior to abandoning the project. Completion Guarantors (or Bonders) promise the investors that there will be a finished film on delivery, and that the project will not go over budget. If the Producer cannot finish the film, the Bonder will step in, take over the production from the Producer, and finish it. There will be a finished film on delivery. This assurance is a lot of comfort to Financiers.

WHEN YOU NEED (OR MIGHT NOT NEED) A BOND

Your Financiers will tell you if you need a bond. It will be a requirement noted in their investment agreements.

Micro-budget films rarely have completion bonds because realistically they cannot afford to buy one, and the budget on a micro-budget film is bound to be so low that the Bonder would look at the budget and say, "Heck, we could never finish the film for that little money!"

And, of course, if you are personally funding most of the money yourself, then you do not need any insurance to assure yourself you will finish the project. It is in your best interest to finish it.

Studios rarely have bonds, because if the show is going over budget, they have the buying power to raise the budget and flow extra money to production to finish it — therefore never going over budget at all. Raising the budget is not an automatic reaction, of course. The studio will have to consider if raising the budget will allow them to recoup the original budget plus the overage when the show is in distribution.

WHO DEALS WITH OR READS A BOND

The Producer will primarily deal with the details of reading the drafts and acquiring the bond, but the Production Manager will end up involved to a point too — as money transactions are critical to the bond coming into place, and some documentation needs signatures that you and the Production Coordinator can arrange. Some Production Managers will be more involved in arranging for the bond due to their experience dealing with the bonding company. In any case, it is good to read the bond and understand its demands and requirements.

HOW MUCH PAPER MAKES UP A BOND?

A completion bond is made up of a veritable ton of legal paper, because the promise the Bonders are giving to the investors is hugely complex. Various bonding companies differ on the actual documents, but here is a guide to the stacks of paper and what the range of documents means. (Some documentation you will need to ensure is, or assist in its being, signed.)

VARIOUS REFERENCE DOCUMENTATION

Bonders need a full and ongoing picture of the production. If they have the ability to take over at any time, they must be kept informed of all facets of the production as it proceeds. You need to furnish them with: incorporation documents, scripts, cost reports, cash flows, production reports, insurance certificate, all financing agreements, interim financing agreement, co-production agreements, Broadcaster agreements, distribution agreements, chain of title, bank account information, cast contracts, key creative crew contracts, key location or studio contracts, prep schedule, shooting schedules, and post schedules. The Coordinator usually keeps the Bonders in the loop of ongoing paperwork, while the Production Manager takes care of the more confidential financing documentation.

THE BOND

The document one can call "The Bond" is an agreement between the Bonder and all the Equity Financiers being insured. It is a thick document that spells out the terms of the bond, how to call in the bond, what specific items the Bonder will deliver for the Financiers to the Distributor and/or the Broadcaster(s) if they have to take over the production, and other details. It is worth reading this document. Each Bonder has a standard template, but each Bonder's is different. To clearly identify the deliverables being promised, the Bonder will mark up the pages that note those deliverables, stating exactly what items are physically being promised in all distribution, broadcasting, and investment agreements. If the agreement says the Producer promised one VHS copy to a certain investor in their agreement, the Bonder will promise that delivery. If the Producer promised an EPK (Electronic Press Kit) — if available — and fifty promotional slides to a Broadcaster in their agreement, the Bonder will promise delivery of the fifty slides. The slides is a firm and specific promise, the EPK is not.

PRODUCER-BONDER AGREEMENT
This agreement spells out the terms of the bond for the Producer's perspective, what is expected of the Producer, the cost of the bond, and what happens if the Bonder takes over.

PRODUCER CONTROL LETTER OR OBLIGATION LETTER
This letter basically gives control of the production from the Producer to the Bonder "right now." The Producer signs this letter, and the Bonder files it away and only produces it again on the day the Bonder walks in to take over the production from the Producer.

BANK-BOND AGREEMENT
Presuming the Bank is also the Interim Financier on the production — and therefore loaning the production money to meet its cash flow needs — the Bank and the Bonder have an agreement that spells out the terms of access to money, taking the interim financing agreement into consideration. The Bank, the Producer, and the Bonder also sign this agreement.

BANK LETTER
The Bank, the Producer, and the Bonder sign this letter. It grants the Bonder access to the production bank account and all the production funds in it in order to complete the film.

LAB ACCESS LETTER
The production lab or transfer facility, the Producer, and the Bonder sign this agreement giving the Bonder access to the negative of the film at the lab in order to complete the film for the Financiers. The Producer retains ownership of the negative, but grants the Bonder access to the negative, just as with distribution agreements. The Producer should never give up ownership of the negative.

DIRECTOR LETTER
The Director of the production has to sign a letter confirming that she believes that this production can be produced with the budget and the shooting schedule provided.

FIRST A.D. LETTER
Depending on the bond, the First A.D. may also be required to sign a letter confirming that the shooting schedule is adequate for this film to be completed on time.

If the Director or the First A.D. does not want to sign this letter, you have a problem. Do they really believe there is not enough time or money to complete this project? It is best you know their options now. Make changes to the schedule or the budget, or replace the crew with people who believe there is enough time and money to complete the project. You cannot afford to start making a film with key crew members already planning to shoot over budget and add extras days to the shooting schedule prior to your shooting the first frame of film.

WHAT IS THE STRIKE PRICE?

No Bonder will take over the production until the "strike price" is met. But what exactly is a strike price? The strike price is calculated as the entire budget minus all deferrals. The Bonder is an insurance company. They do not put any money at risk. If they take over production, they have to have all the money of the budget to complete the film, and cannot afford for a Financier to be so upset the Producer is not finishing the film that the Financier decides to stop flowing money to production. The Bonder tallies what monies have been forwarded from the Financiers to the Producer so far, and deducts them from the full budget price, along with any production deferrals. Then they look at the amounts not yet paid by the Financiers. They will take over production (only if needed) when the Financiers have given their entire investment, or the Interim Financier has given the equivalent as an interim loan, to the production bank account. This procedure ensures the Bonder does not have to front any of their own money to complete the production.

REBATE BONDS VS. REGULAR BONDS

Completion bonds can be structured two different ways. Each affects the production's cash flow differently and dramatically. Most Bonders offer both types of bonds.

"Rebate bonds" charge a high fee in preproduction; if the Producer finishes the film on time and on budget, the Bonder gives back a pre-determined rebate on the cost of the bond. Financiers often let the Producer keep this rebate as a bonus for finishing the production on time and on budget, instead of requiring it be considered production revenue and therefore payable to them to recoup their investment. The downside to rebate bonds is that you must have the cash up front to pay for the hefty fee, which strains your cash flow.

"Regular bonds" charge a lower fee up front, but there is no rebate on delivery. This type of bond is easier on the cash flow, as you require less cash in preproduction to pay for it. As the Producer shoots more and more productions on time and on budget, the fee for the regular bond slowly decreases as added incentive for finishing on time and on budget.

If you and the producing team are relatively new, a rebate bond may be your only choice — as you will be a high risk to the Bonder, since your team does not yet have a track record completing productions on your own, on time, and on budget.

WHAT HAPPENS WHEN THE BOND IS CALLED IN

The Equity Financiers that signed "The Bond" are the only ones who can call in the bond. The Producer cannot decide someday that production is going badly and call in the bond himself. The Financiers have to basically lose confidence in the Producer.

Now, Bonders do not want to take over a show. They are insurance people. They do not want to produce movies. They want to collect premiums. But many of them are ex-Production Managers and ex-Production Accountants. They do know a thing or two about making films. They can finish the film for you. They have also been reading your production and cost reports regularly. They are not stupid, and they will recognize when you are in trouble. If you fail to give them timely production and/or cost reports, they will become concerned. Are you hiding something? You could be hiding what you think is only inexperience or a mild case of incompetence. Well, inexperience might muddle through and go over budget and incompetence may not finish the film at all.

Before the Bonder takes over the production, they will visit your set... often. They will be checking out the problems they may have to inherit and strategizing how to fix them. On these visits they will likely put pressure on the weak links of the production to work harder to finish on time and on budget. Remember, though, that when a Bonder comes on board, they are looking to make big changes. They will not be looking to replace the Third Grip, but they will consider what to do with the key creative personnel: the Director, the First A.D., the DP, the Producers. They may even consider changing the Production Manager and the Production Accountant. These are the people that sweat when the Bonder comes to visit the set.

When the takeover happens, the Bonder will most likely restructure quickly. They have already visited the set a number of times, so they have notes on where the weak links are, and they have already planned how to fix those links. Any or all of the First A.D., the Director, the DP, or the Production Manager may be replaced. The Producer is technically already gone because the Bonder has used the Producer Control Letter on the day of the takeover. Rarely will any of the rest of the crew be replaced. The Bonder needs the crew to complete the film. Indeed, the film carries on. The Bonder will pay for anything over budget that is required to finish the film, and finish it they will.

The Producer will have a hard time finding another Bonder to bond his future productions, so will probably have to produce shows small enough to require no bond at all for a few years or so — until trust can be built up again that he can finish projects on time and on budget.

It may not be the end of the world, but needless to say, you do not want your production to be taken over by the Bond. Do what you can to finish the production on time and on budget. As a Production Manager, that is why you have been hired.

THE PM'S RELATIONSHIP WITH THE BOND

Remembering that Bonders are often ex-Production Accountants or ex-Production Managers, and knowing that Producers can and do call them for advice when hiring Production Managers, it behooves you to get to know the Bonder well, and keep them informed. Let the Bonder know what is going on during production. Never, ever lie to them. They will figure it out, and they will remember you for it.

ALTERNATIVES TO A BOND

Some Financiers on smaller productions allow these alternatives to your purchasing a completion bond:

FEES IN ESCROW

If the production is small enough and the budget is modest enough, but the Financier requires some sort of guarantee that the film will be finished, you may be instructed to put a negotiated amount of cash into a separate escrow account at the Bank — until the Financier allows release of these funds on delivery or audit. It works a bit like a trust fund. Fees in escrow may hinder your cash flow, because you need that cash in the bank for real production costs, not for sitting there untouched. When the fees in escrow are released, the good news is that the cash returns to you. If you get into trouble finishing the film, however, the Financiers will direct you.

WITHHELD FEES

If you have a significant trust level with the Financiers, and the production is small enough and the budget is modest enough, you may be instructed to withhold fees in lieu of purchasing a completion bond. Fees that are targeted for being withheld are primarily Producer fees and Corporate Overhead. The Financier will decide on how much of the fees need withholding, and you will need to draft an agreement or a promissory note that these fees will remain unpaid until the Financier directs you to pay them — usually on delivery. Withheld fees are kindest to your cash flow. You do not need to have cash up front to pay for a completion bond or to put into an escrow account. The Producer and head office company, however, have to survive with partially deferred fees until the production is completed and delivered. If the project gets into trouble and is in fear of not being delivered, or of going over budget, the Financiers can instruct the Producer to funnel the withheld fees to production costs instead of to himself and the head office production company. The incentive to finish the project on budget and on time is huge.

Your production has a completion bond, and you have started to set up your relationship with the Bonder, helping with all the paperwork to be signed to complete the bond's requirements. If you are good at managing the budget and bringing in the show on time and on budget — everything from hiring the right team to managing the cash flow — the Bonder will recognize these skills and respect you for them. You will end up with the pride of a job well done, and you may also find that the Bonder has recommended you to be a Production Manager on future shows with other Producers, because it is in the Bonder's best interest for Producers to hire Production Managers like you who bring in productions on time and on budget. If you are good, word will get around. And it will probably start at the Bonder's office.

Coffee vs. Tea

Coffee people are more decisive than tea people, but they do love to complain a lot.

I mean, you can go to craft service and choose from a host of varieties of teas: English breakfast, Earl Grey, Irish breakfast, peppermint, chamomile, orange pekoe, black, raspberry, strawberry-kiwi, rosehip, orange spice… the list goes on and on. Whatever your tea fancy, it can be addressed and you walk away a satisfied tea-drinker.

But, if you want a cup of coffee, you can have coffee. There it is. In the pot. Coffee drinkers do not look for choice. They look for coffee. They rush to it in the morning as if it were a life-giving liquid. And then they complain about it. It tastes awful. But ask them to change brands, and they will have none of it. This is the best coffee on the market. This is their tried and true brand, and they are loyal.

Well, being a tea drinker myself, I decided that choice was what the coffee drinkers needed. I purchase ordered a selection of coffees from the coffee supplier, and scheduled a blind taste test. Four pots, four cups of coffee each. Let the discussion begin.

They were a bit uncomfortable about all the fuss I was making about this coffee thing. They had a tried and true brand, so why fix something that is not broken? But they were all sports and participated… or at least humored me. Besides, one swallow and they became instant coffee connoisseurs.

Coffee number one was hated by all, without question. It was too bitter and left a kind of dusty residue in the mouth. Mixed reviews came in on numbers two and three. There was serious discussion about which was watery and which was overpowering. But number four… number four. Wow! Now that was a coffee. It sang in their mouths. Just enough bite to wake you up. A balanced flavor. Next to more inferior coffees it shone its best. They all decided this one must be their tried and true brand. They regretted all the insulting they inflicted on this coffee daily. This was their coffee and they were sticking to it, for they were loyal coffee drinkers.

I had to tell them. They had been drinking number one for three years.

They switched brands instantly. By the second week, they were complaining about it already.

CHAPTER 19

PETTY CASH & PURCHASE ORDERS

This chapter could be renamed "How to Spend Money." The Production Manager deals with money a lot, to say the very least. Monitoring money is your day-to-day activity while the rest of the crew is busy finding, buying, and making things. How do you keep track of all the crew spending and their spending promises (for a promise of money is the same as money spent)? Well, first of all, they are spending money two simple ways: with cash and with checks. No different from how you spend money at home, just on a much larger scale.

You trust the crew to spend money wisely, but you still have to monitor the outflow according to the budget. You discuss planned purchases with the crew. You approve all purchases they make, whether it be by cash or by check. Cash can be monitored one way: through petty cash. Checks can be monitored three ways: by direct checks, by purchase order, and by check requisition. Here is a look at all four ways that money gets spent.

PETTY CASH

Checks are best for receipt proof for the audit, but sometimes items can only be purchased with cash: calls on pay phones, time on parking meters, spaces in parking lots, and so on. Some purchases require cash because the seller cannot wait for the time it takes for a check to be approved and written. Most stores will take cash or credit, not check, so cash is the way to go for many, many production purchases.

Petty cash is considered first, because — as mentioned earlier — it is far from petty. When floats go out to single crew members totaling four digits, you will realize the weight and the seriousness of petty-cash purchases.

Ensure that the Production Accountant and you generate an "Accounting Procedures" memo to the crew to inform them how to assemble their petty cash correctly. The crew must sign out the petty cash float assigned to them, then provide either cash and/or receipts for the full value of that float later. Crew should submit their petty cash as often as possible, first for them to stay current with a full float, and second for you and the Accountant to stay current on the costs being charged to production. You will grant a lot of trust to crew members by allowing them to spend money through petty cash, but petty cash allows them to do their jobs more easily. Wardrobe, Sets, and Props have the largest petty cash floats.

Once the petty cash report is submitted, you look it over and approve the costs being spent. Do read the reports when approving costs. Be sure they are detailed, itemizing the reason for each cost so that Accounting can code each cost easily to line items in the budget. Audits will review these reports for accuracy later. Do your due diligence now. Also, you may need to find certain receipts later. When you are trying to remember how much a certain prop item cost when you are selling it in wrap or returning it for being faulty, you need this information. Take time to teach the crew early what you expect for completed petty cash reports. It will serve you well later.

Be sure the petty cash report form has space for each receipt to report the date, company name paid to, description of item, amount with and without tax, and accounting budget code space (for Accounting's use only, of course). If you have ever coded a petty cash report and all its various costs to various budget line items, you will start grouping similar receipts, like all parking receipts, for easier coding next time. Petty cash coding is a lot of work.

While you are approving the petty cash reports, you can monitor petty cash spending on the PM-only cost report. Technically, you do not need to monitor the floats gone out to each crew member, but you do need to monitor the costs as they come in and code them to the PM-only cost report; however, crew do not always keep current submitting and reporting the status of their petty cash spends, and late in production you may find a crew member with a huge petty cash report that comes to you unexpectedly — only because he did not do regular (at least weekly) reports. For this reason, you need to at least note the floats and who has them (like tracking spends through purchase orders), then deduct from the float as the actual spends are reported in.

After your approval of the petty cash reports, Accounting will code each single cost on each report to line items on the cost report, then file each report alphabetically by crew member name. This process is another reason why detailed petty cash reports are essential: When looking for a specific receipt, you will have to remember first who paid for the item, so you can look up the report by his last name, then you have to remember approximately when the purchase was made to find the right report. Because of the wide variety of costs on a petty cash report, it is physically impossible to file by subject matter.

Encourage crew members to submit petty cash reports early and often. You and the Accountant need to keep current on the actual costs to production rather than just the outstanding departmental floats.

CHECKS

Checks are great receipt material for the audit. With checks you can monitor each cost separately and accurately. Using purchase orders, you can even monitor money spent by checks long before the invoices come in, and Accounting can put aside funds to cover the purchase orders to pay those bills.

DIRECT CHECKS

Direct checks are checks for bills that happen regularly, but do not have a purchase order or a check requisition as accounting backup proof for that check. This does not mean that accounting backup does not exist for these checks. All checks require backup as proof for the calculation of the expense.

Since payroll happens weekly or bi-weekly, you do not need a purchase order to requisition each payroll check. You know about it, so you can estimate its costs in advance. Accounting just prepares the actual checks when the time sheets come in. Payroll backup consists of both the time sheets and the crew deal memos.

Rent and telephone and other such regular bills are part of the direct checks that Accounting generates which you approve. Note all expenses as you approve them on the PM-only cost report.

Accounting will file each check with its backup (invoice or time sheet) alphabetically by company or crew name. Payroll files are kept separate from the other direct checks as labor costs are such a huge portion of the production's expenses, and you tend to refer to the labor costs separately from the other costs on a production. Separate payroll files from direct checks let you address labor tax issues easily during wrap.

Crew members who do not write purchase orders nor check requisitions may still charge expenses to the production, surprising you and the Accountant with invoices (usually in wrap) for costs without any accounting backup. Insist on at least a check requisition to explain the cost for the audit. If you have set up and informed the crew of a clear Accounting policy requiring purchase orders or check requisitions for purchases, you have the authority to refuse the cost; sometimes, of course, the expense is valid enough that you will have to pay for it anyway and take the surprise hit to the cash flow. In these cases, you will no doubt remember the crew member who regularly does not supply accounting backup to production costs when you are hiring crew for your next production. Film productions spend large sums of money quickly. There will be enough production surprises to deal with monetarily without your having to deal with surprise costs from lazy crew members who do not fill out proper accounting paperwork.

PURCHASE ORDERS (P.O.s)

You do not want everyone to have piles of cash on them to spend at will. You do not want to give blank signed checks to crew members either. Nor do you want to give them a credit card. You need to control costs. You need to approve purchases before they happen. You especially want to approve large purchases and purchases where the supplier will be invoicing production at a later date. With a warning of these invoices-to-come, you and the Accountant can set the money aside to be able to pay them when they do arrive. You want purchase orders.

Both the Production Manager and the Production Coordinator will become involved in issuing purchase orders.

WHAT IS A PURCHASE ORDER?

If invoices just came flying in through the mail and Accounting wrote checks for them all as they happened, the budget would be overspent in a hot second. You need to know about spends before they happen, to ensure you have enough money in the bank account to cover the costs. No invoice should be a surprise. When an invoice arrives in the mail, the Accountant should be able to say: "Oh yeah, that."

A purchase order (when signed by the Production Manager) is a promise that the production will pay the price listed for the goods or the services ordered, even though no invoice has yet been created. Approved purchase order in hand, the Accountant can set aside the money promised and not spend it elsewhere. Treat purchase orders like contracts. Be detailed so that the Accountant can match the purchase order to the invoice when the invoice comes in days, weeks, or months later. The P.O. will form part of the backup to justify the cost in the accounting files.

FILLING OUT PURCHASE ORDERS

Ensure the crew is detailed in filling out the P.O.s. Have crew members include as much information as possible on the P.O. to prevent misunderstanding. Describe the item, the purchase or rental conditions, and the rental period. Mention if tax is or is not included. Note which department is initiating the purchase, and for which episode and/or set it is going to be used. If there is a work order number to refer to, use it. Any and all of this information will help the Accountant match the purchase order to the invoice when it arrives. Do not forget to note today's date. (See samples of P.O.s on pages 422-423.)

WHAT CAN YOU PURCHASE ORDER?

You can purchase order pretty much anything: equipment rentals with a weekly rate, daily equipment rentals, water bottle delivery, props purchases, construction purchases, car rentals, location rentals, and so on. The list is endless. If you can promise to pay someone prior to their invoicing you, and you know (even approximately) what the cost is, you can purchase order it.

PURCHASE ORDER APPROVALS

As the Production Manager approves purchase orders, jot the information down on the PM-only cost report to track spends before they happen. These costs may not be officially spent yet, but they are costs committed and that is as good as money spent.

TRACKING PURCHASE ORDERS: THE P.O. LOG

The Production Coordinator can track the P.O.s as they are written on a P.O. log form. Accounting can supply the Coordinator with a stack of numbered purchase orders and she can chart why each P.O. was used. This log form is terrific for keeping the Accountant and the PM informed of the costs as they happen, and it also doubles as a terrific inventory list for a quick and easy wrap. Log as much of that information as you

220

can on your P.O. log form. (See a sample on page 424.) When you want to refer to a particular purchase or rental later, you will find that your P.O. log is much more efficient than sifting through the stacks and stacks of P.O.s.

SIGNING OUT PURCHASE ORDERS

The Coordinator can have crew members sign out pre-numbered purchase order forms and note who has which numbers on the P.O. log. Now you can track down any blank P.O.s with as much vigor as signed ones. A blank P.O. is pretty much as valuable as a blank check.

WHEN THE PRICE CHANGES

The objective of the purchase order is to prevent the supplier from invoicing at a higher price than what was originally agreed, but sometimes there are extenuating circumstances and price changes. If the Coordinator is tracking the purchase orders, she can find out about these situations before invoicing happens, then distribute a "cancelled" version of the first purchase order, and create a new one with the correct price.

WHO GETS COPIES OF PURCHASE ORDERS

Once signed by the Production Manager, just like a contract, the Coordinator can distribute the P.O. — one copy to the supplier, one or two to Accounting, and one to the Coordinator's files. The P.O. log may be detailed, but you will still need a copy of the original for reference.

EXPLAIN HOW THE PURCHASE ORDER SYSTEM WORKS

The purchase order system is a great system, and it works. Use it no matter how small the production. Set up a policy that you will not pay invoices without a purchase order. Most suppliers will not invoice without a purchase order anyway. They know that crew rarely has the authority to authorize large purchases, and they want to be paid. Purchase orders ensure that the Production Manager has authorized the payment and production must pay when the invoice comes in.

Beyond setting up the policy, take the time to explain to the crew how P.O.s work. You may have to do so a few times, but you will find the effort worth it, and Accounting (and you) will be grateful. You do not want any surprise invoices.

CHECK REQUISITIONS

Sometimes a check needs writing immediately, like a location or a prop deposit, and you had no time to calculate an estimate of the cost prior to its happening. Since a P.O. is used to say "this invoice will be coming, look out for it," then writing a P.O. at the same time that you write the check is pointless. You still need accounting backup to explain the details of the purchase, so in this case you need a check requisition. Check requisitions give you the opportunity to explain why the item needs to be purchased, and give space for the Accountant to code that cost to a line in the cost report before the cancelled check comes back with the bank statement. Check requisitions give the

Production Manager the opportunity to approve checks before they are written, and to note the cost on the PM-only cost report as it is being spent.

With a check requisition system in place, the Accountant will not write any checks without your approval. The crew will learn this procedure quickly.

The Accountant can ensure there is a supply of check requisitions available for the crew to fill out, either on the distribution table or in a wall envelope for easy access. (See a sample check requisition on page 425.)

A WORD ABOUT CREDIT CARDS

You may have noticed that I have not mentioned credit cards as a form of spending production funds. When it comes to credit cards... don't. You may be cornered into using credit cards on the odd occasion to hold a purchase until the check is cut, or to pay for the odd, difficult purchase — but use them only when you absolutely have to. Write a purchase order for each item charged to a credit card and note on the form that the purchase was paid by credit card, so you will not be surprised when the credit card statement comes in. Pay the entire amount on the credit card when the statement comes in. Production cannot afford the interest rates on credit cards.

Some low-budget filmmakers think that cash flowing the production using credit cards is the easiest way of accessing money while they hope for certain financing contracts to come through. Financing using credit cards is a superbly dangerous way of spending money. The interest rate on credit cards far exceeds any bank interim loan interest rate, so this is the most expensive money you can buy — plus the debt of credit cards follows you personally for as many years as it takes to pay it off, with minimum payments structured to keep you in debt forever.

If you use credit cards for holding an item until it can be paid, like for deposits, then I modify "don't" to "beware." Credit cards are dangerous in one's personal finances; in a company they turn corporate finances into personal problems.

The Auditor will be examining the accounting files for backup to all the costs spent on production. A check alone in a file is not enough information to justify a production cost. Now you are aware of several ways of justifying costs, allowing the PM to approve and track costs as they happen. Even the Coordinator delves into the land of Accounting through tracking purchase orders. Together you are beginning to keep on top of the flow of money on a production.

Buy! Sell!

Co-productions have to deal with currency exchange. A few points change in the currency exchange rate can mean hundreds or thousands of dollars in the exchange if you are receiving a large drawdown check.

In the special circumstances of one particular show, I was set up at the bank to "spot trade" the money as we received it. For spot trading, the money is held at the bank in the original currency until you telephone in and say: "Buy!" Though the bank exchange rate changes once a day, the spot rate changes as the market changes... every few minutes. You basically become a smalltime Trader at the market.

Since it was new territory, I leapt in with both feet. I surfed the Web for information to chart the history of the exchange rate. I researched sites that documented the history on a daily, weekly, and yearly basis, and predicted trends. I had a bookmark to the site at the bank to see what the (somewhat) latest spot rate was. I read the newspapers daily: the finance section. I discussed the financial news with Bank Officials and Professional Traders. I bored my co-workers with my own rhetoric about what I thought was happening to the market.

I was playing the market. Me. I was a player. Wow! My dad would have been proud.

Every now and then I would call the bank for the true latest spot rate. How is the rate? Is it up? Is it down? Can I live with it? How long can I play the market before I really need to trade the money? Do I have hours or days? How long can I handle the stress? How do Traders do this every day when no one ever really knows the future? Uh... uh... okay! Sell! I mean, buy! I'll take it! Trade the money!

We did fine on the exchange. I needed a massage and a holiday.

CHAPTER 20

CASH FLOWS

Financiers give you money to make the film. But they never give you all the money up front. Since you have not even started the film, they are basically purchasing a product that does not exist yet. They are purchasing it based on trust that you will do what you say you will do, and the film will end up a fabulous, marketable film. They will, therefore, have a payment schedule for their investment: a drawdown schedule. When you make it to first day of principal photography, you can drawdown part of the investment. When you make it to the end of principal photography, you can drawdown some more. You will have drawdown triggers all the way through production and post, to delivery and beyond. The question is how much are you spending on a weekly basis, and will the timing of monetary inflows match the outflows you will be spending? You need a cash flow.

The Production Accountant can help create a cash flow, or you as the Production Manager may create it.

CREATING A CASH FLOW

To create a cash flow, you will need: (1) the production schedule, (2) a list of all the Financiers and their drawdown schedules — which you can get from the financing contracts or from the Producer, and (3) the locked budget. Since cash flow creation is a lot of work, it makes sense to generate it based only on the locked budget if you can.

Just like a budget, the cash flow itself is made up of the detail pages and the summary page or top sheet. Each budget line is exploded into multiple columns for you to allocate in which week(s) or month(s) each particular cost will be spent. So open up your spreadsheet program, like Excel, because it is time to get started. (A sample of part of a cash flow is on pages 426 & 427 to help visually explain the document.)

CASH FLOW DETAIL

On a spreadsheet, enter the budget down the left side in the first column (or three to ensure you include a column for accounting codes and another one for descriptions of costs). Next, enter the production schedule across the top, a different week for each column during prep, also weekly during production, and monthly during postproduction. Yes, this will be a very big form. You will, by the way, be publishing cost reports along this same pattern: weekly during production and monthly during post.

EVALUATE AND BREAKDOWN EACH LINE
Now for the big work: Regard each budget line item, and break it down to allocate it to the appropriate week(s) or month(s) in the production schedule columns. This process takes a lot of time, but the thought and the effort you put in at this stage will be worth it for a valuable, considered cash flow.

ENTER COSTS WHEN THEY ARE INCURRED
Enter the costs in the time slots in which the costs are incurred. Your cast members may not need to have their checks for week #1 actually cut until fifteen days later, but once they have finished working in week #1, the cost is already incurred. It will be like you have written a purchase order for their check, and you know that purchase-ordered money is as good as spent; therefore, note the cost during week #1 on the cash flow in the column for week #1.

DIVIDE ALL LINES
Divide fringes into the appropriate categories. Divide contingency between production weeks and post weeks at a reasonable balance. Leave nothing unspent by the end.

DEFERRALS
If someone is deferring fees, enter those fees in the last possible column. Producers may defer some of their fees to cover certain financing restrictions. Find out what any deferrals and restrictions are from the Producer.

SPREADSHEET FORMULAS & REVISIONS
If you are good with using Excel formulas, use equations regarding and references to the budget column numbers to enter all the "scheduled" costs on the cash flow. If you can do this, then you will have the ability to modify the budget, and the cash flow will automatically modify itself through the spreadsheet's references. If you do not know how to use equations and references, do not attempt to do so. The extra work copying and typing the numbers yourself will ensure the integrity of the information in the document. Due to the complexity involved with cash flow formulas on spreadsheet programs, it is easy for novices to miscopy formulas and end up with a cash flow that does not add up correctly. Sometimes you may catch the problem, but it is not worth the mistakes you don't catch.

REFUNDABLE DEPOSITS & BONDS
At the bottom of the budget and cash flow, add a few budget lines each totaling "0" and use these lines to add location deposits, union bonds, and refundable tax outlays. These are the costs you will be outlaying early in production but expecting to get back later in postproduction, so in effect their budget total is "0." They do, however, severely affect your cash flow and bank balance. Be ready for these costs.

TOTALS
Now you can total each column of the cash flow detail for each period (week or month) for the entire production, and know how much you are spending when.

CASH FLOW SUMMARY PAGE

The summary page or top sheet summarizes all inflows and compares them to the out-flows. You can create one on a page or two, depending how many columns you have for the spending schedule.

You have already summarized the outflows on the last line of the cash flow detail. Bring those totals forward onto this page.

Make a new line in the left column(s) for each funding source separately. You could have very few financing sources, or you could have upwards of fourteen. It depends on the complexity of your production. Enter the amounts they pay out on the trigger dates in the cash flow in the various production schedule columns. Total them per period (week or month). This procedure summarizes the inflows.

Now you can find out the difference between inflows and outflows. Subtract the inflows from the outflows on a weekly basis, but remember to keep a "running bank balance" as you calculate. If you have a positive or a negative balance remaining after the first period, you must bring this balance forward into your calculations for the next period. You need to do this so you can see if and when your bank balance is predicted to drop below "0." Once you can identify the week with the most negative bank balance, you will know how much money you will need to borrow from a bank or an Interim Financier in order to finance the cash flow of the project.

Leave a line on this summary sheet to include and summarize the inflow and the out-flow of the interim financing loan, so you can see where it needs to drawdown, and when you have to pay it back. (More on interim financing is in Chapter 21.)

CO-PRODUCTION CASH FLOWS

For co-productions, cash flows can be twice the work. You need a separate cash flow for each co-production partner. Of course, once each partner has locked those budget lines that each company will be accounting and reporting, each company will be responsible for its own cash flow.

AMORTIZATION & PATTERN BUDGET CASH FLOWS

As you know, the amort budget will be made up primarily of preproduction, hiatus, and post costs, whereas the pattern budget will be the repetitive episodic costs. You can create a consolidated cash flow including both pattern and amort costs, since for each period during episodic shooting the pattern budget is pretty much already the cash flow itself. This structure makes for relatively easy cash flow detail breakdown. Be sure to note the two different budgets (amort and pattern) in two separate columns on the left of the spreadsheet.

MICRO-BUDGET CASH FLOWS

Even on micro-budget productions, creating a cash flow is worth the effort. How much will you really need in the bank next week? In the land of micro-budgets, you have to be superbly tight with money. Since your budget is smaller (less line items) and your shooting schedule faster (less cash flow columns), creating a cash flow will be less work anyway.

Now you are clear on both when you are going to spend the money and when you are going to receive it. But what are you going to do about that cash flow deficit? Read the next chapter, then call the Bank or the interim lender.

Bankers & Financiers at a Party

We have an image of Bankers and Financiers. They wear business suits to work. They deal with serious matters and are serious people. The parties they frequent are at glorious mansions overlooking the sparkling lights of the city. They attend these parties in their business suits and, holding a glass of fine wine in one hand (they have the knowledge to choose the very best vintage) and a tantalizing hors d'oeuvre in the other, they discuss matters of great importance with the other guests. All is beautiful. All is serene.

I remember one of these parties. The conversation centered around the food, the wine, the weather, and the view out the window. They were all beautiful, and once we had exhausted trading synonyms to describe them, the conversation dwindled. I found everyone surprisingly uncomfortable being there. No one seemed to know what to say to each other. Boy, we needed an icebreaker.

Well, that was until the goat cheese hors d'oeuvres started to burn in the oven...

whose smoke happened to set off the fire alarm in the house...

whose system happened to be patched directly into the fire department for immediate attention...

and whose sound happened to wake the sleeping baby in the bedroom.

It was mayhem.

But somehow it was good. Every member of the party got involved. Some people rescued the now charcoal hors d'oeuvres from the oven. Another (the mother) attended to the screaming baby. Another was on the telephone to try to stop the fire department's imminent arrival. Others ran to open doors and windows for better airflow. And a cluster of Financiers and Bankers grabbed a chair and took makeshift tools to try to dismantle the fire alarm itself, on the ceiling.

It was obvious not one of them knew how it worked. They tried to figure it out over the screams of the baby. What a feat. They had to remove their jackets to allow freer movement of their arms working over their heads. And no matter how many parts they removed of the alarm, it continued with its ear-piercing shriek... or am I thinking of the baby's screams?

Anyway, finally enough parts were removed and pried off with cheese knives, spoons, and penknives. The alarm was silenced. Soon, too, the baby followed suit and was put back to bed.

We all enjoyed the silence for a moment and then it was over. Conversation struck up and flowed freely now. All jackets were off. No one was uncomfortable being there anymore. No more discussion of the food, the wine, the weather, or the view. We had just had one heck of an icebreaker, and the party really started.

No wonder the fire department showed up anyway.

CHAPTER 21

INTERIM FINANCING

You have a cash flow that tells you that the production bank account will be in the negative by the time you make it to the second week of shooting. You will be receiving enough money to pay for the entire budget by the very end, but you need the money now — before the film is completed, delivered, and audited. You need a Bank or lending institution to loan you money to interim finance the cash flow.

The Production Manager and the Producer deal with the details of interim financing, though the Production Coordinator should be aware of how it works, because it is the production office that keeps the Bank informed of the goings-on of production.

WHO ARE INTERIM LENDERS?

Other lending institutions besides banks provide interim financing for film productions, but for simplicity I will call all interim lenders by the term "Bank."

HOW BANKS FINANCE YOUR PRODUCTION

They don't. Banks do not invest in film productions. They do not provide equity. They do not give grants. They do not provide you interest-free advances against future sales of your production. Banks are, however, in the business of lending money. Though they do not finance your production, they do finance your cash flow if you can prove that 100% of the production budget is covered by "bankable" paper. This is why it is probably better to call Banks interim "lenders" instead of interim "financiers."

HOW AN INTERIM LOAN WORKS OR HOW MUCH CAN I BORROW?

Basically, you look at your cash flow and determine in which period (week or month) your bank account balance is at its most negative. When this happens depends widely on your financing sources and their drawdown schedules. For example, you may find that you go into the hole somewhat in the third week in shooting, but you recover a positive bank balance at wrap and go into a deeper hole just prior to the fine cut. You must look at the most negative number. This is the minimum amount you need to borrow. Now look at the list of final drawdowns from your financing sources. These drawdowns will likely be triggered on delivery and/or the completion of the audit of production after delivery. Choose a collection of these drawdowns to accelerate. For example, choose the "paid-on-audit" drawdown from three financing sources. If these Financiers are considered bankable, the Bank will basically buy these drawdowns from you and loan you the money now. Then, when you reach the audit, these three Financiers pay the Bank, not you, the paid-on-audit money. Your interim loan is paid back, and you stop paying interest on the amount loaned.

HOW THE BANK GETS PAID

The Bank will charge you a bank fee, legal fees, and interest for the privilege of your receiving certain drawdowns in advance. When you are determining the size of interim loan you require on the cash flow, be sure that the Bank's many fees are noted in the cash flow when you expect to pay them. The bank fee and the legal fees are paid up front. The interest is, in a sense, paid up front. The Bank will take an "interest reserve" from you and hold it aside so that when the interest is payable on a monthly basis, they already have a pool of your money from which to deduct the interest amount. Remember that Banks are not in the business of risk, and you have not made the film yet, so technically you have no collateral besides cash in the bank. This is why you will have to pay all the interest up front.

WHAT IS "BANKABLE PAPER"?

Banks are not interested in high-risk loans. Even you do not want them to be: When you put your personal money into a savings account at the Bank, you are not looking for a high-risk investment — you want guaranteed interest income. Therefore, when you buy a house and the bank loans you money through a mortgage, you have the value of the house as collateral to borrow against. When you apply for a personal loan, you have to provide at least equivalent collateral to borrow against. During production, the film has not yet been completed, of course, so a film production technically has no collateral to borrow against.

To provide comfort to the Bank that the interim loan is going to be repaid, you need signed agreements from all your Financiers to support 100% of your financing. Gathering these signed agreements is not an easy feat — because they may not all be signed yet. To help, you can find out what issues might be holding up the signed agreements, and determine if draft agreements are acceptable to the Bank to begin the legal paperwork process to speed up the interim-financing close.

Banks will evaluate the financing sources of your production and will consider some Financiers as "bankable." Government agreements of your country will no doubt be bankable. The Bank is confident that the government will forward the money required to repay the interim loan later in the process when the production triggers dictate. Foreign television stations from small countries which this Bank has never dealt with before are not likely to be bankable. If you want any of their drawdowns accelerated, you will have to find another interim lender to take the higher risk, or the production company has to take the interim burden onto itself somehow.

WHAT PAPERWORK MAKES UP AN INTERIM LOAN

Just like the bond, a Bank requires a veritable ton of paper — agreements and other documentation — to close an interim loan. It takes time to assemble all this paperwork, so begin to gather it as soon as you have locked the cash flow and know how much of a loan you require and when. You will likely need the money quickly. The Producer, or an Executive, will probably deal with arranging for all this paperwork, but do be aware of the documentation required and what it means:

INTERIM LOAN & SECURITY AGREEMENT

This is the agreement between the Bank and the Producer. It sets out the terms of the interim loan, including the interest rate, the bank fee, and the legal fees. The "security" part of this agreement is the Producer's promise to pay back the interim loan no matter what.

ASSIGNMENT OF ACCOUNTS RECEIVABLE (OR OF BOOK DEBTS)

This agreement works in conjunction with the Assignment & Directions noted below. As you are basically selling drawdowns from certain financing agreements you have with third parties, the Producer has to assign these "accounts receivable" or third-party payments to the Bank.

COPYRIGHT MORTGAGE

Since there is technically no collateral, as you have not completed the film yet, the Bank will take a mortgage on the copyright of the production — the only thing the Producer owns about the film — as part of the collateral. This mortgage includes a security interest against all the "intellectual property," against all the contractual agreements (with all suppliers, Performers, crew, and so on), and against all the physical elements of the production as they come into being (like the negative and the original sound rolls as they are produced). The bankable signed financing agreements make up the rest of the collateral.

SECURITY AGREEMENT (OF THE PARENT COMPANY)

Since most production companies are single-purpose companies set up and owned 100% by parent companies to produce one film, the production company itself does not own much to use as collateral against the interim loan. The parent company, then, must promise to abide by the terms of the interim-loan agreement alongside the production company, and if the production company cannot pay back the loan, the parent company will, no matter what. Because of this corporate structure, the parent company signs a security agreement with the Bank.

In certain circumstances where there is no parent company, the Bank may require the individual shareholders to put up a personal guarantee in order to give the Bank sufficient collateral against the loan. A personal guarantee could mean that the individual shareholders will have to use their own houses as the additional collateral.

CERTIFICATE OF OFFICERS
This certificate is primarily a statement of facts about the status of the company, and includes a certification that the company is what is says it is, has no suits against it, and will abide by the terms of the interim-loan agreement.

RESOLUTION OF THE DIRECTORS
The Directors of the production company certify in a resolution that they approve the production company's entering into a financial obligation to the Bank.

INCUMBENCY CERTIFICATE
This document is simply a statement of facts about who the Directors and the Officers of the production company are.

LAB PLEDGEHOLDER AGREEMENT
If the interim loan is not paid back, the Bank would have the right to take the "security" that is held against the loan (for example, to take all the elements that make up the film, including the negative and the original sound rolls). Since the production lab has these physical elements in its possession, this agreement is the lab's promise to keep the elements safe for the Bank, and gives the Bank access to the elements at the lab. The lab cannot release these elements to the Producer until the Bank gives permission.

SUBORDINATION OR STEP-BACK LETTERS
The production company or the parent company may have loans still current with other institutions. If so, remember that the Producer, the parent company, and the shareholders have just guaranteed the Bank that this loan will be paid back, no matter what. They may have also promised other Banks that other loans with them will be paid back, no matter what. There may be a conflict. If money is earned on this production, with "no matter what" type of wording, other Banks with other loans may see this money as income due to them. Therefore, a subordination letter is required from the other lending institutions for them to "step-back" from repayment of their loans when monies come in specifically for this production.

ASSIGNMENT & DIRECTION AGREEMENTS (A&Ds)
As mentioned above, for an interim loan you have technically sold some of the Financiers' drawdowns to the Bank to receive the equivalent money up front. But the Financier agreements bind the Financier to write all checks to your production company. The Bank requires an A&D from each Financier in order to be released from addressing the check directly to the production company. You are basically "assigning" certain drawdowns to the Bank, and "directing" the Financier to pay the Bank instead of you. Some Banks prefer to assign all the drawdowns to the Bank, and the Bank will affect all the cash-flow drawdowns to the company. Other Banks will A&D only certain drawdowns.

INTERIM DRAW REQUEST

The Bank does not automatically start sending you money. You have to officially request the loan on paper, accompanied by a cost report. You may arrange with the Bank to have two or three draw requests, so that you are not paying interest on the entire amount starting in the middle of shooting — when you may need only some of the loan now, and the balance of it closer to fine cut. Minimize interest payable if you can.

INTERPARTY AGREEMENT

Interparty agreements generally happen on international co-productions where some of the international Financiers may participate in the interim financing and others may not. To minimize risk, the Bank needs assurance that to complete the film, all sources of financing will indeed pay per the drawdown schedule they are contracted to honor. This is where the interparty agreement comes in. It covers the agreement of terms between the Bank, the Producer, the Co-Producer, and the Financier(s) not participating in the interim financing. It is a complex document that requires all four parties (minimum) involved in the discussions, and all of them have legal fees associated with drafting the agreement. Enough said.

ADD THE BANK TO THE BOND

The Bank must now be added to the Bond. They are considered a Financier of the production even though they are only financing the cash flow, so they need to be added to the Bond to provide them insurance that the project will be completed.

MINIMIZING THE AMOUNT OF THE INTERIM LOAN

The more money you borrow, the less money you have to produce the film. The higher the amount of the interim loan, the more fees and interest you need to pay. There are several ways to minimize the interim-loan costs payable by the production budget.

First, review the cash flow. Are there any costs that can be pushed to later in production?

The Producer may defer some of the Producer fees or corporate overhead to minimize the interim loan required. On the Producer's instruction, move these costs to the end of the cash-flow schedule.

Also, though you may not be able to minimize the loan amount, you may be able to reduce interest payable if you negotiate with the Bank to receive the interim loan in installments, instead of all up front, generating interest on the entire amount immediately.

Another way to minimize interest payable is to ensure the Bank receives timely draw-downs from the Financiers to pay off the loan. To do this, you have to be sure the Financiers receive all their trigger documentation, including up-to-date cost reports, from you, the Production Manager. Do what you can to minimize any waiting.

Sometimes you will use two different interim lenders to make up the amount you need to borrow. With more players involved, the level of complexity increases. Hopefully you will not have to deal with much of this paperwork, but it is essential that you are informed, because interim financing directly affects your day-to-day cash flow.

The Largest Green-Screen Shot

The CGI Company needed a green-screen shot of Extras walking around, to insert them into an animated background to bring that background to life. It was the "sell shot." In this shot, the existence of real people would make the audience believe that the animated background was a real location, even though it depicted a city in space. The shot was only eight seconds long. What a simple shot... no?

The CGI Company told us the directions for camera perspective on the people: about twenty feet back and twenty feet up. We could rent a big studio. We could paint the floor green. No problem. We started the arrangements.

The CGI Company called us again. Hang on.

The perspective would work better if the camera were back about forty feet and up about forty feet, too. Well, that would mean scaffolding. Perhaps we could choose an overcast day for the even lighting, then lay down a huge tarp we could paint green. Wow. That would be a lot more work and a bigger crew, and the weather would add an element of unpredictability. Not good. We started to make arrangements while we continued to think of other ways of achieving the shot.

Then the CGI Company called again. Hang on.

The perspective on the Extras would still be too close. They would prefer if we could get the shot from about seventy-five feet back and about seventy-five feet up or more. Could we do it? Oh yeah. Sure. Snap our fingers. We can do that. We were stumped. Then it came to us... the local dome stadium has a wonderfully flat-lit green outfield... we could rent the dome stadium!

Hang on. Rent the dome stadium for an 8-second shot? Were we crazy?

With the camera up on the higher level for the right perspective, and the perfectly even lighting courtesy of the flip of a switch, and a bunch of A.D.s and a couple of Wardrobe people on the field with walkie-talkies to direct the Extras, it would be perfect and simple!

CHAPTER 22

OFFICIAL & PM-ONLY COST REPORTS

The cash flow predicts the future when it comes to cost spending: When are we going to spend it? The official cost report reports the past: This is what happened last week. The PM-only cost report is all about the present: What is happening today? What may happen tomorrow that will affect my decisions today?

THE OFFICIAL COST REPORT

The official cost report is a valuable reference to many, since it details weekly the actual spending status of the production, including all actual costs to date, costs promised (or purchase ordered), and all estimated costs yet to happen to finish production. Cost reports are key to triggering drawdowns from Financiers. You, as the Production Manager, need to know how to report costs accurately and efficiently to trigger those drawdowns quickly.

THE DOCUMENTS OF AN OFFICIAL COST REPORT

The cost report is actually made up of three documents: (1) the cost report, (2) the trial balance, and (3) the explanation top sheet. Some Financiers may not require the trial balance unless requested, but that is the exception rather than the rule.

THE COST REPORT OR THE OFFICIAL COST REPORT

Always track costs compared to the locked budget allocations. The accounting software package that comes with the payroll company will generate this document; if you do not have a payroll company, you need to know the cost report's structure to generate the document yourself on spreadsheet software, like Excel. Itemize the locked-budget accounting codes and descriptions down the left side, and then add more columns moving across the page to the right to include columns for:

- Costs This Period: This column shows only the actual costs paid this last week or month, depending on the length of the period. This column is useful reference to see what costs have been happening lately on production.

- Costs To Date: This column shows a grand total of all actual spends to date. To start the audit review, many Financiers require this column to reach a minimum spend of 95% of the budget. Once a cost reaches this column (or the Costs This Period column), you cannot change that cost. It is money out of the bank and is spent and coded. You need to do ledger entries for any costs in these columns you happened to have coded to the wrong budget line, in order to create an accounting trail for the Auditor to understand later.

- Purchase Orders: This column also can be called "committed costs" or just "committed." Here you can report all costs promised by purchase order for which checks have not yet been written. As you know if the purchase order is completed, the cost is as good as spent. On the cost report, you can separate out these "promised" costs — since the money has not left your bank yet, and because the check is not written yet, the cost may fluctuate a little; therefore costs in this column may be modified, unlike costs in the actual columns. This is a valuable column for cost tracking, and it is essential you use it. If the Accountant is not taking advantage of this column, you will never have a true picture of what costs are promised and pending. You do not want to be in the dark about purchase-ordered costs.

- Total Costs: This column is the sum of Costs To Date plus Purchase Orders.

- Estimate To Complete: This column may also be called simply "ETC." Here you can note and revise what you expect to spend to complete the film for each budget line item.

- Estimated Final Costs: This column, which may also be called "EFC," is the sum of Total Costs plus ETC.

- Budget: In this column you transpose the locked-budget line items for comparison to the actual costs.

- Variance: This column shows the difference between the Budget and the Estimated Final Costs. Negative numbers (costs over budget) should be shown in brackets, since minus signs are hard to read on a document with this many columns.

See a sample cost report page on page 428.

TRIAL BALANCE

The accounting software of the production will generate this document. A trial balance is a list of the actual bank transactions as entered into the computer ledger. It is not balanced to the bank statement, because the bank statement has not yet arrived in the mail. This is why it is called the "trial" balance. This is a good document for seeing to whom the actual checks are being written. It has more specific information than the cost report, but there is no reference between this document and the budget, and there is no detail regarding what the checks reference. That is why these two documents work together. Since this document can also go to Financiers, consider what the trial balance may say to the Financiers if the last ten checks written are all payable to the head office of the production company.

COST REPORT EXPLANATION MEMO

Always have an explanation memo accompany the cost report. You will no doubt have overages and savings that will generate questions to whoever will read the cost report. You want to minimize their questions to speed up the drawdown process and also keep the Financiers informed. Make a memo of the items that you think might cause concern or raise questions, addressing the reasons for the overages and the savings on the memo's top page. Doing this regularly will generate a lot of comfort in your cost reporting and will serve you well in dealing with the Financiers on this production and throughout your career.

PREPARING THE COST REPORT

The Production Accountant generates the cost report out of the accounting software (like Vista, Cast & Crew, or Axion) from the payroll company, or on spreadsheet software (like Excel). The Accountant will collect information from actual costs and from purchase orders from the accounting files, and will consult with you, the Production Manager, to iron out the amounts for the ETC column.

DESIGN AND PREPARE FOR AUDIT

Remember as you set up for the first cost report, you need to keep in mind that the final cost report is to be audited or reviewed. You must design an accounting report system with the audit in mind. Speak to the planned Auditor in preproduction to discuss your accounting and reporting procedures. Ensure that the Accountant (or you) collects the various information needed for the audit, including copies of all agreements, copies of all DPRs and call sheets, accurate cost reports and explanation pages, list of Financiers, their investment amounts and contact information, citizenship lists, residency lists, plot synopsis, and so on. Make an audit file now to collect this paperwork. Read Chapter 35 for more information on audit preparation.

THE COST REPORT SCHEDULE

Meet with the Production Accountant and the Producer to discuss the cost report schedule. How soon can Accounting output the first-draft cost report, showing all costs from last week, including payroll? The sooner you can generate the first draft, discuss it, hone it, and publish it, the sooner you can keep the Financiers informed of production's progress, and the less they will worry about the production. The faster the cost report, the faster you can address any financial problem you have — because you will *know* how much production is costing, not just estimating how much it is costing.

As a suggested schedule: Perhaps the Accountant can work on the cost report on Monday and publish the first (internal) draft by Tuesday afternoon, when you two meet to review it. On Wednesday morning you, the Accountant, and the Producer meet to discuss the draft, including your input. The Producer may know of places in the estimates-to-complete to be tightened or that need more money allocated to them for further spending. Then the report is finalized and published as "official" by Wednesday afternoon. Set up a schedule and approval system that works for your producing team.

THE COST REPORT & PRODUCER MEETINGS

Meet with the Producer, and also with the Accountant, at least weekly to discuss costs. You will be meeting them anyway to discuss the progress of production.

When you meet with the Producer regarding the cost report, bring questions. You will use notes from these discussions as notes on the explanation sheet that accompanies the cost report. This is also your opportunity to discuss and strategize with the Producer how to keep production functioning on budget — or bring it back on budget. Discuss how to deal with costs that appear to be going out of control. Are you on budget? Are you over? If so, why? Are the circumstances out of the Producer's control? What are they? How can you bring the production back on budget? Can you wrap an hour early today or tomorrow to help? These are questions that may run through the minds of Financiers reading your cost reports. Address the questions and the issues before the Financiers ask you for explanations and your plans to deal with the issues.

Address all over-budget issues immediately. Waiting before acting costs you money that you cannot afford. If you spend money too quickly on production and do not pull back on costs, the crew may get the false sense that you have money to burn and continue to spend accordingly. The crew does not have the budget in their hands and they cannot tell how much there is to spend unless you tell them.

ESTIMATES TO COMPLETE

In the ETC column of the cost report, you will have the chance to re-budget and re-budget as production moves forward. As you adjust the estimates to complete, you will create overages and will have to take equivalent savings in other budget lines to balance the movement and keep the cost-report total matching the locked-budget total. You want to be minimal in moving costs around from line to line, because each movement of budgeted costs will generate overages and savings that will generate questions of "why" by Financiers that you will have to explain. The more movements you have early in production the less confidence there will be in the accuracy or the integrity of the original budget. See more below in "Dealing with Overages & Savings."

CO-PRODUCTION COST REPORTS

If you are creating cost reports for a co-production, you will have to generate three (not two) cost reports: one covers this country's costs; one shows the other country's costs; and one is a consolidated cost report including both country's costs. Because of this situation, you have to report costs in one currency.

The accounting ledger, however, is divided into five accounts; and yes, the complexity is like a five-episode series shooting simultaneously. The accounts will cover separately: (1) country #1 costs that occurred in country #1, (2) country #1 costs that occurred in country #2, (3) country #2 costs that occurred in country #1, (4) country #2 costs that occurred in country #2, and (5) the consolidated costs. You can then use a transfer account on the trial balance to move the costs from country to country for clean audit tracking.

The reason for this complexity is that there is bound to be overlap in the expenses no matter how you try to keep the two Co-Producer's responsibilities and portions of the budget apart. Technically you can "sell actual receipts" from one country to the other. If you have only three of seventy-five crew members being costed to the other country's budget (due to citizenship), you do not want the checks to come directly from the other country, leaving them to calculate the nuances of crew payroll while you have a payroll company taking care of the rest of the crew. You will end up transferring costs on the accounting books and will need to generate the necessary three cost reports using five ledger accounts.

Using this system, each Co-Producer supplies the other with weekly local cost reports to enter into their respective accounting system (unless you can link the systems by a network) to generate the information for both audits. Yes, you will need to do separate audits for each country.

Though this system may seem a bit excessive for cost tracking, it is not. It is essential that you know what the costs of production are at all times.

SERIES (AMORT & PATTERN) COST REPORTS

If you have a thirteen-episode series, you will be creating fourteen cost reports. One will be the amortization (amort) cost report and the rest will be the thirteen episodic cost reports (based on the pattern budget). This system, which began with the budget structure, allows you to compare costs from episode to episode. When you save money on one episode, you can apply it to the overage on another episode. The further you move into production, the more cost reports you have to print weekly to look at the costs. By the time you are shooting episode #10, you have to print out eleven cost reports to review, because no doubt you will be adding a few costs to previous episodes as you go. You will not necessarily have locked out the costs in episode #2, because it is still in postproduction. If you fail to review all the cost reports regularly, you may not notice the few added costs here and there that eat into your projected savings or increase your projected overages that you were planning to address on later episodes. You may be more over budget than you thought you were.

Also note that only when production is over, can you complete and lock out the costs in the amortization cost report and divide its total across the entire series of cost reports. Though the amort cost report details costs from preproduction, it also covers costs for wrap and postproduction, and these costs remain unspent, and therefore unknown, for some time yet.

THE PM-ONLY COST REPORT

The official cost report comes out weekly. As the Production Manager, you need to know how to track cost spending for yourself during production, prior to issuing the weekly official cost report. The day-to-day spending of production will affect your day-to-day decisions and recommendations regarding issues that inevitably come up. You need to consider, and keep updated, pessimistic and optimistic cost estimates to finish production. For this, you need a system like the PM-only cost report.

COLLECTING INFORMATION FOR THE PM-ONLY COST REPORT

How do you collect and remember all the veritable ton of information from set and office that will update the many lines of the cost report for you to have current ETCs? Think simply. You have to write it down somehow. There is no way you can remember ever-changing numbers without writing them down.

Basically you need to track estimated actual costs, and estimated promised or purchase-ordered costs. Exact actual costs and purchase orders are in the domain of the Production Accountant. Of course, this does not mean you can estimate your numbers badly, it means you can allow yourself more leeway regarding accuracy, because your document is not official.

When you make deals, or you learn information at meetings, or you discuss information on set, note cost details on sticky notes like Post-its®. You can later transpose and gather these bits of information onto the PM-only cost report.

If you have to give priority to some costs over others, target the bigger costs. It is likely that payroll is your largest weekly cost. How much did Accounting spend on payroll last week? Make a notation.

Also target questionable areas. Special effects and stunt costs may not happen daily on your production, but when they do happen, they are significant and many circumstances can increase their cost on the day of shooting to get everything right for the camera.

You need to track these. You will know by the end of preproduction which costs are going to be in the questionable category.

Finally, target areas of the cost report that domino into others. The more film stock you buy and use on set will directly increase the size of your processing and printing or transfer costs, and it also dominos to increase the editing time you will require, increasing your edit labor fees and equipment and suite rental costs. It is therefore good to track the cost from inception: at the purchase of film stock.

Now that you have collected information regarding costs and promises, here are a number of ways of tracking them on paper for reference. Samples are on pages 429-432.

THE PM-ONLY COST REPORT #1 – SPREADSHEET FROM ACCOUNTING

If the Production Accountant outputs the official cost report on a spreadsheet form (like Excel), you can nab a copy of this file and put it on your computer for personal manipulation.

Insert a column for PM-Estimated Costs prior to the Total Costs column and include these PM-estimated costs in the totals. It is also wise to insert a line each time you need to explain the estimate or the reality of the cost in the new column for your personal future reference. Do not rely solely on your memory. There are a lot of budget lines to track and a lot of overages and savings!

It is time to start entering all those costs and promises you collected as information until now. For example, you sign a purchase order for the daily rental of a special piece of equipment for $1,000. Note the $1,000 in the PM-Estimated Costs column in the appropriate line of the PM-only cost report. Insert a line below to describe that special piece of equipment. Later in the same week you sign a purchase order for the daily rental for another piece of equipment for $1,000. If you had not made the notation under the line in the PM-only cost report, you may be confused if you had already entered this new piece of equipment — since the cost happens to match. Now you can add the second $1,000 to this line, and insert another line describing the second piece of equipment. Next week review the official cost report to see if these items are now in the Official Purchase Order column. You will not need to track them anymore. The Accountant is tracking them.

The "under line" notations are also good in case you happen to track a cost that the Accountant has already included in the Total Costs. If the notation is there in words, together you will discover the duplication and correct the error.

The beauty of this system is that the PM-only cost report is the same format as the official cost report, so comparing the two documents side by side is incredibly easy. The drawback of this system is that you have to reformat the document each week (or accounting period) to insert the PM-Estimated Costs column and insert costs and explanation lines that did not make it to the official cost report each week.

THE PM-ONLY COST REPORT #2 – SPREADSHEET MADE BY PM

If the Production Accountant does not work on the same spreadsheet program as you do, but you still like the format of the cost report for notations, and you enjoy taking advantage of the computer's ability to calculate on spreadsheet programs, you can still create a working cost report for yourself. No matter the accounting software, the Production Accountant will likely be able to output a copy of the official cost report to an overall spreadsheet program (like Excel). This procedure will help you get started. The columns you will need to create and/or save are:

- Total (Actual) Costs: Transpose or computer-translate these totals from the latest official cost report.

- PM-Estimated Costs: You will be inserting costs and cost promises in this column, and looking to see these costs are included on the next official cost report.

- ETC: Transpose or computer-translate these totals from the latest official cost report. You will be manipulating these costs, too, taking into account the PM-estimates of the future.

- Estimated Final Costs: The column should have formulas in it to add the Total Costs to the PM-Estimated Costs and the ETC Costs.

- Budget: Again, this column can be transposed from the official cost report, and since it remains unchanged, you only need do this once.

- Variance: Ensure this column is the spreadsheet formula showing the difference between the Budget and the Estimated Final Costs.

You enter costs and cost promises the same way as in the previous spreadsheet system. Insert the PM-Estimated Costs totals on the line to be included in the final calculations, and then insert lines to make explanation notations for the costs you have mentioned.

You can modify this working document to add all the labor costs into one line, if you would like, and if the budget line items permit by their structure, but this is not advisable. The further you modify this document from the original format of the official cost report and all its specific lines, the more you will have to double-check your calculations for errors. You will need to refer to the official cost report alongside the PM-only cost report for the most accuracy. Also, by looking at generalities (like all the payroll on one line) you will lose the specifics of where in the payroll you are going over and need to pull back.

Each week (or period) you will need to update the Total Costs and ETC costs from the official report. Once you create the document, you will be adding lines to the PM-only cost report, so you will no longer be able to insert sections of the official cost report by computer. You will have to enter the updated numbers manually. Still, it is good to become fully familiar with the lines of the cost report. Just as you expect the First A.D., for example, to know the script and the schedule inside and out, you are expected to know the costs of the budget inside and out. It takes working with these numbers and the constantly changing cost report over and over again to assimilate this information. The time you put in will be well spent.

The beauty of this system is that you spend enough time on this document to become fluent with its contents. The drawback is that it does take a good amount of time to keep this document updated and current.

THE PM-ONLY COST REPORT #3 – BUDGET FORM

If you are more comfortable working with and manipulating budget software than you are spreadsheet software, you can create a PM-only cost report in the budget program. Instead of creating a column for the PM-estimates, you add new PM cost estimates only for projected overages and negative estimates for projected savings in each appropriate detail line of the budget.

This is a good system for tracking crew overtime. If the Production Accountant, for example, tells you how much overtime was spent on each crew member this week — or you estimate the costs from the production reports if it is critical you know sooner than by the end of the week — you can add the estimated overages for each crew member in their labor lines in the budget, noting the extra cost was for "overtime week #1," or whatever week it is. Then you can use the subgroup feature of the budgeting program to associate all the labor overtime costs to one subgroup for each week. This way you can see the total of all crew overtime spent in each single week and predict overtime for the following week, or decide how much overtime needs to be cut back to return to budget.

The beauty of this system is that the cost estimates remain on the budget program, a program with which you are most likely familiar, and you can use the features of the budget program to group cost overages to aid in your predictions for future cost spending. The downside of this system is that the budget format does not match the cost report format, so it may be difficult for you to compare the two very different documents to check the integrity of the overage and savings projections.

THE PM-ONLY COST REPORT #4 – PENCIL COPY

Okay, if you are bad working on computers or you particularly like the portability and erasability of a pencil, this system may work for you. With this system you work on a photocopy of the official cost report, penciling overage and savings estimates and notations in any space available around the lists of numbers.

247

Though you can always see what actual costs have been spent, this system does not allow you to accurately predict the costs that are remaining (especially high-budget costs like labor). It is therefore wise to set up a spreadsheet file alongside this system to detail and total labor costs, hours, and overtime. Show each week's overtime costs in a separate column for more detailed analysis.

You need to transpose all your notes weekly from the old cost report to the new official cost report. While doing so, question each notation. Is the rotation still valid, or is it addressed by the new cost report? Through the transposing, the information of the cost report will be reinforced, and you will be reminded of how much — or how little — money is left in each category. You will stay current.

The beauty of this system is that your notations regarding costs are easy to add to and erase from the exact document that the Production Accountant uses, so document comparison and updating is the fastest. The downside to this system is that you still need some sort of spreadsheet file to track costs like labor costs and overtime, forcing you to have two documents to update instead of one. Also, all calculations have to be done manually, and if the official cost report prints out in tiny print, you will have to write in very small letters to add all the information you need to add.

RECORDING PETTY CASH FLOATS ON THE PM-ONLY COST REPORT

Crew often receive petty cash floats, then later return receipts equivalent to the float, and ask for more money to top up their float or return the unused portion of it. You never know how much they have actually spent until they submit their petty cash reports. That is why you want them to submit reports often. If the Production Accountant is noting the floats on the purchase order column of the official cost report, you do not need to track these costs. If the Accountant is not tracking floats here, you can note the float that has gone out to crew members on the PM-only cost report on an appropriate line where you expect most of the receipts to be allocated. When the petty cash reports come in for approval, you can change the notation to report expenses instead of a petty cash float to that crew member. If the float is reimbursed, then you have to note a new line of a refreshed petty cash float to that person, too.

ESTIMATING THE FUTURE WITH THE PM-ONLY COST REPORT

As you can see, with the PM estimates and the adjustments you make to the ETC predictions, you are basically re-budgeting the production over and over again, becoming more and more precise as the costs move from predictions to actuals. Accountants report what actually happened. You need to consider and estimate what might happen for the remainder of the shoot in order to arrive at the end of production on budget. Remember that the PM-only cost report is not an official document. It is only an estimate of what might happen. Since the future is not written yet, you can estimate it either pessimistically or optimistically. Realistically, you need a balance between the two. You have to have some pessimistic projections so that when some things go wrong, you will have the money somewhere in the budget to cover the unexpected, but you do not want to be too pessimistic and end up with a surplus that never makes it to the screen. Use the PM-only cost report to help you keep track of the ever-flowing costs and promises. Keeping on top of the costs as soon as they happen is the only way to look forward.

MANAGING CASH FLOW THROUGH PRODUCTION

What happens when the costs come in, but faster than the anticipated drawdowns and interim-financing inflows to cover them? You are presented with the dilemma of who to pay first in your stack of accounts payable, and who might be able to wait a bit longer before you pay them.

Payroll can never wait and will always be your first priority. Never let the crew know there is a cash-flow problem. Pay payroll. The "problem" is likely a slow drawdown or two that is payable to you now anyway. It is not like you will not be receiving the money, it is only a question of when. The crew, though, has no other means of support other than their paychecks. They have worked for you. You now owe them the money. Period. You never want your company to be known for not paying crew. This label is hard, if ever, to erase, and may even prevent you from hiring crew on all productions in the future.

If cash flow is critical, calculate how critical. Some suppliers may help you at these times. Many of them have given you thirty days to pay their bills anyway. Discuss realistic payment terms with them, and keep them updated if they are helping you through a cash-flow crunch. And though this advice may sound obvious, never promise the same money inflows to several suppliers.

DEALING WITH OVERAGES & SAVINGS

When you were budgeting in the first place, you wanted to be sure there was some "room to breathe" in the budget. Of course, there is a contingency, but you could not predict with exact accuracy every cost yet to come; some of your specific line-item estimates were optimistic and some had to be pessimistic to create a working balance. As mentioned, the closer to end of production, the closer you move to actual costs from estimates. Though you will want to preserve some of these pessimistic predictions, you have to let go of more and more of them every week, or you will end up "surprisingly" under budget by the end of shooting. Your margin for estimates narrows weekly as wrap approaches. The line between pessimistic versus optimistic predictions is a fine line to balance.

You are bound to have savings and overages in the cost report. No one can possibly budget a production and be exactly right in cost predictions for each budget line. You will end up having to move savings from one part of the cost report to cover overages elsewhere.

When you have an overage in a category, increase the ETC in the needy category and decrease the ETC in another category somewhere else in the cost report. Never allocate costs directly to the contingency line. Contingency is not a spending category... it is simply a contingency. If you go over budget in a category where you want to take costs from contingency, increase the ETC in the needy category and decrease the ETC in the contingency line.

Every time you move costs, make a notation of what you are moving and why. You may need notes when completing the explanation memo, or when you are moving costs in the future, and forget why you added money to a particular category.

When moving costs, try to move them to and from similar or logical categories. For example, if you expect to go over $5,000 in studio costs, but you expect a significant savings in location rentals, you can take the $5,000 from location rentals to balance. Or, you are expecting to go over $1,500 in construction labor, but the Construction Manager expects at least at $1,500 savings in construction supplies. This movement is also logical.

OVERAGES BEYOND THE CONTINGENCY

They should not be there yet, but if overages are increasing to the point where all the pessimistic predictions you had in the budget are coming true and the contingency is not going to cover them, you and the Producer, and quite possibly the Executives, must address this problem immediately.

Discuss the situation with the Producer and come up with a plan to stop the excess spending as soon as humanly possible. Meet over the official cost report immediately and bring all your PM-only notes. Draft new official cost reports as soon as possible to keep you current on the outflow of money. You have to know how much production is costing in reality. Where is source of the hemorrhaging? Review the production reports. Talk with the First A.D. and the Producer. If you do not stop the spending now, someone else will... and that could involve replacing you. You may have to suggest to the Producer that someone needs to be fired to effect a real reduction in spending. Do not be afraid of advising radical changes. Just reason it out first. You may have to restructure how to shoot the rest of the production. Are you going to combine locations in a quick rewrite to save on a unit move? The Producer may act, or not, on your advice. "Over-contingency" decisions are weighty ones, and you need to do what you can to help the Producer make informed decisions.

If you do go beyond contingency in going over budget, the Producer may decide to ask the Financiers for more money to finish the film, based on extenuating circumstances. Or the Producer may decide to cover the entire overage himself and recoup that over-budget coverage after all the equity investors have made their money back when the project is sold around the world. The Financiers, however, may decide to call in the completion bond to finish the production and remove the Producer from the picture.

Basically, you want to address any potential budget overages before you end up in this position.

Some completion bonds require less than 50% of the contingency spent by 50% through shooting, some require less than 60% of it spent prior to wrap. Even if the Bonder does not commit you to this type of promise in writing, either system is a good guideline. You will need to reserve a good portion of contingency for postproduction.

DEALING WITH SAVINGS

If you are significantly under budget, you want to know as soon as possible, too. If, at the end of production, delivery, and audit, you come in under-budget, the Producer will likely have to pay back to the Financiers all the money that was not spent. Now, who wants to do that? You want to spend the money on the screen. If you expect significant savings, and know enough in advance, you can augment parts of your budget, adding more special effects or publicity or whatever else to make a better film. You may have to inform the Financiers of your request to apply savings in this manner depending on the amount you are expecting, but if you come up with a good case to spend the money making a better film, they are likely to support you. They have, after all, invested in this film and want it to be the best it can be.

Do not wait until the very end and then spend all the savings at once on capital items the head office company may want to keep. This is not spending it on the screen. You must spend production money on valid production costs. Financiers have the right to refuse costs at the audit stage, and the Producer could end up with a bill instead of the final drawdown check.

Some Production Manager's deals let the PM keep any production savings at the end as a bonus. This deal, however, tempts Production Managers to be extraordinarily cheap in order to line their own pockets, so it not a good idea. If you regularly bring in productions on time and on budget, good word will get around, and you will do very well in your management career without these bonuses.

NEW BUDGET LINES

You can add new budget lines to the cost report when costs come in that do not fit into any of the existing categories. The budget column on the cost report will read zero for these new items since they are items that you have not budgeted for at all. If there are a number of newly created budget lines, anyone reading the cost report (including Financiers) will become rightfully concerned. Why did you fail to budget for an entire item such as this? Address newly budgeted items, with reasons why, on the explanation memo that accompanies the official cost report.

NO NEGATIVE ETCs

No cost report should have a negative number in the ETC column... well, unless you are truly expecting a check to come as income for this budget line. Income on an expense line is very, very unlikely. When reviewing the official cost report, ensure the ETC column shows no negatives. Adjust the Estimated Final Costs to consider the overage and bring the ETC line back to zero or to a positive number. If you do not make this correction, you will gain a false sense of being on or under budget when reading the cost report.

RELATED PARTY EXPENSES (RPTs) & LOCKED EXPENSES

The Producer may have had to report a list of related party expenses to the Financiers. These are expenses paid to non-arm's length companies or people: all costs paid to all Producers, to their families, to companies related to the production company and/or head office. Find out if there is such a declaration. If so, these costs will be locked, and you will not be allowed to spend any overages in these categories without that Financier's approval. Obviously you need to know this information at the start of production prior to monitoring even the first cost report.

ABOUT SPECIFIC COST REPORTS

Since cost reports happen at funding-trigger dates during production, there are certain expenses you expect at different times.

END OF PREP/FIRST WEEK OF PRINCIPAL PHOTOGRAPHY COST REPORT

On the first day of shooting, development is officially over. The project is now a film. You have to pay back all the development loans. Since the development loans are paid back on first day of shooting, you must have these costs paid for on the first shooting week's cost report. You will not see these as expenses yet on the last week of preproduction's cost report.

If you have arranged a "check swap" with the funding company (swapping your paid-back development check with the first day of principal photography's drawdown from the same company), you can at least purchase order the development expenses on the cost report until the actual day the swap happens. Since the first day of principal photography drawdown will also be triggered by other deliverables like this cost report and perhaps other documents, you may not receive this money from the Financier exactly on the first day of shooting. For this reason, you can purchase order the development expenses.

During preproduction be sure the Production Accountant acquires from head office, or from the person who has the receipts, complete and "auditable" backup for all the development costs that you have to expense to the cost report this week. The Accountant cannot list expenses on the cost report for which there are no official, valid receipts.

Refer to the cash flow to check how you are doing on costs that you expected to be spent by now. Other costs you should expect to have paid include: bonding fees or fees being held in escrow; story rights; deposits for various departments; bonds for various unions; and checks for any crew due payable on first day, like the Director, and so on.

Since this cost report will trigger a lot of financial drawdowns, ensure it is created quickly and accurately, and is published immediately. You will need the inflow of money, because now that the camera is rolling, you are spending money faster than ever.

COST REPORTS THROUGHOUT PRODUCTION
Review again the section above on managing cash flow through production for addressing cost-report issues.

The first week of principal photography tends to generate a lot of overages, especially overtime. It is often a wake-up call to the producing team. Deal with these circumstances now and bring costs back on line. Consider, first, that you are all new to this set, including this working team, so production often is somewhat slow to get up to speed that first week. Once on set, you may discover that you have scheduled too much to accomplish in this first week, or that the set you hoped for is not quite ready. The crew, too, will get a wake-up call to get on track. Capitalize on the eagerness and the energy of the crew in that first week, but do not burn them out. Excessive, repetitive overtime will tire a crew, causing less energy as the shoot progresses, that less energy showing up in set delays and accidents. You cannot afford this situation.

As production proceeds, you may find that overages begin to generate in categories such as travel, transportation, construction, the various Art Departments, or any others. Valid overages can happen for any number of unforeseeable reasons. Construction overages, for example, can happen because you have budgeted for certain sets, then when you are on location surveys you find the construction team has to do some modifications to make the locations match the sets. Anticipate what you can, and address what becomes excessive.

FIRST-WEEK-OF-WRAP COST REPORT & THE PM'S LAST COST REPORT
As Production Manager, you will be around for a few weeks of wrap, so you will generate more than one cost report after shooting has ended.

Be sure you are leaving contingency for postproduction, too. In the last production cost reports, most of the shooting ETCs should be minimal to cover the invoices expected shortly, or zeroed out because that category is completed. The set crew, for example, no longer comes to work. A few people are here in wrap, but you can leave a little money in their ETCs to cover the final anticipated payroll. As you zero out accounts, you may discover more savings to reallocate. Is there enough money aside for looping during postproduction? Is the publicity budget in need of a few extra dollars? Find logical places to reallocate the little savings you may have left.

You will be handing your final cost report over to the Postproduction Supervisor, and the Production Accountant may be handing the accounting files over to a Postproduction Accountant. Beyond giving them the cost report and the regular explanation memo, you need to give them as much history about the budget and the cost report as you can, especially if you have moved any budget accounts around related to postproduction. For every ETC cost that is not in the postproduction section of the cost report, make a note of explanation for the person or persons to whom you are handing the responsibility. They need to know if and when they can spend any ETC that never receives an invoice in the future. The more detail you supply now, the less chance you will be bothered at home with questions about your unfinished business. You have been hired to track the spending, but you must hand over the cost report responsibly in postproduction.

You have made it through production — tracking the ever-flowing expenses, predicting the future, and then finding out what the future indeed did bring. This chapter has supplied an overview of the accounting issues in which the Production Manager immerses herself, but this does not end the responsibilities of the job. Even though you are not a lawyer, it is time to move onto business affairs issues that involve you.

V.

MORE CONTRACTING ISSUES

Cover yourself with paper. (Get it in writing.)

Paid Holidays

Film shoots often work weekends and holidays to take advantage of location access and traffic patterns. Otherwise, they go on hiatus to avoid holidays. I can't remember the last time I was actually paid for a Christmas holiday. But there is one holiday-type day I do remember.

The Director of the film was thrilled to find out I was a sailor with my own boat. One of the scenes was in front of the water, and he wanted a boat anchored in the background of the shot. He asked me to do the honors.

Sporting a bikini, I went to work with cell phone and walkie-talkie on board and another sailor to give me a hand. We anchored the boat as instructed on the walkie-talkie to create optimal angle of the boat to the camera. Then settled in for a day's relaxation. I didn't know what my orange bikini would look like from shore until the Director's voice came over the walkie: "Uh… Deb, are you wearing anything out there?" I must have looked naked. Oh boy. I quickly came back over the walkie: "Gee, was I supposed to?" And they all laughed. It was obviously not an issue, since the boat would be so far in the background.

So, for the day, I lounged aboard my sailboat, the sun shining, a sailor to bring me drinks and… getting paid. Then I wondered, how does one declare this on a time sheet?

CHAPTER 23

DEAL MEMOS & LONG FORMS

You have delved into the land of accounting many times. Now that you have mastered dealing with purchase orders, cash flows, and cost reports, you will have no problem with various contracts.

CREW DEAL MEMOS

As Production Manager, your mandate is to sign on the crew as soon as you can, to get them working on the production. For the Production Coordinator, one of the active file folders atop your desk is the "Crew Deal Memos" folder; the faster the crew has signed deal memos, the faster you can create an official crew list and know that production is underway.

THE PM MAKES THE DEALS, THE PC TRACKS THEM

The Production Manager talks to the crew one by one to strike a deal with each of them. Making the deal was covered in a previous chapter. Remember to note the deals and revise the PM-only cost report with the actual numbers instead of the budgeted numbers. How do these deals affect the bottom line of the production costs?

The Coordinator can keep track of the deal memos being signed. Ask the PM daily who is on board and needs a deal memo. Not all crew know where to find deal memo forms.

THE START PACK

The deal memo form itself is only one of the documents you will need to have crew members fill out when they start work. There can be quite a number of forms to complete, so the Coordinator can assemble all the appropriate forms and create a start pack. Discuss with the PM and the Accountant which forms you may need to include in the start pack for this production:

- Union or non-union deal memo: Unions will supply their forms on request. See a sample non-union form on page 433.

- Crew I.D. form from payroll company: The payroll company will supply this form; the information may duplicate much of the deal memo information.

- Tax form for employees: This form is for Accounting or the payroll company to calculate the tax to be deducted from each person's paycheck.

- Corporate form in lieu of the tax form for employees: On this form the Corporation promises to be responsible for payment of all applicable taxes.

- Corporate declaration of tax number: If the Corporation has to charge tax to the production company, it must supply a tax number.

- Copy of incorporation certificate: Actually, the Corporation supplies this form, but a notation in the start pack reminding the crew member is useful.

- Citizenship form for tax credit: You may need each crew member to declare his citizenship for tax purposes later. Do it now.

- Dual Citizenship form declaring citizenship for the other country on a co-production: This declaration allows the Producer to later choose to which country's budget this person's pay is allocated.

- Residency form for tax credit: Again, residency forms may be needed for tax purposes later.

- Permittee form: If this crew member is not a member of the union to which you are signatory, you have to ensure she arranges for a permit to work on the production. Since permittees are new to working on union productions, they often forget to fill out this form. Help them to remember. Production will not pay for the permit, but there is often a form to complete to allow production to deduct the permit fee from the crew member's paycheck.

The start pack becomes quite the package of paper, doesn't it? If it is all assembled for completing at once, then you will not have to chase down the entire crew multiple times to have them fill out all the necessary forms during production. You will save yourself loads of time. Do it now.

Also, as you can see, you may need to make at least two different start packs: one for Employees and one for Corporations.

CORPORATIONS vs. EMPLOYEES

As employees, we are all familiar with source deductions. Taxes and pension fees are deducted from our paychecks at source, giving us a net fee on the paycheck. Corporations are not employees and are responsible for source deductions themselves, so they invoice production for the gross fee. Some crew members will come to production

258

as incorporated businesses; some will not, but would like to invoice production instead of joining on as an employee, so they do not have taxes and other source deductions removed from their paycheck at the source.

WHEN THE CREW MEMBER IS A CORPORATION

Since crew members travel from production to production, contract to contract, throughout the year, they are basically freelance and running their own companies. They can incorporate as a business. An official corporation means that the crew member has a company name that ends with Inc., Incorporation, Corp., Corporation, Ltd., Limited, or Unlimited. Accounting will need a copy of the incorporation certificate from the government as proof of the company's existence, and likely will have another form or two to complete. Incorporated, the corporation takes on the responsibility of paying for all applicable taxes and other source deductions (like pension and unemployment insurance, etc.) from the production company.

WHEN THE CREW MEMBER IS AN EMPLOYEE

Employee status means that Accounting will be making source deductions from the crew member's paycheck at the production company. The production company is the crew member's employer. If the crew member is not a corporation, then he is an employee. Obtain plenty of tax forms from the nearest tax office to include in the start pack, as mentioned above. Filled out, these forms tell Accounting which tax category to use for each employee.

WHEN THE CREW MEMBER IS NOT A CORPORATION

In nearly all cases, if crew members are not incorporated, they must be treated like employees. They cannot invoice like companies. Non-payment of taxes is a serious offense to say the least, and the production company will not want to be party to this ploy by paying non-incorporated employees who invoice. The Production Accountant can explain in detail the tax reasons to crew members who insist on being "employees who invoice."

WHEN THE COMPANY IS REGISTERED

The process of incorporation creates a separate legal entity from the employee. It creates a corporation, and there are a lot of legal and accounting requirements to keep a corporation in business. The process of registration and the nominal fee it takes to register a company is not the same. A registered company is still very much legally attached to and part of the employee. For this reason, registered companies must be treated like employees and are subject to source deductions.

LONG FORM AGREEMENTS

Some crew will have long form agreements alongside their union deal memo. These people may include the Director, the DP, the Line Producer, and the Production Manager. Long form agreements spell out many more specific terms of engagement.

The Production Manager should handle drafting all the deal points for Legal Counsel to draft the official, legal document. Remember, though, that each of these people will have to complete a start pack, too, to accompany the long form.

HANDLING SIGNED CREW DEAL MEMOS

Just another reminder: Signed deal memos are confidential. Never forget this fact. Treat them accordingly.

THE PC OR ACCOUNTING TRACKS CREW SIGNING DEAL MEMOS

On some productions the Coordinator tracks the signing of all crew deal memos, on others it is the Accounting Department that does so. Find out and set up a system to ensure all deal memos are completed fully.

Some crew members will forget to sign their deal memos. When they do forget, they somehow think they will be paid on schedule anyway, even though they have supplied production with no personal information about themselves. Go figure. The Coordinator can use a crew list as a top sheet to track whose deal memo you have and whose has yet to be completed. Note that some crew will take their deal memo straight to Accounting, or leave it in the Production Manager's office. Collect them all for the production files, so see that they all get done. Keep copies for your files, signed and unsigned, in case any are lost in the flow from your desk to Production Manager's signature to Accountant's files.

DEAL MEMOS ARE CONFIDENTIAL

Some crew members will not want the Production Coordinator to see their deal memos, even though the Coordinator is in charge of coordinating and distributing them all to the appropriate departments and unions. If so, be patient and get a copy of the deal memo from the Accountant later, if need be.

THE PC DOUBLE-CHECKS DEAL MEMOS ARE COMPLETE

Before you have the Production Manager sign the deal memos, check them over for completeness. Be sure the crew member has actually signed the forms, the rates are noted, and the proper permit papers are attached, if applicable. Some crew may even fill in the wrong union's deal memo form and not notice. Determine a crew rate sheet from the Production Manager and keep one at your desk for easy reference.

SIGN DEAL MEMOS IN BUNCHES

Of course the PM can sign the deal memos one at a time, but it is more time-efficient to have the Coordinator collect several; then you can sign them a bunch at a time at your daily meetings. It is your choice. The Accountant may be waiting desperately for one particular deal memo, so keep her in the loop about which deal memos are ready for signature. In either case, do not leave the signing of deal memos too long. It can be wise to copy the unsigned deal memos to Accounting immediately, and follow up with signed ones later.

WHO GETS COPIES OF DEAL MEMOS

The Coordinator can copy and distribute the signed deal memos. Treat deal memos like any other contract. Send copies to Accounting, the appropriate union, the crew member, and file a copy in the production files. Ask Legal Counsel if he needs a copy. He will probably want a copy of all contracts with selected key crew. When sending the copy to the crew member, place it in an addressed, sealed envelope. As mentioned, signed deal memos are confidential. The crew will appreciate your care.

HOW TO FILE DEAL MEMOS

As production continues, you will be handling numerous deal memos, for even daily crew who work for a single day need one. Highlight the crew member's last name (not the corporation name) and file the memos alphabetically. If anyone ends up with a deal memo in two different departments, you will find both deal memos together in an alphabetical setup. Note on your crew list cover sheet which deal memos are completed. Though the Production Accountant has a set of deal memos, they are being prepared and filed for the audit. The Coordinator's production files will be referred to more often by head office after production is completed, and when all the accounting boxes are sitting in the auditor's office.

TRACKING DAILY CREW

Keep a log of all daily crew, their jobs, and their telephone numbers. You can attach a sheet to the back of your crew list with this information. Copy it for the A.D.s and for the Production Accountant, too. Daily crew work so briefly that they can easily be forgotten in the flow of paper and not be paid. The list of names and telephone numbers will also jog your, the PM's, and the A.D.'s memories of good daily crew for future reference.

WRAP DEAL MEMOS AT THE VERY END

At some time during production you will have all the deal memos of all the main crew, and you will feel comfortable enough to file this desk folder into the cabinet. Do not remove it from your desk so hastily. Production will be hiring dailies right up to and including wrap. Even you will probably be hiring a daily P.A. to help set up the wrap party.

Daily crew will keep you current on signing deal memos long after you thought you had arranged for the last one, but basically you have now contracted the crew and they are working. Cast have their own issues to deal with, so it is time to consider them next.

One Miracle, Please

Set called in a panic. They needed to change call time for a particular actor to two hours earlier. Today. The actor lived out of town and was no longer at home. He was somewhere in the city. I had to find him wherever he was and get him to set immediately. What am I, a miracle worker?

Think, think. Where could he be? I didn't know any of his friends. I didn't know what he likes to do on his time off. How does one go about finding someone who's just visiting a big city? Where was my crystal ball?

I went over any casual conversation I'd had with him. Any conversation I'd overheard him have with someone else. Topics included: acting, script revisions, the schedule, the weather. I needed something more personal. Sitting next to him at lunch one day, he had talked about getting into acting. About his hometown. About a bar where he used to work in his hometown. The bar was part of a chain. It was a long shot.

I got out the white pages. There were eight of these bars in town. Bar number one thought I was absolutely crazy to try to find him this way. I continued anyway. Bar number two thought I was crazy also... but the staff, surprised, actually found him there and brought him to the telephone.

When the actor got on the line, he obviously thought the bar was playing a joke on him. When I confirmed his identity and mine, and why I was calling, he was stunned to the point of near speechlessness. He would go to set immediately.

I hung up the phone, then paged the set to report the news. Then I sat back, a little stunned myself.

CHAPTER 24

CAST CONTRACTS & IMMIGRATION

For the Production Manager, casting primarily happens under the Producer's supervision, not yours. You need to be involved, though, when it comes to what the deal is in all its costly details. You also may be more involved in casting arrangements for the supporting cast and the Extras.

For the Production Coordinator, one of the file folders on your desk is labeled "Cast Contracts." It was a handy file to keep you abreast of the casting status as it happened, but now that contracting is near, you may be the one striking the actual contracts. You will also be involved in immigration issues should the Performer need a permit to come and shoot on your production.

AUDITIONS

The Casting Director and her company usually set up the auditions. Sometimes, however, the job, or part of it, falls to the Coordinator. The Production Coordinator will be more involved in audition arrangements than the Production Manager. But then again, the PM is probably dealing more with locations issues than the Coordinator.

SET UP THE AUDITION SESSION
Arrange for a room or a casting facility, a video camera, a monitor, videotape, and a person to operate the video camera. The Casting Director will supply you a list of attendees, what parts they are reading for, and times they are coming. Copy this schedule for the Director, the Producer, the Casting Director, the Video Operator, the Receptionist, and whoever else is going to be involved with the session. Keep a spare for the production files.

MAKE AUDITION SIDES
Audition sides, like script sides, are selections of the script for reading during the audition. The Casting Director will choose which scenes are for which character. Make copies, marking the character name boldly on the front page for all the appropriate Performers, for all the crew attending the session, and for a few spares. Do not reduce-photocopy audition sides, and be careful in selecting the pages. For example, if a scene starts on a page before the character's lines start, you will likely need to copy the preceding page or two to give the Performer as much information as possible about his character for the audition. Performers rarely get to read the entire script before auditioning. Give them what help you can.

DISTRIBUTE AUDITION SIDES

Once the sides are made, inform the Casting Director. She will arrange for Performers to come into the office to pick them up. Some agents will ask you to fax the sides to their office. Make absolutely sure that you give each Performer the sides for the correct character.

CAST CONTRACTS

You have a copy of the Performers' union agreement. Read it. It may be dry reading, but it is essential that you are familiar with it. Since the Coordinator may be typing up the cast contracts from the deal memos supplied by the Casting Director, it is imperative that you understand the union agreement as well as the Production Manager does. Attend any union/A.D. meeting in preproduction to meet the union representative. Let the Production Manager shepherd the long form agreements or addendum to the cast contracts with Legal Counsel.

DRAFTING THE CAST CONTRACT

The Casting Director will send you a copy of each Performer's deal memo. Draft a pencil copy of the cast contract for each one on a photocopied union contract. Show both the deal memo and the contract to the PM, who can check it for accuracy and approve the deal. The PM can also note the cost of the deal points on the PM-only cost report. The Coordinator then types up the original agreement and arranges for signatures. Be aware that cast contracts incorrectly completed can cost the production unnecessarily large sums of money. Write them up extremely carefully. Double-check your work. Let the PM triple-check it.

STAR LONG FORM CONTRACTS

Star long form contracts are primarily done by lawyers, but sometimes are generated by you or the PM as addendums to the union agreement, with the lawyer just checking them over. Stars are considered Principal Actors by the union, but their rates are naturally above scale rates. Carefully read the deal memo provided by the Casting Director, then be very clear and very simple completing the draft pencil version of the contract. Let the lawyers use legalese. Note on the union form all the information that relates to the A.D.s (like private dressing room provided), to Transportation (like transport to/from set), and to postproduction (one looping session included, VHS copy of show provided). Do not note any fees on this form — detail the fees on the addendum. Addendums assure privacy of information. You can then copy the union form to the A.D.s, showing the promises but not the money, and copy the whole, more confidential contract with addendum, only to those who need to read the whole thing.

NON-UNION CAST CONTRACTS

Most of the advice for completing union cast contracts still applies to non-union cast contracts, but the form will be of your own making. If Legal Counsel does not make the agreement for you, know that there are two separate items that you must buy from the Performer: the Performer's time on the work day, and the right to use the Performer's recorded images and sounds afterward in the distribution of the production. If you do not specifically note that the fee includes the right for you to use the Performer's images and sounds, then, technically, you do not have the right to sell or show the finished film anywhere. Have Legal Counsel review your form before use.

EXTRAS VOUCHERS

General Extras (or "Background Performers"), Special Skills Extras, and Stand-Ins are cast by an Extras Casting Director and fill in extras vouchers on set from the A.D.s as their contracts. Sometimes you will be involved in finding Extras with specific special skills. Make sure the A.D.s have enough vouchers for use on set. If you are working non-union, you must ensure all Extras have signed an extras release form allowing production the permission to use their images and group sounds in the film, so the Producer can show and sell the finished product. (See a sample extras release on page 434, but remember to consult Legal Counsel whenever finalizing agreements such as these.)

ENSURE CORRECT NAME SPELLINGS

Some Assistants in casting offices do not spell Performers' names correctly. Double-check the exact spelling of the Performer's name with each Performer's Agent. Make sure the contract reads correctly. You will be referring to the contract when drafting the credits. Nothing is more embarrassing that misspelling a Performer's name when the world can read it.

LIST OF TALENT AGENTS

The union will have a list of talent agents. Obtain a copy. Cast contracts are almost always "care of" an agency address, telephone number, and fax number. If the cast deal memos do not have complete talent agency information on them, then the list you acquired will help you.

AGENT vs. MANAGER

Some Performers have Talent Agents plus Personal Managers. Talk to both. Find out where their jurisdictions lie. One may be in charge of contracts, the other publicity. When you have a question, find out whom you should speak to first. Inform the PM.

TYPE RATES TWICE

Typing numbers are difficult. You do not have the luxury of spell check. Always type the Performer's rate twice on a contract: once in numbers and once describing the calculation. A daily rate written as: "$800.00 (Scale Plus 50%)" and an hourly rate as: "$75.00 (Scale)" makes your intentions doubly clear, just in case you make a mistake in typing the numbers.

WORK PERMITS
All non-union Performers working on a union production need work permits from the union. New Performers will pay for the permits themselves; established Stars will likely have negotiated for production to pay for them.

CAST CONTRACT SIGNATURES
Either the Production Manager or the Producer signs the cast contracts on behalf of the production company. As PM, decide with the Producer who is going to be signatory. It should be the person who can double-check the accuracy of all the deal points. A signed cast contract that has not been checked for accuracy to the deal points can easily reveal a very expensive or very insulting mistake. Do due diligence.

DISTRIBUTE CAST CONTRACTS
If the union form is 3-part carbon, each copy will note where to be sent: the Performer, the production company Accounting office, and the union office. Make sure that both Legal Counsel and you also get copies. Assistant Directors often ask for copies to keep up with contracted promises. Mask the rates section to keep confidentiality.

PICTURES AND RESUMES
Ask each agent for pictures and resumes for each cast member on production. Publicity, Wardrobe, Hair and Makeup will be appreciative. Post your copies of the photographs in the production office with character names added at the bottom. For Stars, you may need extra copies for autographs. Discuss the Performer's attitude toward autographs with the Agent.

"CHANGE OF DATE(S)" MEMOS
If the dates as listed on the contract change, note the time and the date you spoke with, and got confirmation from, the Agent or the Performer. Draft a memo detailing this confirmation and refer to the contract number (if applicable). Then copy the memo to all the people who get the cast contract. The union agreement specifies how many hours notice is required for various changes and cancellations without penalty. Consider this memo to be a new addendum to the contract. By noting the time and the date you spoke to the person, the memo becomes very useful to Accounting in determining if a Performer has to be paid for the day cancelled or changed. (See a copy of a change of date form on page 435.)

IMMIGRATION & TRAVELING STARS

The Production Coordinator handles the logistics of immigration for cast and crew, since immigration permits can of course apply to both. The Production Manager needs to note and track the costs associated with the immigration process.

ARRANGING FOR AN IMMIGRATION PERMIT

Procedures for bringing a Star across borders follow: (If you are traveling a crew member, adapt the information below.)

INFORM THE IMMIGRATION OFFICE

Warn the immigration office as soon as you know that a non-national worker will be coming to work on the production. Give them the opportunity to be prepared for production to decide on a Performer very shortly before filming begins. Discuss the latest procedures.

COLLECT IMMIGRATION INFORMATION

Collect this information from the Agent, the Performer, or from yourself:

- Complete Legal Name (some Performers have stage names)
- Permanent Home Address
- Home Telephone Number (immigration may/may not need this)
- Agent's Address (for the union work permit)
- Agent's Telephone Number (for the union work permit)
- Date of Birth
- Country of Birth
- Citizenship
- Union Work Permit (to prove union's permission)
- Job Description (character name and film title)
- Arrival Travel Date
- Flight Company, Flight Number, Arrival Time & Air Terminal
- Departure Travel Date *

* Add at least two months onto the departure date in case of emergency. If production shoots an extra day or two and the permit has expired, you will have to take the Performer across the nearest border to arrange and pay for another permit.

PAY FOR THE PERMIT

In some countries, you have to get the Performer to pick up and pay for the permit at the local embassy or consulate. In other countries you can meet the Performer at the airport and pay for the permit on arrival.

MEET PERFORMER AT AIRPORT

Whether the Performer has the permit in hand or not, always have a representative of the production company meet him at the airport. Be there for emergencies, be there for hospitality, and be there for professionalism. Often the Transportation Coordinator or the Star Driver will be that contact person.

MORE ABOUT TRAVELING STARS

While the Coordinator asks questions of the Star for immigration purposes, she can also find out his various preferences. You are probably the first person the Performer will be dealing with on the production, so now is the time to make a good first impression.

RESEARCH PLACES TO STAY

The Production Manager knows how many people will require a hotel for production. Research the places people can stay so you can strike a deal with one hotel to house them all. Does the hotel you choose have both rooms and suites to match all the deals you are making regarding travel and living? Who is paying for the incidental costs, like telephone and in-room movies? Is the stay long enough to warrant renting a furnished apartment instead of a hotel room? Go and see these places, or ensure the Coordinator goes and sees them and photographs them, not unlike a Location Scout. You want to know what the visiting cast or crew is going to experience before you ask them to stay there.

HOTEL ROOM PREFERENCES

The Coordinator can ask the Performer about hotel room preferences. Does the Performer like lots of or little sun exposure? Does he need a pool, fitness facility, or smoking/non-smoking room? Would he like to be in a particular area of town? Know your options before calling and promising the world.

AIRPLANE PREFERENCES

Does the Performer want a bulkhead, aisle, or window seat? Is there a frequent-flyer number to attach to the ticket sale?

FOOD PREFERENCES & ALLERGIES

For Craft Service and Catering, ask about food preferences and allergies. Does the Performer want lots of fresh food or does he have a penchant for dark chocolate? Are there any food allergies?

AUTOGRAPH PREFERENCES

If you have not already discussed how the Performer likes to deal with autographs, discuss his preferences now. You may be asked to store the names of people who wish autographs, so that the Performer can sign them all at once at the end of the shoot.

SEND SCRIPT PACKAGE

As with any cast member, as soon as a Star in on board, send him a script package with all the latest in paperwork from scripts to crew list to cast list. Include a personal letter of welcome, and if he has not traveled to your city before, include some travel information.

MEDICAL

Likely you will need to arrange for the Star to have a medical in his town in order to add him to the production's insurance policy. Arrange for this examination right away. (More on Insurance is in Chapter 17.)

ADR SESSIONS & CONTRACTS

ADR stands for "Additional Dialogue Recording," and is the recording of voices to match picture during postproduction. ADR is also known as Looping. Since ADR usually happens after wrap, you may not have to deal with it, but if you are working on a series, you will.

ARRANGING FOR ADR

The Post Supervisor or the Post Coordinator will handle most of these booking arrangements with assistance from the Production Coordinator. The Production Manager needs to note the appropriate costs involved, as some ADR sessions will be covered by inclusive deals on the cast contract. The Production Coordinator not only needs to check that the paperwork is completed to ensure the Performers will be paid for the session, but also needs to report the session on the DPR.

BOOK & CONTRACT PERFORMERS

The Post Supervisor or the Post Coordinator usually arranges for the ADR studio, while the Production Coordinator arranges for the Performers' attendance. Make sure there is a signed contract for each Performer who is going to be recorded. Performers who have performed on set already have contracts. New voices may be added during postproduction. Generate these voice-only contracts as you would cast contracts. Refer to your union agreement, if applicable.

PERFORMER WORK REPORTS

As the A.D.s fill out work reports daily for the Performers on set to report what hours the talent worked, someone at the ADR session must fill out the form for each session. Send a blank report to the session. You can help by filling in the production company name, title, date, and Performers booked.

MAKE A MEMO ANNOUNCING THE ADR SESSION

Send a memo confirming the details of the ADR session to Postproduction, Accounting, Producer, and Production Manager. Accounting, now aware of the session, can track down the work report if it does not come back speedily.

KEEP A COPY OF ALL INFORMATION

Keep a copy of all the information about the ADR session in your desk file folder in case you have to track down anything, like missing work reports. Send a copy of all appropriate information to the Performers' union office.

Cast contracts seem overpowering when you first start working with them. They are legally binding and do promise a lot of the production. When you have contracted your

final cast member, you may find that Stunt contracts, being under the same union jurisdiction, keep the Coordinator busy making new contracts all the way through production. To prevent costly mistakes, accuracy is key in the completion of any and all cast
contracts. If the Production Manager has to spend time with the Coordinator to ensure
she is up to speed on the intricacies of cast contracts, it will be time well spent and
money well controlled.

Set Food Extravagance

You know you work in the film industry when...

You sit down to a lunch in the middle of a field in the middle of nowhere to dine on roast beef and Yorkshire pudding, and you have a choice of at least two salads and at least two desserts.

It's four o'clock in the morning, and it's time for lunch.

You get tired of having grilled salmon... again.

The milk in your fridge at home expired in June... and it is now August.

CHAPTER 25

SUPPLIER AGREEMENTS

Anytime you make an agreement with a supplier, whether you are the Production Manager or Coordinator, you should commit to the deal on paper and have it signed by both parties as soon as possible. Writing commits both you and the supplier to the terms of the deal. The Accountant, too, will have excellent reference and backup for when she is calculating and writing the appropriate checks.

SUPPLIER LETTERS OF AGREEMENT

When the Production Manager makes a verbal deal with a supplier (like the Caterer or the Casting Director), make a letter of agreement immediately to confirm the details. If you relate the details of the deal to the Production Coordinator, the Coordinator can create the first draft letter of agreement. You can then tweak the document both as a second set of eyes for accuracy to the deal points, and to approve the document. Being the signing authority, the Production Manager should have all letters of agreement.

HOW TO MAKE A LETTER OF AGREEMENT
Since you are not a lawyer, do not try to write the way you think a lawyer sounds. Be simple and direct. Use letterhead to type a letter to the supplier, including their name, address, telephone and fax numbers. Address the letter to the person signing the agreement. Start the letter with: "This letter confirms the following:", then proceed to explain very plainly what the details of the agreement are, what the production company is promising, and what the supplier is promising. End with: "Your signature below indicates your agreement to the above," and mark spaces for the Production Manager and the supplier's representative to sign. Ensure copies of these letters go to the Production Accountant, the supplier, the Legal Counsel, and to the production files with the Production Coordinator. (See a sample catering letter agreement on page 436.)

WHEN TO USE LETTERS OF AGREEMENT
Letters of agreement can be for Caterers, Casting Directors, Animal Handlers, someone giving permission to use his name in the script, or even non-union crew members. The options are endless.

PM & LEGAL APPROVES WORDING
The Production Manager should review all letters of agreement before sending them

out for signature. Since you are signing them all, this procedure will be easy to accomplish. Depending on how complex the letter is, you may elect to forward it to Legal Counsel for rewording. The simple, direct phrases presented will be a terrific start for a more formal contract. Collect the wordings of successful simple letters of agreement for reference on future productions.

WHERE TO FILE LETTERS OF AGREEMENT

If these letters are with crew members, file with the crew deal memos. If they concern clearances or the contact list, file them with the clearances or the contact lists, respectively. Use logic. File Catering agreements in the Catering file. Since the Production Accountant will file these letters by alphabetical order, the Coordinator can afford to file them by subject matter. When head office looks through the files later, they may not know the specific company names, but they will be able to look up agreements filed under "Catering," "Equipment House," "Casting Director," and "Animal Handler."

Committing to agreements assures how much is being spent, and what the deal terms are. Since nearly everything related to production has a price tag attached to it, once these deal letters are signed, you will have comfort to move forward. The deal has been made and agreed to.

Audience for a Fall

I came to set one day just before lunch. We were filming in a generating station. Lots of pipes, large machinery, tall metal staircases, and cement floors. The place was laced with atmosphere. It was a perfect place to film this scene.

The crew was hard at work preparing for the shot. Tension was high. Concentration was focused. The Assistant Directors called for the set to be locked up. Silence fell and all eyes turned to the shot. The sound rolled. The camera rolled. "Action."

There was a scuffle at the top of the stairs. A cast member slipped and fell onto the stairs. But he did not fall down just one step. He fell down more. Two, three, ten, twenty, thirty. Smack, crunch, thunk, he seemed to hit every stair on the way down with sickening crunches. Thunk, crunch, wham, smack, splat. He landed on the cement floor face down. He did not move a muscle. The crew stared in anticipation; it was a painful fall to watch. The camera kept rolling. "Cut."

A sigh of relief, and the crew broke into applause for the man in the crumpled heap at the base of the staircase. Then the Assistant Director called out, "That'll be lunch, one hour!" And everyone left.

At the sound of lunch, the Stuntman stood up and headed off with the crew. Not a scratch on him. Heaven knows why.

CHAPTER 26

THE SPECIAL DEPARTMENTS

The special departments, like special effects, CGI, stunts, and shots starring children and animals, are often the "sell" shots of the film. We love to talk about them. We impress ourselves with how inventively we made movie magic become reality on the screen. Anything is possible... for a price. I will not discuss how much certain shots cost, because the world of imagination is open, and you might as well ask how long is a piece of string. You do need to consider, however, the following issues when dealing with the special departments:

PREP & RESEARCH

Preparation is unmistakably key to successful special shots. By the time you go to camera, you and the crew should be so familiar with what is about to happen that you feel like you have already completed the shot. You have researched it. You have talked about it. You have planned it. You have rehearsed it. Now: You do it for the camera.

PLAN & STORYBOARD THE SEQUENCES
Special shots take a lot of set time to capture on film properly and dynamically. When you realize how much prep time and cost is required for each special shot, you do not want to shoot footage that will end up on the cutting room floor. Ensure storyboard panels are planned and drafted for the special sequences. This preparation makes everyone think through the sequence in specific detail — from the edited shot sequence, back to the requirements on set to capture the shots, back to the planning behind capturing the shots. You want the eyelines to match for continuity, and you want the duration of the shot to be as specific as possible.

RESEARCH SUPPLIERS
Carefully research potential suppliers prior to committing to one. You need to know without a doubt what production needs from the supplier for the sell shots. The storyboard plans will help you in discussions. Be specific when interviewing suppliers. What is their track record? What special shots have they done for other films that may be related to what you need? You do not want to be a training ground for these suppliers. What exactly have they done for the shots on their show reel, and which of those shots have been done partially by them with another supplier embellishing the effect somehow? Know what you are getting before you commit.

SAFETY

In all cases, safety issues come first. The suppliers should be well aware of safety issues, so discuss safety with them. The Workers' Compensation Board is another source for safety preparation, but you may find the crew unions are more up on the specific safety requirements for film-related safety — even publishing safety requirements for certain special shots — because this is a very specialized industry. Be sure all safety precautions being taken are clearly identified and explained to the crew, both verbally at a meeting and in detail on the call sheet for their reference. Again, safety is a first priority. You want to see "special" on set, not "surprise."

PREP TIME FOR SUPPLIERS

There is no such thing as a "spur-of-the-moment" special shot. If the supplier thinks he can promise you this, find another supplier. Still, you are responsible to commit to the supplier early enough in preproduction to allow the supplier enough prep time to prepare and practice for the special shots. Animals need time to train; they cannot "cram for exams." Special effects suppliers need time to test their explosions so they know ahead of time how big the blast will be, and how much smoke it might generate. You will also need time to arrange for the permits required for certain special shots.

SPFX – SPECIAL EFFECTS

Special effects are on-set flash. They can range from the use of dry ice, steam, or smoke as atmosphere, to the creation of a waterfall, snowfall, rainfall, wind, blazing fire, or explosions — all on set. Some special effects may be simple enough for the Props Department to handle, but as the complications increase, you will need a reliable, experienced supplier: a special effects company.

Most of their equipment has some kind of motor that will blot out your sound. Sound will record guide track anyway during the take, and should get wild lines of the Performers running their lines in the same sound atmosphere of the set — without the camera and the special effects equipment running. The Editors may be able to match the wild sound enough with the picture in post using the guide track as, obviously, a guide. Be prepared to pay for an ADR session later for the Cast anyway.

For special effects, the Production Manager needs to liaise often with the SPFX Supervisor. The Supervisor is the key person for design and preparation of the shot, so he will know if the costs are increasing to achieve the result wished for by the storyboard. (Complications during preproduction, and redesigning of the storyboard sequences can easily increase the costs of these special shots.) This person is also the key safety person on the day.

CGI – COMPUTER ANIMATED EFFECTS

CGI stands for "computer-generated image" or "computer-graphic imagery." Some may be 2D computer effects — like painting in smoke and painting out animal tethers — while others may be 3D computer effects, like painting in a solid object — like a car falling off a cliff. If you have complicated CGI on your production, you may even have two separate departments, one for 2D effects and one for 3D effects, and if you have a huge number of effects on the production, you may even have two or three different CGI suppliers to deal with the workload in time to complete the film.

When one first mentions CGI, you tend to think of making animals talk and creating computerized mechanical characters to star alongside the cast. You do not often think of enhancing an explosion that the SPFX team has already made on set, or of painting out animal tethers, or of removing the sound boom from the shot. Well, these are CGI shots, too, even though they appear invisible when the final film is done — and they are just as expensive as other fancy visible CGI shots. Try to minimize the invisible CGI fixes to ensure the CGI money in the budget goes toward the most dynamic effects shots.

As mentioned before: Beware! When the crew knows you have a CGI supplier on board, they may get lazy when shooting the set special effects and when working with animals. To increase shooting speed and do less preparation themselves, they may leave all sorts of tethers and other visual items in the shot, figuring you can "fix it in post." Remember CGI fixes are the most expensive way you can fix problems. The few minutes saved on set not doing a proper rehearsal may cost you hours and tons of money in post to fix.

For this reason, CGI shots must be storyboarded and well planned. Shooting extra footage that gets cut out of the film is one expensive thing, but animating extra footage is unthinkable.

Again, the Production Manager needs to liaise often with the CGI Supervisor. Find out if the crew is adding shots to the CGI list on an ongoing basis. This person should also be the one on set supervising the shots that are going to be combined with the CGI animation.

If you are setting up the CGI room for the animation team, ensure you have enough air conditioning and airflow in the room. This much computer equipment in a small space generates an awful lot of heat.

MOTION CONTROL

Motion control is related to CGI animation, as motion control shots involve synching the camera action with animation to be painted on afterward. If the camera is stationery, animation is easy to paint onto the shot, because neither the shot nor the drawing board (computer screen) is moving. Once camera movement is involved, the animation has to move at exactly the same rate that the camera does, so the animation does not "slip or slide" across the screen. For example, if you dolly toward a Performer who is holding a CGI-animated snow globe, you need motion control to ensure the snow stays inside the globe. Motion control shots can be truly dynamic indeed.

Your first question with motion control should be: Does the camera really need to move? If camera movement on this shot is not critical to the story, it is much, much more affordable to animate the shot without adding the complexity of motion control. Is this really the best place to spend a good chunk of production's budget? Of course, if all the shots of the film are moving camera, and every single time you cut to an effects shot the camera is static, this will look terribly obvious and certainly far from impressive. Be sure the style of shooting and the effects match the size of budget you have.

The Motion Control Supervisor will be key in planning all the various elements required for the shot using motion control. On the day, the motion control team will hook up a computer to the camera to record and program the camera movement for repetitive playback both on set, and later on the computer screen for the animation. As for elements, the Supervisor may need a shot of the action complete with Performers on the set; a separate shot of the set using the camera movement, but seeing no Performers (a background plate); and a separate shot of the Performers doing the action against a blue or a green screen using the camera movement but not seeing any background. Because of this level of technical complexity, the Motion Control Supervisor may need to direct the shot instead of the Director. Placement of every element and Performer in the screen, along with the camera movement, is critical to the success of the blending of the animation into the shot in postproduction. This need for exacting technical accuracy, however, may result in somewhat stale screen performances, as the Performers are asked to act in a hugely sterile, technical-first environment. Be ready for this possibility.

BLUE SCREEN OR GREEN SCREEN

Blue screen or green screen is an old effects process, but it is still used. Since skin color is so far opposite the blue or the green you use on these screens, you can "key out" the flat blue or green from behind Performers to insert a background, like a fantastic planet, behind them — to give the audience the illusion that these Performers are actually on that planet. This process is sometimes still called "chroma key"; its colors are chroma-key blue and chroma-key green. Old chroma keys used to leave a blue halo around the Performers — especially around their hair where the line between action and background is uneven; computers have advanced significantly, so blue-screen shots are less visible than they ever used to be.

Of course, using blue screen, the Performers may not wear any blue in their wardrobe, or if using green screen, they cannot wear any green. If they do, the blue or the green color will also be keyed out, and the background will be inserted where their blue jeans or green sweater was, too. As technology advances, it has become possible to key out only certain shades of blue or of green, but there is a limitation. For this reason, ensure that the Wardrobe Designer is involved in conversations about blue-screen or green-screen shots. And be sure that the costume design and shooting schedule does not have you painting the screen from blue to green to blue to green every other day.

Painting an even color of the blue paint or the green paint is critical to being able to key out all the color in postproduction. Be sure the screen is painted early enough in advance in case there is streaking and you have to have it painted again. It goes without saying that you need to hire professionals to paint these screens. Even lighting is also critical to a successful key. Arrange time for a pre-light crew to get it right without the shooting crew waiting around to watch them work.

WORKING WITH ANIMALS

We love animals, and we remember fondly many shots with animals from various films. The script calls for a fox, dog, cat, owl, rat, spider, horse, rabbit, ferret, squirrel, otter, ant, monkey, trout, chicken, goat, duck, pig, lama, alpaca, or whatever to do something specific or to be somewhere specific. You need a trained animal (or insect) and a Wrangler (or Trainer or Handler). Remember, though, that animals will be animals whether they are trained or not. It is in their nature.

Show the Wrangler the storyboard plan. In your early meetings, professional Wranglers will tell you what a particular animal may or may not do on command. Ensure you commit to an Animal Wrangler early enough for them to complete the weeks of training they will need to train their animals to do the specific tasks you require in the script. Some animals are more trainable than others. Even within species, like dogs, some breeds are more trainable than others.

Just like with any of the special departments, be specific in what you need of this supplier. Negotiate a fee based on specifics. That is why you ensured a storyboard plan was in place early.

Prepare, too, to schedule around the animals. They get tired. They do not understand how important this film is to you, so they will not work beyond their tiredness to complete the shot. When they get tired, they get tired — and it shows. If they are transported a long distance, they need time to adapt to their new surroundings. They may need time on set in their new environment to become comfortable before performing. Ask the Wrangler.

Shooting multi-camera when animals are on set is helpful. Animals cannot repeat performances the way Performers can. Use a reduced Second Unit (or animal unit) to capture animal reaction shots. Why have the entire main unit crew standing around waiting for the animal to perform — or not — for the camera? Be sure the animal unit is scheduled to gather shots after main unit has captured the main action of the same scene. If the animals and main cast have to interact, you want the animal unit to capture shots to fit into main unit's shot plan, not have the animal unit shoot reaction shots first and dictate to main unit (and to the Director) how to film a certain scene.

Some animals are dangerous and may panic with lots of people around. Most animals are not used to the number of people required to be on a film set. This is another reason that Second Unit is helpful. If animals need to be on main unit, ensure that safety issues for the crew and for the animals are addressed, and ensure the crew is fully informed both verbally and on the call sheet. Remember that most animals have a more highly developed sense of smell than people, so certain smells in the location's environment will affect them and therefore their performance. As I said, animals will be animals. Research and be prepared.

STUNTS

Stunt Performers are more predictable than animals, to say the very least. But the stunts themselves are filled with uncertainties no matter how you plan for them. Weather may even play a factor. Imagine you have arranged for a stunt over a raging river. When you arrive at the river, it is covered in ice, and the Stuntman could just walk across it instead of swinging over it. This is not a very exciting stunt anymore.

As Production Manager, when you know the details and the plans of the stunt, you will need to negotiate a stunt adjustment fee based on the danger level of the stunt, and the number of times you have asked the stunt to be performed. Since you have to pay for each take, and no two takes will look alike, you will undoubtedly need a second camera or two on the day.

Liaise with the Stunt Coordinator, and ensure he comes to relevant preproduction meetings to keep in the loop of preparation for camera. To properly prepare, this person will need to walk through the locations where all stunts are going to be performed.

One last word about stunts: Never allow safety to be jeopardized to have more "flash." Be smart.

WORKING WITH CHILDREN

Working with children is not unlike working with animals. They are not the same, of course, because you can talk with children, but there are some distinct similarities between the two. Children tire. They do not have the attention span that adults have, so you cannot expect them to work effectively for hour after hour. They cannot duplicate a performance take after take, but will fade around take two.

On a film set, when children are performing, they are working. Yet in most places there are no laws to control the working conditions of children, because most governments simply state that employing children is illegal. Governments are now dealing with this dilemma, though some more quickly than others. You may find that on a co-production the two governments have directly conflicting laws governing the working conditions of children. Address this problem early.

If you are in an environment where there are no laws to govern you when you hire children, know that Performer unions have had very strict rules about working with children of different ages for a long time. They stipulate how long children are allowed for a work day, how much tutoring time is required each day, how many rest periods for how long are required, and that no overtime is allowed. If when you hire children there are no governmental working conditions, abide by the union rules, whether you are a union shoot or not. These rules were designed to protect the children. As you are technically hiring them illegally, you may need to prove that the working conditions you provided them were thoughtful and protective. Do not get yourself or the production into trouble when hiring children.

During the school season, you will have to hire a Tutor for children you have working on your set if you are shooting on school days. If the Child Actor has worked before, her parent may have a specific choice of Tutor. If you have a number of children of varying ages, you may have to hire more than one Tutor. Check the rules with the Performer union you are signatory to, or whose rules you choose to follow.

Always meet the Parents and/or Guardians. One of them is bound to be on set with the Child Actor anyway, but meet them ahead of time to give them comfort that this production is professional and thoughtful to the needs of children on set. Think about what you are going to do to be true to your word. Film sets are not child-friendly in general. There are many safety hazards for children all over, and the hurry-up-and-wait nature of film set is very boring for children. Have you hired a crew that is child-friendly? How is the Director's patience with children?

As animals will be animals, so children will be children. Do not expect them to act or react like adults. They are children and act accordingly. Allow them their childhood. You are only a child once.

OTHER SPECIAL DEPARTMENTS

Other special departments can include: television synch (since you need special equipment to synch the television 30 frames per second to the film 24 frames per second), helicopter flying shots, shots from boats, and so on. The issues are the same as for the departments noted above. Plan. Research. Hire professionals. Safety comes first.

When it comes to special shots or sell shots, think simple, even if you are using a special department. Simple can be well done. For example, a wire being pulled off screen can move objects as well as CGI can in postproduction, but is much cheaper. This is a creative industry. Be creative in problem-solving and creating the magic. Use the special departments when you have exhausted the simple effects and want to spend the money on something spectacular. That will be using the budget wisely and putting the money where it belongs: on the screen.

VI.

MORE PRODUCTION & COORDINATION ISSUES

Fast, good, cheap… pick any two.

I Won't Go Back to White

When it comes to revising a script, I hate going back to white. I will search high and low for every pastel-colored paper on the market to postpone the inevitable "return to white."

It was very close to end of production, and I was happy that we had never had to return to white. We had survived numerous script changes and I was certain the revisions were at an end. We had been from white to pink to blue to green to yellow. The standards. Then on to buff to salmon to gray to goldenrod to sand and at last to lavender.

Then one more revision came in. It was a short two-pager. I couldn't bear the thought of going back to white for such a short revision. But we had exhausted every pastel paper in existence. So, I got out red and green highlighters, and with the help of the office staff drew a pattern on each page to publish... the plaid revisions.

CHAPTER 27

SCRIPT FORMAT & REVISIONS

Script revisions happen for many reasons. Watching a scene in the editing room, it is decided that some more dialogue needs to be added to a previous scene to explain this scene's reason for being. Another scene ended up with longer-than-planned screen time, so the solution is to shorten a different scene again. The list goes on.

THE PRODUCTION MANAGER & SCRIPT REVISIONS

Some script revisions affect the budget with the addition of locations or props or whatever, others save the budget money, and others have no effect at all on the budget. As the Production Manager, you are probably already in the loop concerning what revisions are about to happen, so you have anticipated the costs or savings associated with the script revisions yet to come. When the revisions are published, read them immediately. Do the changes really reflect what you expected, or are there other surprises for you and the budget? There may be.

THE PRODUCTION COORDINATOR & SCRIPT REVISIONS

The Coordinator is responsible for the typing and publishing of accurate script revisions, though the Production Secretary may be the person assigned to the actual typing. What the Coordinator needs to know inside and out is script format and how to manipulate it.

TYPING THE EARLY DRAFTS

There are many wonderful books on the market that can explain script formatting in great detail. There are also many lovely software programs that help Writers format scripts as they type. This chapter will not attempt to replace them, but will present you with a nutshell version of what you need to know or learn. Because, even if you use script-formatting software, you still have to understand script format to generate what you need for the shooting set. As the Production Coordinator, you must know script format even better than the Writing Department. A well-formatted script is essential to clearly and easily explain the story to the crew for filming.

CHOOSE A SCRIPT FORMAT
Of the several formats used, and endless versions on those formats by Writers and Producers, choose between two of the basic kinds: feature film format and comedy format. Get the Writing Department's and the Producer's approval in choosing a script format.

FONT
Always use courier font, as each character of the typeface has the same spacing. You need this consistency for the written word so that the script is entirely legible, and so that one script page will equal about one minute of screen time for every script.

WHO TYPES THE SCRIPT
The fastest typist in the office should type scripts on condition that he is also the person who best knows script format. Reformatting pre-typed pages takes almost as long as retyping an entire script.

MAKE THE FORMAT & LABELING CONSISTENT
Be consistent about labeling scene locations, about identifying character names, about everything. This advice cannot be repeated too many times. The reason: If a script notes Ken's living room as: KEN'S LIVING ROOM, LIVING ROOM, INT. KEN'S HOUSE, and as THE ELLIOTT LIVING ROOM, the crew will be confused over how many locations the script actually needs. Script-formatting software will consider this one location as four separate locations because each of the names is slightly different.

INFORM THE PM & THE CREW OF CHANGES WHILE TYPING
When you type the script, you are reading it word for word. You are bound to notice that, for example, seven new props have been added to a certain scene. Write this down and talk to the Props Department soon to find out if they are aware of the forthcoming change. Mention it also to the Production Manager. Since the script itself will take a few more hours to type, print, copy, and distribute, informing the crew as you type can give them added time to address the new changes.

WHAT TO LOOK FOR	WHOM TO TELL
Changes That Affect Today	Appropriate Department(s)
Changes That Affect Tomorrow	Appropriate Department(s)
New Characters	Producer/Casting Department
Changed Character Names	Clearance Company/Legal Counsel
Changed Location Names	Clearance Company/Legal Counsel
New Locations	Locations Department
New Props	Props Department
New Wardrobe	Wardrobe Department
New Action (Stunts, Effects)	Appropriate Department(s)
Changed Dialogue	Performers affected

IF THE PC IS NOT THE TYPIST
If you choose a typist other than yourself, have a copy of the source file (or handwritten script pages) to read as the typing is happening. Keep atop the revisions. Make notes. Inform the crew.

TYPING FROM VARIOUS FORMATS
Writers will give you scripts on anything from computer disk to handwritten sheets of paper torn from a binder. It is your job to make each script format the same (especially on a series).

- <u>Typing from Handwriting</u>: If the Writers give you script in handwritten form, you will learn to be very good at reading their individual handwriting. Most Writers are so fast to get the idea onto paper, they may overlook proper spelling and grammar. In this case, do not always type word for word. Read the script as you type to determine if the "mistake" you are reading is an intentional style of writing or a typo. Proper scene breaks can be missing, too. Do not have characters walk from room to room or flash forward in time without breaking for a new scene heading.

- <u>Formatting from a Computer Disk</u>: Even if the script is given to you on computer disk, the Writer's word-processing program or script-writing program may not be the same as yours. On translating the file into your word processor, you will either find yourself reformatting the entire script or, at worst, needing to retype every word. Whichever you do, print out a copy for the Producer and the PM first, then read the script as you work to be sure correct scene breaks occur.

- <u>Formatting from a Plain Text File</u>: If the Writer and you do not have compatible computer programs, the file you receive attached to email will certainly be readable as ASCII, DOS, or plain text. All word-processing formatting will be lost in the transfer. Print out a copy for the Producer to review as is, then begin the process of formatting the plain text into a legible script.

WHEN NOT TO REFORMAT OR RETYPE
The Producer may suggest that you do not immediately re-format or re-type the first script that you have received from Writer, who may want to radically revise the script from its present state. Save yourself the work. Find out.

IF YOU NEED HELP FORMATTING
If you are worried about script format or have a question about where to break a scene, go to the A.D.s. They have to schedule the script scene by scene, and so will be happy to advise you.

WHEN IS A DRAFT FINAL?
All early (pre-final) drafts should not have scene numbers. Only when the script is

declared by the Producer to be a "final draft" should you number the scenes. This system ensures that the crew does not do heavy breakdowns of what they need for their department on a draft of the script that has yet to go through more major changes. Keep in touch with the Producer and the Writers about how close to "final" the script is.

WHO NUMBERS THE SCENES?
Some A.D.s like to number the scenes in the script themselves. Most expect the Coordinator to do the job. If you are unsure about how to number a sequence, ask the A.D.s. You have the knowledge of script formatting, and they have the knowledge of how they plan to shoot this collection of scenes.

SAVE AT LEAST TWO COPIES
The script in your computer is a long document. Save it, along with a backup copy. If you do not backup, just imagine having to type the whole script over again from scratch.

TITLE PAGES

There are about as many versions of title pages as there are versions of script formats. Be clear. Be consistent.

TITLE & WRITING NAMES
Center the title and the Writer(s) names, and place them about one-third the way down from the top of the page. The title is underlined or put in quotation marks. Identify all the Writers of the project as they are to be credited contractually, ensuring spelling and name order is correct. If in doubt, check with the Producer.

PRODUCTION COMPANY NAME, ADDRESS & TELEPHONE
To identify ownership of the property, note the production company name, address, and telephone number at the bottom right or the bottom left of the title page.

SCRIPT STATUS & DATE
Is the script a first, second, final draft, or pink revision? For early drafts, type which early draft and the date. For any script after the first final draft, list all the revisions and dates in a growing list. This list will remind crew of all the different parts they need to collect to make a single complete script. Place the list at the top right or the bottom right of the title page. Leave enough room for at least twelve different colored revisions.

COPYRIGHT AND/OR DISCLAIMER
Some production companies require a copyright notification and/or a disclaimer on the title page. Ask the Producer or the Legal Counsel. If you need one, place it at the bottom center of the page. If it is long, use small print.

SAMPLE TITLE PAGES

Since pictures can speak more than words, see two samples of title pages on pages 437and 438. The first is for a very revised single production script, and the second is an early draft of one episode of a comedy series.

FEATURE FILM SCRIPT FORMAT

This format can be used for feature films, Movies of the Week, and any type of drama program. It can also be used in a series format, but for this case, presume that the production is solitary.

PAGE HEADER

For page one, center the title at the top of the page. Specify the color and the date of the latest revision at the top right. For all other pages, make a header at the top left that reads title, color, and date. The redundancy is especially important to identify pages when they are faxed, copied onto the wrong-colored paper, or found separate from the script.

PAGE NUMBERS

Scene numbers and page numbers can be similar or even identical, depending on the pace of the script. If you use a dash before and after page numbers, you will find it harder to mistake page numbers for scene numbers (which are also on the right side of the page). You can also choose to have a period after all page numbers to differentiate them from scene numbers.

TAB SETTINGS

Listing them from left to right, these are the tab settings you will need:

• 0.5" left of left margin	Scene #
• Left margin	Scene Headings & Action
• 1" in from left margin	Dialogue
• 2" in from left margin	Parenthetical
• 2.5" in from left margin	Character Name
• 5" in from left margin	Transitions
• 0.5" in from right margin	Page #
• Flush Right	Scene #, Revision Marks

SCENE HEADINGS

Make scene headings bold and in capitals so that you and the crew can find them quickly. Scene headings are made up of three parts: inside/outside, where, when. Begin with INT. (Interior) or EXT. (Exterior), then describe the location, then use a dash, then end with DAY or NIGHT. Always include all three parts. Read the script carefully, if need be, to gather the information for all three parts. Do not use more than one dash. Script-formatting software tends to consider a dash as an indication that the location description is completed; the information after the dash will be considered the time of day. You do not want to have LIVING ROOM as your time of day description. Finally, be consistent about the location descriptions. Do not give one location more than one descriptive name.

SCENE NUMBERS

Place scene numbers far into the margins at both sides of the page for fast, double reference. You can precede the number with "Sc." if you like, so that crew will quickly differentiate between the scene and the page numbers.

ACTION

Description of action is generally very sparse in a script. Ensure you use hard returns at the end of each line instead of letting the computer do the line scrolling. This tactic will be useful when you come to revise the script line by line on a word processor.

WHEN TO CAPITALIZE IN ACTION

Character names, technical action, and sounds can be capitalized, but with action description being sparse, capitalizing words can get out of hand.

- Character names: Capitalize a character name only the first time it appears in a scene. This will help crew to determine who plays in the scene.

- Technical Action (left margin): Terms like ANGLE ON:, DIFFERENT ANGLE:, MUSIC:, and SFX (Sound Effects):, SPFX (Special Effects): are all capitalized and placed on the left margin for notice. These are specific requirements of Camera, Sound, and other technical departments.

- Technical Action (within description): When technical effects are not highlighted by placing them on the left margin and are written in the middle of a descriptive paragraph, capitalize the feature for notice. These include: BANG!, LIGHTS ON, and so on.

DIALOGUE

Dialogue margins are rather flexible. How wide or how narrow they are depends on the intended pace of the dialogue. Discuss this issue with the Producer or the Writing Department. As with the action, use hard returns at the end of each line so that you can revise each line individually later.

CHARACTER NAMES

Capitalize all character names and be consistent. The script may give a character several names throughout the course of the story, but you should let each character have only one name. If a character changes names during the script, keep using one name and add the new name in parentheses beside the character name later. Do not center character names if you are using any formatting software, because the software relies on specific tab settings to find the character names.

PARENTHETICALS

You will see words in parentheses beside character names and underneath character names. Parentheticals are the ones underneath. They are descriptions of how the dialogue is to be read, or what is to be acted simultaneously. These tend to be in lower case.

	MAX
• How words are said	(whispers)
• Whom words are said to	(to computer screen)
• Where words are said to	(to off screen)
• Actions to be performed	(waves hand)
• Laughter & sighs	(chuckles)

Directions in parentheses beside the character name are production explanations, not directions for the actor. These tend to be in uppercase.

• The dialogue continues	MAX (CONT)
• Location of the character	WOMAN (ON TV)
• Speech is voice over or narration	MAN (V.O.)
• Dialogue is heard from off screen	VOICE (O/S)
• Alternate character name	PERSON WITH HAT (MAX)

TRANSITIONS

Transitions are editing commands that carry you to an entirely different scene. These include CUT TO:, DISSOLVE:, and SWISH PAN TO:. Do not confuse these with on-set technical commands, like ANGLE ON:, that instruct you to a new camera angle within the same scene.

CONTINUED

Note CONTINUED in parentheses at the bottom and the top of each scene that continues onto the next page. This makes each page clear about whether the scene ends at the bottom of the page or not. When noting CONTINUED at the top of the next page, add the scene number for clarity.

SCRIPT PAGE SAMPLE

Review the two samples on pages 439 and 441. They show all the formatting notes mentioned above.

COMEDY SCRIPT FORMAT

This format can be used for comedy, sitcoms, or any fast-paced dialogue scripts. Since single-episode productions have already been addressed, presume that the comedy script is for an episodic television series. Basically, use the same format as the feature film script format, incorporating a few changes:

PAGE HEADER
Add the episode number to the header. With a series, you will be handling revisions for many episodes at the same time, and will need to identify each page separately.

ACTION
Action is completely capitalized for this type of format.

DIALOGUE
Dialogue is still upper and lower case, but is double-spaced for easy, fast reading.

SCRIPT PAGE SAMPLE
Again review the sample script pages on pages 439-441 to see the differences between the feature film script format and the comedy script format.

SCRIPT REVISIONS

When you revise a script, you need to highlight to the crew exactly what has changed without asking them to re-read the entire script every single time. Here is a step-by-step process to keep atop the many revisions that flood the Coordinator's desk:

COLLECT SCRIPT REVISIONS IN DESK FILE FOLDER
You collect notes for script revisions from many sources. The Producer and the Writers give you marked-up copies of the script. You have taken notes during production meetings as future script changes are discussed. You have notes from the script clearance company about changes that need to be made. You have heard the A.D.s mention that a scene will be shot in a different way than what was originally written. Make a note about this, too. Store all your notes in the desk file folder labeled "Script Revisions." When you come to revise the script, all your notes will be in one place.

WHO APPROVES THE REVISIONS
Though revisions and requests for revisions come from far and wide, they must all be approved by the Producer. Review them with him.

WHEN TO REVISE A SCRIPT
Publish a new script or a new set of pages only when there are enough revisions to warrant their publishing, or when the change is drastic enough to require that you inform the crew immediately. Ask the Producer. If you have been informing the crew of changes before they happen, publishing the pages daily or hourly is not crucial.

WHY USE COLORED PAPER FOR REVISIONS?

Colored revisions are for instant and distant recognition. If a crew member shows up on set and sees everyone with a yellow script while hers is blue, she will be instantly aware there are script revisions to be had and will seek them out.

WHEN IS IT REVISED PAGES vs. REVISED SCRIPT?

Consider the number of pages that you need to revise. If revised pages account for more than 70% of the script, you will do better to publish an entire new draft on the new paper color, reformatting the pages as you go. You cannot, however, revise an entire script once shooting has begun. Continuity is already using the script to make notes to the editors, and is sending the script page by page to the editors as the film is being shot.

TYPING THE REVISIONS

When it is time to revise the script, here is how to tackle the job:

CHANGE THE TITLE PAGE

Add the new revised color and date to the list of revisions on the title page.

CHANGE THE PAGE HEADER

Change the header on each page to note the correct new color and date for the revision.

MAKE CHANGES AND MARK NEW REVISIONS

Every time you change a word in the script, mark the changed material with an asterisk (*) flush right on that line. There is no limit to the number of asterisks you can use on a page. With this system, crew can immediately see which lines to read on the revised page to look for the new material.

REVISING A REVISION – CLEAR OLD REVISION MARKS

Before revising a script that has been previously revised, erase all previous revision marks (asterisks). If not, you will find a build-up of asterisks, and finding the latest revision on the page becomes increasingly difficult.

SOFT RETURNS vs. HARD RETURNS

Because you revise the script one line at a time, you need hard returns at the end of each line to allow you to flush right and place the asterisks. If soft returns (automatic word wrapping) are still in the script at this point, search and replace them on the computer with hard returns.

A & B SCENES

Once a script is marked "final," the scene numbers cannot change. To insert new scenes in between two existing ones (like between scene 6 and 7), you must number the new scenes with As and Bs: Sc.6, Sc.6A, Sc.6B, Sc.7. Hope you never have to insert a scene between scene 6A and 6B. If you do, try: Sc.6A, Sc.6AA, Sc.6B. If you have to insert a scene prior to scene 1, use: Sc.A1.

OMITTED SCENES
Once a scene is added to the script, it must always be listed, even if it is omitted. Like any scene header, note the scene number and OMITTED beside. Keep this notification in every revised draft that follows.

A & B PAGES
As the scene numbers remain fixed in a final draft script, so do the page numbers. If the revised page becomes shorter due to omissions, leave the rest of the page blank. If the revised page becomes longer, continue the revision on an "A" page. Your page numbers can therefore look like this: page 12, 13, 14, 14A, 14B, 14C, 15, 16, and so on.

OMITTED PAGES
When the new material has you removing one or several pages from the script, mark the span of page numbers missing atop one of the revised pages. Your new page number sequence could, therefore, look like this: page 12, 13-14B, 14C, 15, and so on.

You will liken keeping up with script revisions to trying to catch a waterfall. As soon as you finish getting through one colored revision, another — or the plan for another — lies waiting in the wings. Be ready for the effect revisions have on the budget, so than you can get the information out to the crew as soon as possible. You can do it.

What Meaneth Nine to Five

There is nothing whatsoever nine to five about working in film — except, maybe, one thing.

Renting an ice rink in the middle of hockey season means that your set time starts at 3:00 a.m. at the rink, and you have to travel to the nearby production office at 2:30 with the radio in your car cheerfully announcing, "And here's a song to get you home safely tonight."

When you get to the production office and the boiler breaks at 3:00 a.m., you won't be able to get in touch with the landlord before 7 or 8. String all baseboard heaters into the smallest office you can, and gather any people into that office for the early-morning huddle. Keep your parkas on for added warmth. Draw straws to find out who is the next person to walk down the icy hallway to make the next photocopy.

Then, think about it. Who is going to call the production office at 3:30 in the morning? The set. Go to the set with the Production Manager. It's an ice rink. It might be warmer. Just remember to be back in time to arrange for the fixing of the boiler.

Have lunch at nine in the morning, and an afternoon snack around noon. Start fading about three, but the end of the workday is nearing. Be prepared for this. Driving home is one of the few times you get to mingle with all those nine-to-fivers. It's five o'clock rush hour.

CHAPTER 28

PRODUCTION SCHEDULING

There are preproduction schedules, production schedules, one-line schedules, shooting schedules, and Second Unit schedules. The Production Manager and Coordinator need to be up to speed on all the types of schedules.

The PM especially needs to be able to read and review the shooting schedule to evaluate its plausibility for the show's being able to be completed on time and on schedule.

The Coordinator may not need to type the schedule anymore, only photocopy and distribute it. The Assistant Directors tend to create and generate all the schedules with their scheduling software. If there is no access to this software, the Coordinator wil have to be prepared to lend a hand.

PREPRODUCTION SCHEDULE

Pretty much every day in prep the Assistant Directors revise a list of the events that are scheduled to happen during preproduction. This list includes times of meetings, location surveys, and wardrobe fittings, and is usually drafted in the form of a memo.

The PM needs to know what meetings are being scheduled, and be involved in as many as possible. Who is meeting with whom? Are the special-effects prep issues being addressed?

The Coordinator's job is to distribute the prep schedule to the crew daily. If the schedule is given to you handwritten, you are to type that, too.

PRODUCTION SCHEDULE

The Coordinator can make this schedule with input from the PM. Collect information from the PM, the Producer, and the A.D.s to generate a one-page week-by-week breakdown of the entire production's schedule. For each week note if the production is prepping, shooting, on hiatus, on holiday, or wrapping. Also note which days of the week are shoot days. At a glance the crew can now understand the entire schedule, even which weeks are non-Monday-to-Friday workweeks. Include dates for post events like the dates for rough cut, fine cut, delivery, and audit. When this schedule revises, copy it onto colored paper just like a script revision for notice. Long after production has completed, the Accounting, the Publicity, and the Legal Departments will be referring to this schedule. Be accurate. Here is an obviously hypothetical example for production dates only:

- MON.SEP.01   Labor Day Holiday (off)
- TUE.SEP.02 - FRI.SEP.05   Prep
- SUN.SEP.07 - THU.SEP.11   **SHOOT EPISODE #1**
- MON.SEP.15 - FRI.SEP.19   Hiatus
- MON.SEP.22 - FRI.SEP.26   **SHOOT EPISODE #2**
- MON.SEP.29 - FRI.OCT.03   Wrap

PRODUCTION BOARD (STRIP BOARD OR THE BOARD)

The A.D.s create the shooting schedule by first making a production (or strip) board. The board can be a physical board, or created on computer. If it is a physical board, it is large and black, and when opened, displays many colored vertical strips coded with numbers and words. There is also a large white "header board" strip that displays the legend for the number codes. The entire board is written in pencil. Get familiar with looking at and reading a board. (See a sample Strip Board on page 442.)

"DECODING" OR READING THE STRIP BOARD

Since the A.D.s are the ones that create the board, you do not need to know all the details of creating one yourself. But, since the board always depicts the schedule in its latest form, you should know some of the basics of the language and the codes of a strip board:

EACH STRIP IS A SCENE IN THE SCRIPT

Each colored strip on the board represents one scene of the script, no matter how long each scene is. Though the information on each strip can vary from A.D. to A.D., you can read on each strip: the scene number, whether the scene is day or night and interior or exterior, a written description of the location, a micro synopsis of what happens in the scene, and a list of the characters needed for that scene (with each character represented by a number code).

THE HEADER BOARD

The header board is the first panel of the board and it tells you: the film title, the key crew names, the version of the script used for this schedule, and a legend of which character has been assigned to which character number. These character numbers are the same ones you use on the cast list and the call sheets.

WHY DIFFERENT COLORS FOR EACH STRIP?

The colors of each strip tell you at a glance if the scene is day or night, interior or exterior. A legend that is often used:

White:	Exterior day	(bright light, like the sun, appears white)
Yellow:	Interior day	(the color of household lights is yellowish)
Blue:	Exterior night	(films often light night scenes blue)
Green:	Interior night	(yellow "interior" plus blue "night" equals green)

Black and red strips serve as borders between the days. Red identifies a weekend. Black strips usually have a white space to summarize the date and the total number of pages scheduled to be shot for that day.

Every strip is written in pencil, since the board changes with every script revision. You will notice that computer-software strip boards are set up to emulate the physical board right down to the color codes, so if you can read one, you can read any of them.

WHY DIVIDE THE PAGES BY EIGHTHS?

You see the scene page counts are listed in eighths of pages and wonder why anyone would choose fractions that are difficult to add and subtract to use as numerical totals. Eighths are a good fraction for division. You can divide a page in half, and in half again, and in half again, and still have a readable fraction. Always list page counts in eighths (use 4/8 instead of 1/2) because, as you know, you can more readily add and subtract the fractions with a common denominator.

When the schedule changes, if a manual scheduling system is being used, the Coordinator should take the time to double-check the daily page count totals. Sometimes these totals are forgotten when it comes to recalculation. Computer-scheduling software removes the need to do this. Make your primary math teacher proud.

READING THE SCHEDULE

The A.D.s schedule a production taking into account many factors, so there is no "right" and "wrong" when it comes to scheduling, but there are a number of limitations and questions you as Production Manager can address and discuss with the A.D.s to make some schedules more workable than others:

PERFORMER AVAILABILITY

Performer availability will be your first limitation when deciding which scenes you are filming when. If you can only get your Star for the first three weeks of filming, then you will have to schedule all his scenes then. Period. You may even find that your first day of principal photography is based on the yet-to-be-announced wrap day of your lead Performer on another shoot. If this is the case, of course, keep in daily contact with the other shoot, and try to relax amid the stress. For Child Actors and Animals, you will have to schedule shorter days, as they tire quickly.

LOCATION AVAILABILITY

Location availability is at the top of the limitation list, along with Performer availability, for dictating your schedule. It is logical, though, to shoot all the scenes at a single location at one time — no matter when they occur in the script — saving the unit company move and setup time.

TRAFFIC PATTERNS

Does the schedule take into account traffic patterns or work schedules? If you need a downtown office, do you need to shoot during a weekend day to gain access? If you are closing a street, do not plan to do it during rush hour on a weekday.

NUMBER OF SCENES PER DAY

How many scenes are you targeting to achieve daily on the set? Keep in mind the next two sections, because some scenes take longer to complete than others. Still, if you are planning a large number of small scenes, ensure that the schedule addresses all the required time needed for costume changes and set-decoration changes to achieve all the scenes.

NUMBER OF SETUPS PER DAY

Consider the Director's shot list for each scene when planning for how many scenes to target each day. Some scenes can be covered in one setup, and others take plenty more. If the camera has to move a number of times to new positions on set during the day, remember that lighting too will have to change, and together preparation for these two take up a lot of set time. Crack television crews may achieve about 20-27 setups per day, and perhaps 40-45 setups if there is a second camera running, while new Directors may manage to complete only about 9-11 setups in the same time. IMAX 3D is so technically complicated that you may expect to achieve only 4-5 setups per day.

NUMBER OF EIGHTHS OF PAGES PER DAY

Make sure the schedule addresses a reasonable number of pages for you to achieve each day. Feature films may plan for about 2-3 pages per day, while television movies and series plan for about 7-10 pages per day. Dialogue scenes may be high on page count but not difficult to film, while other scenes that involve complicated special effects may be very low on page count, but will take you an enormous amount of time to capture. Remember the extenuating circumstances of various scenes when you determine a reasonable page count for the day.

WEATHER COVER

Weather issues have to be addressed by the schedule, even though weather is unpredictable. You can, however, predict tides, so you can be sure not to schedule a scene at the beach when the tide is so far out it would be a scene at the mud flats. For the unpredictable part of weather, how is weather cover being addressed? It is best to schedule exterior scenes early in the schedule so that if the weather is bad, you can reschedule them later and shoot some other scenes at an interior "weather-cover" location. Is production prepared for weather cover, or is the set still being built, so there is nowhere to shoot if the weather is bad? Have a contingency plan all the way through the shoot.

SUNRISE & SUNSET

Sunrise and sunset is also somewhat predictable, as you can look up the times on a chart. The quality of that particular sunrise and set is, of course, the wild card. The further from the equator you shoot, the longer days you can shoot outside in natural light in the summer, and the shorter days in the winter. Be sure the schedule does not try to achieve too many scenes for the light available. No A.D. can hold the sunset for the Director.

TURNAROUND

If you are shooting nights, then want to flip back to days, you have turnaround issues to consider. Has the crew had enough time to go home, get rested, and return to work, or do you need to take a day off to give them enough turnaround time? For this reason it is best to schedule day scenes first, then night scenes later, if you can. That way, as you do an hour or two of overtime during the shoot, you will not be in danger of biting into turnaround time (very costly overtime) because you are planning on shooting later and later anyway as the schedule proceeds.

COMPANY MOVES

Limit the number of company moves during your shoot days. You want to spend the prime portion of the shoot day shooting film, not paying for the crew to pack up, move to a new location, and unload over and over again.

DAILY TARGETS

Though the schedule plans certain scenes on certain days, should production happen to get ahead of itself, is there a plan for targeted scenes each day, so you do not have to wrap early and still pay the crew for a full day's work?

SCRIPT ORDER

Because of the cyclical nature of scripts, where the first scene and the final scene are often in the same location, you will never shoot a film in script order. But you can address some internal script order if need be. Some scenes may need to be played before other scenes, and the Director may request certain scenes be filmed before others to help the Performers with their characters' emotional arcs. It does help the cast (and the crew) to shoot the script in as close an approximation to story order as possible to develop their characters as the story develops. At the beginning of the shoot, the cast is not very familiar with each other, so consider scheduling scenes where characters are unfamiliar with each other at the beginning of the schedule. Another reason why script order may need to be considered is: If someone needs a huge change in makeup from young to old, you cannot afford the set time to have the makeup applied, removed, applied, and removed again during the shoot.

FLEXIBILITY

Above all, the schedule needs to be flexible. The unexpected happens during a film shoot. The schedule needs to be able to change if circumstances dictate. How is the schedule flexible?

THE IDEAL SCHEDULE

You get to shoot all the day exteriors first, all the night exteriors next, then all the day interiors, and finally all the night interiors — staying in script order from beginning to end with no availability problems for cast or locations. Well, we can all dream...

A.D. BREAKDOWN PAGES

Aside from the board, the Assistant Directors make a breakdown page for each scene, detailing all the needs of each scene (from props to stunts to Extras to anything else), not just the list of characters. On scheduling software, the A.D. enters the information onscreen, but never really needs to print out the onscreen breakdown pages; the program will use the breakdown information when printing the many formats of schedules and specific departmental breakdowns. When the schedule is created manually, the A.D.s need to generate one breakdown page per scene to ensure the information is transferred to every schedule and departmental breakdown they are yet to create. Once the breakdown pages are shuffled into order (or rather placed into order), you have a schedule that just needs typing. The Coordinator, in this case, may be the one typing the many schedule forms. (See samples of A.D. breakdown pages on pages 443 and 444.)

ONE-LINE SCHEDULE

Scheduling software will output a one-line schedule for the A.D.s, but if the Coordinator needs to create one instead, refer to the A.D. breakdown sheets and remember that each line equals one scene. With that you will have a "one-liner." When you look at it later, it will probably remind you of a strip board typed sideways.

WHAT TO PUT ON A ONE-LINER

Think minimal information. For each scene on the one-liner, include: the scene number, scene location description, specified interior or exterior, day or night, the continuity day number, list of characters in that scene (by number code), page count, and the shooting location. Note Extras by using an "X." If you have a number of scenes on one set, include a micro-short synopsis to differentiate the scenes from each other. Also include a legend to explain the number codes you used. Revise the schedule on colored paper, just like you would a script revision. (See a sample one-liner on page 445.)

WHY MAKE A ONE-LINER?

The one-line schedule is good to display the scene order (with minimum necessary description) of the entire shooting schedule in the shortest possible format. Because it is very short, more of the crew will likely read it and all its revisions in detail. Depending on the speed of production, this schedule sometimes is not created, and you will go straight to making a shooting schedule.

SHOOTING SCHEDULE

Again, scheduling software will output a shooting schedule for the A.D.s, but if the Coordinator needs to create one instead, combine all the information from the one-line schedule with all the breakdown information from the A.D. breakdown pages. Include the scene synopses, all the various departmental set requirements, and list the characters by name as well as by number. Depending on the detail of the A.D. breakdowns, the shooting schedule can easily become as thick or thicker than the script. Revise it using colored paper, like a script — even page by page if necessary. And since you will use all this information again on the call sheet, consider designing the shooting schedule to be in a similar format to the call sheet, so you can cut and paste the information daily, creating fast-draft call sheets. Be sure, though, you design a schedule that suits both you and the A.D. team. (See a sample shooting schedule on page 446.)

SECOND UNIT

Second Unit has its own shooting schedule separate from Main Unit, so clearly define it and print it on another colored paper for identification. Since Second Unit is often picking up shots that main unit did not achieve or that the Editor requests, the Second-Unit schedule may change rapidly. The unit may stick to a simple format for their shooting schedule, or just have a several-day advance schedule noted on their Second - Unit call sheets to remind them of the ever-changing future.

SCHEDULING FOR LOW-BUDGET PRODUCTIONS

If the production is very low-budget, you will not want to publish a revised, thick shooting schedule every time there is a small schedule order change. Instead, make a "shooting schedule" (complete with all the set requirements) in script order and call it the "script breakdown." Now you are free to revise the much shorter one-line schedule every time there is a schedule change, minimizing photocopying, and revising the script breakdown only when the set requirements change.

SPECIALITY BREAKDOWN MEMOS

The A.D.s will write up a series of mini-schedules directed toward specific departments, like a listing of all the stunts and on what day each stunt will be. If there is no scheduling software to generate these breakdown memos, the Coordinator can design the form as he pleases, keeping clarity in mind. A version of the one-line schedule is best for familiarity. Using a graphic or small drawing code at the top of each specialty breakdown will help to identify each breakdown at a glance. Here are some of the specialty breakdowns you will use, and why:
  • List of Extras (what scene they are in, what day they play)
  • List of Stunts (who plays them, what day they play)
  • List of Picture Vehicles (what day they play)
  • List of... (whatever else the A.D.s think of!)

With your knowledge of schedules and how they work, you (the PM and the Coordinator) and the Assistant Directors are a team now. You can even add eighths of pages blindfolded. Better than that, you can see the plan for production ahead of you, and can now foresee finishing on time as well as on budget.

For the Crew Only

Few Executives read all the credits in the memos you generate. They have very little time to worry about anything beyond the contractual and the financing credits. It's up to you to check most of the names and the spellings on your own. That is until the credits hit the screen. I learned this when the Production Secretary and I decided to put our nicknames on a very early draft of the credits.

Working on a French co-production, the Production Secretary decided that our names were not in keeping with the French flair of the show. We needed appropriate nicknames. We included these names on an early draft of the credits. The Production Manager and the Producer chuckled but didn't oppose the inclusion, so the credits went forward.

Executive Producers and financing companies on both sides of the Atlantic reviewed draft after draft of the credits. No one changed or deleted our "French" names. We were thrilled that all the Executives supported the little fun we injected into the credits.

Then came the first crew screening of the film. It was a heavy dramatic film. At its inevitable conclusion the credits began to roll. The crew was suitably depressed until the office staff credits rolled by. Chuckles and lightness filled the room. The Production Coordinator was credited as "Miss Paté" and the Production Secretary as "Babette."

A memo came to the office from the Executives the next day to remove our nicknames from the credits. Well, at least we got to see them once on the big screen.

CHAPTER 29

CREDITS

You start gathering information for them in prep, the Production Coordinator makes a first draft of them on first day of shooting for the PM's and the Producer's eyes only, and on your last day in wrap you are still trying to finalize them. They are the screen credits.

SCREEN-CREDIT DESIGN

The Production Manager needs to discuss with the Producer the design for the credits — both head and tail credits. Sure, a company may be contracted for the design or the look of the credits, but you need to know which names are required in what order and which logos are to be included where, to satisfy all contracts, as well as ensure that the look of the credits works for the film.

Watch credits on TV or on rental features as research. What credits can you include realistically, especially for the tail credits? Does the production have limited allowable screen time, like on television series, where you only have enough time to display the names of the department heads, or is there enough time to display the entire crew and their assistants? Is production a low-budget feature with so many donated items that you need to credit everyone's generosity? What logos need to be included and what union requirements dictate credit order and inclusion?

Know that credits on cards can show more names on the screen in less time than a credit roll or a crawl. Cards are also cheaper than a roll, though a credit roll is a standard credit format for feature films. Do know that white letters on a black background are the most affordable credits when it comes to film, as credits over the moving picture of the film is an expensive optical effect process. Credits over pictures on video, however, is completely simple and totally affordable. You can play with the fonts available, but ensure the font you choose is unmistakably readable. At the end of the day, everyone wants to be able to read his credit clearly.

Know how much screen time you plan to have, or are restricted to, for both opening and closing credits.

THE PREVIEW DRAFTS

The Production Coordinator has been collecting notes and copies of pages of contracts in the desk file folder associated with credits. On or near day one of principal photography, make a preview draft of the credits to review with the Production Manager and the Producer only. The PM and the Producer need to give their input before the draft is distributed to the many other people necessary for approvals, because credits are a very sensitive issue. It is all too easy to offend someone by omission, incorrect title and/or placement, and by incorrect spelling. With the Coordinator, the PM, and the Producer reviewing the draft and double-checking each other, the initial design ideas of credits can be ironed out, and an excellent first draft of the credits will be distributed as the first official draft. It may take a few preview drafts to get there, but that is to be expected.

THE PC COORDINATES THE PREVIEW DRAFTS
The Coordinator generates the actual drafts and gathers input from all sources to consolidate the credits.

MAKE A LIST OF CREDIT PROMISES
To begin the preview draft, consolidate your notes to make a list of who and what credits have been promised in all contracts, deal memos, and letters of agreement. Ask Postproduction and the Legal Counsel for credit promises in contracts or agreements that you do not handle.

APPROVE A CREDIT-LIST FORMAT OR DESIGN
The Producer may have a preferred format for the credits, or may want to choose from several formats that you present. When making a format, find out as much as possible from the Producer and the Production Manager. Which positions require a head credit? Are there a limited number of head credit cards? What positions begin the tail credits? Will the tail credits be a roll or on cards? Find out from Postproduction how many lines can fit on a card where the names remain legible. Just like the PM, watch feature films and television movies and series to write down the templates of their credits. You will find that productions vary greatly in style. (See two samples of credit styles on page 447 and page 451.)

INCLUDE CARD OR ROLL TIMINGS
When assembling any draft of the credits, include the screen timings of each card or of the duration of the roll. Then those approving the credits can see instantly if there is a timing problem with all the people and the companies they would like to, or have to, credit. Find out any and all timing restrictions from the PM and the Producer.

CHECK SPELLING
Checking spelling cannot be stressed enough. Double-check! Triple-check! Be absolutely certain that every single name is spelled correctly. Call the Performers' Agents and confirm again how to spell each Performer's name if need be. There is no computer spell-check program that can check the spellings of names.

MAKE THE FIRST PREVIEW DRAFT
Combine the information and the format to create a first preview draft. The Production

Manager and the Producer may revise this draft several times before allowing it to be called the "first" draft and presenting it to the countless Executives and companies involved for approvals. Everyone is relying on you to present the credits honoring all contracted promises. Note each contracted promise in the far right margin in brackets along with the card timing (if applicable). Since few will read all the contracts and deal memos you do, these notations will be a critical reference when anyone wants to change certain credits. Here is an example:

Card #1	starring KEN ELLIOTT	0:03 ("starring," single card)
Card #2	with LAURA FISHER RICHARD PATZ	0:03 ("with," head credits, shared card) ("with," head credits, shared card)
Card #3	and MO DANIELS as "Spitfire Mo"	0:03 ("and...as," last head credit, single card)

REVIEWING THE PREVIEW DRAFTS

As Production Manager, review the preview drafts of the credits with the Producer. Is there enough screen time for all the credits at both head and tail? Is the design and the format acceptable at this stage? Do the credits as presented abide by the union rules for screen credits that stipulate both who must be credited and placement of certain credits? Double-check any spellings of which you are the slightest bit unsure. Carefully check the financing agreements: Have you honored their credit requirements in wording, logo placement, and credit duration? Discuss, too, with the Producer if there is anyone else you need to have in the preview loop of credits to ensure credit completeness, like Postproduction and the Legal Counsel.

After the Production Manager and the Producer give their input, the Coordinator may be up to the second or third preview draft. Be sure all preview drafts are marked clearly as "preview" (as opposed to "official") to avoid alarm if someone finds something critical missing.

THE EARLY DRAFTS

Now that the first round of information has been collected, make the first draft of the credits. These are not final drafts by any means, but you need to be sure you have considered all possible credits before paring down to the final, approved version.

THE PC COORDINATES THE EARLY DRAFTS
Again the Coordinator will generate and track each draft.

MAKE A COVER-PAGE MEMO
Mark clearly on a cover-page memo to whom these credits are going and which draft it is. The cover-page memo is designed to keep the confidentiality of the credits underneath, and to clearly keep track of who is giving input to these credits.

WHO GETS THE EARLY DRAFTS
The first and early drafts are sent to Executives and companies for approvals. The PM will know which companies will need credits for approval. These people also include all Producers, the Legal Counsel, Postproduction, and anyone else the PM and the Producer so deem. Guilds and unions need to approve credits specific to their members. Though you may not want to send them an entire draft, you can lift appropriate sections of the credits to them with a letter announcing and describing the credit(s) being granted.

CALL FOR AND RECORD APPROVALS OR REQUESTS FOR CHANGES
Everyone on the cover-page memo must respond to the credits with approvals or requests for changes. If some of them do not respond, call for the information. Note all changes on your copy of the credits, and code each request to the person requesting. Some requests will be in direct opposition to others. When the Producer reviews all these requests together, she can identify who is asking for what, and can deal with the conflict. Let the Producer handle all issues that come up regarding the credits.

WHEN PEOPLE CHANGE THE SPELLING OF THEIR OWN NAMES
Some people will ask for spellings of their names that are different than the ones contracted. If this occurs, confirm each new request in a letter or a memo to that person, with a copy sent to the Producer and the Legal Counsel. If that person changes his mind after the credits are completed, you (and Legal Counsel) will have written proof of the credit requested.

HOW MANY EARLY DRAFTS DOES IT TAKE?
It takes many, many drafts to approve credits. The more Executives, the more drafts it will take. This is why you need to start the credits process as early in production as possible. When it seems to you and the Producer that the credits are approved from all sources, you are ready to make the first of the "final" drafts.

THE FINAL DRAFTS

The heading reads "drafts" for a reason. As soon as you publish a final draft of the credits, someone is bound to call in with a change.

THE PC COORDINATES THE FINAL DRAFTS

Put off finalizing the credits until the last possible moment. Postproduction will be able to tell you the date the credits are typeset, then go to camera. Find out the last possible date from them.

WHO GETS THE FINAL CREDITS

Final credits go to the same people as the earlier drafts, but also go to government agencies, Financiers, Publicity Departments, Distributors, Broadcasters, and to other people that the Producer or the Production Manager advises. (See a suggested list for the distribution of final credits in Chapter 30.)

DATE THE FINAL DRAFTS

Note the words "final draft" along with the date on the cover-page memo and on the credits themselves. When there are several final drafts published, the date will be the only way to discern them from each other. If not, revised final drafts will have to be labeled creatively, like "revised final draft," then "final and approved draft," then "very revised final draft."

KEEP POSTPRODUCTION INFORMED

Especially if there are several final drafts, keep in touch with Postproduction. Make sure they typeset and go to camera with the latest of the final draft credits. Warn them, even by telephone, when you know changes are going to be made to the credits.

Your eyes will grow tired from looking at the same names over and over again. The Coordinator can still have an Assistant help by double-checking using her own fresh eyes. You will get no thanks for correctly spelling each person's name in the credits, but you will certainly hear about the one name you misspelled and forgot to check. Any oversight you make will be displayed brilliantly on the big (or little) screen. Do everything you can to be letter-perfect.

Memory Lane

As technology advances, one forgets its origins.

One show I worked on had no money to rent computers, so my office equipment consisted of a typewriter. The show also had no money for a typing table, so I sat on a telephone book to get the right angle for typing.

When it came to revising the scene order on the shooting schedule, I stared in wonder at the pages: How to do the job? Without a computer and without retyping, how does one revise the information and get it out to the crew quickly? I was baffled. And then it hit me. Scissors and tape. I cut each scene into strips and retaped them into the correct order. How primitive, I thought. And after several revisions, this job could get really messy. But then it occurred to me: This is exactly why a computer calls its function "cut and paste."

CHAPTER 30

PAPERWORK DISTRIBUTION

The Production Manager may stand in awe of the Coordinator amid the wonder of flying paper, and well you should, because the PC certainly knows how to generate and distribute paperwork. But as for remembering who got which version of what paperwork, the Coordinator needs help. That is what this chapter is for. No one's memory can retain such ever-changing lists of information. This system will help the PC track all the paperwork that needs to be circulated during production.

TRACKING SYSTEM

Setting up a tracking system for paperwork may seem insignificant at first, but as production proceeds, copious amounts of paperwork and revised paperwork must be distributed to a growing list of recipients both on the crew and in offices around the world. At any given time, you must be able to know who has what information. A tracking system is essential.

WHO KEEPS TRACK OF DISTRIBUTION
Though the job of keeping the records is often delegated to the Production Secretary, the Coordinator is ultimately responsible for the working of the system. Work together.

MAKING A TRACKING SYSTEM
You need a system that is quick, simple to update, and easy to read. Here are two different systems that work well:

THE PAPER DISTRIBUTION BINDER
Devote one binder to paper distribution. Use divider tabs to mark the differing types of paperwork (each episodic script, crew list, cast list, call sheet, etc.). In each section, create a chart that lists the names of the people or the companies to receive this paperwork in the first column, and mark the rest of the columns for each revision of that paperwork, labeling color and date. When distributing the paperwork to each recipient, note in each appropriate box the date of sending. You can also use codes to note the method used, like "D" for delivered, "F" for faxed, and "C" for couriered. This system requires the tracking binder to be close at hand for several people to use. This system effectively keeps all the information in one spot, but you cannot see each company's list of paperwork without flipping many pages. (See a sample on page 454.)

317

CHARTS ON THE WALL ENVELOPES

Remembering you have wall envelopes collecting paperwork for various companies, you can create a chart to post on each one to use as your tracking system. List the paperwork that each company requires in the first column, and mark the rest of the columns for each revision of that paperwork, labeling color only. When delivering the contents of the envelopes, note the date in each appropriate box. Though this system shows you at a glance which paperwork each company receives, not every company you will distribute to will have a wall envelope — you will require a separate written log elsewhere for them. This system is good for showing each company's list of paperwork at a glance, but the information of all companies is spread out around the office. (See a sample on page 455.)

KEEP EXTRA COPIES OF PAPERWORK ON STANDBY

You will discover very quickly that some people have a natural tendency to lose paperwork over and over again. Other people will take the last copy from the distribution table and not inform you. Especially keep an extra copy or two of collated fully-colored scripts on standby (but not on the distribution table) for these purposes. You will welcome these standby copies when you are rushed and have to generate a collated seven-colored script for someone immediately.

TWO COLLATED SCRIPTS IN OFFICE FOR SIDES

Besides any standby copies of the script, keep two fully-collated scripts in the office for use when making the daily sides for the set. At the end of the production, these scripts, if well kept, can serve as master copies for any final scripts that you must photocopy for Executives and companies.

STORE LEFTOVER COPIES IN AN "ARCHIVE" BOX

As some people tend to lose paperwork, so other people and companies will remember at a later date which paperwork they require. Keep old versions of all paperwork in an archive box instead of throwing them out. Often people will be satisfied with an older copy of the script because they just want to have an idea of the plot.

STARTER DISTRIBUTION LISTS

The checklists that follow will jog your memory when distributing anything, paper or otherwise. The Production Coordinator and the Production Manager should review these lists to jointly decide who needs to receive what.

DEPARTMENT HEADS

When you have something to go to all department heads, refer to this list. When creating your own distribution lists, review this list to be sure you address the entire crew.

- ❑ Producer (any and all)
- ❑ Director
- ❑ Story Editor
- ❑ Production Manager
- ❑ Production Coordinator
- ❑ Production Accountant
- ❑ 1st A.D.
- ❑ Location Manager
- ❑ Continuity Supervisor
- ❑ Casting Director
- ❑ Publicist
- ❑ Production Designer
- ❑ Art Director
- ❑ Set Decorator
- ❑ Props Master
- ❑ Wardrobe Designer
- ❑ Hair Stylist
- ❑ Makeup Artist
- ❑ Director of Photography
- ❑ Sound Mixer
- ❑ Gaffer
- ❑ Key Grip
- ❑ Special Effects Supervisor
- ❑ Stunt Coordinator
- ❑ Construction Manager
- ❑ Transportation Coordinator
- ❑ Postproduction Supervisor

OFFICE KEYS LIST

Okay, keys are not paperwork. But you do need to hand out many of them to the crew and need to monitor who has what. Ensure the PC and the PM decide who really needs which key. Do not just copy tons of keys and hand them out. Use a key sign-out list. Know who will actually be using the office after hours. If you have an alarm system, make sure each person with a key knows how to use the alarm system properly. Here is a starter list for discussion:

Producer
Production Manager
Production Coordinator

Production Secretary
Office Production Assistant
1st A.D.
2nd A.D.
3rd A.D.
Location Manager
Location Scout
Production Designer
Art Director
Set Decorator
Props Master
Wardrobe Designer
Construction Manager
Transportation Coordinator
Driver Captain
Head Driver
Craft Service

THE JOY OF PAPERWORK DISTRIBUTION LISTS

It is time to move onto the majority of the paperwork distribution lists that you will require. Again, the PM and the PC need to examine and fine-tune these lists to create your own "Joy of Distribution" lists. When completed, give copies of your lists to all the office staff, and to the A.D.s (for set-related distribution).

SCRIPT-RELATED PAPERWORK

Scripts are generally very long documents; therefore, keep an accurate list of who gets each script to prevent over-photocopying.

SCRIPT – EARLY DRAFTS

If the draft is very early in preproduction, some of the people on this list may not be hired yet. Even though this list is large, check with the Producer to determine which of these people really requires the current early draft of the script.

Script Research Company
Executive Producer
Producer
Director
Story Editor
Casting Director
Director of Photography
Production Manager

Production Coordinator
Production Designer
1st A.D.
2nd A.D.
Location Manager
Art Director
Set Decorator
Props Master
Wardrobe Designer
Continuity Supervisor
Sound Mixer
Gaffer
Key Grip
Special Effects Coordinator
Stunt Coordinator
Transportation Coordinator

SCRIPT – MAJOR REVISIONS ONLY
This distribution list is for those who may not need every little revision of the script.

Publicist
Performer Unions
Government Agencies

SCRIPT – EVERY REVISION
At this point, it is too obvious to list the entire shooting crew on this list, so these are recipients BEYOND the set crew to consider.

Distributor or Broadcaster
Funding Agencies
Executive Producer & Head Office Personnel
Editors
Completion Bond Company

SCRIPT RESEARCH REPORT
The clearance company responds with notes of character names that must change, songs that must be cleared before singing on set, and warnings of any copyrights and trademarks that are being infringed. (More on script clearances is in Chapter 32.) Distribute this report to:

Executive Producer
Producer
Director
Story Editor/Story Department

Legal Counsel
Production Manager
Production Coordinator
Production Accountant
1st A.D.
Production Designer
Art Director
Set Decorator
Props Master
Wardrobe Designer
Continuity Supervisor

SCHEDULE-RELATED PAPERWORK

You are already familiar with numerous kinds of schedules. BEYOND the set crew, these are other people to keep informed. Call them first to confirm which paperwork they require.

CALL SHEET (SENT VIA FAX DAILY)
Distributor or Broadcaster
Performer Unions
Crew Unions
Extras Casting Director
Funding Agencies
Government Agencies
Completion Bond Company

ONE-LINE SCHEDULE & PRODUCTION SCHEDULE
Executive Producer & Head Office
Editors
Publicist
Distributor or Broadcaster
Funding Agencies
Government Agencies
Completion Bond Company

SHOOTING SCHEDULE
Executive Producer & Head Office
Editors
Publicist
Performer Unions
Funding Agencies
Government Agencies

Completion Bond Company
Performers (who are not on set)

OTHER PAPERWORK

This section is made up of lists, contracts, and breakdowns. Since you, as the Coordinator, are responsible to disseminate information to those not on the crew, these lists cover those people and companies.

CREW LIST
    Executive Producer & Head Office
    Editors
    Publicist
    Distributor or Broadcaster
    Crew Unions
    Performer Unions
    Funding Agencies
    Government Agencies
    Completion Bond Company

CAST LIST
    Executive Producer & Head Office
    Editors
    Publicist
    Distributor or Broadcaster
    Performer Unions
    Funding Agencies
    Government Agencies
    Completion Bond Company

PERFORMER CONTRACTS
    Talent Agent for Performer
    Production Accountant
    Production Coordinator
    Legal Counsel
    A.D. (with pay rates masked)

PERFORMER PICTURES & RESUMES
    Production Coordinator
    Publicist

EXTRAS BREAKDOWN MEMO
    Performer Union

Extras Casting Director
Executive Producer & Head Office
Production Coordinator

CREDIT LIST – FINAL

Executive Producer & Head Office
Producer
Legal Counsel
Production Manager
Production Coordinator
Production Accountant
Publicist
Postproduction Supervisor
Distributor or Broadcaster
Funding Agencies
Government Agencies
Completion Bond Company

THE PRODUCTION REPORT & ALL ITS BACKUP PAPERWORK

As you know, the DPR is actually a compilation of reports from each of the departments. Each departmental report has its own set of recipients for distribution, as does the daily production report itself. Start with these distribution lists, and consult each department and the Production Manager to create your own set of report distribution lists for the production. Determine and note who keeps the original of each report.

PRODUCTION REPORT – DRAFT COPY

Be sure the Production Manager has approved even the draft copy before distributing this document.

Production Accountant
A.D. (who writes the report on set)
Executive Producer
Completion Bond Company
Production Coordinator

PRODUCTION REPORT – TYPED AND SIGNED COPY

Now approved by all parties, the production report has a wider distribution. It remains a confidential report. Treat it as such.

Production Coordinator (keeps the original)
Executive Producer
Producer
Production Manager

Production Accountant
1st A.D.
A.D. (who writes the report on set)
Funding Agencies
Completion Bond Company

CONTINUITY TOP SHEET

This report is the Continuity Supervisor's summary of all scenes shot or not, and an update on the timing of the entire script. This is the form to refer to when completing the continuity section of the production report.

Continuity Supervisor
Editors
Executive Producer
Producer
Production Manager
Production Coordinator
Production Lab (copy may go straight from set)

OTHER CONTINUITY PAPERWORK

Shot reports, log forms, wild sound reports, and any other continuity paperwork detail even further all the information the Editors need to know for postproduction.

Continuity Supervisor
Editors
Production Coordinator
Production Lab (copy may go straight from set)

SOUND REPORT SHEETS

The Sound Department reports on the quality of the contents of each roll of sound stock they use. They usually use a two-part form that enables them to keep a copy of their paperwork upon sending you the editing copy. These are the forms you count when completing the "sound stock used" section of the production report.

Editors
Production Coordinator
Production Lab (copy may go straight from set)

CAMERA REPORTS

Just like the Sound Department, the Camera Department reports to the lab and to the Editors the contents of each roll of film, and which take or takes to print.

Editors
Production Coordinator
Production Lab (copy will go straight from set)

DAILY FILM STOCK SUMMARY

The Camera Department also reports to production the amount of film used to date and the amount of unused film on hand. This is the form to refer to when completing the "film totals" section of the production report.

> Production Coordinator

PERFORMER WORK REPORTS

Already discussed, this form is a time sheet for Performers. Refer to it when completing the Performer's section of the production report.

> Production Accountant
> Performer Union
> Production Coordinator

EXTRAS VOUCHERS

These forms serve as both contracts for Extras and as time sheets. Refer to these when completing the Extras section of the production report.

> Production Accountant
> Performer Union
> Production Coordinator

DRIVER TIMES

Since the Transportation Department often wraps at the end of the day after the last A.D. does, they forward their daily work times into the production office later. Sometimes you have to call for this information. These timings will complete the crew attendance section on the production report.

> Transportation Coordinator
> Production Accountant
> Production Coordinator

You have noticed that the Production Coordinator keeps a copy of every piece of paper that is distributed. Paperwork gets lost now and then. The production office needs to have the backup copy for anything the PC or the office handles. It is the Coordinator's production files that end up going to head office as a complete set of what happened during production. With every piece of information and report you file now, and the record you have of everything that has been distributed in the office, you will be assembling that set from day one — with a little "joy" in the distribution, because you have a system that works to help you.

VII.

ONGOING SPECIAL ISSUES

Find out how much "free" costs.

The Box at Customs

When it comes to shipping props, you can ship an incredibly wide variety of items. You have to know how to handle each one separately when it comes to customs clearances. One missing word can stop a shipment and delay a shoot.

On one show, we had to ship crates and crates of props to New Zealand for a period piece. All parts of the paperwork were carefully reviewed over and over again for accuracy and completeness. At the border one crate stopped dead.

But customs refused to open the case to examine the contents. They asked the shipper if the contents were real or fake. The documents did not specify. The shipper refused to open the case to find out, too. They telephoned me back home to ask if I had forgotten to include the word "fake" on this contents list. I asked them to be more specific. They said they refused to open the case to find out; they just wanted my answer, and read to me the list of contents.

I held back my laughter and apologized for the oversight and insisted that yes, the props were indeed fake. The two items that had concerned them so deeply were: one human ear... and one baby's head.

CHAPTER 31

COURIERS & CUSTOMS

When production decides that there is a very special item for set that needs to be imported from another country, you know you cannot ship it as easily as you can across town. Knowing also that the item is required on set in a day or two, it is time to make friends with a Customs Broker. The Production Coordinator organizes the shipment, and the Production Manager tracks the costs associated with shipping, duties, and taxes.

COURIERS (LOCAL & INTERNATIONAL)

The Coordinator tends to be the one both to set up the account with the local and international couriers and to deal with the day-to-day business of shipping and receiving packages. The PM can trust the Coordinator to this job and become involved in more complex shipping issues, as noted below.

TRACKING COURIERED PACKAGES

As the Coordinator, you are comfortable with the services of the courier companies you have chosen. You can call them after hours, they are quick to respond, and they are reasonably affordable. They have pre-printed your company name on a series of waybills. There is a bit more you should know to track the many packages you send daily and weekly:

FILL OUT WAYBILLS COMPLETELY

Get into the habit of filling out each waybill completely, whether local or international. If you think that packages are delivered without a telephone number, the date, or a complete description of the contents, you are right most of the time. Realize, however, that noting the telephone number aids the courier if it cannot find the address or the person, and noting the date and the contents aids you if someone forgets to enter the information into the distribution binder. Completed waybills only help you.

LOG OR KEEP WAYBILLS

Use a log form to record each couriered envelope or package. You will refer to this log. You send a lot of packages to numerous people and companies. Your memory cannot retain the information. Your memory cannot help you when you have to trace lost packages.

KNOW YOUR COURIER'S SERVICES

Know when the last pickup is for your courier. Know where the drop boxes are and those last pickup times. Know the latest time you can take a package to the courier's airport location and still get it on the plane. Due to the nature of the film industry, you will almost always be working on those last minute times.

TAXIS AS LOCAL COURIERS

Taxis deliver people or packages in town. They can be faster than the fastest service your courier can provide, but they tend to be more expensive. Taxi companies can set you up with an account and give you chits to fill out instead of handling cash. They charge an administration fee atop the price of each ride for this convenience.

THE EFFICIENT OFFICE P.A.

If you have an efficient Office Production Assistant, you will find you do not need your local courier very often. An Office P.A. who knows the city and can manage time, will cut your courier bill down to minimum. He is also equipped with more knowledge about production, and therefore production's priorities, than any courier or taxi driver could be. Use the Office P.A. to your advantage.

THE CUSTOMS BROKER

Documents easily cross borders, bypassing customs. Documents have no commercial value. Working for a film company, you will rarely be shipping only documents. There are many restrictions and many forms for items that have to pass through customs to enter your country. You need a Customs Broker to help you. The Production Manager tends to choose the Customs Broker. When choosing one, talk about its services, including accessibility after hours, as well as its rates. Dealing with shipping and receiving, the Coordinator will more often be the one to deal with the Customs Broker on a day-to-day basis.

POWER OF AUTHORITY LETTER

When a Customs Broker is chosen, the Coordinator can produce a letter addressed to that Broker giving it the power of authority to clear packages through customs for you. The Production Manager needs to be the signing authority for this letter, of course, being a signing authority for the company. The letter is very short and can read like this:

(On letterhead)

Customs Broker
Customs Broker Address

To whom it may concern:

This letter authorizes (Customs Broker company) to act on our behalf of FILM COMPANY INC. ("FILM TITLE") relating to all customs clearances.

Sincerely,

(Production Manager Name)
Production Manager

COURIERS KNOW SIMPLE CUSTOMS PAPERWORK

International couriers know about the customs paperwork to be completed for many shipments. If you ask, they will supply you with appropriate forms and directions for the do-it-yourself approach. Use this approach for repeated simple packages, like the daily videotapes you may be shipping to some of the Executives. If you are ever concerned about the correct paperwork or customs procedure, call your Customs Broker for advice.

VIDEOTAPES (OR EXPOSED FILM) CROSSING BORDERS

Rushes, rough cuts, and delivered shows may have you shipping your share of videotapes across international borders. Confirm with the courier or the broker that no more paperwork is needed than a commercial invoice and a videotape declaration to accompany the waybill. The commercial invoice describes in more detail what the waybill explains, and the videotape declaration is your assurance that the videotapes do not contain material that is pornographic or treasonous. Some countries have censors from whom you will need approval at the border.

COMMERCIAL INVOICE – SMALL SHIPMENTS

The waybill often has a section that is called "commercial invoice." Completing this section is sufficient for international videotape shipments, except for very large shipments. Note how many videotapes and which format are in the package, then mark in large letters in this section that the tapes are: "FOR REFERENCE ONLY; NOT FOR RESALE." Presuming, of course, that you are sending rushes or cut shows for approvals, then "for reference" is what they are.

COMMERCIAL INVOICE – LARGE SHIPMENTS

For large shipments, make a secondary, more detailed commercial invoice on letterhead, as shown here:

(On letterhead)

Date of shipment: (date)

To Whom: (name, address, phone, fax)

Description of Contents: (e.g., one VHS videotape)

Value of Contents: (note value and currency)

Reason for Export: (e.g., daily rushes of "Film" for reference only; not for resale)

How Shipped: (courier company name & waybill number)

Signed: (Production Coordinator name & title)

VIDEOTAPE/FILM DECLARATION

If you cannot get a form from the courier or the broker, make one on letterhead like this:

(On letterhead)

Date of shipment: (date)

To Whom: (name, address, phone, fax)

Waybill Number: (number)

Description of Contents: (e.g., one VHS videotape)

Length of Videotape or Film: (e.g., 30 minutes)

Reason for Export: (e.g., daily rushes of "Film" for reference only; not for resale)

I/we declare that the FILM(S)/VIDEO(S) contain no obscene or immoral matter, nor any matter advocating or urging treason or insurrection against (country of destination), nor any threat to take the life of or inflict bodily harm upon any person in (country of destination).

Signed: (Production Coordinator name & title)

WARDROBE CROSSING BORDERS

Imagine sending a knife wrapped in a t-shirt (for safety) from one country to another, complete with customs documents for the knife. You may wonder why the package stops at customs. Customs will be looking for the proper documentation for the t-shirt. Okay, an overstatement, but at the border, they do need to know what the article of clothing is, its value, why you are shipping it, what fibers makes up the fabric, and where each fiber was made in the world. Each piece of information requires a separate form. When you ship clothing, get the help of your Customs Broker.

REQUEST FOR REDUCTION OF DUTY LETTER

When you courier large shipments of rental wardrobe internationally, large duties and taxes are triggered because customs presumes the wardrobe is arriving to stay. To apply for reduction of these duty and taxes, because production is only renting the wardrobe, draft a letter to the customs office with the help of your Broker (who will know the latest procedure). Start with the following draft letter, customizing the information to your production:

(On letterhead)

Date: (date)

Collector
Customs Office

Dear Sir/Madam:

Please consider this letter an application for reduction of duty and taxes for the wardrobe (see attached lists). I am applying on behalf of the importer, FILM COMPANY INC., whose address is listed here. We are a (country of nationality) crew currently in production of a (type of film) entitled, "FILM TITLE," for (note where it will be distributed or broadcast). Below please find our responses to the questions regarding responsibility of the importer:

a) Name and address of importer:
(film company's name, address, telephone, fax, email, Web address)

b) Contact within company:
(Production Coordinator name, Head of Wardrobe name)

c) Financial Hardship:
We believe that full duty and taxes would be excessive considering the short period of time that the wardrobe will be in the country. These goods are obtainable only from (the country of export) and will be returned immediately.

d) Why goods are required:
We are filming "FILM TITLE" that requires authentic (describe originality of wardrobe).

e) Goods not available from national suppliers:
The above-mentioned goods could not be obtained from the top costume houses in (your country) due to their peculiarity within the time and budget allotted.

f) List of companies and persons contacted:

Name at least three companies you contacted for this wardrobe. Include letters from these companies reporting that they do not have this particular wardrobe. (The letters are described on page 335.)

g) "Public Interest":

This production employs many people from the shooting crew to the support industries, such as (note appropriate suppliers you use, like: equipment houses, hotels, restaurants, airlines, limousines, postproduction laboratories and sound facilities, telephone systems, studio rentals, the unions and guilds, etc.). If we cannot obtain the goods within the required time and budget, we will have to shut down production until such time as we can have appropriate wardrobe made for filming, which would mean a shutdown of at least (mention an estimated time frame). This shutdown will affect in excess of (number of employees) people with a loss of income.

h) Statement:

See attached letter from Production Manager. (The letter is described on page 335.)

i) National Competitors:

We have contacted everyone possible to obtain the required costumes and they are unable to provide the goods. Nor can anyone suggest anyone in (your country) that can.

j) Any objections to reveal company's name:

FILM COMPANY INC. does not have any objections to its name being revealed.

k) Description of what makes them special in nature:

(Describe the costumes.)

l) Use of goods:

As wardrobe for a (feature film or television movie).

m) Where goods to be used:

"FILM TITLE" movie currently filming in (city).

n) Value of goods:

(note overall value and currency)

o) Estimated date of arrival:

Shipment from (costume company name) in (city, country) on (date of arrival).

If you require further information, I can be reached at the production number listed below. I look forward to hearing from you in the near future.

Signed, (Production Coordinator name and title)

WARDROBE SUPPLIER LETTERS (Item f. above)

The Head of Wardrobe will usually arrange for these letters for you. If the supplier asks you to draft the wording, since they are busy, start with the following: "FILM COMPANY INC. has requested the rental of (specify costumes). We do not have such costumes in our stock and do not know of another company in (your country) that can assist them with this rental."

STATEMENT LETTER FROM PM (Item h. above)

Create and attach a letter addressed to customs from the Production Manager that promises the film company will cover all duty and taxes should the request for reduction of duty be denied. Begin with the following wording: "This letter is to confirm that FILM COMPANY INC. would accept responsibility for payment in full of duties and taxes applicable under the (appropriate tax act), if the request for reduction of duty and taxes is not approved."

COMMERCIAL INVOICE

Type up a commercial invoice on letterhead, just as you do for videotapes, detailing exactly what items are being imported. The costume company will have a detailed list since they have to generate one for rental and accounting purposes anyway. Do not simply photocopy their forms (which you will also use for customs). Make the commercial invoice easy to read, listing the items clearly, and noting the overall value rather than individual values.

FILM EQUIPMENT CROSSING BORDERS

If you take film equipment to certain countries for the filming period and return with it, your Customs Broker will help you to obtain a "carnet." If it is the whole equipment package, the equipment rental house will arrange for the carnet. A carnet is a document that lists every single item of film equipment (right down to each filter), all the serial numbers, every separate value, and every source country for each separate piece. This document is a promise to customs that this equipment will be in the country temporarily. It works like a bond, which is why you need to return home with each piece of equipment you imported. This is a complex form to get. Beyond that, not all countries recognize a carnet, so you may have to arrange for another type of certificate of temporary import/export. When you are planning on shipping large quantities of equipment for the duration of (or part of) the shoot, talk first with your Customs Broker and with the equipment rental house you are using. They will both be of great help.

FILM STOCK CROSSING BORDERS

Security at the airports may say that unprocessed film is unaffected by the security x-ray machine, but they are wrong. There is a very real risk of x-ray radiation on your raw stock or unprocessed rushes every time you pass them through a security x-ray machine. X-rays are also cumulative in effect. Consider this effect when you add up all the machines you need to pass through on the journey. And, yes, the higher the ASA of the film, the higher the risk, as ASA measures the film's sensitivity to light (which is a kind of radiation). Therefore, as you cannot afford to have raw stock or unprocessed rushes exposed to x-rays, it behooves you to send the film in lead cases when crossing borders, or arrange for some other cross-border arrangement wherein the film is not x-rayed. If you are hand-carrying unprocessed film across the border, remember to bring along a black changing bag in case you need to open a can at security. You likely will.

OTHER ITEMS CROSSING BORDERS

You can ship almost anything: contact lenses, animals, props, antiques, and so on. Since countries have different restrictions and requirements for each shipment, contact your Customs Broker for the latest procedures for each item.

HAND-CARRYING ITEMS ACROSS BORDERS

Due to time constraints, sometimes the only remaining alternative is to fly a person across a border to hand-carry the item to its destination. Because this is a last resort method of shipping, any delay at the border is critical. Paperwork must be perfectly complete and accurate. Review all the paperwork necessary with the Customs Broker. It may arrange for someone at the airport to aid you through customs. Along with all that paperwork, give a letter of identification to the person hand-carrying:

(On letterhead)

Date

To whom it may concern:

(Hand-Carry Person name) is hand-carrying (describe item) for the film entitled: "FILM TITLE." (Describe reason for the export and if the item is being returned to the country.)

The value of (the item) for customs purposes is: (amount and currency).

Signed, (Production Coordinator name and title)

As the Coordinator, you will get used to foreign shipments, growing amazed by how similar the various customs forms actually are. Each one requires so much of the same information over and over again with one or two extra items. You may never stop being amazed, but you will soon learn which forms are appropriate to which packages, and amaze the Production Manager, and the crew, on your knowledge about customs. The PM will feel a level of comfort with the Coordinator shepherding anything and everything across town and across borders. When whatever it is needs to be on set, the PC is dealing with the details to ensure it shows up on time.

Sing to Me in Public Domain

Actors often invent unscripted business on set for their characters, to add depth and personality to their performances. That's wonderful, unless the unscripted business is singing unscripted, copyrighted songs.

One Actor I worked with had this tendency, and the first two songs did not prove to be a big problem. After watching the rushes, I arranged for licenses to use the songs that he sang. Both licenses were reasonable. Twice lucky. But the third song...

Watching the rushes, I was relieved that the actor had chosen to hum a piece of his own making. It was a totally unintelligible, nonsensical collection of sounds. Not so, apparently.

The day before broadcast, the Production Secretary was dubbing a copy of the show and commented how long it has been since she'd heard that song. "Song?" I asked. She told me the title and the artist. It was no collection of sounds, as I originally thought; it was an obscure, old, and very copyrighted song.

The Producer asked me to get a quote on the license. I discovered a catch. The particular Broadcaster we were using was not signatory with the performing rights company that covered the song. The performing rights company did not want to grant a license at any cost. They wanted the Broadcaster to become signatory.

So, to this day, lawyers speak with lawyers about this song, and the particular Actor was never allowed to sing or hum unscripted songs on set again, unless it could be proven before call time that the songs were indeed in the public domain.

CHAPTER 32

LEGAL CLEARANCES

Sometimes the Producer does it. Sometimes Legal Counsel does it. Often either of you, the Production Manager or the Production Coordinator, does it. "It" is the clearing of the rights to copyrighted works, like songs or photographs, for use in a film production. This chapter cannot be an exhaustive description of legal rights and clearances, and does not intend to be — but it will guide you on this facet of film-making. Keep in contact with Legal Counsel for advice as you enter the world of rights and clearances.

THE SCRIPT CLEARANCE REPORT

Script clearance has been mentioned several times so far. You need to find a script clearance company to read and report on the script as it is, when you are close to production.

E&O INSURANCE

As mentioned previously, in order to distribute or broadcast a film production, the Producer needs to arrange for E&O insurance (errors & omissions insurance) for the film. E&O insurance is a kind of "malpractice" insurance for Producers in case the Producer has mistakenly represented a real person or a company in this fictional film, and the actual person or company feels the representation is derogatory and harmful enough to them to sue the Producer. Now, these types of lawsuits never result in the suing party only suing the Producer; the party will also sue the Distributor and the Broadcaster and the Studio and anyone else who has money to compensate them. This is why you cannot distribute the film without E&O insurance. Everyone needs to be protected.

Of course, the Producer (through the production company) must have done all the research during the scriptwriting process to ensure that this fictional film indeed does not happen to portray a real person or company or take place in real locations. This is where the script research report comes in. Clearance companies read scripts and report on all the names, trademarks, logos, and other potentially litigious items in the script and comment on them for the Producer. The Producer must then act and change the references to keep the script legally clear. The Producer may consult with Legal Counsel to determine which of the clearance report references need to be changed and which ones are clear enough as they are.

HOW SCRIPT CLEARANCE REPORTS WORK

If, for example, the script has a character named John Smith who is a dentist from a particular city, the clearance company will research to see if such a man exists. If there are many John Smiths in that city, of which none are dentists, then the name "John Smith" is clear for use in the film. If, however, there is one John Smith who is a dentist in all of North America, or if there is only one John Smith in that city, then the clearance company will suggest your changing the character name in the script to avoid any possible lawsuit. The real John Smith may see the film, decide that his character is a derogatory portrayal of himself, and sue. Production needs to use clear names in the script. The same goes for names and trademarks on props, locations, set dressing, and wardrobe (like logos on baseball caps). These references will be in set descriptions and in dialogue references.

FIRST CONVERSATION WITH A CLEARANCE COMPANY

Decide between the Production Manager and Coordinator who is going to be the contact with the script clearance company. Then, when you first talk to the script clearance company, know where and when the script takes place. Is the film fictional or is it based on a true story? Where is the film going to be distributed or broadcast? From this information and other questions they will ask, the clearance company will determine the scope of the clearance you need, and the two of you can negotiate a price.

THE CLEARANCE COMPANY AND SCRIPT REVISIONS

It is truly important to keep the clearance company abreast of all script revisions as soon as possible. Once you are aware of how they read a script, you as the Coordinator — while you are typing the next script revision — can telephone in script changes as they happen. This process will give the clearance company extra time to research the new material.

THE RELUCTANCE OF CHANGING NAMES

Writers, Story Editors, and Producers may be reluctant to change names they deem either trivial or absolutely essential to the story as is. Changing names is legal preventative medicine, so if you need to, involve the Legal Counsel for persuasion. Together the Legal Counsel and the Producer can evaluate the potential legal risk and come up with a decision to change the names or not, and take the risk of this item being an exclusion from the E&O insurance.

ADDRESSING THE SUGGESTIONS ON THE CLEARANCE REPORT

After distributing the clearance report, read it carefully and ensure that, somehow, the production team addresses each suggestion for change.

CHARACTER NAMES THAT DO NOT CLEAR

Have the Writers or the Story Editor generate a list of replacement names in descending order of preference to send to the clearance company for "re-clearing" immediately. Once a replacement name is cleared, send a memo to everyone who gets the clearance report. The Coordinator needs to place an extra copy in the script revision desk file to remind him to include it when next revising the script. The immediacy of the memo will help the Wardrobe Department (for example) build clothing labels using correct, cleared names.

LOCATION NAMES THAT DO NOT CLEAR

If the script is fictitious, the names of the locations must also be fictitious. If an actual location (like a restaurant) with its name is used onscreen, then the script, legally, is no longer located in a fictitious place. Actual locations make the clearing of character names more complex and iffy. Get replacement names to the clearance company as soon as possible. The Art Department will likely have to build signs to identify these fictitious buildings on screen.

TRADEMARKS THAT DO NOT CLEAR

Trademarks like "Kleenex" and "Xerox" are often mentioned in early drafts of scripts when what is actually meant is "facial tissue" and "photocopy." The clearance report will note these trademarks for you. If you do not change these words in the script, you must contact each company to negotiate written permission to use their trademarked name onscreen. Since most corporate companies do not work at the speed of film companies, permissions can take up to six or eight weeks. For trivial onscreen references, your time and effort are not worth wasting. Make the change.

REFERENCES THAT ALMOST DO NOT CLEAR

People who work at clearance companies seem to have seen every film ever made, read every book on the market, and speak every language in the world. These people are amazing. You may see a comment in the clearance report that notes a certain visual look is particularly like that of another film already made, or a certain phrase has been published in a book already on the market, or that a certain work or character name actually means something terribly rude in another language. Discuss these comments with the Producer and the Legal Counsel. Find out how these notes will be addressed.

CLEARANCES REFERENCES NOT IN THE SCRIPT

As you can imagine, not all references that need clearing are listed clearly in the script. While out shopping for production, the Wardrobe Department has the opportunity of purchasing clothing that features copyrighted logos; the Set Dressing team has the opportunity of purchasing or renting televisions and stereo equipment with copyrighted logos on them, too; and the Locations Department has the likelihood of showing other company names in the background of shots by the location's proximity to other businesses. As a Production Manager, you cannot rely totally on the script clearance report; you need to hire a professional crew who are conscious of clearance issues. If in doubt, discuss these issues at the beginning of production, especially with the Art Department.

WHERE TO ASK FOR PERMISSION

You have a copyrighted name that you really want to use in the film but you do not know whom to ask for permission. If the contact name and the number are not already on the clearance report, telephone and ask the clearance company. Though they are not negotiators for you, they will find out where you have to go to obtain permission.

USING ACTUAL NAMES

In stories based on real people or companies, it is obvious that you need each person's and each company's permission to depict them in the film. But even in fictional films, you will sometimes use the names of real people or locations:

USING AN ACTUAL PERSON'S NAME

When the script uses the name of a person, be it a crew member or a friend who gives permission to the production company to do so, draft a short letter from that person confirming that permission. Legal Counsel needs all such permissions in writing in order to obtain the E&O insurance. Be simple in creating the letter with wording like: "I give FILM COMPANY INC. permission to use my name in the film 'FILM TITLE.' I understand that my name will not be used in a derogatory manner." Review the wording with Legal Counsel for simplicity and full legal coverage.

USING AN ACTUAL LOCATION OR COMPANY NAME

Location agreements usually contain a clause to give the film company permission to use the company name onscreen when filming there. Do not assume all location agreements specify this. Check with the Location Manager. If there is no such clause and you intend to see the company's name onscreen, generate a letter granting the permission you need and review the letter with Legal Counsel.

MUSIC CLEARANCES

If there are a lot of songs in the script and the film company has the funds, hire a music clearance company to clear the songs for you. They will identify songs that are in the public domain (and are therefore free) and will save you from an enormous and time-consuming job. If, however, you have to (or want to) clear the music in the script, here are a few things you should know:

WHAT IS PUBLIC DOMAIN?

Songs in the public domain are free to use. When the owner of the copyright has been dead for a certain length of time, his work is put into the public domain. The required number of years varies from country to country from fifty to 100, so check with Legal Counsel to determine how many years is required for the distribution plans for your production. Be aware that there are many familiar songs that are not in the public domain. "Happy Birthday To You," for example, is still a very copyrighted work.

TYPES OF RIGHTS
Once you select a song to use, there are four types of rights you may need to buy before using that song:

PUBLISHING OR SYNCHRONIZATION RIGHTS
As the name suggests, you must contact a Music Publisher to purchase a publishing rights license. This license grants you permission to use the "sheet music" for a particular song. This license in hand, you can hum that song, sing that song, play that song, or arrange your own version of that song onscreen and play that song in synchronization with the film you are producing.

RECORDING RIGHTS
As the name suggests, you have to contact a Record Company to get a recording rights license. This license grants you permission to play a particular recording of a song onscreen. This license does not include the Publisher's permission. You must obtain a publishing rights license separately.

ARTIST RIGHTS
Sometimes the Record Company does not hold all the rights to a recording, because the Artist has retained some rights. Ask the Record Company if Artist's rights are applicable to this recording. Artist's rights are negotiated through the Record Company or through the Artist's manager. Again, you still have to obtain a publishing rights license separately.

ARRANGEMENT RIGHTS
Not all songs in the public domain are free to use. Some have arrangement rights attached to them. An Arranger can take a song in the public domain, publish his own arrangement, and copyright that arrangement. As the description suggests, you will need to contact a Publisher to negotiate arrangement rights.

SO, WHAT ARE MASTER RIGHTS?
You will hear the term "master rights" used frequently. "Publishing rights" are technically called "master rights" and "recording rights" are technically called "master recording rights" (but are often incorrectly called "master rights"). By using the terms "publishing" and "recording" instead of "master" for both, you cannot mix up the two licenses, and people in the industry will understand you.

WHERE TO LOOK FOR MUSIC RIGHTS
For publishing rights, call the Index Department of the music performer rights associations (ASCAP, BMI, SOCAN, or the similar CMRRA) with the name of the

song. They can furnish you with the name of the Publisher and will also know if arrangement rights apply.

For recording rights, simply refer to the CD cover for the name of the Record Company. Contact the Permissions or Legal Department and request permission. Postproduction will consider a CD adequate from which to duplicate the recording onto the soundtrack. If there is no CD of the song, ask the Record Company to supply you with a master of the recording.

TERMS, TERRITORIES, USAGE, FEES

When you are set to negotiate for the rights, address the following criteria:

TERM

Often license fees are for a 5-year term, 10-year term, or perpetuity. Naturally, the longer the term is, the higher the price. Buy as much as you can afford. Distributors and Legal Counsels love the words "in perpetuity," so that a few years from now they do not have to buy the rights all over again.

TERRITORY

You can get a license to cover one country or pay more and cover the world. Find out from the Producer the plan for the film's distribution. Will production or the Distributor pay for all those foreign territories?

USAGE

Is the song to be hummed, sung, or played as an instrumental? Is it heard as a record playing or does a band mime to the recording? Is the song atmosphere in the background or a critical part of the scene's action? Have some script pages handy to demonstrate the song's usage in the scene when you ask for permission. The owners need to know how the song is to be handled to be certain it is not being used in a derogatory manner.

FEES

A character hums an identifiable song in the script as he walks in the door. The Producer wants to know how much the use of that song will cost. Fees vary drastically, taking into consideration the range of terms, territories, and usages; the budget of your production; and the particularities of each Publisher. Each song will be different. A price quotation is time-consuming for you and the Publisher, so be sure you really want that song before you start the process of asking for permission.

STOCK MUSIC

Stock music is generally low-copyright music. If you are specific about a song you want but not about a particular arrangement or Artist, contact a Stock Music Supplier to source stock music that will suffice. They charge research fees, so be specific. They also charge transfer fees, so be sure Postproduction tells you exactly which delivery format is acceptable. The license fee is sold to you at a very discounted price compared to that of the big Publishers, and the license will be for the use throughout the world and in perpetuity.

PROMISE OF A SCREEN CREDIT

Song credits are not short. For each piece of music, count on three to four lines of text to credit any or all of the song title, the Composer, the Publisher, the Artist, and the Record Company. Be up front with the record company about credits. It is standard to credit songs, but if the production is too small to warrant many credits of any kind, address this issue early. Do not wait for the license to arrive with credit wording expected and specifications defined.

WHEN YOU CANNOT FIND THE OWNER

Rights change hands. They expire. They revert back to the Composers. Publishers buy out other Publishers. Sometimes you cannot find the rights to a song no matter how hard you try. Keep notes of everyone you contact in your search for the owner. If after a few weeks your search has still been to no avail, Legal Counsel can review your notes and decide that enough effort went into the search, so the song can be used anyway.

SINGING UNSCRIPTED SONGS ON SET

As mentioned earlier, performers can be asked to adlib a song on the set. Talk to the A.D.s and do not let any Performer hum a song that is not in the public domain! Clearing a song after it has been cut into the film is a nearly impossible task. With the film completed, you are no longer in a bargaining position. If the owner does not want to sell you the rights, your only way out is to cut the offending song from the film.

CUE SHEETS

Postproduction is aware they have to forward cue sheets to the music performer rights associations (ASCAP, BMI, or SOCAN), as well as to the Distributors, the Broadcasters, and other places. Cue sheets report how many seconds of each song is played in the production and identify the respective owners. The associations use this information to calculate royalty payments to the Composers. Read the licenses you have purchased. They may also require that a copy of the cue sheets go to the Publisher and/or the Record Company. If so, send a memo to Postproduction relating this information.

PHOTOGRAPHIC CLEARANCES

When you are getting permission to use a photograph from a stock library or a magazine, note that there are two kinds of rights that may apply: "magazine rights" and "photographer rights." Treat these clearances much in the same way as music clearances. As the Magazine Company is like a Publisher, so the Photographer is like the Music Artist. The Magazine's Legal Department will know if the Photographer has retained any rights to the photograph you wish to use, not unlike Artist's rights. If the people depicted in the photograph are unrecognizable, there are no more rights to buy. Note, however, that if the people are recognizable, you must seek permission from each one of them, too. A simple letter granting permission to the film company will suffice, but it is wise to discuss this situation with Legal Counsel before pursuing photographic clearances.

In some cases, Stills Photographers you hire on set retain rights to the photographs they take (not unlike Artist's rights). In these cases, you will have to address these rights issues in their agreement/deal memo when you hire them.

OTHER CLEARANCES

Rights can be attached to numerous items: radio shows, posters, artwork, and so on. The script clearance report will note these copyrighted items and lead you to the source for chasing down the appropriate permissions.

TITLE SEARCHES

A title search is different and separate from script clearances. You need a legal firm that specializes in title searches to clear the title for your production. Again, this search is another requirement for the E&O insurance application, and you most certainly do not want your production to have the same name as another film just recently, or soon to be, released. Internet research can help you do the initial title search yourself, so you do not end up purchasing several title searches looking for a title that just will not clear.

PRODUCT PLACEMENT

Product placement is when a company pays the production to show its logo onscreen. It is a form of advertising for the company and a source of revenue for the production. Not all productions, however, want to advertise products in the course of telling a story, and not all Broadcasters appreciate what is basically a commercial during the story. If production allows for product placement, you can approach companies directly or contact a Product Placement Agent from your reference books. Product placement is rarely the source of income it appears to be, and you have to ensure the product's logo is clearly on the screen, which the Director may find restrictive.

Legal clearances no longer mystify you. Though this chapter has not been an exhaustive explanation, the complexity of rights here should inspire you to not be a stranger to your Legal Counsel. She, too, will appreciate your contact and will be happy to share knowledge with you, as she will be up on the latest when it comes to intellectual property rights. Just be sure that you have all the necessary rights before committing anything to screen.

VIII.

POSTPRODUCTION

Do not fix it in post… create magic in post.

Who's in Charge?

Though the hierarchy of a film production deems the Executive Producer most in charge, that is not true all of the time. At the wrap party, the Coordinator rules.

One wrap party, we rented a cruising boat to tour the harbor. The several decks supplied us with a wonderful buffet, danceable music, and incredible views of the city. The party was a great success, and the Executive Producer, along with the Producer and the Production Manager, decided that it should continue for another hour. The Executive Producer was willing to cover the expense on his own credit card.

The boat crew refused their request. They needed the permission of a woman named Deborah. This must be the boat's manager, the producing trio presumed. So a search went out for this Deborah. When she was found, she was escorted to the scene of the request.

The Executive Producer, the Producer, and the Production Manager were rather surprised to find out that the person who appeared was not the boat's manager, but their own Production Coordinator. In front of the trio, the boat crew asked Deborah for permission to extend the party. I quickly said, "Yes, of course!" then turned to the Executive Producer and said: "Sir, you have my approval to spend your own money."

CHAPTER 33

WRAP & WRAP PARTY

The last day of principal photography is here. Crew members are talking about their next jobs. But your mind is concerned with the last phase of production: wrap. In wrap you must return everything that you rented, sell everything that you bought, and pack all the files for head-office storage. It is time to hand over your files of ongoing issues to head office and to Postproduction. It is time to empty the office. It is also time to arrange a celebratory party.

THE PRODUCTION MANAGER WRAPS

Wrap does not mean production is completed. It is far from completed. Only principal photography is done. Postproduction continues. The Production Manager is responsible to wrap up the files of production and hand over the cost-reporting responsibilities to the Postproduction Supervisor. Here is what will keep the PM busy during wrap:

- ❑ Meet with the Coordinator Daily
- ❑ Wrap Main Unit
- ❑ Wrap Second Unit
- ❑ Wrap the PM Files
- ❑ Seek Out and Collect Final Invoices
- ❑ Wrap Out Petty Cash
- ❑ Final Production Cost Report
- ❑ Wardrobe & Set Sale or Storage
- ❑ Check In with Accounting
- ❑ Prep for Audit
- ❑ Hand-Over Memo
- ❑ Post Mortem
- ❑ Tie Up Loose Ends
- ❑ Move Files to Head Office

MEET WITH THE COORDINATOR DAILY
First things first: Meet with the Coordinator daily, even — or especially — during wrap. The PC was key to setting up the office in the first place, and will be heading up wrapping the office now. The PC will also be organizing the wrap party, so you will both need to speak frequently about wrap issues.

WRAP MAIN UNIT
How is the studio strike of the sets proceeding? How is the return of the equipment going? Are there any broken or lost items that need to be found or paid for by production? In

everyone's rush to complete within days, and your needing to be at the office for a week or two, you must remember to supervise and be available during wrap to discover potentially costly issues. You want to be immediately available so you can corral crew into helping you deal with issues before departing to new shows and holidays. Note anything that will cost you money on the PM-only cost report.

WRAP SECOND UNIT
Second Unit may be shooting a few days or a week into wrap. Do not forget about them. Have they achieved all their pickup shots? Their wrap issues will happen later, and you still need to be fresh to deal with them. Find out if they are having trouble getting access to key crew for decision-making while wrap of main unit is underway.

WRAP THE PM FILES
It is time to sift through all the PM files and remove the paperwork that is unnecessary for future reference. Fax top sheets with "2 pages attached" as the only notation are basically useless now. You can integrate the PM files into the Coordinator's production files now, if you would like, so that head office will have fewer sources of files to refer to when they are seeking information in the future.

SEEK OUT AND COLLECT FINAL INVOICES
You want to have all payables in the cost report as soon as possible. The Postproduction Supervisor should not have to chase down production invoices for you. Ask companies for invoices, even if they are supplied by fax, so that you can at least purchase order and close out all production costs on the cost report. Most companies will be thrilled to be able to invoice you quickly.

WRAP OUT PETTY CASH
As with invoices, it is time to ensure all crew have completed their petty cash and balance out. They will be eager to supply you with their petty cash anyway, unless they owe production money. Some crew will surprise you with receipts you never expected because they have been hoarding them throughout production. Expect this conduct now and then. The Production Accountant will no doubt hold onto the crew's last paychecks until their last petty cash receipt is in.

FINAL PRODUCTION COST REPORT
All the final invoices and final petty cash reports you have been collecting enable you and the Production Accountant to generate the final production cost report. You want to zero out as many production line items as possible, so everyone knows how much money and contingency is left for postproduction.

WARDROBE & SET SALE OR STORAGE
Are you arranging for a wardrobe and set dressing sale or putting this material into storage? If production is a television series, you will most likely want to keep the sets and wardrobe in case the show is picked up for the next season. Make a notation to the

Producer of how long you are storing the materials, because the budget will only pay for so many months. On other shows you may want to sell the items to generate a little income for the production company to offset some production overages in those categories. Sets are hard to sell, but you can always contact film companies starting up soon; they might be interested. The Art Department and the Coordinator will be pleased to arrange for and publicize the sale.

CHECK IN WITH ACCOUNTING
The Production Accountant will be busy wrapping the accounting files and preparing them to move to the Postproduction Accountant, and preparing the production reports for the audit. She will also ensure the payroll company completes all the tax forms for the crew. If the cast were paid on flat rates, the Accountant will have to calculate the union scale rates of the actual hours each Performer worked, to be sure the flat rate encompassed all those hours and all that overtime. You may find you will have to pay extra for even flat-rate cast because of this situation. Do what you can to help the Accountant wrap all the accounting issues of production.

PREP FOR AUDIT
Prep for the audit has been mentioned, but will be discussed in more detail in Chapter 35.

HAND-OVER MEMO
Create a hand-over memo to the Producer, the Postproduction Supervisor, and the Postproduction Accountant, summarizing anything and everything you would like to know if you were to take over the production from here. Include cost report notes, because the Postproduction Supervisor and the Postproduction Accountant will be generating the cost reports from now on. What is the history they need to know? What invoices may yet come in? What issues about unpaid bills do they need to know? Include a list of all accounts payable with explanations for why each is remaining unpaid. Include notations for issues that may arise in your absence. Discuss this memo with the Production Accountant, because she can help with information from her perspective. The Coordinator will be generating his own ongoing-issues memo. Be sure your hand-over memo works well with it.

POST MORTEM
Whether production went well or did not, it is always good to do a post mortem so you can learn from both your good and bad experiences. Hindsight is a wonderful teacher. Knowing what you know now in wrap, if you could go back and do everything all over again, what would you do the same, and what would you do differently? Summarize these thoughts in a memo for the Producer and for yourself. If you are on a series, there may be another season where you can use this memo in early preproduction decisions. Encourage other keys to do post mortems too, or at least interview them during wrap about what would have been done similarly or differently: the First A.D., the Production Designer, the Production Accountant, others. Every job is a learning experience. Capitalize on that experience. Remember to be insightful. This is an opportunity to think and analyze, not to rant.

TIE UP LOOSE ENDS

Many other issues of an unpredictable nature will form in wrap. You will spend time chasing things down, calling people and companies, and basically tying up loose ends. The days will slow down, but you probably will not notice for a week or so. There will be fewer and fewer people every day. Include whatever you cannot tie up in the hand-over memo.

MOVE FILES TO HEAD OFFICE

At the end of your wrap, move the files back to head office. You may end up moving back to head office yourself to complete wrap and to tidy up the last few loose ends. Remember to say your goodbyes.

THE PRODUCTION COORDINATOR WRAPS

You brought it all together here in the office. It is time to dispose of it all. Return it, sell it, close it out, hand it out, or accomplish whatever needs to be done. You also need to report on everything you are about to do.

- ❑ Meet the PM Daily
- ❑ Arrange the Wrap Party
- ❑ Refer to Chapter 5 (Setting Up the Production Office)
- ❑ Report to the "Wrap" File
- ❑ Inventory List
- ❑ Summary Memo of Returned Items & Ongoing Issues
- ❑ List Items for Sale
- ❑ Wardrobe & Set Sale or Storage
- ❑ Crew Gifts Arrived and Distributed
- ❑ Crew Photograph
- ❑ Seek Out and Collect Final Invoices
- ❑ Close Accounts
- ❑ Be Careful Ordering Office Supplies in Wrap
- ❑ Box Up Files for Head Office
- ❑ Forward Telephone to Head Office
- ❑ When You Do Not Have to Empty the Office Entirely
- ❑ Take Your Kit Home

MEET THE PM DAILY

As mentioned to the PM, you both need to meet daily. In wrap, the office quickly becomes a busy place again; then as people wrap day by day, the activity slows down. You both have to be on top of wrap issues immediately — before the crew goes home and can no longer help you with answers.

ARRANGE THE WRAP PARTY
Arranging the wrap party is discussed in more detail below.

REFER TO CHAPTER 5 (SETTING UP THE PRODUCTION OFFICE)
Since Chapter 5 lists all the items you arranged, such a list will not be repeated here. Review and reverse the items you acquired in that chapter.

REPORT TO THE "WRAP" FILE
You already have a file in the cabinet called "Wrap." In this file, keep all the memos and the copies of letters reporting what happened to everything (from the furniture to the linen delivery) at the end of the film.

INVENTORY LIST
Back in preproduction you created an inventory list (or kept a detailed P.O. log) of everything that you bought and rented as it happened. This list is invaluable to you now to double-check that all items indeed get wrapped. Much time has elapsed since the beginning of preproduction, and your memory will need the assistance. The Production Accountant may be able to add to this list after reviewing the petty cash reports for inventory-type purchases.

SUMMARY MEMO OF RETURNED ITEMS & ON-GOING ISSUES
As you return items (from walkie-talkies and coffee machines to telephones and furniture), keep notes of when and how everything gets returned. Draft a memo combining all these notes, sending it to the Producer, the Production Manager, the Production Accountant, and to yourself. Also note last working dates for all the office staff, and the status of issues that could not be completed by the end of your last workday. This memo will be a wonderful reference after your departure.

LIST ITEMS FOR SALE
Note every saleable item that production bought and each item's original purchase price. Other production companies just starting up will buy pretty much everything from folding tables to office supplies. Approve and price the sale list with the Production Manager, then contact other Production Coordinators to peddle your goods.

WARDROBE & SET SALE OR STORAGE
If production is a television series, you may have to help with arrangements to store the wardrobe, sets, set dressing, and props until the next potential season. If not, there may be a wardrobe & set sale to rid production of all their goods. Find out when other sales are planned and coordinate the office sale simultaneously. This tactic will help for attendance. You may even help with publicizing the sale by faxing or telephoning your contacts and other production companies starting up soon.

CREW GIFTS ARRIVED AND DISTRIBUTED
Whether they are hats, bags, sweatshirts, pins, watches, or bathmats with the show title on them, make sure the crew gifts are delivered on time. Keep in touch with the supplier.

The Producer may want them handed out on the last day of principal photography or at the wrap party. Handing them out without missing a crew member is actually a large undertaking, so here is advice on how to coordinate it.

- <u>Make Labels For Distribution</u>: Handing out crew gifts sounds easy, until you see the mountainous heap of crew gifts left on the office floor by the courier. If you have 200 sweatshirts to hand out, some will go to the set crew, some to the postproduction crew, some to cast that wrapped weeks ago, and some to Executives in another country. It is very easy to give too many gifts to one person, and run out before you have finished. If the gift is free, many crew members will ask you for an extra one or two for their families and friends. So here's what to do: Just like scripts, label each gift before distribution. You have a list of who is entitled to a crew gift. On file folder labels, write one crew name per label (include size, if applicable). Then pre-organize the labels in groupings of: (1) those to be couriered out of country, (2) those to be delivered around town, (3) those to be distributed on set, and (4) those to be held for people coming into the office to pick them up. When the stacks of crew gifts arrive, slap a label on each one. Done. If not, have several spare gifts on hand, because those 200 identical sweatshirts after distribution on set are just that: identical. Some will get lost. Some people will take two.

- <u>Make Boxes For Distribution</u>: Though the crew gifts are labeled, they still may be a large bundle to handle. Decorate old photocopier paper boxes with wrapping paper and put the crew gifts into the boxes in roughly alphabetical order (i.e., clump all the As together in any order). Then label the boxes with the appropriate letters. Now you can hand out the gifts or let the crew pick them up on their own.

- <u>When Crew Gifts Are A Surprise</u>: It is next to impossible to keep a surprise from an entire crew. If you want to try, use a code word with the supplier on the telephone to inform him that you cannot talk presently because someone else is in the room. On arrival, whisk the crew gifts into a pre-designated solitary room (with a lock) to store, label, and box them in private. You can also encourage a red-herring rumor to steer the crew off track in guessing what the gifts might be.

- <u>When Handing Out Free Gifts On The Last Day Of Shooting</u>: Check with the Producer if the daily crew and the daily cast on the last day should receive a crew gift. Know the company's position before being put on the spot when someone who has worked for the company for nine hours asks to have a crew gift.

- <u>When "Crew Gifts" Are Purchased By The Crew</u>: Purchased crew gifts are not really gifts at all, but "gift" is the only term that covers such a wide range of items. Review the choices and the prices with the Production Manager, and decide on an item or two. Make and distribute a flyer to the crew presenting all the information necessary, including a picture or drawing if possible. Get payment in advance, or ask Accounting if paycheck deductions can be effected. Keep a separate file to track the orders and the money. Because of the number of people involved and the sporadic way the money will filter in, this job will become very time-consuming. Be prepared.

CREW PHOTOGRAPH
A crew photo may be taken on the last day or during the shoot, and copied for distribution on the last day. Distribute these the same way you do crew gifts (with labels).

SEEK OUT AND COLLECT FINAL INVOICES
Now that you are emptying the office, telephone your suppliers — especially suppliers to the wrap party — to ask for final invoices immediately. Have them fax the invoices so that payment can be effected while you are still in the office (to make sure it happens).

CLOSE ACCOUNTS
Discuss with the Production Manager which accounts need to be closed (from the office cleaners to the water delivery) and which ones remain open for head office and Post-production to use. Fax letters to those suppliers confirming that the account has been closed because production is completed. Copy these letters to the Production Accountant and file them in the wrap file. The courier account should remain active for use during postproduction. Send the remaining blank waybills to the Accountant and/or the Postproduction Supervisor.

BE CAREFUL ORDERING OFFICE SUPPLIES IN WRAP
Double-check the crew requests for office supplies as you get close to wrap. You will be ordering many storage boxes, but should not be ordering staplers and rulers. Ensure that production does not furnish crew home offices.

BOX UP FILES FOR HEAD OFFICE
The filing cabinet is currently filled with reams of paperwork. As you box up the files for storage at head office, make a point of looking through each file one by one. Pull out any duplicate or extraneous material. You may find that up to one third of the paper in the filing cabinet is expendable. The Production Manager may hand over his files to incorporate into the production files, too. Label each file box clearly with the film title, your title, and the date. Include a disk of all your computer files that relate to the project. Finally, find out the name of the person to receive these files at head office. Have the Office P.A. personally deliver the file boxes to that person. These files are important. They tell head office everything that happened on the production. These files will be the reference about production for years to come.

FORWARD TELEPHONE TO HEAD OFFICE
When arranging for the telephone disconnection, forward the telephone number to the head-office number. This procedure helps people trying to find the company in the next month or two.

WHEN YOU DO NOT HAVE TO EMPTY THE OFFICE ENTIRELY

If the office is a permanent production office, or if another production company is moving in when you are done, you may not have to empty the office down to the bare walls. You are lucky. With the Production Manager, decide what of the office can be emptied or simplified, and then do a scaled-down version of wrap.

TAKE YOUR KIT HOME

At the end of your last day, take home your kit. The longer you are on production, the more you will have brought in during the past weeks or months, so make sure the Office P.A. is still around to give you a hand. Do not forget to say your goodbyes.

THE WRAP PARTY

Though the wrap party is not the very last thing you do in wrap, it does signify the end of production; therefore, it is addressed last in this chapter. The Coordinator does most of the work arranging and hosting it, but the PM gets involved too, as every design and decision has its price.

THE UNEDITED INVITATION LIST

The Coordinator creates the unedited invitation list. Start with all the lists (crew lists, cast lists, credit lists) to create a mega first-draft invitation list to the wrap party. Include absolutely everyone you can think of so that you do not forget a soul. This list will be enormous.

DISCUSSIONS WITH THE PM

Review the first-draft invitation list with the Production Manager and narrow it down to reality. Decide if spouses and guests are invited. Decide on a day of the week and discuss possible venues. Get an idea of the money you are allowed to spend.

SEE POTENTIAL PARTY VENUES

Research places to hold the party. Visit these venues. Just like hotel rooms, there is nothing like seeing the place in person to make discussing the party location easier.

WRAP PARTY BUDGET & CHECKLIST

It is your turn to generate a budget and track the costs. A wrap party has many costs associated with it. Make the party come in on budget, but with flare. Use the following checklist to prepare the wrap party budget: (See a wrap party budget form on page 456.)

- ❑ Date of Party
- ❑ Invitations

❑ Party Room
❑ Decor of Room
❑ Catering
❑ Bar
❑ License
❑ Notifications
❑ Music
❑ Other Entertainment
❑ Total

DATE OF PARTY

Note the planned date for the wrap party on the wrap party budget/checklist.

INVITATIONS

You can create invitations on the photocopier, or convince the Art Department to design invitations for professional printing. Decide if you will fax, mail, or deliver invitations. Invitations that people have to surrender at the door (for door prizes) are great both to ensure people bring them and to cut down on gatecrashers.

PARTY ROOM

Make sure the room is big enough for the crowd. Note the features of the room, like a fireplace or billiard tables. These features may help sway you on choice of venue. Rental is usually free if a bar is supplied with the room. Know when you have to vacate at the end of the evening. Estimate the costs involved of supplying washroom supplies and/or a cleaning service. Find out if you or the venue will supply security.

DECOR OF ROOM

Is the lighting appropriate to the party? You may want to arrange lights from your equipment supplier or buy miniature Christmas lights to create a mood. Decide how many tables and chairs you will need and price their rental. Table cloths and ashtrays are often supplied by the caterer, if you ask for them. Some decoration ideas to spark your imagination are: helium balloons strung onto film cores, film cans as ashtrays, and, of course, flowers. Budget some money to hire a Production Assistant or two to help you with the set-up and to do the clean-up. You will be so busy hosting the party, you will not have any time to "work" the party as well. Hire Assistants that have not worked on the show until now, so that they will not be tempted to drink and socialize with the cast and crew.

CATERING

Decide what food you want to serve. Will you have a serve-yourself buffet of pizza or oysters shucked by catering staff? Order food for sixty percent of the attendees, as people do not eat as much as they drink. For dessert, a cake with the film title in icing looks wonderful. To ensure people will actually eat the cake rather than just admire it all evening, arrange for the Producer (or someone) to cut the cake, then arrange for other people to physically hand out the slices. The caterer can supply napkins, plates, and cutlery for this purpose. Will you use paper plates or the real thing? Confirm when the caterer needs to set up, and when they will return to clean up.

BAR
Are you arranging for your own bar or will you use the room's bar? If you choose the room's bar, discuss the prices and deposit. Buy wine by the bottle instead of by the glass, if you can. Decide how many bartenders you will need. Who is getting the ice and the ice containers? If you choose a full bar (beer, wine, and liquor), who is getting the mixers? The caterer can supply you with more napkins and glasses if you ask. Know who is in charge of setting up and cleaning up the bar.

LICENSE
If you arrange for your own bar, you need a "no sale" liquor license. You cannot charge money for the drinks. Contact your local licensing office for the procedure and the fee.

NOTIFICATIONS
To have a large party, you should also notify the police, the fire department, the health department, and the buildings & inspections department. You may need these letters to complete your liquor license application. They do not cost anything and you can fax or deliver them. You are showing these departments that you know how to run a safe party and when you are going to do it. Include in each letter when, where, and how many guests; also describe security, mention that you will be serving food, and explain that the party is an end-of-production party.

MUSIC
Will you have a band or a disk jockey? If a band, confirm if they are providing their own lights and equipment; ask if they can supply recorded music in between sets. Be clear when the music is to start and end. Discuss with the band or the disk jockey how they may feel about a possible extension to the end of the evening if the party is going well. Ask when they need access to the room for set-up and clean-up.

OTHER ENTERTAINMENT
Other entertainment could be door prizes, access to a skating rink, the showing of an out-take reel, or whatever your imagination can dream up. If you choose an outtake reel, give the editors enough time to complete one. When you rent the equipment to show the reel, hire enough technicians to take care of the set-up, testing, and clean-up of the equipment.

TOTAL
Approve the party choices and the prices with the Production Manager. Total the budget and copy it to the PM, the Production Accountant, and you, the PC. You have to monitor and keep to these costs.

PC HOSTS THE PARTY

Now that the party is budgeted, arranged, and happening, the PC steps into the shoes of host. Be obvious so that your "party" Production Assistants can find you if they need to. Socialize and welcome everyone. But above all else, have a great time! This is your party, too! Tomorrow you will get to hear how wonderful the party was all over again as the crew talk about it. Enjoy!

After the wrap-party night, both the PM and the PC return to the office to complete wrapping the office. The hours slow down again and you eventually adjust to the pace of wrap. Soon, you too will be going home or moving onto your next production. Congratulate yourself for a job well done. You deserve it!

Small, Dark Rooms

You have to wonder about postproduction people. They spend an awful lot of time alone and in small, dark rooms.

One Picture Editor comes to mind with a particularly difficult scene to cut. Apparently the editing was a more painstaking process than ever — the matching, the timing, the best performances, the reveal, the joke. The Editor had meeting after meeting with Director and Producer to work it through. He worked long and hard hours tweaking the scene over and over again. He would get it right. He was determined. The heat from the editing equipment in the small room was almost unbearable. But he ventured on. He was striving for editing perfection and nothing less.

Then it happened. Perfection.

He leapt out of his editing room into the middle of the production office to celebrate... sporting only Spandex pants, swinging shoulder-length hair that would do any rocker proud, and playing the air guitar.

You have to wonder what those small, dark rooms do to a person. Still, it was quite a rocking good tune.

CHAPTER 34

POSTPRODUCTION

Postproduction officially starts after principal photography wraps, but the Editor and his Assistant have been on board already, synching and cutting film from the second day of shooting. Postproduction does stretch on long after production is done, and it is usually up to the Postproduction Supervisor to shepherd the film through the final critical stages of post — to deliver the film to all the contracted sources on time and on budget. As Production Manager, you need to understand a little bit about postproduction, so that it does not become a "black hole" of knowledge to you. You do, after all, have to budget for post knowledgeably.

THE UNIQUENESS OF POSTPRODUCTION

There may be a Postproduction Supervisor or a Postproduction Coordinator or both. You have budgeted for them, and you will hand over the issues of production management (like the creation and the distribution of regular cost reports) to them to follow up and continue during postproduction.

There is a whole different set of concerns during postproduction than during production. The pace is different, for starters. While production spends heavily day by day, postproduction spends week by week, or event by event. You may have a five-week shoot, but a ten-week post. You may have a crew of 75, while they may have about six. Production spends its time getting the movie magic "into the can," basically collecting the parts of the movie. Postproduction, however, is making movie magic in the editing room; they are literally making the movie from the parts production supplies. Postproduction is indeed unique. Hire a Supervisor or a Coordinator who understands the unique issues of postproduction and of technical acceptances by various Distributors, Broadcasters, and countries.

THE STAGES OF POSTPRODUCTION

You can divide a film production into basically three technical stages: the shooting stage, the postproduction stage (editing), and the finish or delivery stage. You can use film or video/digital in any of these stages, but basically this section deals with the three most commonly used combinations. We will look at each separately from a postproduction point of view:

SHOOT ON FILM – POST ON VIDEO/DIGITAL – FINISH ON FILM

Most feature films shoot in this manner: shooting on film stock like 35mm, then transferring to a video or a digital format for editing, and conforming back to film stock again for the finished product. More and more features are being shot on digital, but there is still a need to transfer to film for the delivery in order to distribute the film worldwide and to show at film festivals. The cost of the digital-to-film transfer is still quite hefty, so at the end the day, you may find that your budget savings are nominal, as all you have done is delayed costs until the time of the delivery and the film transfer.

SHOOT ON FILM – POST ON VIDEO/DIGITAL – FINISH ON VIDEO/DIGITAL

If you do not need a film finish for a festival or a Distributor, and you are delivering video/digital tapes to Broadcasters, then this works. Most television series and MOWs (Movies of the Week) are produced in this manner.

SHOOT ON VIDEO/DIGITAL – POST ON VIDEO/DIGITAL – FINISH ON VIDEO/DIGITAL

The most economical way of completing a film is to start on video/digital and end on video/digital. Most documentaries and low-budget television-only projects are shot in this manner.

THE POSTPRODUCTION PROCESS

Since you are the Production Manager, the best way to understand post is to run through the issues of production in reference to the budget. The budget is generally set up to look at the costs chronologically.

ABOUT "SHOOTING ON FILM"

Before moving into official postproduction, there are a number of post-related issues you deal with during production. First, we will look at shooting on film:

RAW STOCK
Raw stock is what unprocessed film stock is called before it is run through the camera.

EXPOSED FILM
Once the film has been through the camera, raw stock is now exposed film. Camera Assistants will label film cans accordingly, and production will ensure exposed film is dropped off at the lab every night. You do not want to be responsible for storing exposed film in uncertain weather conditions and risk ruining the original film.

ORIGINAL NEGATIVE

Once it was called raw stock, then exposed film, now that it has been through the processing at the lab, the same stuff is called original negative. This is *it*. Immediately you want to strike a print (or a video/digital transfer) from this negative and store the original negative safely at the lab, where there are environmentally-controlled storage facilities for negatives.

NEG CHECK

Labs process film overnight and print (or video/digital transfer) early in the morning, which is why you can have a negative check the next morning. Early the next morning, the lab can report if the negative is okay or scratched.

I/P (INTERPOSITIVE) AND I/N (INTERNEGATIVE)

If you are planning a film finish, and have the money to backup all your negative, process an I/P and I/N immediately from the original negative. By doing this you are creating a new original negative, the I/N. You will now do all your post work from this negative, not from the original. Every time any film or negative runs through a process of any sort at the lab, you are risking more scratching and damaging. Regular wear and tear. With an I/N in hand, if damage happens to the I/N, you still have an I/P to go back to in order to create another I/N. And, if damage happens to the I/P, only then do you need to return to the original negative to strike another I/P. Remembering that the original negative is *it*, you want to do all you can to preserve the film for future use. Budget-wise, however, it is more likely you will strike your I/P and I/N after you have cut the negative.

WORKPRINT (ONE-LIGHT) OR VIDEO TRANSFER

If you are posting on film, you need to strike a workprint from the negative. It will be a one-light (one exposure) workprint because you are not terribly concerned about pretty exposure; the Editor just needs to see the image to cut the story. If you are finishing on film, you will want to strike a workprint of some of the early rushes of production to project, see, and analyze at least some of the film on a big screen. Likely you are posting on video or digital, so you can transfer from the negative directly to video/digital for picture editing. The Editing Assistant then needs to digitize those rushes onto the computer to access the footage in the computer-editing software. Sound is also transferred at this stage from the original format into the computer.

RECORDING AND TRANSFERRING SOUND

Sound has been busy recording, most likely to DAT tapes, or onto 1/4" tapes if using the Nagra. Just as the picture needs transferring to the editing format, so does the sound.

SYNCHING THE RUSHES OR DAILIES

Every day during the shoot, an Assistant Editor synchs the picture to the sound, using the clapboard or the time-code slate (a clap board with electronic numbers on the front of it) at the beginning of each scene as reference. The Editing Department outputs the final rushes when they are done later that day (onto VHS and higher quality video/digital formats) for reference and analysis. These are the rushes. They have been rushed through processing and synching to be seen here and now.

EDGE CODING OR EDGE NUMBERING

If you are about to edit on film, you have made a workprint of the film, and transferred and synched the sound with the picture. You now need to go through a process where tiny numbers that match each other are printed on the far edge of both the print and the sound stock. This way, no matter which piece of sound or picture you have, you can match them picture to sound in synch anywhere along the miles of footage you have. It is obvious how essential this coding is for tracking shots during the editing process. There are already other tiny numbers along the edge of the workprint, but these numbers have been printed in the lab from the original negative. These are reference numbers used when cutting the negative later in the postproduction process.

TIME CODE SLATE VS. BURNED-IN TIME CODE

You will hear a lot about time code during postproduction. There are several times you use it, each one being different. Time code is audio/visual reference that runs like a clock giving a time/frame address to every frame of the digital/video and audio to enable you to synch the two.

On set, the time-code slate shows the audio time code on the slate and therefore is recorded on the picture. After processing, the audio can be synched quickly with the picture by simply calling up the visually noted audio time code as seen on the picture. This time code will have huge gaps in its numeric sequence since time code runs like a clock, and on set you are never shooting 100% of the clock time.

As you are synching the rushes, you will be laying the "synched" rushes down to a new master tape. In order to have a visual time-code reference in the picture-editing process, you need a new time code "burned-in" to the picture to give a visual address to each frame. As this time code is laid down all at once, it will be sequential from the beginning of the tape to the end, and will therefore differ from the numbers used on the time-code slate for synching.

There is a third time code you will create, but that is later in the video/digital editing process — after you lock the picture edit.

ABOUT "SHOOTING ON VIDEO/DIGITAL"

Shooting on video/digital appears much simpler than shooting on film, but there are some unique issues you must consider:

TAPE STOCK

As raw stock is to film, tape stock is to video/digital. What you use during the shoot day becomes your "original tapes" which are in fact *it* — as precious as original negative. Instead of dealing with scratches on film negative, you may have to deal with tape drop-outs.

ISO TAPES

ISO stands for isolation. These are the tapes used by the second camera or B-camera on production. By shooting two cameras or more, you can capture multiple angles at the same time, but will need to reference this material differently to know which is which.

BACKUP TAPES

While you are shooting, you also create backup tapes immediately. If not, it behooves you to dub backups immediately. Backups work the same way as I/Ps and I/Ns.

TRANSFER TO EDITING FORMAT

The editing team needs to digitize the original scenes onto the computer to cut the show using the computer-editing software.

RUSHES DUBS

Synching may or may not be required, depending how sound was recorded on the original tapes, but dubs of the original tapes need to be made for reference. These are rushes.

Now that you have the rushes in hand — whether you shot them on film or on video/digital — you are technically finished with production costs and are off in the land of official postproduction.

ABOUT "PICTURE POSTING ON FILM"

Though you may not do picture post on film, you need to understand the process, because video/digital picture posting was set up to emulate how it has been done on film for years.

ASSEMBLY

When you put all the master shots in order, to see the entire film and to get an initial sense of the story and the timing of the entire show, you have an assembly. This is the fastest way to see the overall picture.

ROUGH CUT

Since the Editor usually starts just after shooting has begun, he can edit scenes while the film is still being captured. The Editor will start with an assembly, then add close ups to highlight story points and emotions. There is no fine-tuning in the rough-cut editing process; this stage is about creating the film in broad strokes. The rough cut is where you experiment in the editing process. For feature films, if you have the time, you can have rough-cut screenings complete with rough sound mix using music similar to what you may end up using, to give you a better sense of the film onscreen. There is nothing like seeing the film onscreen with rough music to best examine the outcome of the story as it is forming. Because the rough cut is filled with broad strokes, big changes can happen from cut to cut. The film may have slugs (black leader with white text headings) to fill in for unfinished scenes or undelivered CGI or effects shots. Financiers and others may have approval of the rough cut, so the post schedule needs to address time for these people to review the cut and give their approvals, and possibly include time to make required changes.

DIRECTOR'S CUT & PRODUCER'S CUT
Editor is allowed a cut of the film, as are the Director and the Producer. Who has the final cut (i.e., final decision) will have been contracted prior to shooting.

FINE CUT
The final cut is the fine cut. This is where the fine-tuning happens. Scene timing is tightened. Missing CGI shots are included. Other minor changes occur. Even though there may be more than one fine cut, as financiers may have a say in fine-cut approvals, the changes from cut to cut are basically minor by this stage.

PICTURE LOCK
The last fine cut is picture lock. Picture editing is completed and the picture will have no more changes from here on. This procedure allows the Sound Department to work to this "locked picture," to add sounds and synch them frame for frame to the picture. Since no more changes may happen to the picture after picture lock, you can have negative cut into this order while the sound team works on the soundtrack.

TRANSFER TO VIDEO FOR SOUND POST
You will not be cutting sound on magstock anymore (the old film way), unless you can find a place that still has the facilities to mix it. Since it is so hard to find the equipment and the facilities to do this now, I will assume all sound post will be considered computerized with a video-picture reference. Transfer the locked picture to videotape for the sound team to set to work.

ABOUT "PICTURE POSTING ON VIDEO/DIGITAL"
AVID, Lightworks, and Final Cut Pro are three editing systems where the Editor can cut the film on computer. Computers have adapted the film-cutting process to the computer screen and have allowed Editors to edit faster and to save and examine several different cuts at the same time. This freedom to look at more choices, faster, has naturally made computers the best way of editing films.

COMPUTER LOAD LIST
The Continuity Supervisor takes notes of which shots are "printed" on set. The computer load list identifies these shots, so that the Editors can digitize only the "printed" takes into the computer.

OFFLINE
The offline is basically the same as the rough cut and the picture fine cut. Since computers can store several versions and give the editing team more choices to evaluate, you may find that offline editing actually takes longer than usual, unless you have decisive

people in the approval process.

DIRECTOR'S CUT & PRODUCER'S CUT
Just as on film, the Editor, the Director, and the Producer all are allowed a cut of the film. Who has the final cut (i.e., final say) will have been decided prior to shooting and committed to on paper.

PICTURE LOCK
You need to lock the picture for the same reasons you lock it for film. Picture lock is the final, approved fine cut. Give a video copy of the locked picture to the sound team to work on the soundtrack; if finishing on film, give another video copy to the negative cutter to "conform" the picture from video to film again.

EDL
This is an "Edit Decision List." It is a printout of all the chosen shots in the chosen order, and a notation of exactly which frame each shot begins and ends. Obviously, this list is essential for the negative cutter to cut the film to match the videotape cut.

ABOUT "SOUND POSTING ON VIDEO/DIGITAL"
Posting sound "on film" means using magstock that is in synch with a film workprint, but as this process is now so rare, I will not discuss it. Posting sound on digital has [open]ed up many more possibilities than posting sound on magstock could offer, and it [is] more affordable. You can arrange with a sound facility to set up a package to [hir]e the sound-edit staff as well as the equipment, or you can hire people separately [de]al with the sound facility only for the studio time.

[You] can accumulate a host of sound tracks to be mixed together. The more [sound] tracks, the richer the sound landscape is to the ear. It is not unusual to hear [pro]ductions having from 75 to 200 tracks of sound: dialogue, sound effects, foley, atmosphere, and music tracks. To orchestrate such a wide, rich sound track, you may hire a Sound Designer.

DIALOGUE EDITING
Dialogue tracks need to be split into several tracks to separate the various voices, so the sound quality of each can be treated separately during the sound mix. Dialogue Editors may even steal sound from another take to apply to this take because the sound or the voice performance is better.

ADR/LOOPING
When the dialogue is unacceptable in the sound edit, you may need to call in the Performer to re-do some of his lines. ADR is done in a sound studio where the picture is looped to repeat over and over again, so the Performer can lip synch his lines to the picture. More on the specifics of the ADR session and contracts needed is in Chapter 24.

NARRATION OR VOICE OVER RECORD

Voice over may also be recorded during post for the dialogue edit. This is a Performer's voice that does not synch with any picture, so you can use a simpler sound studio to record the voice.

WALLA

Walla is a team of Performers who work together in a sound studio providing you with background group sounds for the sound track, sounds like cheers and background restaurant mumbling.

SFX EDITING OR SOUND EFFECTS EDITING

Sound Effects Editors gather sounds from various sources to match to the picture. The sound of a gun on a sound track is way too tinny to sound good for the film, so Sound Effects Editors are inventive about creating sounds the way we think they should sound. There are many sound effects libraries to tap into as a resource. So that each sound can be treated separately during the mix, Sound Effects Editors use multiple tracks to lay down these effects. Sound effects can also be layered and layered from separate tracks to make one sound incredibly rich and complex.

ORIGINAL FX RECORDING

When Sound Effects Editors are not sourcing sounds from libraries, they are outside recording and being their inventive best.

ATMOSPHERE TRACKS

Sound Effects Editors also add separate atmosphere tracks for every room or space. Atmosphere is the background "white noise" that every room possesses and that would be noticeably missing if absent.

FOLEY EDITING

The Foley Artist is the person in a foley studio at the sound facility who, while watching the film, supplies another layer of sounds to add to the richness of the sound track. A foley studio, for example, has several floor sections of differing qualities: one of gravel, one of pavement, one of tile, and another of wood, so the Foley Artists can time footstep sounds to the picture on appropriate surfaces. They also add clothing sounds, door sounds, kissing sounds, and a host of others.

MUSIC COMPOSER

The Music Composer and the Sound Designer will come on board rather early in production to discuss the way the music is planned to fit into the final film. At no later than rough-cut stage, the Music Composer needs to do the music spotting with at least the Director to decide what music needs to be added where. A spotting session basically generates a work list for the Music Composer. Then she writes and/or sources the music for each of those screen moments and transitions. Often you can hire a Composer who has her own studio and will create the music for the soundtrack as a one-stop supplier.

MUSIC EDITING

The Composer does not supply the music cut to the picture frame-ready. The Music Editor needs to lay the music onto various tracks so the fades and the dissolves and the other sound treatments to the music can be addressed during the mix. The Music Editor may also move some of the music around to fill in spaces that need to be filled to smooth out a scene or a transition.

PRE-MIX

The Sound Editors have created timing sheets, graphically plotting where each sound is laid on each separate track for reference for the Sound Mixer as the tracks are mixed together. Since it is expensive to rent a mixing theater for the final sound mix, you will end up doing a pre-mix to iron out the problems that always seem to show themselves when you combine all the tracks of sound for the first time. You will fire through the sound mix like a dry run during a pre-mix, merely identifying the problems to address now.

SWEETENING

After the pre-mix you have some editing time to fix the problems identified in the pre-mix, or replace sounds that just do not work. This process is sweetening.

MIX

The final mix is when all the various sound tracks finally come together to match with the final picture. There is a rocking motion to sound mixing. The film moves forward and some tracks are mixed together for a few seconds or minutes, then the film is rewound to review the mix or to take another pass at getting it right. This routine happens over and over and over again. It can be a bit hypnotic if you arrive at the mix sleepy, so get a good night's sleep beforehand.

Today's modern mixing theaters have total recall of all the sound-editing decisions made to date, enabling easy revisions and the automation of hundreds of sound elements at the mix. If, however, you have many, many tracks, the mix may take a few passes as you mix several tracks down to a few, then the few down to one or two.

You can mix in mono or stereo, or if you have arranged for a license, you can mix in Dolby Stereo, THX, or other noise-reduction systems. The Sound Designer, the Sound Editors, and the Music Composer will have addressed preparing for these noise-reduction systems prior to the mix, of course, but here is where it all comes together.

M&E TRACK

You need to generate a Music and Effects track separate from the dialogue track, so that you leave the project available to international sales. With an M&E track, any country can dub the voices into any language accompanied by the rich M&E track underneath. This is usually a required deliverable to distributors.

BACKUP OR PROTECTION COPY
Just as you have backups for the picture throughout postproduction, always create a master backup of the final mix on DAT or 1/4" or some other protection format.

TRANSCRIPT
The transcript is another necessity for international dubbing and is nearly always a required deliverable. It goes with the M&E track, allowing other countries to translate the script for dubbing purposes. Ensure the transcript is made from the final, locked picture and sound track.

MARRY SOUND TO PICTURE
If you are finishing on film, it is time to arrange for the optical negative of the sound track to print it to, and combine it with, the finished film. If you are finishing on video/digital, it is time to lay the sound down onto the master video picture.

ABOUT "FINISHING ON FILM"
If the film is going to a film festival, or going to be screened in a theater somewhere in the world, you obviously need a film finish. For some of the following activities, sound may still be posting. The objective is to have the sound mix done in time to create the optical sound track and marry it to the finished film.

CONFORM TO NEGATIVE OR PREPARE FOR NEG CUT
On film, the Editor has to mark up the workprint with black wax to show all the fades and the dissolves and the other optical effects to the negative cutter, who will be using this workprint as the blueprint to permanently cut the negative. The workprint will be split into A&B rolls, separating each shot onto the next roll to be dealt with separately in the rest of the completion process. When you see the shot on roll A, you will see black leader on roll B, then when you see the next shot on roll B, black leader will be on roll A, and so on. It ends up looking rather like a checkerboard of shots between the two rolls.

On video/digital, the Editor needs to ensure that the EDL is correct and the fades and the dissolves and the other optical effects are noted for the negative cutter, who will be using this EDL as a blueprint to permanently cut the negative.

NEGATIVE CUT
If you have an inter-negative, you cut it, saving the original negative. The process of negative cutting removes a frame on each side of the shot for each cut, as the negative is literally cut, the emulsion is scratched off the frame prior to and after the shot, and the now-clear negative is glued onto other film for permanence. Once the negative is cut, there is no turning back. The negative will be A&B rolled, just like the workprint, to allow for changing colors and exposures from shot to shot later in the completion process — without affecting the preceding or the next shot.

INTERPOSITIVE & INTERNEGATIVE
If you have decided to strike a backup I/P and I/N of the cut negative only, now is the time to do it. Store the original cut negative safely in the lab's vault.

CHECK PRINT
This is the first print of the cut negative, used to see if there are any problems that need to be fixed. It also gives the opportunity to make notes on the color timing needed to fix certain shots, or to bathe certain sequences to complete the look of the film.

OPTICALS & TITLES
White on black titles are simple on film, but if you want to superimpose titles over picture, then you need an optical effect. Though superimposition is cheap for a video/digital finish, as it can be done during the online, it is an expensive optical process for a film finish.

COLOR CORRECTION OR COLOR GRADING
The DP tends to come back to deal with the color timing of each scene. Just as in a sound mix where you addressed the sound level and the quality of each sound, in the color timing you adjust the color and the exposure on each shot of the film.

PRINT OPTICAL TRACK
Once the soundtrack is mixed, it needs to be printed to optical track to marry to the final finished film.

ANSWER PRINT (& WET GATE)
The first answer print (a wet-gate answer print) is the first time sound and picture are printed together and you have a completed film you can screen... if the colors are acceptable. You will find you need to fine-tune the color timing and will end up printing more than one answer print in the process.

WET GATE
Every time film goes through a process at the lab, there is always the danger of light surface scratches appearing on the acetate side of the negative. The film goes through a lot of equipment, so it is only natural that this type of wear and tear will happen. To prevent seeing these light scratches on the finished film, you can send the film through a wet-gate process every time you print the film. A wet-gate literally prints the film through a printing gate filled with a clear solution that fills in the light scratches temporarily.

RELEASE PRINT (& WET GATE)
The release print (a wet-gate release print) is the final answer print. Once you have a release print you like, it is time to print multiple copies for the Distributor, film festivals, and other sources who require a film deliverable. If you have used the original negative

all the way through the process, you may well have sent the original negative through the lab's equipment at least six times already (for processing, workprinting, check printing, answer printing twice, and release printing), exposing it each time to the danger of permanent scratches. You are well on the way to wearing out the original negative when now you need to have a pristine negative to create all those release prints. If you had printed an IP/IN immediately, your original negative will only have been through the lab's process twice by now (for processing and inter-positive printing). The IP/IN process is invaluable, as you cannot replace damaged original negative without shooting the film again.

BLOW-UP PRINT

If you shot on Super 16, you cannot finish the film until you blow it up to 35mm. Super 16 uses the space where the optical track should be to expose more picture. The proportions of the frame on Super 16, however, better match that of a 35mm negative than regular 16mm does. If money is driving the choice of using Super 16 instead of 35mm, remember to check into the cost of the blow up. You may find the cost is high enough to warrant your shooting the film on 35mm in the first place.

ABOUT "FINISHING ON VIDEO/DIGITAL"

If the final product is planned only for television broadcast, or for video festivals, then you do not need a film finish and can finish on video/digital. Again, sound may still be posting while some of the picture finishing happens.

With the use of film, you aim to preserve the finest source of the film: the original negative; likewise, in video/digital you need to preserve the master videotape. It is most clear when you dub from VHS to VHS to see the generational loss in resolution from original to copy. VHS, however, is not a broadcast format, and you will find that the formats you use during postproduction (Betacam SP, Digital Beta, etc.) have remarkably less generational loss with each copy — but the principal still applies. Preserve the master video, and make duplicate masters in case something should happen to the original master.

ONLINE OR CONFORM

Once the picture is locked, online or conform can begin. This stage is like a video/digital version of the negative cut. You go back to the master videotapes to edit together the master tape of the film. The information on the EDL details all cuts, fades, dissolves — and where to find all the original material. You will likely have to move into a higher-end editing suite (at the post facility) to do the online. Here you can also add final CGI shots and effects like fades, dissolves, super-impositions, and titles. On older online systems, you have to allow for time for the computer effects to be rendered (created on the computer from the plans you have inputted). The more complex the effects, the more rendering time is needed.

TIME CODE

As mentioned previously, you will be laying down a new (third) time code at picture lock. Since the rushes tapes had their own consecutive time code, by the time you get to picture lock, there is a complete mishmash of time codes from all the edits. During the online, you are laying down the final edit to a new tape, so lay it down with a new, continuous time code.

COLOR CORRECT

Many color correction notes are taken during the online, but it is afterward in a separate session that you can commit to the color corrections. You may wish the DP to be involved at this stage.

TITLES

Also at this stage, you can add titles to the video picture. Being on video/digital, superimpositions over picture are very easy to do. You can input text from the lab's computer, add video clips from other tape sources, and add computerized or videotape logos of Financiers at this stage. This is the last time to ensure the credits are correct. Input errors are not infrequent, so beware. Once done, you have to layback to ensure the title video layer matches the length of the videotape.

LAYBACK SOUND TO VIDEO

Now the final sound mix is added to the final video/digital picture onto a new master videotape.

VERSIONING – TRANSFER TO PAL, NTSC, OR SECAM

Different countries have different video/digital formats. You know from travel that electricity is different in various countries; the differing cycles of electricity require different videotape formats. NTSC is used in North America, whereas PAL is used in the UK and Western Europe, and SECAM is used in France, Asia, Africa, and Eastern Europe. Basically, each format is hugely different from each other. Due to electricity being 60 cycles per second in the UK and 50 cycles per second in North America, PAL runs 4% longer in screen time than NTSC if you were to do a straight transfer. You can either remove a frame here and there to match length during the transfer, or transfer the videotape expecting the different length, as long as you are not too picky about the change in pitch of the sound being either higher or lower at the new speed.

DELIVERY MASTERS

With all the postproduction parts assembled, you can now make the delivery masters or delivery clones. To prevent the loss of generations, you need to dub them all from the same master tape.

BACKUP OF MASTER OR PROTECTION COPIES

For each delivery dub you send out, you need to dub a backup master or protection copy in case something goes wrong with the one sent. If you have a number of delivery requirements, this process can mean a lot of protection copies: one in NTSC on Digital

Beta, one in NTSC on Betacam SP, one in PAL on Digital Beta, one with commercial blacks, one without, one version at 23 minutes, one version at 28:30 minutes, and so on.

VIEWING COPIES

Viewing copies are made on VHS. You will need plenty for all the Financiers, the Producers, and other crew or cast or suppliers to whom you promised tapes of finished product. To ensure the best bulk dubbing rate, Publicity may wish to order their promotional copies at the same time you are creating the viewing copies.

CLOSED CAPTIONING

If you are broadcasting the program, you may need a closed-captioned version as another deliverable. There are facilities that will do this as a one-stop supplier. Closed captioning, however, is a two-step process: one to create the captions and the other to encode the captions onto the tape.

VERSIONING – OTHER LANGUAGES

If you are versioning to other languages, you can also find suppliers that do this process as a one-stop package. Even if you are not versioning to other languages in the production budget, you will likely need a transcript of the final edited film so that distributors in the future can arrange for dubbing or subtitling.

TRANSFER TO FILM

Even if you shoot on video/digital and post on video/digital, you may want to transfer the final product back to film. This is an expensive process, but it becomes more accessible in price and quality every year.

VAULTS & STORAGE

Whether you have an original negative or a master videotape, you need to consider storage of the original in an environmentally-controlled vault for safekeeping. The production lab will have facilities for short-term storage while you are making the film, but after delivery, arrangements need to be made for long-term storage. Who is going to pay for these extended storage costs? Ensure the information about the storage is given to head office.

DELIVERY

Delivery triggers more cash flow to production, so you will be especially concerned that the show is delivered on time to all parties. Of course, delivery does not only mean you have to deliver one master tape to each party. The various financing agreements will list a host of items required as deliverables that may include master tapes, an M&E track, a transcription, publicity photos and slides, biographies of the key cast and crew, a cost report, and a host of other possibilities. The Postproduction Supervisor should have a list of all the deliverables, but it is wise to go over the list to be sure all elements make it to the appropriate parties in a timely manner to affect a quick turnaround of the delivery payments.

Broadcasters may reject delivery for technical reasons once they have screened the tape. Delivery is not considered completed until the broadcaster accepts the finished show. Be sure the technical issues are addressed immediately. Have technical folk talk with technical folk to ensure a speedy resolution. The Postproduction Supervisor will head dealing with these issues.

It is possible to arrange for a technical evaluation of your final delivery tapes prior to delivery. This procedure will help you address technical issues before they become a real problem after delivery to the Broadcaster.

AIR DATES & RELEASE DATES & FESTIVALS

On a series, you may still be working in production when the show has begun delivery and even airing. If the information becomes available to you, publish a memo to all concerned informing them of the airdates. Crew and cast love to pass around this information to family and friends. If you are aware of a festival screening date, also inform "All Concerned" via memo.

Also on a series, if you are working on a later season, you may find that you will become involved in submitting the show to festivals, as production and Postproduction have all the paperwork and technical contracts to arrange for speedy dubs and copying or printing of historical information.

It is unlikely you will be around for the release date of a feature, but you can keep in touch with the Producer to find out when the film will be released. Prepare a telephone/fax/email list to spread the word when you do have information about the film's release or broadcast. Word of mouth attracts larger audiences, and you want the film to be seen.

This chapter has been a mere nutshell look at postproduction. Recognize the importance of the Postproduction Supervisor and the Postproduction Coordinator in dealing with these many complex issues. They are part of the team.

Well-Traveled Wardrobe

Cost report pop quiz:

You're on a multi-international co-production. You have to keep track of costs being spent in Toronto, Nova Scotia, New Zealand, and the UK — all separately.

You rent costumes in London, England. Ship them to Toronto, Canada, for fittings, organization, and repackaging. Then ship them to Nova Scotia for shooting. Ship them back to Toronto for further organization and repackaging. Then ship them on to New Zealand for shooting. Ship them back to Toronto for further organization and repackaging. And finally, ship them back to London, England, at the end of the shoot. Got it?

The question is... on which cost report do you report the wardrobe costs? Ugh.

CHAPTER 35

AUDIT

The audit. It happens long after production. It happens after delivery and all the costs of production are being reported as really and totally final. Neither the Production Manager nor the Coordinator are involved on a production when it comes to audit, but the Production Manager — being so involved in reporting production costs — needs to be aware of the audit, as you and the Production Accountant are basically preparing for the audit from your first day's work.

MUST YOU ALWAYS AUDIT?

You may not always have to go to audit. On very small films, you may only need a final cost report at audit stage; on others you may be allowed a review engagement; but most of the time you will be arranging for an audit.

A final cost report is just that: a report from the Production Accountant on the final costs. A review engagement is a review of the books by an outside, unrelated accounting source to double-check the plausibility of those numbers. A full audit is also conducted by an outside, unrelated accounting source, where they not only check the plausibility of the books, but examine all the accounting files — spot-checking to cross reference the numbers in the books to original receipts, to see if all the official backup is present to validate those numbers. Naturally, the more work an outside accounting source has to do, the more expensive the report.

The Financiers will determine if production requires a final cost report, a review engagement, or a full audit. Their decision will be influenced by the budget size of your production, and by the experience and the past history of the producing team. Find out what your production will require at the very end of the day.

THE VARIOUS REVIEWS OF AN AUDIT

There may be more than one type of review to make up your audit. You are designing the accounting system and, in essence, preparing for the audit in preproduction. Factor in the requirements of all the financing sources. Do your financing sources require the Auditor to only review the final costs, or do they also require the Auditor to do one of many possible compliance reviews, to see that you really did do what you promised to do in the financing agreements? Compliance reviews can vary from a review of Writers Guild payments (as in the USA), to a review of third country costs and of the creative contribution by nationals (as in the UK), to a review of related party costs, a nationality list of key creative personnel, and a list of the financing sources (as in Canada). If tax incentives based on labor are part of your financing, you may also need the Auditor to review the labor costs during the audit. Basically, the audit can easily become very complex. In preproduction, factor in these "end of the day" needs so that you can extract this information quickly and easily. Have you factored in the accounting complexity of a multi-country co-production? Take time to think through the accounting needs of your production and talk it through with the Production Accountant and with the chosen Auditor.

THE PAPERWORK NEEDED FOR AN AUDIT

Since the audit is the most detailed of reports, here is a list of the paperwork generally required for an audit review. Prepare to assemble this paperwork during production. Prepare the production accounting files to collect and display this information clearly and easily. Neither you nor the Production Accountant will be around for the audit review or will want an Auditor calling you at home for an explanation of accounting anomalies or incomplete files and reports.

AN OVERVIEW OF THE GENERAL LEDGER
The Production Accountant can write an explanation of how the general ledger was set up and any other notes the Auditor may need to easily read the general ledger, especially notes on what coding system was used for various type of costs.

CHART OF ACCOUNTS
A bit like a table of contents, this is a printout of the budget account codes (and account descriptions) used in the general ledger. The Production Accountant can generate this report.

GENERAL LEDGER
This is obvious, because this is "the books." It is generated from the accounting software.

FINAL COST REPORT
The Postproduction Accountant will be generating this final cost report, because it happens after delivery to the Distributor and/or the Broadcasters. By the time you leave production, the final production cost report (complete with explanation memo) should be in this file.

VARIANCES FROM ORIGINAL BUDGET
You have made many explanation memos for the cost reports. Look them over and summarize why the large variances happened on various budget lines.

LIST OF DEFERRALS INCLUDED IN PRODUCTION COSTS
No deferrals should be counted as production costs, but in case they are, the Auditor

needs to know what "non-costs" you have considered to be money spent, so he can deduct this amount from true production costs.

LIST OF NON-CASH TRANSACTIONS

If there were any production costs that were non-cash transactions, you have to declare them to the Auditor.

SYNOPSIS OF THE PLOT

If there is no brief synopsis of the plot already, it is likely that the Producer or the Publicity Department have one that you can use.

INVENTORY LIST OF THE ACCOUNTING BOXES SENT TO THE AUDITOR

Since the accounting files will take up a number of boxes, create an inventory list for each accounting box, so that the Auditor can refer to this list to quickly find any information.

COPY OF ALL PRODUCTION REPORTS

As production is done, all the DPRs will be done, too. You can assemble this set of production reports in wrap, or the Production Accountant has already prepared a file in prep, and the DPRs are already in the accounting files because he has been collecting them during production. Do not forget to include Second Unit's production reports.

COPY OF ALL CALL SHEETS

Just like the production reports, you can assemble a set of call sheets in wrap, or have the Production Accountant prepare a file and collect them for the audit during production. Again, do not forget Second Unit's call sheets. These are usually optional, but can be helpful to the Auditor.

LIST OF FINANCIERS

List all the Financiers of production, complete with their names and all their contact information.

COPY OF ALL FINANCING AGREEMENTS

Ensure the accounting files have a complete set of all the latest in financing agreements, co-production agreements, distribution agreements, broadcasting agreements, interim loan agreements, and tax credit approvals or certificates.

COPY OF ALL DEFERRAL AGREEMENTS

Whenever you defer funds, you have an agreement. Copy all of these in one place and summarize the deferrals for the Auditor. If you have deferrals on all the crew, this is a long report and a big file.

ORIGINALS OF ALL BANK STATEMENTS WITH CANCELLED CHECKS

These originals justify the general ledger. The Production Accountant will ensure that they are filed appropriately and accessibly.

VIDEOTAPE OF THE COMPLETED FILM
Yes, the Auditor needs to see the actual film. Send a VHS.

OTHER PAPERWORK THAT MAY BE NEEDED

As mentioned, there may be a few or many more compliance reviews that need to take place during the audit. Discuss what is needed with the Auditor, but here is a sampling of other reports you may need to generate prior to the audit for review:

- A list (or cost report) of non-country charges

- A calculation of the Writer's or the Performer's payments

- A list of key creative personnel, their nationality, screen credit & total remuneration

- A copy of all screen credits

- A delivery schedule to all Distributor(s)/Broadcaster(s)

- A list of related party expenditures (costs associated with non-arm's length companies, the Producers, their relations, and companies related to them)

- A list of labor costs (detailing crew names/companies, employee/corporate status, company ownership status [single-owned or multi-owned], citizenship[s], residency, total labor cost by country and state or province)

The more work the Production Accountant and you do to prepare for the audit, the faster — and therefore cheaper — the audit will be. The Producer will not have excess funds after delivery to pay for an Auditor to sort through badly prepared accounting files, to find out officially what happened to all that money. Remember that the audit review triggers the final drawdowns that will pay back a lot of the interim-financing loan. If you have prepared for the audit well, you will save the Producer money even in your absence. Only when the audit review is done, can you really, truly say your job as Production Manager is really, truly done.

CLOSING NOTES

Congratulations! You did it! You have just managed or coordinated a film production!

As the PM, you were trusted with the production's money to see that the production was produced on time and on budget. As the Coordinator, everyone looked to you to keep production running. As a team, you made it happen. Be proud. If you feel like you have just dealt with absolutely everyone and everything during the course of making the film, you are right. You did. Both Production Management and Coordination can be all-encompassing and stressful experiences. When the stress gets to you, remember: It is only a movie. Take a deep breath and try to relax. You do not have to be an expert, but you do need to think clearly. You have the ability and you are prepared. You can carry on.

Keep a balance between working on paperwork and keeping in contact with the crew. Though you have a desk in the production office, your job is much more than shuffling paperwork. Recognize your job as one critical part of the magical wheel of making a film come to life. No matter what your job, you will always be learning. Ask questions. Adapt this book to create your own personal style of management or coordination. Make the job yours.

Congratulations again as you embark on a very exciting adventure: the exotic lifestyle of filmmaking! Get the most out of it. "Now" will never happen again, so enjoy every minute of it... from prep all the way to post.

But before I go, I have one more story for you...

The Exotic Lifestyle

Many of us get into the film industry because we are looking for an exotic lifestyle. None of this nine-to-five work complete with benefits for me! Oh no! I want an interesting job! An exotic career!

So we work in film. Black becomes the key color of our wardrobes. We work so many hours on set or in the production office that most of our friends are filmmakers. We date filmmakers. We watch films. We talk about films. We make films. We eat on set or at film parties. We swap film rumors with our friends and help each other with contacts for future work.

Yet, no matter how much we work from contract to contract, at the end of every job we wonder... will I ever work again? Exotic equals unstable. We recognize that now. So that's why our parents always wished we'd find a "real" job! Never mind. We love it here. We are filmmakers.

So when I go to film parties, I naturally bring my fellow along with me. He dresses in black just like me and everyone else. Little do they know he is here in disguise. For the time always comes during conversation when they ask him what department he works in. Of course he is a film-maker. Aren't we all? But my fellow smiles and says that he doesn't work in film. He works in Parks & Recreation.

Shock comes to their faces first. Then they respond: "Wow. You have a real job." You can see their eyes light up and a look of admiration come to their faces. A "real" job... with benefits! How exotic!

Now go out and enjoy YOUR exotic lifestyle!

IX.

APPENDIX -
SAMPLE FORMS

A list of these forms can be found in the Table of Contents on pages xv-xvi.
These forms can be downloaded in full size (8.5" x 11") at
www.mwp.com/pages/booksfilmprod101.html

DEVELOPMENT TO PRODUCTION BUDGET SAMPLE #1

"Film Title"
Development to Production Budget Sample #1
The figures on this form are for demonstration purposes only and are not to be taken as financial advice.

Acct	Description		Sub-Total	Total
1.00	**STORY RIGHTS / ACQUISTIONS**			
1.01	Story Rights	7,500		
	Paid in Development	(7,500)	0	
	TOTAL STORY RIGHTS			**0**
2.00	**SCENARIO**			
2.01	Writer	75,000		
	Paid in Development	(25,000)	50,000	
2.20	Story Editor	6,000		
	Paid in Development	(4,500)	1,500	
2.25	Research	5,000		
	Paid in Development	(2,532)	2,468	
2.27	Clearances / Title Search	2,000	2,000	
2.60	Writer Travel & Living	2,968		
	Paid in Development	(2,968)	0	
	TOTAL SCENARIO			**55,968**
3.00	**DEVELOPMENT COSTS**			
3.95	Story Rights	7,500		
	Writer	25,000		
	Story Editor	4,500		
	Research	2,532		
	Travel & Living	2,968		
	Producer Fees	3,750		
	Overhead	3,750	50,000	
	TOTAL DEVELOPMENT COSTS			**50,000**

DEVELOPMENT TO PRODUCTION BUDGET SAMPLE #2

"Film Title"
Development to Production Budget Sample #2

The figures on this form are for demonstration purposes only and are not to be taken as financial advice.

Acct	Description		Sub-Total	Total
1.00	STORY RIGHTS / ACQUISTIONS			
1.01	Story Rights	7,500		
	Paid in Development	(7,500)	0	
	TOTAL STORY RIGHTS			0
2.00	SCENARIO			
2.01	Writer	75,000		
	Paid in Development	(25,000)	50,000	
2.20	Story Editor	6,000		
	Paid in Development	(4,500)	1,500	
2.25	Research	5,000		
	Paid in Development	(2,532)	2,468	
2.27	Clearances / Title Search	2,000	2,000	
2.60	Writer Travel & Living	2,968		
	Paid in Development	(2,968)	0	
	TOTAL SCENARIO			55,968
3.00	DEVELOPMENT COSTS			
3.95	Financing Company #1	10,000		
	Financing Company #2	35,000		
	Financing Company #3	5,000	50,000	
	- Story Rights ($7,500)			
	- Writer ($25,000)			
	- Story Editor ($4,500)			
	- Research ($2,532)			
	- Travel & Living ($2,968)			
	- Producer Fees ($3,750)			
	- Overhead ($3,750)			
	TOTAL DEVELOPMENT COSTS			50,000

BLANK BUDGET TOP SHEET #1

"Film Title"
Type of Production (ie: Feature Film, # Episode Series   )

Shoot Format / Post Format
List of Unions or Non-Union
Budget prepared by Name

Shoot Month & Year
Location vs Studio
Budget dated Date

Acct	Description	Total
1.00	Story Rights / Acquisitions	
2.00	Scenario	
3.00	Development Costs	
4.00	Producer	
5.00	Director	
6 00	Stars	
Total "A" (Above The Line)		
10.00	Cast	
11.00	Extras	
12.00	Production Staff	
13.00	Design Labor	
14.00	Construction Labor	
15.00	Set Dressing Labor	
16.00	Property Labor	
17.00	Special Effects Labor	
18 00	Wrangling Labor	
19.00	Wardrobe Labor	
20.00	Makeup / Hair Labor	
21.00	Video Technical Crew	
22.00	Camera Labor	
23.00	Electrical Labor	
24.00	Grip Labor	
25.00	Production Sound Labor	
26.00	Transportation Labor	
27 00	Fringe Benefits	
28.00	Production Office Expenses	
29.00	Studio / Backlot Expenses	
30 00	Location Office Expenses	
31.00	Site Expenses	
32.00	Unit Expenses	
33.00	Travel & Living Expenses	
34.00	Transportation	
35.00	Construction Materials	
36 00	Art Supplies	
37 00	Set Dressing	
38 00	Props	
39.00	Special Effects	
40 00	Animals	
41 00	Wardrobe Supplies	
42 00	Makeup / Hair Supplies	
43.00	Video Studio Facilities	
44.00	Video Remote Technical Facilities	
45.00	Camera Equipment	
46 00	Electrical Equipment	
47 00	Grip Equipment	
48 00	Sound Equipment	
49.00	Second Unit	
50.00	Videotape Stock	
51.00	Production Laboratory	
Total "B" (Below The Line Production)		

60.00	Editorial Labor	
61.00	Editorial Equipment	
62.00	Video Post Production (Picture)	
63.00	Video Post Production (Sound)	
64.00	Post Production Laboratory	
65.00	Film Post Production (Sound)	
66 00	Music	
67 00	Titles / Opticals / Stock Footage	
68.00	Versioning	
69.00	Amortization (Series)	
Total "C" (Below The Line Post Prdn.)		
70 00	Unit Publicity	
71 00	General Expenses	
72.00	Indirect Costs	
Total "D" (Other)		
80.00	Completion Guarantee (%)	
81.00	Contingency (%)	
82.00	Cost of Issue (%)	
GRAND TOTAL		

BLANK BUDGET TOP SHEET #2

"Film Title"
Type of Production (ie· Feature Film, # Episode Series...)

Shoot Format / Post Format
List of Unions or Non-Union
Budget prepared by. Name

Shoot Month & Year
Location vs Studio
Budget dated. Date

Acct	Description	Total
801-00	Story & Other Rights	
803-00	Writing	
805-00	Producer & Staff	
807-00	Director & Staff	
809-00	Talent	
810-00	Fringe Benefits (ATL)	
Total Above The Line		
811-00	Production Staff	
813-00	Camera	
814-00	Art Department	
815-00	Set Construction	
816-00	Special Effects	
817-00	Set Operations	
819-00	Electrical	
821-00	Set Dressing	
823-00	Action Props	
825-00	Picture Vehicles & Animals	
826-00	Computer Graphics	
827-00	Special Photography	
829-00	Extra Talent	
831-00	Wardrobe	
833-00	Makeup & Hair	
835-00	Sound	
837-00	Location	
838-00	Video Tape	
839-00	Transportation	
841-00	Film & Lab	
843-00	Tests	
845-00	Facility Expenses	
847-00	Second Unit	
848-00	Special Unit	
849-00	Fringe Benefits (Prdn.)	
Total Below The Line Production		
851-00	Editing & Projection	
852-00	Video Tape Post	
853-00	Music	
855-00	Sound (Post Production)	
857-00	Film, Tape & Library	
858-00	Visual Effects	
859-00	Titles & Opticals	
860-00	Fringe Benefits (Post Prdn.)	
Total Below The Line Post Production		
861-00	Insurance	
862-00	Publicity	
864-00	Product Placement	
865-00	General Expenses	
866-00	Fringe Benefits (Other)	
867-00	Insurance Claims	
869-00	Completion Costs	
870-00	Contingency	
Total Other		
GRAND TOTAL		

BLANK BUDGET TOP SHEET #3

"Film Title"

Type of Production (ie. Feature Film, # Episode Series..)

Shoot Format / Post Format
List of Unions or Non-Union
Budget prepared by Name

Shoot Month & Year
Location vs Studio
Budget dated Date

Acct	Description	Total
A	Story & Script	
B	Producer / Director	
BE	Main Cast	
Total A+B+BE (Above The Line)		
C01	Production Management	
C02	Assistant Director / Continuity	
C03	Technical Advisors	
C04	Camera Crew	
C05	Sound Crew	
C06	Editorial Staff	
C07	Stills Camera Staff	
C08	Wardrobe Staff	
C09	Makeup Staff	
C10	Hair Dressing Staff	
C11	Casting	
C12	Production Accountancy	
C13	Projectionists	
C14	Miscellaneous Studio Staff	
C15	Foreign Unit Technicians	
D	Art Department	
E1A	Cast (Non-Principals)	
E2	Stand-Ins / Doubles / Stunts	
E3	Crowd	
F	Music	
G	Costumes & Wigs	
H	Miscellaneous Production Store	
I	Film & Laboratory Charges	
J	Studio Rentals (Prdn. & Post)	
K	Equipment	
L	Power	
M1	Travel & Transport	
M2	Studio & Other Transport	
N1	Hotel & Living Expenses	
N2	Studio Hotel & Living	
Total C01 thru N2		
O	Insurances	
P	Social Security & Fringes	
Q	Publicity	
R	Miscellaneous Expenses	
S1	Construction Labor	
S1A	Construction Materials	
S2	Set Dressing Labor	
S3	Operating Labor	
S4	Striking Costs	
S5	Lighting / Spotting Labor	
S7	Foreign Labour	
S8	Properties	
T	Special Effects	
U	Location Facilities	
Total O thru U		

Y	Finance & Legal	
Z	Overheads	
Total Y+Z (Other)		
	Completion Insurance (%)	
GRAND TOTAL		

Budget Breakdown Sample #1 - "The Lists"

Locations	Cast
Hilary's Galley - I I I I Huw's Workshop - I N N I I I I Hilary's Livingroom - I I I N N I I I I I I N I I I I I Park - I I I I I I I I N N I I I Ext. Max's House - I N N N N I I N Max's Office - I I I I I N N I I I Indoor Playground - I I I I Classroom - I I Hospital Room - I I I City Establishing - I Max's Back Porch - I I I N N N N I N Huw's Forge - N N N N Solarium - I I	Hilary - I I I I I I I I I I I I I I I I I I I I I I I I I I I I I I I I I I I I I I I I I I I Huw - I I I I I I I I I I I I I I I I I I I I I I I I I I I Max - I I I I I I I I I I I I I I I I I I I I I I I I I I Thug - I I I I I I I I Friend - I I I I I I I I I I I I I I I I I I I I I
Extras	Vehicles
Man with Dog - I I Indoor playground kids - I I I Classroom Kids - I Teacher - I Drivers of passing cars - I I I I Nurse - I I Gardening Grandmother - I I I I I I I 4 Bridge players - I	Max's car - I I I I I I I I Hilary's car - I I I I I I I I I I I Huw's Truck - I I I I I I I I Mini-bus - I Backhoe - I I Tank - I I I

Other pages may track: Children, SPFX, CGI, Stunts, Songs, Animals, Other Special Notes...

BUDGET BREAKDOWN SAMPLE #2 "THE SPREADSHEET"

Budget Breakdown Sample #2 - "The Spreadsheet"

Sc#	Set	D/N	# Pg	Cast	Extras	Animals	Vehicles	Other Notes
1	City Skyline	N	0.5	-	peds,drivers		cars	
2	Office	N	1	M,Hw		ferret		
3	Parking Lot	N	2.5	M,T			M,T,cars	gun fire
4	City Streets	D	1	M,T,Stunt drivers	peds,drivers		M,T,cars	car chase
5	Indoor Playground	D	2	M,Hw,Hy,F	kids,parents	dog		
6	Forge	N	2	Hw,Hy				
7	Kitchen	D	1.5	M,Hy		dog,ferret		smoke

Legend
M = Max
Hw = Huw
Hy = Hilary
T = Thug
F = Friend

Detail Page of Budget

"Film Title"
Sample detail portion of a budget
The figures on this form are for demonstration purposes only and are not to be taken as financial advice.

Acct	Description	Amount		Rate	Sub-Total	Total
						59,438
10-0	CAST					
10-1	Principal Cast Members					
	Character #1					
	- Shoot Days	20	days	500	10,000	
	- OT	20	hours	100	2,000	
	Sub-total				12,000	
	- Rights Pre-buy	50	%	12,000	6,000	
	- Prep Fittings/Rehearsals	2	days	250	500	
	- H/M/W	20	hours	65	1,300	
	Character #1 - Total				19,800	
	Character #2					
	- Shoot Days	15	days	300	4,500	
	- OT	15	hours	50	750	
	Sub-total				5,250	
	- Rights Pre-buy	50	%	5,250	2,625	
	- Prep Fittings/Rehearsals	2	days	150	300	
	- H/M/W	15	hours	35	525	
	Character #2 - Total				8,700	
	Total 10-1 Principal Cast Members					28,500
10-4	Casting Director		Allow			10,000
10-4.5	Casting Facilities		Allow			1,500

... and elsewhere in the budget ...

Acct	Description	Amount		Rate	Sub-Total	Total
20-2	Production Manager					
	- Prep	5	wks	2,000	10,000	
	- Shoot	5	wks	2,000	10,000	
	- Wrap	2	wks	2,000	4,000	
	- Hiatus	0	wks	2,000	-	
	- Stat Holidays	0.2	wks	2,000	400	
	See Fringes in Category 45-0					
	Total 20-2 Production Manager					24,400
20-5	Production Coordinator					
	- Prep	4	wks	1,000	4,000	
	- Shoot	5	wks	1,000	5,000	
	- Wrap	2	wks	1,000	2,000	
	- Hiatus	0	wks	1,000	-	
	- Stat Holidays	0.2	wks	1,000	200	
	See Fringes in Category 45-0					
	Total 20-5 Production Coordinator					11,200

Checklist of Questions/Notes for Budget Creation

Project Title \
Type (MOW, FF, series, #eps) \
Budget size (estimate) \
When shoot \
days shoot \
When delivery/# months post \
Shoot: digital, video, 16 or 35 \
For Distributors/Broadcasters

ATL - Script Rights
Original vs. cost of rights/who \
Nationality of original work

ATL - Writer(s)
Names/rates/nationality \
Union \
Rights to be bought \
Travel: who/when/where

ATL - Development
Spent to date/by who \
To be spent/by who \
Budget/bkdn _____; Travel _____; Tax estimates _____; Loc scout _____

ATL - Producers
List names/Co's/rates/nations \
 /restrictions (ie: 5% of budget) \
XP(s) \
Producer(s) \
Assoc Producer(s) \
Line Producer \
Other(s) \
Producer Asst(s) \
Travel: Who/When/Where

ATL - Director
List name/confirmed?/rate \
Rights to be bought \
Union \
Travel: When/Where

ATL - Stars
List names/Roles \
 /Rates/Nationality \
Rights to be bought \
Travel: who/when/where \
Rehearsal/wdb/MU tests

CHECKLIST OF QUESTIONS/NOTES FOR BUDGET CREATION (PAGE 2 OF 2)

Budget Questions/Notes - 2

BTL - Production
Union for cast _____
Union(s) for crew _____
SPFX _____
Stunts _____
Animals _____
Night shoots _____
Location vs. studio _____
Distant location _____
Period wdb/sets _____
# of Extras _____
Child Actors _____
Second Unit _____
B-Camera _____
Cranes/camera cars/etc _____
Other special notes _____

BTL - Post
Union for post crew _____
Facilities deals? _____
Music Composer - name/rate _____
Music rights _____
Stock footage _____
Titles - how fancy _____
Opticals _____
Delivery version(s) _____

BTL - Other
Publicity - how much _____
Insurance - E&O # of yrs _____
Legal - how much _____
Post Acctg - how much _____
Audit - how many _____
Corporate overhead - how much _____
Interim financing - what items _____
Est. interim loan size _____
Foreign currencies _____

Completion Bond
Company history _____

Contingency - % _____

Which Financiers involved? _____
_____
_____

Contact info _____

TIME SHEET

Production Company Ltd.
TIME SHEET

Soc.#: _____

Name/Company: _____

Address: _____

Rate: _____ FOR WEEK ENDING: _____

Approvals:

Exec.Prd: _____ P.M.: _____

Dept.Head: ___ Acct.: ___

DAY	CALL	LUNCH		DINNER		WRAP	HRS	ST	1.5	2.0	2.5	3.0	MP	TA	HRS
SUN															
MON															
TUE															
WED															
THU															
FRI															
SAT															

TOTAL HOURS WORKED:

EQUIVALENT ST HOURS:

NOTES:

ITEM	ACCOUNT	AMOUNT
AMOUNT PAID:		

ACCIDENT REPORT FORM

ACCIDENT REPORT	
Date of Accident:	Time of Accident:
Date/Time Reported:	By Whom:
Description of Location:	
Injured Person (Full Name):	
Age:	Occupation:
Address:	Telephone:
Nature/Extent of Injuries:	
Attending Physician:	Address:
First Aid Rendered: Y / N	By Whom:
Hospital Name:	Conveyance (Name):
Witnesses Names/Addresses:	
Description of Incident:	
Reported by:	Signature:

WALKIE-TALKIE SIGN-OUT FORM

Film Title: WALKIE-TALKIE SIGN-OUT   Page:

Name/Dept	Walkie #	Serial #	Accessories	Date Taken	Date Return	Sign

KEY SIGN-OUT FORM

Film Title: KEY SIGN-OUT   Page:

Name	Dept	Key(s)	Date Taken	Sign	Date Return	Sign

EQUIPMENT RENTAL LOG

Film Title: EQUIPMENT RENTAL LOG   Page:

Date	Rental Co.	Eqt Rented	Dept	Ep#	Start/End Rental Dates	Price

Courier Log

Date Sent	To Whom (From)	Reason/Contents	Ep#	Dept	Courier Co / Waybill #

LONG DISTANCE LOG

Film Title: LONG DISTANCE LOG   Page:

Date	Time	Phone Number	Your Name	Personal	Business

POLAROID FILM SIGN-OUT FORM

Film Title:　　　　　POLAROID FILM SIGN-OUT　　　　Page:

Date	Name	Department	Ep#	600 Taken	Spectra Taken

Copier Paper Count Form

Film Title: COPIER PAPER COUNT   Page:

Date	white	pink	blue	green	yellw	gold	purpl	LEGAL	11x17	no-hole
Fri.										
Fri.										
Fri.										
Fri.										
Fri.										
Fri.										
Fri.										
Fri.										
Fri.										
Fri.										
Fri.										
Fri.										
Fri.										
Fri.										
Fri.										
Fri.										
Fri.										

DEVELOPMENT COST REPORT

"Film Production Adventure"
Development Cost Report
as of 1 Dec 2004

The figures on this form are for demonstration purposes only and are not to be taken as financial advice.

Code	Description	Actual Cost	Dev Budget	Difference
1.00	Story Rights	10,000	10,000	-
2.00	Script Writing & Fringes	30,000	30,000	-
3.00	Story Editor & Fringes	5,000	5,000	-
4.00	Research	1,794	2,000	206
5.00	Budget/Breakdown	3,000	3,000	-
6.00	Travel & Living	2,312	2,000	(312)
7.00	Office Overhead & Accounting	4,894	5,000	106
8.00	Producer Fees	13,000	13,000	-
	TOTAL	70,000	70,000	-

CREW LIST (PAGE 1 OF 2)

"Film Production Adventure"

Production Company Ltd. Address Telephone/Fax/Email/Web Page	Parent Company Ltd. Address Telephone/Fax/Email/Web Page
Co-Production Company Ltd. Address Telephone/Fax/Email/Web Page	Key Funding Company Ltd. Address Telephone/Fax/Email/Web Page

CREW LIST

GREEN REVISED

3 Dec 2004

executive producer	NAME c/o Company name	office phone # email address
executive in charge of production	NAME c/o Company name	office phone # email address
supervising producer	NAME c/o Company name	office phone # email address
associate producer	NAME c/o Company name	office phone # email address
producer	NAME home address	home phone # email address
line producer	NAME home address	home phone # email address
director	NAME home address <u>Agent</u>: Agency & address Agent's name	home phone # email address agency phone # agency fax #
writer	NAME home address <u>Agent</u>: Agency & address Agent's name	home phone # email address agency phone # agency fax #

Continuing with contact information for:

<u>PRODUCTION OFFICE</u>
production manager
assistant production manager
production coordinator
production secretary
office P.A.
assistant to producer
tutor

<u>ACCOUNTING DEPARTMENT</u>
production accountant
assistant accountant

CASTING DEPARTMENT
casting director (leads)
casting director (on location)
extras casting

PUBLICITY
publicist
stills photographer

PRODUCTION - ON SET
1st assistant director
2nd assistant director
2nd 2nd assistant director
3rd assistant director
set production assistant
continuity supervisor

LOCATION DEPARTMENT
location manager
assistant location manager
location assistant

ART DEPARTMENT
production designer
art director
1st assistant art director
2nd assistant art director
computer graphics
draftsman
storyboard artist

SETS DEPARTMENT
set decorator
lead set dresser
set dresser
on-set set dresser

PROPS DEPARTMENT
property master
lead props
props buyer

VISUAL EFFECTS
effects supervisor
computer animation
special effects
prosthetics

WARDROBE DEPARTMENT
costume designer
assistant costume designer
wardrobe mistress
assistant wardrobe mistress
seamstress

HAIR/MAKEUP DEPARTMENT
hair designer
makeup artist

CAMERA DEPARTMENT
director of photography
camera operator
1st assistant camera
2nd assistant camera
camera department trainee

SOUND DEPARTMENT
sound recordist
boom operator

ELECTRICAL DEPARTMENT
gaffer
best boy
electric
generator operator

GRIP DEPARTMENT
key grip
dolly grip
grip

STUNTS DEPARTMENT
stunt coordinator

TRANSPORTATION DEPARTMENT
transport coordinator
picture vehicle coordinator
transport captain
head driver
driver

CATERING/CRAFT SERVICE
caterer
craft service

CONSTRUCTION DEPARTMENT
construction manager
head carpenter
carpenter
scenic painter
construction labour

POST-PRODUCTION
post production supervisor
music composer
picture editor
assistant editor
sound effects editor
dialogue editor

Cast List

(On Letterhead)

"Film Production Adventure"

CAST LIST

BLUE REVISED - 2 Dec 2004

1. Max   ACTOR'S NAME   Talent Agency
                        Home address   (Agent's Name)
                        Home phone   Agency address
                        Home email   Agency phone / fax
                                            Agency email

2. Huw MacConneach   STAR'S NAME   Talent Agency/Manager
                        c/o Hotel   (Agent/Manager Name)
                        Hotel address   Agency address
                        Hotel phone   Agency phone / fax
                                            Agency email

3. Friend   ACTOR'S NAME   Talent Agency
                        Home address   (Agent's Name)
                        Home phone   Agency address
                        Home email   Agency phone / fax
                                            Agency email

4. Little Boy   ACTOR'S NAME   Talent Agency
                        Home address   (Agent's Name)
                        Home phone   Agency address
                        Home email   Agency phone / fax
                        (Parent's names)   Agency email

STUNTS - Stunt Agency, address, phone, fax, email, web page

51. Stunt Coordinator   STUNT PERFORMER NAME   Home phone
                        Home address
                        Home email

STAND-INS

Female Stand-in   STAND-IN'S NAME   Home phone
                        Home address   Email

Male Stand-in   STAND-IN'S NAME   Home phone
                        Home address   Email

N.B. Character numbers match A.D. character number assignments (i.e., on all schedules and call sheets).

"Film Production Adventure"

Contact List

PINK REVISED   4 December 2004

Air Conditioning   Company Name   Telephone #
                      Address   Fax #
                      Web Page   Email
                      Contact Person

Apartment Rental   Company Name   Telephone #
                      Address   Fax #
                      Web Page   Email
                      Contact Person

Batteries   Company Name   Telephone #
                      Address   Fax #
                      Web Page   Email
                      Contact Person
                      Account #

*Continuing with this format, list suppliers, contact names, and
account numbers for the following subjects:*

Casting Facility

Cel Phones

Cleaners

Coffee Machine/Supplies

Computer Rental

Conference Operator

Courier (in town)

Courier (international)

Customs Broker

Doctor

Disposal & Containers

Drafting Equipment

Electrian

Equipment (camera/grip/elec.)

Equipment (scaffolding)

Contact List - page 2

Expendables (gels, etc.)

Film Stock

Florist

Funding Agencies

Furniture Rental

Guarantor Company

Hotel

Immigration

Internet

Limousine

Location Supplies

Music Rights Clearances

Moving & Storage Company

Nurses

Office Rental

Office Supplies

Pagers

Payroll Service

Photocopier & Fax Machine

Photofinishing

Plumber

Post: Laboratory

Post: Editing Facility

Post: Sound Editing Facility

Post: Video Transfers

Printing Company

Product Placement
Recycling

Safety Supplies

Script Research Company

Security

Stock Footage

Studio

Tables & Chairs Rental

Taxi

Telephone Rental

Telephone: Long Distance

Towel Service

Travel Agent

Tutors

Unions & Guilds

Vehicle Rental

Vehicles: Honeywagons

Vehicles: Winnies

Vehicles: Winnie pump-out

Vehicles: Road/Traffic Info

Vehicles: Tow Truck/Repairs

Video Rental

Video Stock

Walkie-Talkies

Wardrobe Supplier/Builder

Washer/Dryer

Water Machine

Weather Information

```
"FILM PRODUCTION ADVENTURE"      CALL SHEET      Day:  11
Production Company Inc.                          Date: SATURDAY 30 OCTOBER 2004
Office #: 555-1212
                                 BREAKFAST READY:  0630
Producer/Director:    (Name)     LEAVE FOR SET:    0730
Production Manager:   (Name)
Assistant Director:   (Name)        On Location:   0800
                                 Shooting Call:    0915
LOCATION: MAPS HANDED OUT AT BREAKY      Lunch:    1300

WEATHER: Cloudy, windy, light rain, hi:14, lo:6, POP:70%SUNRISE/SET: 0749-1816
```

POLICE: (Telephone #)	AMBULANCE: (Telephone #)	FIRE: (Teleponе #)

SC#	SET	D/N	CAST	PGS	SYNOPSIS
*** MORE "DRIVING & PROCESS" BLOCK SHOOTING THE FOLLOWING "HUW CAR" SCENES ***					
8pt	INT HUW'S CAR	Day	2.4.	6/8	Next day, same route
9pt	INT HUW'S CAR	Day	2.4.	1 0/8	Hilary gives advice on better sleep
10pt	INT HUW'S CAR	Ev'g	2.4.	1 0/8	Magic hour: Arriving to work
15pt	INT HILARY'S CAR	Night	2.	1/8	Huw looks for Hilary
Reduced unit...					
26	INT HILARY'S CAR	D4N	4.	---	Isn't that the same street sign?
Target of opportunity...					
1	INT HUW'S CAR	Morng	2.4.	2/8	Gosh, ya gotta love these hours
2	INT HUW'S CAR	Ev'g	2.	1/8	Home so soon?

¿ ¿ ¿ C L O C K S   G O   B A C K   O N E   H O U R   T O N I G H T ¿ ¿ ¿

CHARACTER	ARTIST	LV.COTT	H/M/W	SET
2. HUW	(Name)	0730	0800	0900
4. HILARY	(Name)	0730	0800	0900

SET REQUIREMENTS

VEHICLES		-Huw's car on tow rig for block shooting, then home for processing
		-Hilary's car on set for "Flashlight scene"
		-Hilary's car on standby for reduced unit
LIGHTING/GRIP	9:	Glare of sun passes
	10:	Door opens to beam of diffuse light, Car moves into sun
ART DEPT	8-10:	Huw's littered car dressing
	8:	Bug splat on windshield
	9:	Hilary's candies
	26:	Street sign: "The Middle of Nowhere"
MAKEUP/HAIR	15:	Huw looks haggard
WARDROBE	8:	Huw's gym clothes, Huw's watch
	9:	Huw's watch
	15:	Huw's gym shoe (left)
NOTES	26:	Dry ice

CALL SHEET SAMPLE #1 (PAGE 2 OF 2)

	TUESDAY ADVANCE SCHEDULE		Cloudy windy cool hi:10 lo:2 POP:60%(0650-1714)		
4	EXT MAX'S HOUSE	Morng	---	1/8	Establishing shot
23	INT LIVING ROOM	Morng	1.	4/8	Max breaks in to his own house
25	INT LIVING ROOM	Morng	1.	2/8	Max asleep out on the couch
24	INT KITCHEN	Morng	1.	3/8	Max learns all about hot chocolate
28	INT LIVING ROOM	Night	1.	2/8	Max slept through the whole day?!?

Call sheet joke here...

"FILM PRODUCTION ADVENTURE" **CALL SHEET** Day: 14
Film Company Inc.   Date: WED., FEBRUARY 16, 2005
Address
Telephone   CALL: 3:00am
Night Line Telephone   Gennie Op x2: 2:30am
                                           Honeywagon: 2:30am
Exec. Producers   (Name)   MU/Hair: 3:00am
                   (Name)   Wdb: 2:30am
Producers   (Name)   Craft: 2:15am
                   (Name)   Substantials: 5:30am No:85
Prdn. Manager   (Name)   Lunch: 9:00am No:85 Box:300
Director   (Name)
                                              Sunrise: 7:08am
Episode #5 "It's a N-Ice World"   Sunset: 5:56pm
                                              Weather: sunny, windy, warmish
Set Cel: (Tel.#)   POP 0% Lo:-5 Hi:+5
Loc Cel: (Tel.#) LOCATION: (SEE MAP)
                  1. Hockey Arena, (Address)

SC#	SET/DESCRIPTION	CAST	D/N	PGS	LOC
34-B	INT ICE SURFACE The dream-game	1,4,6,12,Black team x15, White team x12,Refs x3,Coach x1, Fans x298, Photographer x1	N10	3 4/8	1
34-F	INT STANDS Fans cheer them on	12,Fans x300	N10	1/8	1
34-A	INT BLACK BENCH But we're bad guys?	1,2(vo),4,6,Black team x15, Fans x300	N10	1 0/8	1
34-D	INT BLACK BENCH Somebody wake me?	1,2(vo),4,6,Black team x15, Fans x300	N10	3/8	1

* 2ND CAMERA DAY   TOTAL: 5 0/8

CHARACTER	ARTIST	PU	H/M/W	SET	LOC
1 Max	(Name)	3:15am	3:30am	4:00am	1
2 Huw V/O	(Name)	--	N/A	N/A	
4 Hilary	(Name)	--	3:30am	4:00am	1
6 Thug	(Name)	--	3:30am	4:00am	1
12 Reporter	(Name)	--	3:00am	4:00am	1
PHOTO DOUBLES					
1A Max Double		--	2:30am	3:00am	1
4A Hilary Double		--	2:30am	3:00am	1
6A Thug Double		--	2:30am	3:00am	1

EXTRAS
Cast of thousands! ... uh, hundreds! Fans x298 --   4:00am 1
Coach x1, Photographer x1   --   4:00am 1
Black team x15, White Team x12   2:30am   3:00am 1
Refs x3   3:00am   4:00am 1

1st AD:(Name/Phone)   2nd AD:(Name/Phone)   Transport:(Name/Phone)

CALL SHEET SAMPLE #2 (PAGE 2 OF 2)

DAILY CREW
2:30am - P.A. Daily x1, TAD Daily x1 to report to set.
3:00am - 2nd Camera x1, 2nd Focus Puller x1 to report to set.

TRANSPORTATION
2:30am - Honeywagon hot and cooking!
3:15am - Transport to pick up "Max" at the hotel

ADVANCE SCHEDULE - **DAY** 15 - THURSDAY, FEBRUARY 22, 2001
30	INT ARENA STANDS	1,4	D9		4/8	1
45-A	INT STANDS	12,Fans x35	N11	1	0/8	1
45-C	INT STANDS	Fans x35	N11		1/8	1
45-B	INT WHITE BENCH	1,2(vo),4,7,Fans x35	N11		7/8	1
35	INT ARENA CORRIDOR	1,2(vo),7	N10		1/8	1

RUSHES OF DAY 13
4:30pm - at the Lab

Crew Rep: (Name)   Actor's Union: (Name/Phone)   Safety Rep: (Name)

Callsheet joke here...

Map to location (with closest hospital noted) here...

Production Report Sample #1 (Blank)

| DAILY PRODUCTION REPORT - Prdn Company: | | | | DAY | | of | |

Title: _____ **Date:** _____

Producer/Director: _____ **Scheduled Dates:** _____

Sets: _____

Locations. _____

Weather

Crew Call- ☐ **Lunch-** ☐ **Wrap -** ☐

#1 Shot AM ☐ **#1 Shot PM** ☐

	Scenes	Pages		Minutes		Setups
Script -			Prev -		Prev -	
Taken Prev-			Today -		Today -	
Today -			Total -		Total -	
To Date -			Avg -		Avg -	
To be taken-						
Avg/Day -			Script Running Time			

Scene #'s

Wildtracks

#	Cast	Character	SWF	Call	Set	Lunch out	Lunch in	Wrap	Sound Stock Usage
									of
									Avg Total Film Use/Day:

Position	Crew Name	Set	Wrap	Lunch out	Lunch in	Film Stock Usage	B/W	100ASA	400ASA
Director						Received Previous			
Prdn Mgr						Received Today			
Loc Mgr						Total Received			
1st AD						Used Previous			
2nd AD						Used Today			
Continuity						Total Used			
DOP						On Hand			
1st A.Cam						NOTES:			
2nd A.Cam									
Gaffer									
Electric									
Key Grip									
Grip									
Sound									
Boom Op									
Art Dir									
Set Dec									
Prop Master									
Wardrobe									
Wdb Asst									
Hair/MU									
Photographer									
PA's						1st AD:		PM·	

416

PRODUCTION REPORT SAMPLE #2 -BLANK- (PAGE 1 OF 2)

Production Company

DAILY PRODUCTION REPORT

MAIN UNIT DAYS	_____ of _____
2ND UNIT DAYS	of
TOTAL DAYS	of

Title·

Producer·

Start Date.

Date

Director

Finish Date·

Sets·

Locations.

Weather.

Crew Call-	
#1 Shot AM	

Lunch-	
#1 Shot PM	

Wrap -

Script Running Time

Scene #'s

	Scenes	Pages
Script -		
Taken Prev-		
Today -		
To Date -		
To be taken-		

	Minutes
Prev -	
Today -	
Total -	
Avg -	

	Setups
Prev -	
Today -	
Total -	
Avg -	

Wildtracks

FILM USE		Prev	Today	Total
100 ASA	Gross			
	Print			
	NG			
	Waste			
400 ASA	Gross			
	Print			
	NG			
	Waste			

FILM INVENTORY	Total Rec'd	Today	Total Used	On Hand
100 ASA				
400 ASA				
GRAND TOTAL				

#	Cast	Character	SWF	Call	Wrap	Lunch out	Lunch in

SOUND 1/4"	Prev -	
	Today -	
	Total -	

Cash Extras	Wdb-Set	Wrap	Amt

Qty	Act/Per/App	Type of Extra	H/M/W	Set	Wrap	Lunch out	Lunch in

TOTAL AMT CASH EXTRAS

Asst Director

Prdn Mgr.

417

PRODUCTION REPORT SAMPLE #2 - BLANK - (PAGE 2 OF 2)

		Title:	
Director	_____	Day:	Date
1st AD	_____		
2nd AD	_____	Prdn Coord _____	Gun Wrangler _____
3rd AD	_____	Coord Asst _____	Animals _____
Set PA	_____	Office PA	Wrangler
Continuity	_____	Art Director _____	Nurse
Craft Serv	_____	1st Asst Art _____	Ambl. Attend
DOP	_____	2nd Asst Art _____	Security
Cam Op	_____	Art Trainee	Policemen
1st A.C	_____	Set Dec _____	ETF
2nd A.C	_____	Lead Sets _____	Vehicles (list) _____
Cam.Trainee	_____	Set Dresser _____	_____
Gaffer	_____	On Set Dress _____	_____
Best Boy	_____	FX Super _____	_____
Electric	_____	FX Asst _____	_____
Gennie Op.	_____	3D Artists _____	_____
Key Grip	_____	2D Artists _____	_____
Best Boy Grip	_____	Computer Artist _____	_____
Grip	_____	Prosthetics _____	_____
Sound Mixer	_____	SPFX _____	
Boom Op	_____	SPFX Asst _____	Pic.Vehicles: _____
Props Master	_____	Stunt Coord _____	_____
Lead Props	_____	Stills Photog.	_____
Props Buyer	_____	Post Super. _____	Substantials at: _____ x
Cost. Design	_____	Editor _____	Lunches at: _____ x
Ast Cost.Des.	_____	Asst Editor	Dinners at _____ x
Wdb Asst	_____	DAILIES:	
Seamstress	_____		
Hair Design	_____		
MU Artist	_____		
Trans Coord	_____		
Trans Captain	_____		
Drivers	_____		

NOTES

LOCATION RELEASE

(This form is a sample to inspire you to design one with your own legal counsel appropriate to your production, and is not to be taken as legal advice.)

To: Production Company Inc.
      Address
      Telephone / Fax
      Email / Web Page

In consideration of the sum of _____, and for other good and valuable consideration, the receipt and sufficiency whereof is hereby acknowledged:

I hereby grant Production Company Inc., its affiliates, licensees, successors and assigns (hereinafter collectively the "Company") the irrevocable right, in perpetuity, to use the footage taken of the premises (the "Footage") located at:

_____ (the "Premises")

on the following date(s):

_____

in connection with the production, distribution and exploitation of the feature film presently entitled "Film Production Adventure" (the "Film"), to edit, delete, alter and amend the Footage in any manner and to juxtapose the Footage with any other material. The Film and/or the Footage may be exploited throughout the world, in perpetuity and in any and all media now or hereafter devised without any further payment to me. The Company has no obligation to use the Footage in the Film.

The Company will insure the Premises for damages as a result of accident or negligence on the part of the Company.

Should the Company need to return to the Premises for retakes for whatever reason, I agree to accept terms no less favorable than the terms stated herein.

I do hereby release and forever discharge the Company of, from and against all actions, causes of action, claims, suits, judgments and demands which may by made against the Company by virtue of the appearance of the Premises, in any manner whatsoever, in the Film.

I warrant that I have the right to grant the above rights to the Company and enter into this Release.

Dated this _____ day of _____, _____.

Witness: _____   Signature: _____
                                   Name: _____
                                   Title: _____

                                   Address: _____
                                   _____

                                   Tel: _____

PRODUCTION MANAGEMENT 101 / *Patz*

LOCATION LETTER

(on letterhead)

(Date)

TO THE BUSINESSES, PATRONS AND RESIDENTS OF MAIN STREET, FILM AVENUE AND NEW STREET:

Film Company Inc. is presently filming scenes in and around (City) for an independent feature film presently entitled "Film Production Adventure." This production is a family comedy about an unlikely threesome who while making a movie about Grandma's bad cooking, they learn how to live life to the fullest at the same time.

On January 4, 2005, we will be filming at 123 Main Street on the corner of Main Street and Film Avenue. We will also be filming in the park on Main Street at the same corner. The shots at 123 Main Street will be exterior shots of the building. The shots in the park will be of our hero, Max, confronting his nemesis with hilarious results.

We will be filming between the hours of 3:30 p.m. and 10:00 p.m. We will be parking our vehicles on Film Avenue and on New Street.

We are an experienced crew and we are aware of the need for street access and a calm atmosphere with as little disruption as possible while working in your neighborhood.

We hope that our presence does not cause you any inconvenience and appreciate your patience in this matter. If you have any questions, please call me on my cell phone (telephone #) or my assistant (Name) at the production office (telephone #). On the day, either I, or my assistant, will be on site during the set-up and shooting if you have an immediate concern.

Sincerely,

(Name)
Location Manager
contact number(s)

PETTY CASH REPORT

Petty Cash Report

Name: _____   Film Title: _____

Dept: _____   Date: _____

#	DATE	TO WHOM	PURPOSE	ACCT	NET AMT	TAX	TOTAL
1							
2							
3							
4							
5							
6							
7							
8							
9							
10							

APPROVALS				
		TOTALS:		
EX.P:	P.M.:	MINUS ADVANCE:		
DEPT:	ACCT:	BALANCE/DUE:		

DISTRIBUTION:

Purchase Order (P.O.)

"Film Production Adventure"
Production Company Ltd.
Production Company Address
Production Company Phone
Production Company Fax

Purchase Order No. ___001___

To: SUPPLIER COMPANY SUPPLIER ADDRESS SUPPLIER PHONE SUPPLIER FAX	Ship to: STUDIO STUDIO ADDRESS CONTACT PERSON
Contact Name: PERSON NAME	Delivery Date: **7 DEC 2004**
Ordered by: WILHELM	Tax #: ATTACHED EXEMPTION FORM
Date ordered: **5 DEC 2004**	Terms: INVOICE

Qty	Description	Unit	Total
5	REALLY NECESSARY ITEMS (RENTAL) 2 WEEK RENTAL (3-DAY WEEK) DELIVERY TO STUDIO PICK UP FROM OFFICE ON 21 DEC 2003 RE: LOCATION DEPARTMENT	7.50/DAY	225.00 N/C N/C
Approval: DP			225.00

Copy - Supplier   Copy - Production Company   Copy - Accounting

PURCHASE ORDER (BLANK)

"Film Production Adventure"
Production Company Ltd.
Production Company Address
Production Company Phone
Production Company Fax

Purchase Order No. _____

To:	Ship to:
Contact Name:	Delivery Date:
Ordered by:	Tax #:
Date ordered:	Terms:

Qty	Description	Unit	Total

Approval:

Copy - Supplier   Copy - Production Company   Copy - Accounting

P.O. Log

PO#	To Whom	For What	Ep#	Dept	Date	Amt

Film Title: P.O. LOG   Page:

CHECK REQUISITION

"Film Production Adventure"
Production Company Ltd.
Production Company Address
Production Company Phone & Fax

CHECK REQUISITION

Date:_____   Required:_____   Amount/Currency:_____

PAYABLE TO: _____

               _____

               _____

TELEPHONE: _____

CONTACT: _____

FOR: _____

Mail Check:_____   Hold for P/U: _____   Give Check to:_____

APPROVALS:

Dept. Head:_____   PM: _____   Allocation:_____

Do not write below this line - for Accounting use only
****

425

CASH FLOW SAMPLE (DETAIL)

Cash Flow Sample (Detail)
(The figures on this form are for demonstration purposes only and are not to be taken as financial advice.)

Acct	Description	Budget	Dev/Prep4	Prep 3	Prep 2	Prep 1	Shoot 1	Shoot 2	Shoot 3	Shoot 4
1-1	Story Rights	7,500	7,500							
1-0	**STORY RIGHTS**	**7,500**								
2-1	Writer	75,000	25,000				50,000			
2-3	Story Editor	6,000	4,500	1,500						
2-4	Script Clearance	2,000			2,000					
2-9	Fringes	12,480	4,360	120			8,000			
2-0	**SCRIPT WRITING**	**95,480**								
4-1	Executive Producer	75,000	3,750				10,000			
4-2	Producer	75,000	3,750	4,000	4,000	4,000	4,000	4,000	4,000	4,000
4-7	Producer's Assistant	15,000	800	800	800	800	800	800	800	800
4-8	Producer Travel/Living	7,500	2,968			2,000	1,000			
4-9	Fringes	2,100	112	112	112	112	112	112	112	112
4-0	**PRODUCERS**	**174,600**								

... and further down the cash flow ...

Acct	Description	Budget	Dev/Prep4	Prep 3	Prep 2	Prep 1	Shoot 1	Shoot 2	Shoot 3	Shoot 4
						7,500	7,500	7,500	7,500	7,500
75-1	Contingency	100,000								
75-0	**CONTINGENCY**	**100,000**								
79-1	Union Bonds - out	40,000			40,000					
	Union Bonds - in	(40,000)								
	Location Deposits - out	20,000		10,000	10,000					
	Location Deposits - in	(20,000)								
	Art Deposits - out	10,000	7,500	2,500						
	Art Deposits - in	(10,000)								
79-0	**REFUNDABLES**	**-**								
	TOTAL OUTFLOWS	**1,500,000**	68,430	32,038	63,774	101,673	298,386	115,385	133,124	119,130

CASH FLOW SAMPLE (SUMMARY TOP SHEET – WITH INTERIM FINANCING CALCULATION)

Cash Flow Sample (Summary Top Sheet)
[Boxed numbers are Financier's drawdowns assigned to the Bank for the interim financing loan]

(The figures on this form are for demonstration purposes only and are not to be taken as financial advice.)

Acct	Description	Budget	Dev/Prep4	Prep 3	Prep 2	Prep 1	Shoot 1	Shoot 2	Shoot 3	Shoot 4
	TOTAL OUTFLOWS	**1,500,000**	**68,430**	**32,038**	**63,774**	**101,673**	**298,386**	**115,385**	**133,124**	**119,130**
	INFLOWS									
	Financier #1	750,000	10,000	187,500			187,500			150,000
	Financier #2	375,000	35,000				225,000			
	Financier #3	150,000	5,000				45,000			
	Financier #4	175,000	20,000		20,000		20,000		20,000	
	Producer Deferral	50,000								
	TOTAL INFLOWS	**1,500,000**	**70,000**	**187,500**	**20,000**	**-**	**477,500**	**-**	**20,000**	**150,000**
	Inflows Minus Outflows		1,570	157,032	113,258	11,585	190,699	75,314	(37,810)	(6,939)
	INTERIM FINANCING	246,250							46,250	
	Running Balance		**1,570**	**157,032**	**113,258**	**11,585**	**190,699**	**75,314**	**8,441**	**39,311**

Acct	Description	Shoot 5	Shoot 6	Wrap 1	Wrap 2	Post Mo1	Post Mo2	Post Mo3	Post Mo4	Total
	TOTAL OUTFLOWS	**131,346**	**110,117**	**57,745**	**18,778**	**41,249**	**64,803**	**87,890**	**56,133**	**1,500,000**
	INFLOWS									
	Financier #1			112,500			56,250		46,250	750,000
	Financier #2						75,000		40,000	375,000
	Financier #3			50,000			25,000		25,000	150,000
	Financier #4	20,000		20,000		20,000		20,000	15,000	175,000
	Producer Deferral								50,000	50,000
	TOTAL INFLOWS	**20,000**	**-**	**182,500**	**-**	**20,000**	**156,250**	**20,000**	**176,250**	**1,500,000**
	Inflows Minus Outflows	(118,285)	(228,402)	(103,647)	(122,425)	(143,674)	(52,227)	(120,117)	(0)	
	INTERIM FINANCING	100,000	100,000				(100,000)	(20,000)	(126,250)	-
	Running Balance	**27,965**	**17,848**	**142,603**	**123,825**	**102,576**	**94,023**	**6,133**	**(0)**	

COST REPORT SAMPLE (TOP SHEET AND DETAIL)

Cost Report - Sample Top Sheet (showing sample numbers, and sample cell references/formulas)
(*The figures on this form are for demonstration purposes only and are not to be taken as financial advice.*)

COST REPORT

Film Title _____
Production Company _____ For Period Ending _____

	Budget Code	Description	Costs This Period	Costs To Date	P.O.s	Total Costs	ETC	EFC	Budget	Variance
1	1.00	Story & Writer				=D+E	=H-F			=I-H
2	2.00	Producer				=D+E	=H-F			=I-H
3	3.00	Director				=D+E	=H-F			=I-H
4	4.00	Star				=D+E	=H-F			=I-H
5		Total Above-The-Line	=C1+2+3+4	=D1+2+3+4	=E1+2+3+4	=F1+2+3+4	=G1+2+3+4	=H1+2+3+4	=I1+2+3+4	=J1+2+3+4
6	10.00	Cast								
7	11.00	Crew								
8	12.00	Location/Studio								
9	13.00	Equipment								
10	14.00	Supplies								
11	15.00	Production Lab								
12		Total Below-The-Line Production								
13	20.00	Pic & Sound Edit	-	2,500	5,000	7,500	147,500	155,000	150,000	(5,000)
14	21.00	Music & Rights	500	1,500	960	2,460	124,540	127,000	125,000	(2,000)
15	22.00	Post Lab	4,500	12,500	2,250	14,750	30,250	45,000	45,000	-
16	23.00	Publicity	3,756	48,224	-	48,224	399,776	448,000	450,000	2,000
17	24.00	General Costs								
18		Total Below-The-Line Post/Other	8,756	64,724	8,210	72,934	702,066	775,000	770,000	(5,000)
19	30.00	Contingency	-	-	-	-	30,000	30,000	35,000	5,000
20		GRAND TOTAL	=C5+12+18+19	=D5+12+18+19	=E5+12+18+19	=F5+12+18+19	=G5+12+18+19	=H5+12+18+19	=I5+12+18+19	=J5+12+18+19

Cost Report - Sample Portion of Detail Page

COST REPORT

Film Title _____
Production Company _____ For Period Ending _____

Budget Code	Description	Costs This Period	Costs To Date	P.O.s	Total Costs	ETC	EFC	Budget	Variance
21.10	Music Composer	-	1,500		1,500	83,500	85,000	85,000	-
21.50	Music Rights	-	-	750	750	34,250	35,000	32,500	(2,500)
21.75	Stock Footage	500	-	210	210	6,790	7,000	7,500	500
21.00	**MUSIC & RIGHTS**	500	1,500	960	2,460	124,540	127,000	125,000	(2,000)

428

PM-ONLY COST REPORT - SPREADSHEET FROM ACCOUNTING

PM-Only Cost Report - Version #1 (Spreadsheet From Accounting)
(The figures on this form are for demonstration purposes only and are not to be taken as financial advice.)

COST REPORT
Film Title _____
Production Company _____
For Period Ending: _____

Budget Code	Description	Costs This Period	Costs To Date	P.O.s	PM ONLY	Total Costs	ETC	EFC	Budget	Variance
218 10	Props Labor	2,650	5,300	-		5,460	18,550	24,010	24,750	740
	Shoot Wk 2 Overtime				160					
218 50	Props Purch/Rentals	1,250	19,576	350	160	21,926	3,074	25,000	20,000	(5,000)
	#1 Petty Cash Float				2,000					
	#2 Petty Cash Float				1,000					
218 80	Props - Kit Rental	200	400		1,000	400	800	1,200	900	(300)
218.0	PROPS	4,100	25,276	350		27,786	22,424	50,210	45,650	(4,560)
220 10	Camera Labor	9,050	18,100	-	544	18,644	45,250	63,894	62,300	(1,594)
	Shoot Wk 2 Overtime				544					
220 50	Camera Eqt Rental	7,200	7,200			7,200	36,000	43,200	45,000	1,800
220 55	Camera Daily Rentals			225	1,500	1,725	775	2,500	2,500	-
	Steadicam (maybe)				1,500					
220 70	Camera Expendables	1,294	1,339	37		1,376	1,124	2,500	2,500	-
220 80	Camera Kit Rentals	425	-	210		210	2,340	2,550	2,700	150
220.0	CAMERA	17,969	26,639	472		29,155	85,489	114,644	115,000	356

and further down the cost report

Budget Code	Description	Costs This Period	Costs To Date	P.O.s	PM ONLY	Total Costs	ETC	EFC	Budget	Variance
400 10	Insurance		23,500	-	(1,500)	22,000	8,500	30,500	30,500	-
	Pkg Insurance savings				(1,500)					
400 15	Medicals	150	675	75		750		750	750	-
400 50	Corporate Overhead					-	150,000	150,000	150,000	-
400 60	Legal		7,500	-		7,500	32,500	40,000	40,000	-
400 70	Post Accounting					-	4,800	4,800	4,800	-
400 75	Audit						5,000	5,000	5,000	-
400 90	Bank/Financing		374	-	54,000	54,374	20,626	75,000	75,000	-
	Interim Interest Estimate				54,000					
400.0	GENERAL COSTS	150	32,049	75		84,624	221,426	306,050	306,050	-

PM-ONLY COST REPORT - SPREADSHEET MADE BY PM

PM-Only Cost Report - Version #2 (Spreadsheet Made By PM)
(The figures on this form are for demonstration purposes only and are not to be taken as financial advice.)

Film Title: _____
Production Company: _____

For Period Ending: _____

COST REPORT

Budget Code	Description	Total Costs	PM ONLY	PM + Total	ETC	EFC	Budget	Variance
218.10	Props Labor	5,300	160	5,460	18,550	24,010	24,750	740
	Shoot Wk 2 Overtime		160					
218.50	Props Purch/Rentals	19,926	2,000	21,926	3,074	25,000	20,000	(5,000)
	#1 Petty Cash Float		1,000					
	#2 Petty Cash Float		1,000					
218.80	Props - Kit Rental	400		400	800	1,200	900	(300)
218.0	PROPS	25,626		27,786	22,424	50,210	45,650	(4,560)
220.10	Camera Labor	18,100	544	18,644	45,250	63,894	62,300	(1,594)
	Shoot Wk 2 Overtime		544					
220.50	Camera Eqt Rental	7,200		7,200	36,000	43,200	45,000	1,800
220.55	Camera Daily Rentals	225	1,500	1,725	775	2,500	2,500	-
	Steadicam (maybe)		1,500					
220.70	Camera Expendables	1,376		1,376	1,124	2,500	2,500	-
220.80	Camera Kit Rentals	210		210	2,340	2,550	2,700	150
220.0	CAMERA	27,111		29,155	85,489	114,644	115,000	356

... and further down the cost report .

Budget Code	Description	Total Costs	PM ONLY	PM + Total	ETC	EFC	Budget	Variance
400.10	Insurance	23,500	(1,500)	22,000	8,500	30,500	30,500	-
	Pkg Insurance savings		(1,500)					
400.15	Medicals	750		750	-	750	750	-
400.50	Corporate Overhead	-			150,000	150,000	150,000	-
400.60	Legal	7,500		7,500	32,500	40,000	40,000	-
400.70	Post Accounting	-			4,800	4,800	4,800	-
400.75	Audit	-			5,000	5,000	5,000	-
400.90	Bank/Financing	374	54,000	54,374	20,626	75,000	75,000	-
	Interim Interest Estimate		54,000					
400.0	GENERAL COSTS	32,124	54,000	84,624	221,426	306,050	306,050	-

PM-ONLY COST REPORT - BUDGET FORM

PM-Only Cost Report - Version #3 (Budget Form)
(The figures on this form are for demonstration purposes only and are not to be taken as financial advice.)

"Film Title"

Acct	Description	Amount		Rate	Sub-Total	Total
218.0	**PROPS**					50,210
218.10	**Props Labor**					
	PROPERTY MASTER					
	- Prep	2 4	weeks	1,800	4,320	
	- Shoot	6	weeks	1,800	10,800	
	- Wrap	0.6	weeks	1,800	1,080	
	SHOOT WEEK 2 - OVERTIME				*104*	
	Total Property Master				16,304	
	PROPERTY ASSISTANT					
	- Prep	2 4	weeks	850	2,040	
	- Shoot	6	weeks	850	5,100	
	- Wrap	0.6	weeks	850	510	
	BUDGET AT $950; AGT AT $850					
	SHOOT WEEK 2 - OVERTIME				*56*	
	Total Property Assistant				7,706	
	Total 218.10 Props Labor					24,010
218.50	**Props Purchase/Rentals**		Allow		20,000	25,000
	ESTIMATED OVERAGE		*Allow*		*5,000*	
	(N.B. PETTY CASH FLOAT $1,000 X2)					
218.80	**Props Kit Rental**					
	2 kits x $75 each	6	weeks	150	900	1,200
	KITS @ $100 EACH (+$25 X2/WK)	*6*	*weeks*	*50*	*300*	

... and further down the "budget-format" cost report .

Acct	Description	Amount		Rate	Sub-Total	Total
400.0	**GENERAL COSTS**					304,550
400.10	**Insurance**					
	Entertainment Package		Allow		23,500	
	ENT. PKG BUDGET $25,000 - SAVINGS					
	E&O Insurance		Allow		5,500	
	Total 400.10 Insurance					29,000
400.15	**Medicals**	10	Meds	75	750	750
400.50	**Corporate Overhead**		Allow		150,000	150,000
400.60	**Legal**		Allow		40,000	40,000
400.70	**Post Accounting**		Allow		4,800	4,800
400.75	**Audit**		Allow		5,000	5,000
400.90	**Bank/Interim Financing**		Allow		75,000	75,000
	INTEREST RESERVE EST $54,000					
	$21,000 ALLOWABLE FEES/LEGALS					

431

PM-Only Cost Report - Version #4 (Pencil Copy)
(The figures on this form are for demonstration purposes only and are not to be taken as financial advice.)

PRODUCTION MANAGEMENT 101 / *Patz*

PM-ONLY COST REPORT - PENCIL COPY

Film Title.
Production Company

COST REPORT   For Period Ending

Budget Code	Description	Costs This Period	Costs To Date	P.O.s	Total Costs	ETC	EFC	Budget	Variance
218 10	Props Labor	2,650	5,300	OT WK2=$ 160	5,300	18,550	23,850	24,750	OT OVG $ 160 / 900
218.50	Props Purch/Rentals	1,250	19,576	Float $ 1000x2 350	19,926	5,074	25,000	20,000	(5,000)
218 80	Props - Kit Rental	200	400	-	400	800	1,200	900	(300)
218.0	PROPS	4,100	25,276	350	25,626	24,424	50,050	45,650	(4,400) OT OVG $ 544
220.10	Camera Labor	9,050	18,100	OT WK2=$ 544 -	18,100	45,250	63,350	62,300	(1,050)
220.50	Camera Eqt Rental	7,200	7,200	S/cam $ 1500 ?	7,200	36,000	43,200	45,000	1,800
220 55	Camera Daily Rentals	-	-	225	225	2,275	2,500	2,500	-
220 70	Camera Expendables	1,294	1,339	37	1,376	1,124	2,500	2,500	-
220.80	Camera Kit Rentals	425	-	210	210	2,340	2,550	2,700	150
220.0	CAMERA	17,969	26,639	472	27,111	86,989	114,100	115,000	900

and further down the cost report

Budget Code	Description	Costs This Period	Costs To Date	P.O.s	Total Costs	ETC	EFC	Budget	Variance
400.10	Insurance	-	23,500	-	23,500	7,000	30,500	30,500	Sav $ 1500 ?
400.15	Medicals	150	675	75	750	-	750	750	-
400 50	Corporate Overhead	-	-	-	-	150,000	150,000	150,000	-
400 60	Legal	-	7,500	-	7,500	32,500	40,000	40,000	-
400 70	Post Accounting	-	-	-	-	4,800	4,800	4,800	-

Non-Union Crew Deal Memo

DEAL MEMORANDUM

BETWEEN: Prdn. Company: _____

_____

AND: Company/Name: _____

Address: _____

_____

Telephone: _____

Co.Tax#/Soc.#: _____

* *

CONCERNING THE FOLLOWING FILM PRODUCTION:

_____

* *

CATEGORY: _____

SHOOT DATES: _____

START / END WORK DATES: _____

PAY RATE: PER DAY: _____

OTHER: _____

_____

PAYABLE BY: _____   INVOICE: _____   PAYROLL: _____

* *

_____   _____
Company/Employee   on behalf of
                                     Production Company

_____   _____
Date   Date

EXTRAS RELEASE FORM

EXTRAS RELEASE FORM

(This form is a sample to inspire you to design one with your own legal counsel appropriate to your production, and is not to be taken as legal advice.)

To: Production Company Inc.
      Address
      Telephone
      Fax
      Email
      Web Page

For good and valuable consideration, the receipt and sufficiency whereof is hereby acknowledged:

I hereby grant Production Company Inc., its affiliates, licensees, successors and assigns (hereinafter collectively the "Company") the irrevocable right, in perpetuity, to use the footage taken of me (the "Footage") in connection with the production, distribution and exploitation of the feature film presently entitled "Film Production Adventure" (the "Film"), to edit, delete, alter and amend the Footage in any manner and to juxtapose the Footage with any other material. This grant of rights includes the right to use my image, voice and all instrumental, musical or other sound effects produced by me contained in the Footage without restriction of any kind or nature whatsoever. The Film and/or the Footage may be exploited throughout the world, in perpetuity and in any and all media now or hereafter devised without any payment to me. The Company has no obligation to use the Footage in the Film.

I do hereby release and forever discharge the Company of, from and against all actions, causes of action, claims, suits, judgments and demands which may by made against the Company by virtue of my appearance, in any manner whatsoever, in the Film.

Dated this _____ day of _____, _____.

Witness: _____   Signature: _____

                                   Name: _____

                                   Address: _____

                                   _____

                                   Tel: _____

CHANGE OF DATE FORM

PERFORMER'S CHANGE OF DATE FORM
(to attach to all copies of Performer's Agreement)

To: _____
Person Spoke To

_____
Talent Agency

_____
Talent Agency Address / Telephone / Fax

RE: _____
Re: Performer's Name playing "Character Name"

From: _____
Production Company

_____
Address

_____
Telephone / Fax / Contact Name

This is to confirm our TELEPHONE CONVERSATION of:

_____   at   _____
Date   Time

concerning a change of date(s) for the following work day(s):

From: _____   To: _____

From: _____   To: _____

and/or additional work day(s) as follows:

_____

_____

_____
Signature

_____
Name

_____
Date

435

CATERING DEAL LETTER

LETTER OF AGREEMENT

(This form is a sample to inspire you to design one with your own legal counsel appropriate to your production, and is not to be taken as legal advice.)

between:

PRODUCTION COMPANY LTD.	AND	CATERING COMPANY LTD.
Address		Address
Telephone		Telephone
Fax		Fax

Date

This is to confirm that Catering Company Ltd. ("The Caterer") agrees to cater **"Film Production Adventure"** Television Movie for Production Company Ltd. ("The Production") for the period: __Start Date - End Date__.

The Caterer agrees to provide meals for cast and crew for __Price__ plus tax per person and substantials for __Price__ plus tax per person.

In addition, The Caterer will provide their own vehicle.

The Production agrees to supply tables and chairs and all beverages.

The Production agrees to provide The Caterer with a deposit of __Amount__.

With regard to changes in location, meal time and number of meals to be served, The Production agrees to give The Caterer best effort for twenty four (24) hours notice.

Invoices to be submitted weekly.

Signed and agreed,

Production Manager
on behalf of
PRODUCTION COMPANY LTD.

Name: _____
on behalf of
CATERING COMPANY LTD.

Date

Date

FEATURE FILM TITLE PAGE

```
              FINAL (WHITE) DRAFT  -  1 December 2004
              PINK REVISED         -  2 December 2004
              BLUE REVISED         -  3 December 2004
              GREEN REVISED        -  4 December 2004
              YELLOW REVISED       -  5 December 2004
              ORANGE REVISED       -  6 December 2004
              BUFF REVISED         -  7 December 2004
              TAN REVISED          -  7 Dec 2004 (PM)
              GOLDENROD REVISED    -  8 December 2004
              LAVENDER REVISED     -  8 Dec 2004 (PM)
              WHITE AGAIN REVISED  -  9 December 2004
            * PINK AGAIN REVISED   - 10 December 2004



              "Film Production Adventure"


                      written by

                   Deborah S. Patz


                   based on a story by

                   Laura J. C. Fisher
```

```
                        Production Company Ltd.
                        Address
                        Telephone
                        Fax Number
                        Email
                        Web Page
```

```
      Copyright notice & disclaimer
```

TV Series Title Page

FILM PRODUCTION ADVENTURE

Episode #2

"It's a N-Ice World"

teleplay by

Deborah S. Patz

based on characters by

Laura J. C. Fisher

Second Draft - 26 April 2005

Production Company Ltd.
Address
Telephone
Fax Number
Email
Web Page

Copyright notice & disclaimer

"Film Production Adventure"   Blue-3 Dec 05
by Deborah S. Patz

FADE IN:

Sc.1 **EXT. HILARY'S HOUSE - NIGHT**   Sc.1

Establishing shot. It is raining softly.

CUT TO:

Sc.2 **INT. LIVING ROOM - NIGHT**   Sc.2

HILARY (30) sits amid piles of scripts and script notes,   *
working on them, but the biscuit tin on the coffee table   *
keeps drawing her attention.   *

> HILARY (V/O)
> After she died, I inherited my
> grandmother's recipe tin. Now, for
> most people, this would be a precious   *
> gift. My only problem was: my
> grandmother couldn't cook.

> YOUNG HILARY (V/O)
>   (sniffing)
> What's that smell?

> GRAN (V/O)
> Oh! The roast!

The SOUND of footsteps rush up stairs.

CUT TO:

Sc.3 **INT. KITCHEN (FLASHBACK) - NIGHT**   Sc.3

Smoke is seeping out of the oven. GRAN (55) puts on oven
mitts and opens the oven door, removes a blackened char
of meat on a platter. Smoke billows from the oven.

> GRAN
> Ooo, just in time!

YOUNG HILARY (8) watches, unbelieving, from the kitchen
door.

(CONTINUED)

3. CONTINUED:

                     HILARY (V/O)
       It never was.

                           CUT TO:

Sc.4 **INT. KITCHEN (FLASHBACK) - NIGHT (LATER)**   Sc.4

   A questionable meal, including the blackened meat, is
   placed on the table. YOUNG HILARY tests the meat with a
   fork, starts eating the vegetables.

   HILARY'S MOM (33), HILARY'S DAD (37) and GRAN are also
   at the table, eating. Everyone has trouble cutting the
   meat, but no one addresses the issue.

                     HILARY (V/O)
     There was a reward, though, for making it
     through one of Gran's meals, and that was
     dessert. As much as Gran couldn't cook.
     She sure could bake.

                       DISSOLVE TO:

Sc.5 **INT. KITCHEN (FLASHBACK) - NIGHT**   Sc.5

   GRAN serves up a slice of lemon meringue pie, spilling it in
   pieces onto the plate.

                     HILARY (V/O)
     And Lemon Meringue Pie was my all time
     favorite.

   YOUNG HILARY grins, widely.

                        CUT TO:

Sc.6 OMITTED   Omit Sc.6 *
                                *
                                *
                                *
                                *
                                *
                                *
                                *
                                *

COMEDY SCRIPT PAGE

```
     "Film Production Adventure: Ep.#2" - Blue - 23 Dec 05    -5-

6. CONTINUED:

   MAX ROUNDS THE CORNER AND COMES FACE TO FACE WITH
   HUW, ALREADY WITH FOOD IN HAND FROM THE 'FRIDGE.

                         HUW
                A little hungry, perhaps?

                         MAX
                Sort of...

                         HUW
                Would that be "sort of yes" or

                "sort of no?"

                         MAX
                Uh... "sort of yeah."

   HUW DIVES INTO THE 'FRIDGE FOR SOME FOOD FOR MAX. HE
   PASSES OUT ITEM AFTER ITEM FOR AN AMAZING SPREAD.
   MAX RELAYS THE FOOD TO THE TABLE.

                         HUW
                You know, I've heard all the stories,

                but faced with her Gran's cooking,

                it takes a braver man than me to eat it.

                         MAX
                Yeah. Me too.

   HILARY ENTERS THE KITCHEN AND SURVEYS THE FEAST IN THE
   MAKING. SHE LOOKS HUNGRY.

                         HUW (CONT)
                You got our invite to the midnight feast?

                         HILARY
                What amazes me, is that I had actually

                forgotten what her food really tasted

                like. Gosh, I miss those days.
                                        (CONTINUED)
```

STRIP BOARD

			Sc.#	1	26	Day 1 - End - 2 5/8 pages	14	11	6	Day 2- End - 4/8 pages
			Day/Night	N	D		D	D	D	
			Int/Ext	Int	Int		Int	Ext	Ext	
			Continuity Day #	1	3		3	2	2	
			Pages	1 1/8	1 4/8		1/8	2/8	2/8	
Title:	Film Prdn Adventure			INDOOR PLAYGROUND	INDOOR PLAYGROUND		KITCHEN	DRIVEWAY	MAX'S HOUSE	
Director:	Jane Doe									
Producer:	John Smith									
A.D.:	John Doe									
Script date:	Pink									
Character	Artist	No.								
Max		1		1	1		1	1	1	
Huw		2		2	2		2			
Friend		3		3	3		3			
Hilary		4		4	4		4			
Roommate		5		5	5				5	
Thug		6			6			6		
Mother		7		7	7					
Father		8		8	8			8-vo		
		9								
		10								
		11								
		12								
Spot (dog)		13						13		
		14								
Extras				X	X			X	X	
				Max sure knows how to play!	Everyone celebrates... big time!		Chocolate milk... shaken, not stirred	Making friends with thug... not dog	All is quiet arriving home	

A.D. Breakdown Page

BREAKDOWN SHEET #	SCRIPT BREAKDOWN SHEET	SCENE #
28	FILM TITLE: FILM PRODUCTION ADVENTURE	23

INT / EXT	SET COORDINATOR'S KITCHEN	DAY / NIGHT N-4	PAGES 2 3/8

DESCRIPTION COORD. DESPERATELY TRIES TO MAKE DINNER	LOCATION	STUDIO STUDIO 1

CAST	EXTRAS	STUNTS
1. COORDINATOR	STAND-IN FOR COORD.	51. STUNT-COORDINATOR COORD. SLIPS ON BANANA PEEL CRASH PAD

PROPS	WARDROBE	VEHICLES
LOTS OF COOKING POTS, BLACKENED FOOD, NON-SLIP BANANA PEEL, SMOKE IN OVEN, BRIEFCASE, COMPUTER IN BAG, PENS & PENCILS (TO FALL OUT OF BRIEFCASE), PHOTO OF KEN & JORDAN	DOUBLES FOR STUNT, NEVER-USED APRON, NEVER-USED OVEN MITTS	

NOTES

ANIMALS: BIRD AT WINDOW WATCHES THE MESS, WRANGLER

ELECTRICS: DAY FOR NIGHT

NOTE TO ALL: SMOKE IN OVEN

MAKEUP: COORDINATOR LOOKS VERY, VERY TIRED

A.D. Breakdown Page (Blank)

BREAKDOWN SHEET #	SCRIPT BREAKDOWN SHEET FILM TITLE:	SCENE #

INT / EXT	SET		DAY / NIGHT	PAGES
DESCRIPTION			LOCATION	STUDIO

CAST	EXTRAS	STUNTS
PROPS	WARDROBE	VEHICLES
	NOTES	

One-Line Schedule

"Film Production Adventure"
One-Line Schedule

Blue Revised
Date: 9 Dec 2004

Sc#	Description	D/N	Cast	Pages	Loc

DAY 1 - MON. JAN. 03, 2005   1.=STUDIO, 2.=123 MAIN ST

24	INT HOME OFFICE	N5	1,2,3	1 4/8	1.
4	INT HOME OFFICE	N1	1,3-vo	1 0/8	1.

* * * * * * U N I T   M O V E * * * * * *

2	EXT HOUSE	D1	1,X	1/8	2.

END DAY ONE - 2 5/8 PAGES

DAY 2 - TUE. JAN. 04, 2005   1.=FUN PARK, 2.=CITY PARK

1pt	EXT WATERPARK	D1	1,2-vo,4,X	6/8	1.
26	EXT WATERPARK	D7	1,2,3,4,X	4/8	1.

* * * * * * U N I T   M O V E * * * * * *

8	EXT PARK	D2	1,4,X	2/8	2.
12	EXT PARK	D2	1,2,X	1 2/8	2.

END DAY TWO - 2 6/8 PAGES

DAY 3 - WED. JAN. 05, 2005   1.=123 FIRST AVE

6	INT/EXT MAX'S CAR	D2	1,51,X	4/8	1.
10	EXT/INT MAX'S CAR	D2	1,2,51,52,X	2/8	1.
9	EXT CITY STREETS	D2	51,52,X	3/8	1.
11	EXT CITY STREETS	D2	1,2,X	1 0/8	1.

END DAY THREE - 2 1/8 PAGES

DAY 4 - THU. JAN. 06, 2005   1.=STUDIO

1pt	INT LIVING ROOM	D1	1-vo,2	3/8	1.
3	INT LIVING ROOM	N1	1,2-vo	3/8	1.
19	INT LIVING ROOM	N4	1,2,3	7/8	1.

* * * * * * TARGET OF OPPORTUNITY * * * * * *

18	INT LIVING ROOM	N4	2,3	1 2/8	1.

END DAY FOUR - 2 3/8 PAGES

DAY 5 - FRI. JAN. 07, 2005   1.=STUDIO, 2=COOL GARDEN

18	INT LIVING ROOM	N4	2,3	1 2/8	1.

* * * * * * U N I T   M O V E * * * * * *

21	INT INDOOR WATERFALL	D5	1,2,3,4	1 3/8	2.

END DAY FIVE - 1 5/8 PAGES

Characters
1. Max
2. Huw
3. Hilary
4. Little Boy
X Extras

SHOOTING SCHEDULE

<u>**"Film Production Adventure"**</u>   Pink Revised
Shooting Schedule   Date: 13 Dec 2004

DAY 1 - MON. JAN. 03, 2005
                    LOC.#1 - STUDIO - 111 FILM ST.

| 24 | <u>INT HOME OFFICE</u>
Max figures it all out | N5 | 1 4/8 | 1.MAX
2.HUW
3.HILARY | <u>Props</u>: Really cool
computer, Homework,
Stacks of paper,
Flowers, Tapioca
pudding to eat
<u>Set Dressing</u>: Secret
wall switch
<u>Lighting</u>: Computer
light effect
<u>Music</u>: Radio gets
turned off |

| 4 | <u>INT HOME OFFICE</u>
Getting the mission | N1 | 1 0/8 | 1.MAX
3.HILARY'S
  VOICE | <u>Props</u>: Really cool
computer, Homework,
Stacks of paper
<u>Lighting</u>: Computer
light effect
<u>Sound</u>: Fax bell |

---

               * * * UNIT MOVE TO LOC.#2 - 123 MAIN ST. * * *

| 2 | <u>EXT HOUSE</u>
Max arrives home, wet | D1 | 1/8 | 1.MAX
EXTRAS
Man with
  dog x1 | <u>Props</u>: Max's cel
phone, Wet towel
roll, Knapsack
<u>H/M/W</u>: Max is wet
from water park |

                    END DAY ONE - 2 5/8 PAGES

DAY 2 - TUE. JAN. 04, 2005
                    LOC.#1 - FUN PARK - 1001 PLAY WAY

| 1pt | <u>EXT WATERPARK</u>
Max gets a phone call | D1 | 6/8 | 1.MAX
2.HUW'S
  VOICE
4.LITTLE
  BOY
EXTRAS
Kids x30
Parents x7
Lifeguard x2 | <u>Props</u>: Max's cel
phone, Water to
splash on Max, Pool
toys a'plenty,
Max's towel (dry)
<u>H/M/W</u>: Max gets wet
(triples of Max's
dry clothing) |

            (Day 2 - cont'd Page 2...)

446

CREDIT STYLE #1 (PAGE 1 OF 4)

"Film Production Adventure"

Credits - 4th Draft (Version #1)

December 15, 2004

OPENING CREDITS

CARD #

1	Company Name Presents	0:03
2	Script Revision Nightmare	0:03
3	Actor	0:02
		(single card, 1st)
4	Actor	0:02
		(main titles, 2nd)
5	Actor	0:02
		(single card, 3rd)
6	Actor	0:02
	Actor	*(shared card)*
7	and Actor Name as Character Name	0:02
		(single card, last, "and-as")
8	Written by	0:02
9	Directed by	0:02

Total= 0:20

CREDIT STYLE #1 (PAGE 2 OF 4)

"Film Production Adventure"   Credits Ver.1 -2

Credits - 4th Draft (Version #1)

END CREDITS (CRAWL)   Total= 2:00

Executive Producer

Producer

Co-Producer

Director Of Photography

Production Designer

Costume Designer

Editor

Music

Featuring
(in alphabetical order)

Actor Name	as	Character Name
Actor Name	as	Character Name
Actor Name	as	Character Name
Actor Name	as	Character Name

With special thanks to
(List a few special names)

Associate Producer

Associate Director

Production Manager
First Assistant Director
Casting Director
Legal Advisor
Executive in Charge of Production

Production Coordinator
Assistant Coordinator
Production Accountant
Assistant Accountant

Production Secretary
Office P.A.
Assistant to the Producer

Unit Manager
Location Manager

CREDIT STYLE #1 (PAGE 3 OF 4)

Credits Ver.1 - 3

Second Assistant Director
Second Second Assistant Director
Third Assistant Director
Continuity Supervisor

Camera Operator
Focus Puller
2nd Assistant Camera
Trainee

Gaffer
Best Boy
Electric
Generator Operator
Key Grip
Best Boy Grip
Grip
Sound Recordist
Boom Operator

Art Director
Set Decorator
Assistant Art Director
Trainee
Model Builder
Lead Set Dresser
Set Dressers
Property Manager
Props Assistant
Props Buyer

Construction Manager
Head Carpenter
Carpenters
Scenic Artist
Painters
Construction Labor

Assistant Wardrobe Designer
Wardrobe Mistress
Assistant Wardrobe
Seamstress
Hair Designer
Key Makeup Artist

Special Effects
Stunts
Location Casting
Extras Coordinator

Transportation Coordinator
Driver Captain
Drivers
Boat/Vehicle Wrangler

CREDIT STYLE #1 (PAGE 4 OF 4)

Credits Ver.1 - 4

Post Production Supervisor
Second Editor
Assistant Editor
Negative Cutting
Color Timing
Laboratory

Sound Supervisor
Sound Effects Designer
Dialogue Editor
Sound Mixer
Sound Mix Facility

Music Director
Music Engineer
Soloist
Additional Vocals

Location Catering
Craft Service Company
Nurse
Unit Publicity
Stills Photographer
Titles Design

Filmed on (film stock)

The producers gratefully acknowledge
the support and assistance of

Produced by (Co-Production Companies)

A (list countries) Co-Production

Produced with the participation of

Produced in association with

Developed with the assistance of

(Legal disclaimer, ie:
This film is based on true events, however, some of the names in
this film were changed and some events fictionalized for dramatic
purposes. This motion picture is protected under the laws of the
United States, Canada and other countries, and its unauthorized
duplication, distribution or exhibition may result in civil
liability or criminal prosecution.)

© (year, in Roman numerals) Production Company Ltd.

(Union and Guild logos)

(Co-Production Companies logos)

"Film Production Adventure"

Credits (Version #2)

EPISODE #2 - "Oh no! Not Again!"

Opening Credits

FONT STYLE: VENETIAN 521 GOUDY EXTRA BOLD

Final Draft - 20 Dec 2004

Card #

1	Film Production Adventure	0:02
2	starring Lead Actor	0:02 *(single card, 1st,* *"starring")*
3	Lead Actor	0:02 *(single card, 2nd)*
4	and Lead Actor as Character Name	0:02 *(single card, last,* *"and-as")*
5	series created by	0:02
6	based on characters by developed for television by	0:02
7	supervising producer	0:02
8	producer	0:02

Shown over the first frames of Act One:

9	Oh No! Not Again!	0:02
10	written by	0:02
11	directed by	0:02

Total= 0:22

"SCRIPT REVISION NIGHTMARE"   Credits Ver.2 - 2

Credits (Version #2)

EPISODE #2 - "Oh no! Not Again!"

Tail Credits   Total= 1:00 +logos

Final Draft

Card #

1	executive producer	0:02
2	executive in charge of production	0:02
3	guest starring Star Name as Character Name and featuring Actor Name as Character Name	0:03
4	director of photography production designer	0:02
5	editor music theme by performed by	0:02
6	casting director wardrobe designer	0:02
7	production manager assistant production manager first assistant director second assistant director third assistant director continuity supervisor	0:02.5
8	art director 1st assistant art director 1st assistant art director art department trainee set decorator lead set dresser lead set dresser set dresser	0:02.5
9	special effects design props master props builder props assistant art department coordinator	0:02.5

CREDIT STYLE #2 (PAGE 3 OF 3)

		Credits Ver.2 - 3
10	camera operator 1st camera assistant 2nd camera assistant camera department trainee sound mixer boom operator	0:02.5
11	assistant wardrobe designer wardrobe mistress makeup artist hair designer	0:02.5
12	key grip dolly grip gaffer best boy construction manager head carpenter scenic painter	0:02.5
13	production coordinator production accountant business affairs production secretary production assistant craft service catering	0:02.5
14	post-production supervisor post-production coordinator post-production assistant sound editors 1st assistant editor foley artist sound assistant	0:02.5
15	rerecording laboratory rerecording studio post-production facilities on line editor colorist sound editing facility	0:02.5
16	© (Year) Production Company Ltd. (Disclaimer) (Piracy Clause) (Union and Guild logos)	0:02.5
17	Produced with the participation of	0:03 x2
18	produced by in association with	0:03 x5
19	Co-Production Company logos	0:03 x3

PAPER BINDER DISTRIBUTION TRACKING FORM

PAPER BINDER DISTRIBUTION TRACKING FORM

SCRIPT	White-Dec.1	Pink-Dec.2	Blue-Dec.4	Green	Yellow
Research Company	C - Dec 1	C - Dec.2	C - Dec 4		
Exec Producer	D - Dec 1	D - Dec.2	D - Dec.4		
Producer	D - Dec.1	D - Dec.2	D - Dec.4		
Director	D - Dec.1	D - Dec.2	D - Dec 4		
Story Editor	D - Dec 2	D - Dec.2	D - Dec.4		
Casting Director	C - Dec.2	N/A	N/A		
DP	D - Dec.1	D - Dec 2	D - Dec 4		
"Rest of Crew"	D - Dec.1	D - Dec.2	D - Dec 4		
"The Cast"	D - Dec.1	D - Dec.2	D - Dec 4		
Distributor	C - Dec.1	C - Dec.7	C - Dec.7		
Broadcaster	C - Dec.1	C - Dec 7	C - Dec.7		
Funding Agency	C - Dec 1	C - Dec.7	C - Dec.7		
XP/Head Office	C - Dec.1	C - Dec.7	C - Dec.7		
Editors	D - Dec 1	D - Dec.2	D - Dec.4		
Completion Bond	C - Dec 1	C - Dec.7	C - Dec.7		
Publicist *(major only)*	C - Dec.1	N/A	N/A		
Performer Union *(major only)*	C - Dec.1	N/A	N/A		
Gov't Agency *(major only)*	C - Dec.1	N/A	N/A		

"C" means "sent via courier"
"D" means "hand-delivered"
"F" means "sent via fax"

WALL ENVELOPES DISTRIBUTION TRACKING FORM

WALL ENVELOPES DISTRIBUTION TRACKING FORM

HEAD OFFICE (Contact Name)	White	Blue	Pink	Yellow	Green
Script (Ep. #1)	C – Dec 1	F – Dec 2	F – Dec.4		
Script (Ep. #2)	C – Dec 5				
Script (Ep. #3)	C – Dec 7				
Script (Ep. #4)					
Script (Ep. #5)					
Script (Ep. #6)					
Research Report (Ep. #1)	F – Dec 8				
Research Report (Ep. #2)					
Research Report (Ep. #3)					
Research Report (Ep. #4)					
Research Report (Ep. #5)					
Research Report (Ep. #6)					
Crew List	C – Dec 1	F – Dec.7			
Cast List (Ep. #1)	C – Dec 1				
Cast List (Ep. #2)	F – Dec 5				
Cast List (Ep. #3)					
Cast List (Ep. #4)					
Cast List (Ep. #5)					
Cast List (Ep. #6)					
One Line Sched. (Ep. #1)	F – Dec.3				
(etc.)					

"C" means "sent via courier"
"D" means "hand-delivered"

WRAP PARTY CHECKLIST & BUDGET

Date of party:	

	Description/Notes	Price
WRAP PARTY INVITATIONS		
Number invited		-
Invitation costs		
Mailing costs		
PARTY ROOM		
Room rental		
Capacity		-
Special features		
Closing time		-
Security		
Washroom supplies		
Clean up		
DECOR OF PARTY ROOM		
Lights rental		
Tables/chairs		
Linen/Ashtrays		
Balloons/Helium		
Flowers		
Other decorations		
Set up/clean up		

Wrap party Checklist & Budget Form (page 2 of 3)

WRAP PARTY CATERING		
Food/buffet type		
Specialty food		
Catering staff		
Cake		
Napkins (type)		
Plates (type)		
Cutlery (type)		
Set up/Clean up		
BAR & BEVERAGES		
Bartenders		
Deposit required		-
Beer		
Wine		
Liquor		
Mixers & others		
Ice & containers		
Glasses (type)		
Napkins & access.		
Set up/clean up		
LICENSE		
Liquor license		

NOTIFICATIONS		
Police		-
Fire Department		-
Health Department		-
Build ' g/Inspect ' n		-
MUSIC		
Band		
D.J.		
Set up needed		-
When clean up		-
OTHER ENTERTAINMENT		
Entertainment type		
Outtake reel avail		
Video equipment		
Set up/clean up		

GRAND TOTAL PARTY COSTS:	

DEBORAH PATZ

A filmmaker since 1984, Deborah S. Patz is president of Golden Arrow Productions Ltd. She has a diverse film production background on video, 16mm, 35mm, and IMAX 3D. Her shows include family and children's programming, low-budget features, and science fiction extravaganzas. She has filmed in several countries, including Hong Kong and China, and worked on co-productions with such countries as the US, Canada, the UK, France, Japan, and New Zealand.

A selected filmography includes: *The Magician's House* (an Emmy Award-winning family mini-series, as Executive In Charge of Production); *These Arms of Mine* (a dramedy series, as Executive In Charge of Production); *Ruffus the Dog & Panda Bear Daycare* (a pre-school series, as Line Producer/PM); *Automatic Writing* (a feature film, as Line Producer); *L5: First City In Space* (an IMAX 3D feature, as Unit Manager); *The Big Comfy Couch* (a children's series, as Line Producer/PM); *William Shatner's TekWar* (4 Movies of the Week, as APM); *Maniac Mansion* (a comedy series, as PC); *The Sound & The Silence* (mini-series, as PC); *Alfred Hitchcock Presents* (a mystery series, as APC); *Ewoks & Droids* (2 animated series, as Casting Agent); *The Edison Twins* (a youth series, as Casting Agent).

Beyond hands-on production, Ms. Patz has also been an Investment Analyst at Telefilm Canada for the development and production of feature film, television, and new media, including numerous drama, children's, youth, documentary, variety, and performing arts projects.

The author of the internationally successful *Surviving Production*, Ms. Patz continues to share her knowledge of production and business with this expanded second edition, *Film Production Management 101*, to further educate and inspire the filmmakers of today and tomorrow.

When not making films and writing books, Ms. Patz — through Golden Arrow — offers seminars and workshops on producing and production management skills, including workshops on beginner and advanced use of Movie Magic software. She also offers consulting services, reading and reporting on scripts, and creating and evaluating production budgets.

Ms. Patz currently resides in Vancouver, BC, Canada.

Golden Arrow Productions Ltd.

www.goldenarrowproductions.com
patzelliott@canada.com

INDEPENDENT FILM & VIDEOMAKER'S GUIDE
2nd Edition
Expanded & Updated

Michael Wiese

This is the new, completely expanded and revised edition with all the information filmmakers need, from fundraising to marketing and distribution. This practical and comprehensive book will help you save time and money and inspire you to create successful projects.

Contents include:
- Writing a business plan
- Developing your ideas into concepts, treatments, and scripts
- Directing, producing, and market research
- Distribution markets (theatrical, home video, television, international)
- Financing your film
- How to do presentations and write a prospectus
- An appendix filled with film cash flow projections, sample contracts, valuable contact addresses
- And much more!

"Wiese covers the most important (and least taught) part of the job: creative deal-making. The book is full of practical tips on how to get a film or video project financed, produced, and distributed without sacrificing artistic integrity."
— *Co-Evolution Quarterly*

Michael Wiese has over 30 years experience in film, television, and home video in production, marketing, and distribution. He is currently preparing to direct a feature in Bali, Indonesia, based on his novel (see page 35) and a television documentary on extraterrestrial communication (see page 9). Additionally, he presents his independent filmmaking seminar throughout the world. He may be contacted at *mw@mwp.com*.

$29.95, 480 pages
Order # 37RLS
ISBN: 0-941188-57-4

FILM & VIDEO BUDGETS
3rd Updated Edition

Deke Simon and Michael Wiese

Over 40,000 Sold!

For over 15 years *Film & Video Budgets* has been the essential handbook for both beginning and professional filmmakers. Written by two pioneers of do-it-yourself filmmaking, this book outlines every element of production.

Updated and revised for digital video productions (and video-to-film transfers), this definitive book contains detailed formats and sample budgets for many different kinds of productions, from "no budget" digital movies to documentaries to a $5 million feature — along with all the crucial practical information that's made it an industry bible. Also includes new and highly useful materials, such as a comprehensive master list of line items for just about everything that could possibly be put into a production, and information-packed chapters on handling pre-production and setting up a production company. Also provides Excel sample budget templates downloadable for free from the Web.

Budget samples include:
- $5 Million Feature Film
- Documentaries (both film and video)
- Industrial
- Music Video
- Student Film
- No-Budget Digital Feature
- Digital Video Feature
- Video-to-Film Transfer
- And much more!

Deke Simon and Michael Wiese are veteran filmmakers who have had extensive experience in film, television, and video.

$26.95, 462 pages
Order # 9RLS
ISBN: 0-941188-34-5

SETTING UP YOUR SHOTS
Great Camera Moves Every Filmmaker Should Know

Jeremy Vineyard

Written in straightforward, non-technical language and laid out in a nonlinear format with self-contained chapters for quick, on-the-set reference, *Setting Up Your Shots* is like a Swiss army knife for filmmakers! Using examples from over 140 popular films, this book provides detailed descriptions of more than 100 camera setups, angles, and techniques — in an easy-to-use horizontal "wide-screen" format.

Setting Up Your Shots is an excellent primer for beginning filmmakers and students of film theory, as well as a handy guide for working filmmakers. If you are a director, a storyboard artist, or an animator, use this book. It is the culmination of hundreds of hours of research.

Contains 150 references to the great shots from your favorite films, including *2001: A Space Odyssey*, *Blue Velvet*, *The Matrix*, *The Usual Suspects*, and *Vertigo*.

"Perfect for any film enthusiast looking for the secrets behind creating film. Because of its simplicity of design and straightforward storyboards, *Setting Up Your Shots* is destined to be mandatory reading at film schools throughout the world."
— Ross Otterman, *Directed By Magazine*

Jeremy Vineyard is a director and screenwriter who moved to Los Angeles in 1997 to pursue a feature filmmaking career. He has several spec scripts in development.

$19.95, 132 pages
Order # 8RLS
ISBN: 0-941188-73-6

DIRECTING & VISUALIZATION

FILM DIRECTING: SHOT BY SHOT
Visualizing from Concept to Screen

Steven D. Katz

Over 150,000 Sold! International best-seller!

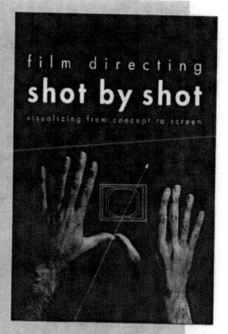

Film Directing: Shot by Shot — with its famous blue cover — is the best-known book on directing and a favorite of professional directors as an on-set quick reference guide.

This international bestseller is a complete catalog of visual techniques and their stylistic implications, enabling working filmmakers to expand their knowledge.

Contains in-depth information on shot composition, staging sequences, visualization tools, framing and composition techniques, camera movement, blocking tracking shots, script analysis, and much more.

Includes over 750 storyboards and illustrations, with never-before-published storyboards from Steven Spielberg's *Empire of the Sun*, Orson Welles' *Citizen Kane*, and Alfred Hitchcock's *The Birds*.

"(To become a director) you have to teach yourself what makes movies good and what makes them bad. John Singleton has been my mentor... he's the one who told me what movies to watch and to read *Shot by Shot*."
— Ice Cube, *New York Times*

"A generous number of photos and superb illustrations accompany each concept, many of the graphics being from Katz' own pen... *Film Directing: Shot by Shot* is a feast for the eyes."
— *Videomaker Magazine*

Steven D. Katz is also the author of *Film Directing: Cinematic Motion*.

$27.95, 366 pages
Order # 7RLS | ISBN: 0-941188-10-8

24 HOURS/ 1.800.833.5738   LOWEST PRICES AVAILABLE ONLINE AT WWW.MWP.COM

SOUND DESIGN
The Expressive Power of Music, Voice, and Sound Effects in Cinema

David Sonnenschein

The clash of light sabers in the electrifying duels of *Star Wars*. The chilling bass line signifying the lurking menace of the shark in *Jaws*. The otherworldly yet familiar pleas to "phone home" in the enchanting *E.T.*

These are examples of the many different ways in which sound can contribute to the overall dramatic impact of a film. To craft a distinctive atmosphere, sound design is as important as art direction and cinematography — and it can also be an effective tool in expressing the personalities of your characters.

In addition to introducing basic theory and analyzing specific examples of sound design in well-known films, this groundbreaking book shows you how to use music, dialogue, and sound effects to provoke an emotional reaction from your audience. Interactive, simple exercises nurture your creative ability to hear and compose the most effective sounds to express the story and then seamlessly integrate them with all the other cinematic elements.

"A comprehensive guide... with detailed analysis and straightforward commentary on one of the least understood areas in filmmaking: sound."
> — George Watters II, Supervising Sound Editor
> *Pearl Harbor, The Rock, The Hunt for Red October*

"The need for such a book is great indeed, fulfilled in this obviously heartfelt project."
> — Gary Rydstrom, Academy Award-Winning Sound Designer
> *Terminator 2, Titanic, Jurassic Park, Saving Private Ryan*

David Sonnenschein is an award-winning Sound Designer who directs feature films and teaches vibrational healing and sound design.

$19.95, 245 Pages
Order # 11RLS | ISBN: 0-941188-26-4

PRODUCTION

STORYBOARDING 101

James O. Fraioli

Storyboarding 101 is written especially for those looking to break into storyboarding but don't know where to start. The book gives you clear and concise information on both the mechanics of the art and the way the business works.

$19.95, 133 pages | Order # 46RLS | ISBN: 0-941188-25-6

HITTING YOUR MARK
What Every Actor Really Needs to Know About Working on a Hollywood Set

Steve Carlson

Even experienced actors doing their first film gig can be caught off-guard by the unfamiliar terminology, equipment, and production procedures unique to film sets. Includes discussions of technical basics, camera awareness, blocking techniques, on-set etiquette, reshoots, auditioning on camera, and much more.

$16.95, 198 pages | Order # 44RLS | ISBN: 0-941188-69-8

COSTUME DESIGN 101
The Art and Business of Costume Design for Film & Television

Richard La Motte

Here is all you need to know to launch a career in professional costume design. Richard La Motte (*Pearl Harbor*, *Gods and Generals*, *The Mark of Zorro*) gives a full overview of the industry, with an emphasis on practical information such as on-set protocol, running a set operation, and the challenges of working on large-scale productions with a high number of extras. Comprehensive, with crucial insider tips.

$19.95, 178 pages | Order # 18RLS | ISBN: 0-941188-35-3

CUT TO THE CHASE
Forty-Five Years of Editing America's Favorite Movies

Sam O'Steen as told to Bobbie O'Steen

Eclectic and unpredictable films such as *The Graduate, Cool Hand Luke, Chinatown,* and *Who's Afraid of Virginia Woolf?* ushered in what many historians and movie buffs call The Golden Age of Cinema. As diverse as these films are, they have one thing in common: They were all edited by one man, Sam O'Steen.

Sam O'Steen was a world-renowned editor whose talent, smarts, and desire to get the truth out of the film propelled him to an amazing level of success. He helped shape many of the most influential movies in motion-picture history.

This groundbreaking book takes the reader behind the closed doors of the editing room where Sam O'Steen controlled the fate of many celebrated films. Sam's absorbing stories — from on and off the set — are spiced with anecdotes about producers, directors, and such stars as Frank Sinatra, Elizabeth Taylor, Jack Nicholson, Meryl Streep, and Harrison Ford.

"Everything I know about film editing I learned from Sam O'Steen."
— Roman Polanski, Director, *Rosemary's Baby, Chinatown, Frantic*

"Sam was listening to the currents that flow underneath human events."
— Mike Nichols, Director, *Who's Afraid of Virginia Woolf?, The Graduate, Catch-22*

"Sam O'Steen was an American master and this book tells you where and how."
— Robert Benton, Writer/Director, *Kramer vs. Kramer, Places in the Heart, Nadine*

Bobbie O'Steen is a writer with a background in story and film editing. As a film editor, she received an Emmy nomination for *Best Little Girl in the World*.

$24.95, 249 pages
Order # 19RLS | ISBN: 0-941188-37-X

DIRECTING FEATURE FILMS
The Creative Collaboration between Directors, Writers, and Actors

Mark Travis

The director is the guide, the inspiration, the focus that can shepherd hundreds of artists through the most chaotic, complex collaboration imaginable. But how does one person draw all these individuals together to realize a single vision?

Directing Feature Films takes you through the entire creative process of filmmaking — from concept to completion. You will learn how to really read a script, find its core, determine your vision, and effectively communicate with writers, actors, designers, cinematographers, editors, composers, and all the members of your creative team to ensure that vision reaches the screen.

This edition of the best-selling *The Director's Journey* contains new material on all aspects of filmmaking, taking the reader even deeper into the process.

"A comprehensive and inspired examination of craft. A must read for any serious professional."
> — Mark Rydell, Director
> *On Golden Pond, The Rose, James Dean*

"With astonishing clarity Mark Travis articulates the techniques and skills of film directing."
> — John Badham, Director
> *Saturday Night Fever, War Games, Blue Thunder*

"Mark Travis is the only practical teacher of directing I've ever met — and simply the best. I learned more from him than I did in four years of film school."
> — Cyrus Nowrasteh, Writer/Director
> *The Day Reagan Was Shot*

Mark Travis has directed motion pictures, television programs, and stage shows. A graduate of the Yale School of Drama, Mark has shared his techniques on directing in courses around the world. He has served as a directing consultant on many feature films and top-rated television series.

$26.95, 402 pages
Order # 96RLS
ISBN: 0-94118-43-4

ORDER FORM

To order these products please call 1-800-833-5738 or fax (818) 986-3408 or mail this order form to:

MICHAEL WIESE PRODUCTIONS
11288 Ventura Blvd, Suite 621
Studio City, CA 91604
1-818-379-8799

BOOKS:

_____
_____
_____
_____

Subtotal $ _____
Shipping $ _____
8.25% Sales Tax (Ca Only) $ _____

TOTAL ENCLOSED _____

Please make check or money order payable to
Michael Wiese Productions

(Check one) ____ Master Card ____ Visa ____ Amex

Company PO# _____

Credit Card Number _____
Expiration Date _____
Cardholder's Name _____
Cardholder's Signature _____

SHIP TO:

Name _____
Address _____
City _____ State ____ Zip _____
Country _____ Telephone _____
Ask about our free catalog

VISIT OUR HOME PAGE www.mwp.com

Please allow 2–3 weeks for delivery.
All prices subject to change without notice.

CREDIT CARD ORDERS

CALL
1-800-833-5738

or FAX
818-986-3408

OR E-MAIL
mwpsales@earthlink.net

SHIPPING
ALL ORDERS MUST BE PREPAID

UPS GROUND SERVICE
One Item - $3.95
For each additional item,
add $2.00.

Special Reports-$2 ea.

EXPRESS DELIVERY
3 Business Days
Add an additional
$12.00 per order.

OVERSEAS
Surface - $15.00 ea. item
Airmail - $30.00 ea. item

9 780941 188456